WE THE
CORPORATIONS

OTHER WORKS BY
ADAM WINKLER

Gunfight: The Battle over the Right
to Bear Arms in America

WE THE CORPORATIONS

HOW AMERICAN BUSINESSES WON THEIR CIVIL RIGHTS

ADAM WINKLER

LIVERIGHT PUBLISHING CORPORATION

A Division of W. W. Norton & Company

INDEPENDENT PUBLISHERS SINCE 1923

New York   London

For information about permission to reproduce selections from this book, write to
Permissions, Liveright Publishing Corporation, a division of W. W. Norton & Company, Inc.,
500 Fifth Avenue, New York, NY 10110

For information about special discounts for bulk purchases, please contact
W. W. Norton Special Sales at specialsales@wwnorton.com or 800-233-4830

Manufacturing by LSC Communications Harrisonburg
Book design by Barbara Bachman
Production manager: Lauren Abbate

Library of Congress Cataloging-in-Publication Data

Names: Winkler, Adam, author.
Title: We the corporations : how American businesses won their civil rights / Adam Winkler.
Description: First edition. | New York : Liveright Publishing Corporation, a Division of
W. W. Norton & Co., 2018. | Includes bibliographical references and index.
Identifiers: LCCN 2017051893 | ISBN 9780871407122 (hardcover)
Subjects: LCSH: Civil rights of corporations—United States.
Classification: LCC KF1386.C58 W56 2018 | DDC 346.73/066—dc23
LC record available at https://lccn.loc.gov/2017051893

Liveright Publishing Corporation, 500 Fifth Avenue, New York, N.Y. 10110
www.wwnorton.com

W. W. Norton & Company Ltd., 15 Carlisle Street, London W1D 3BS

1 2 3 4 5 6 7 8 9 0

To Margo and Irwin Winkler
for their generous love, infinite support,
and enduring inspiration

CONTENTS

—

STATUE OF ROSCOE CONKLING, FRAMER OF THE FOURTEENTH
AMENDMENT AND ATTORNEY FOR THE SOUTHERN PACIFIC
RAILROAD, IN NEW YORK'S MADISON SQUARE PARK.

Are Corporations People?

IN DECEMBER 1882, ROSCOE CONKLING, A FORMER SENATOR and close confidant of President Chester Arthur, appeared before the justices of the Supreme Court of the United States to argue that corporations like his client, the Southern Pacific Railroad Company, were entitled to equal rights under the Fourteenth Amendment. Although that provision of the Constitution said that no state shall "deprive any *person* of life, liberty, or property, without due process of law" or "deny to any *person* within its jurisdiction the equal protection of the laws," Conkling insisted the amendment's drafters intended to cover business corporations too. Laws that referred to "persons" have "by long and constant acceptance . . . been held to embrace artificial persons as well as natural persons," Conkling explained. This long-standing practice was well known to "the men who framed, the Congress which proposed, and the people who through their Legislatures ratified the Fourteenth Amendment."

Conkling's claim was remarkable. The Fourteenth Amendment had been adopted after the Civil War to guarantee the rights of the freed slaves, not to protect corporations. Conkling, however, had unusual credibility with the justices. For two decades, he had been the leader of the Republican Party in Congress and was often said to be the most powerful man in Washington. He had twice been nominated to the Supreme Court himself, most recently in the spring of the same year he appeared on behalf of the Southern Pacific Railroad. The Senate voted to confirm him but he declined the position, citing poverty from his career in public service—becoming the last person to turn down a seat on the Supreme Court after having been confirmed. More than most lawyers then, Conkling was considered by the justices to be their peer. And when it came to the history surrounding the drafting of the Fourteenth Amendment, Conkling's expertise was unparalleled. As a member of Congress during Reconstruction, Conkling had been on the very committee that wrote the amendment. If anyone could testify to the intent of the Fourteenth Amendment's drafters, it was Conkling, who was one himself.

To back up his improbable story, Conkling produced a musty, never-before-published journal that purported to detail his committee's deliberations. A close look at the journal, Conkling suggested, would show that while the nation was focused on the rights of the freedmen, he and the other members of Congress had also been worried about laws that unduly burdened business. It was for this very reason that the Fourteenth Amendment used the word *person*. An early draft of the amendment had guaranteed the rights of "citizens," Conkling said, but the language was later changed specifically to include corporations, which were often deemed by the law to be persons for various purposes. As a result, Conkling argued, the Fourteenth Amendment guaranteed the Southern Pacific Railroad the same rights of equal protection and due process as the former slaves.

There was just one small problem with Conkling's account of the drafting of the Fourteenth Amendment: it was not true. The drafters of the Fourteenth Amendment did not try to secret into the Constitution broad new protections for corporations, nor was the wording of the amendment ever altered in the way Conkling suggested. As we will see, one of the preeminent figures in American politics had attempted to deceive the justices of the Supreme Court in an effort to win constitutional protections for the Southern Pacific Railroad.[1]

Although a procedural snafu prevented the Supreme Court from issuing a final ruling in Conkling's case, the justices soon after embraced Conkling's argument that corporations had rights protected by the Fourteenth Amendment. In the years that followed, the Supreme Court would invoke those corporate rights to invalidate numerous laws governing how businesses were to be run, supervised, and taxed. Between 1868, when the amendment was ratified, and 1912, when a scholar set out to identify every Fourteenth Amendment case heard by the Supreme Court, the justices decided 28 cases dealing with the rights of African Americans—and an astonishing 312 cases dealing with the rights of corporations. At the same time the court was upholding Jim Crow laws in infamous cases like *Plessy v. Ferguson* (1896), the justices were invalidating minimum-wage laws, curtailing collective bargaining efforts, voiding manufacturing restrictions, and even overturning a law regulating the weight of commercial loaves of bread. The Fourteenth Amendment, adopted to shield the former slaves from discrimination, had been transformed into a sword used by corporations to strike at unwanted regulation.

* * *

WE THE PEOPLE. Revered by so many, those three words that begin the Constitution have also been criticized for being inaccurate. When the Constitution went into effect in 1789, African Americans were enslaved in eleven states, and women were not allowed to vote in any. The Framers used the phrase *We the People* to identify who was responsible for enacting this charter of liberty and self-government, but their description was misleading. More than half the nation's population was prohibited from participating in the process by which the Constitution was adopted; most were also denied many of the rights the Constitution purported to guarantee. For those left out, the phrase was not a description but an aspiration, and American history has often pivoted around their struggles to gain equal rights, their fight to finally take their rightful place among *We the People.*

While the civil rights movements for women, racial minorities, and other oppressed groups have been thoroughly studied, there has been another centuries-long push for equal rights that has remained largely unnoticed: the "corporate rights movement." Roscoe Conkling's case was neither the first nor the last time corporations asked the Supreme Court to recognize their constitutional rights. Despite the fact that corporations have never been subjected to systemic oppression like women and minorities, they too have pushed to gain constitutional protections since America's earliest days. Indeed, today corporations have nearly all the same rights as individuals: freedom of speech, freedom of the press, religious liberty, due process, equal protection, freedom from unreasonable searches and seizures, the right to counsel, the right against double jeopardy, and the right to trial by jury, among others. Corporations do not have every right guaranteed by the Constitution; they have no right to vote or right against self-incrimination, and none to date has gone to court asserting a right to keep and bear arms. Yet corporations have won a considerable share of the Constitution's most fundamental protections. Corporations, too, have fought to become part of *We the People*.

In the past decade, the issue of constitutional rights for corporations was thrust into the public spotlight by the Supreme Court's controversial 2010 decision in *Citizens United*. By a narrow 5–4 majority, the justices ruled that corporations have a First Amendment right to spend their money to influence elections. The decision was wildly unpopular, with polls showing an overwhelming majority of both Democrats and Republicans opposed. *Citizens United* also helped inspire Occupy Wall Street, where protestors carried signs declaring "Corporations Are NOT People." "I don't care how many times you try to explain it," President Barack Obama said. "Corporations aren't people. People are people." As of 2016, sixteen states and hundreds of municipalities had endorsed a constitutional amendment to overturn *Citizens United* and clarify that constitutional rights belong to human beings, not corporations.[2]

The backlash had little effect on the justices. Four years after *Citizens United*, the Supreme Court expanded the rights of corporations once again in the *Hobby Lobby* case. The court held that Hobby Lobby Stores, a chain of craft stores with 23,000 employees and over $3 billion in annual revenue, had religious liberty rights under a federal statute.

The company, which was founded by a religious family and remains closely held, was allowed an exemption from a federal rule requiring large employers to include birth control in their employees' health plans. The *Hobby Lobby* decision has since been cited to support the claims of businesses whose owners do not wish to provide wedding services to same-sex couples on grounds of religion.[3]

These Supreme Court decisions came as a surprise to many people, lawyers included. Law students are taught about civil rights, women's rights, Native Americans' rights, gay rights, even states' rights—but not about corporate rights. Yet, as the corporate transformation of the Fourteenth Amendment in the wake of Conkling's deception suggests, the *Citizens United* and *Hobby Lobby* decisions are just the proverbial tip of the iceberg, the most visible manifestations of a larger, and largely hidden, phenomenon. Over the course of American history, corporations have pushed relentlessly, and with noteworthy success, to gain the same rights as individuals under the Constitution.

* * *

CORPORATIONS DID NOT WIN their constitutional rights in quite the same way as women, racial minorities, or gays and lesbians. Historians of those more familiar civil rights movements emphasize how activists pursued their claims in both courts of law and the court of public opinion. To achieve lasting constitutional change, scholars say, required more than just judicial victories. These movements also had to change public opinion. Lawsuits were backed up by broad-based, popular social movements that demanded rights for those who had been denied the original promise of *We the People*. Activists mobilized the masses, and through protests, marches, and public advocacy persuaded not just judges but the larger society that these excluded groups deserved equal rights. According to one scholar, the Supreme Court "usually pays attention to an actual or emerging moral consensus, certainly with respect to fundamental rights."[4]

Corporations, in contrast, gained their rights without winning over hearts and minds. Ronald McDonald and the Pillsbury Doughboy never marched on Washington or protested down Main Street with signs demanding equal rights for corporations. Corporations unquestionably benefited from popular mobilizations for states' rights, small government, and free markets. Yet there was never an effort to convince the public that corporations, as such, should have individual rights too. Corporate rights were won in courts of law, by judicial rulings extending fundamental protections to business, even in the absence of any national consensus in favor of corporate rights. As Adolf Berle and Gardiner Means, two especially influential thinkers about the corporation, once wrote, "It is the essence of revolutions of the more silent sort that they are unrecognized until they are far advanced." The corporate rights revolution was not exactly silent; in fact, the controversies that led to these important judicial rulings were often well publicized in their day. The larger pattern, however, remained hidden—at least until *Citizens United*.[5]

We the Corporations focuses on one central element of the corporate rights movement: how corporations pursued and won constitutional protections through the courts, especially the Supreme Court. Although Americans often think of the Supreme Court as a bulwark to protect minority rights against the tyranny of the majority, the court's record of protecting women and racial minorities was dishearteningly bad prior to the 1950s. For most of American history, the Supreme Court failed to protect the dispossessed and the marginalized, with the justices claiming to be powerless in the face of hostile public sentiment. As we will see, however, the court's record on corporate rights was much different. In 1809, the Supreme Court decided the first case on the constitutional rights of corporations, decades before the first comparable cases for women or racial minorities. And unlike women and minorities, who lost nearly all of their early cases, corporations won that first case—and have compiled an impressive list of victories in the years since. For corporations, the court has insisted that broad public sentiment favoring business regulation must bend to the demands of the Constitution. To the extent the Supreme Court is a bulwark against the tyranny of the majority, powerful and wealthy corporations have been among the primary beneficiaries.[6]

In our daily discourse, Supreme Court justices are often labeled "liberal" or "conservative." Yet what has often united justices across the left/right spectrum is a tendency to side with business. In recent years, scholars have increasingly noticed that even in the ideologically divided Roberts court, the justices regularly find common ground in business cases. This pattern, however, is not unique to the contemporary Supreme Court. For most of American history, the court has been decidedly favorable to business, regardless of whether the majority of justices was liberal or conservative. There are a number of ways this business tilt can be measured, from the number of cases business interests win to the adoption of legal rules that promote free enterprise. One prominent yet understudied illustration is the historic and self-conscious expansion of constitutional rights for corporations.[7]

Corporate constitutional protections were not merely, however, a product of a business-friendly Supreme Court. In many instances, corporations gained constitutional rights when their cases became tangled up in larger political battles or jurisprudential developments. In the early 1800s, for example, the renowned Chief Justice John Marshall sought to protect corporate rights as a way of enhancing the power of the fledgling federal government. After the Civil War, Justice Stephen Field, undoubtedly the most colorful justice to sit on the nation's highest court—he remains the only sitting justice ever arrested, for murder no less—saw corporate rights as necessary to stem the rising tide of socialism. As the Supreme Court embraced new, more libertarian understandings of free speech a century ago, the justices also extended First Amendment rights to newspaper corporations, without which the freedom of the press would be much less meaningful in a modern society.

Indeed, the history of corporate rights sheds new light on, and complicates, our understanding of "liberal" and "conservative" Supreme Courts. Chief Justice Roger Taney, the author of the infamous *Dred Scott* case, whose reactionary views on race have left him one of the most reviled figures in the history of the Supreme Court, was one of the most forceful advocates for limiting the constitutional rights of corporations. In the early twentieth century, the *Lochner* court, which became notorious for its frequent rulings siding with business against government regulation, was also the first to articulate clear boundaries to corporate constitutional rights. Corporations were entitled to property rights, the *Lochner* court said, but not rights associated with personal liberty, like free speech. Ironically, it was the famously liberal New Deal and Warren courts of the mid-twentieth century that first extended liberty rights to corporations.

This long view also illuminates the nuanced role of corporate personhood in the story of corporate rights. Many critics of *Citizens United* believe that corporations have the same rights as individuals because the Supreme Court defines them as *people.* The proposed constitutional amendment to overturn *Citizens United* is based on this idea, declaring that only human beings are people under the terms of the Constitution. Yet corporate personhood has played only a secondary role in the corporate rights movement. While the Supreme Court has on occasion said that corporations are people, the justices have more often relied upon a very different conception of the corporation, one that views it as an *association* capable of asserting the rights of its members. This alternative way of thinking about the corporation has paved the way for the steady expansion of corporate rights. Indeed, as we will see, corporate personhood has traditionally—and surprisingly—been used to justify limits on the rights of corporations.

* * *

CORPORATIONS AND THE CONSTITUTION are more intimately linked than one might imagine. Our story will begin in the colonial era, when even before corporations sought individual rights in the Supreme Court, they nonetheless exerted considerable influence on American ideas of government. It was a corporation, after all, that planted the first seeds of democracy in the colonies, and the goal was to secure profit, not promote liberty. Moreover, the Framers built from what they knew, and the colonies had been originally organized as corporations operating under written charters that, like the Constitution, set the rules for lawmaking and imposed limits on the power of officeholders. As a result, numerous distinctive features of the American Constitution can trace their roots to the nation's corporate origins.

After the Constitution was ratified, corporations quickly sought to gain the rights it guaranteed to individuals. Although there was never a broad-based popular movement for corporate rights, throughout American history the nation's most powerful corporations have persistently mobilized to use the Constitution to fight off unwanted government regulations. The Bank of the United States, the brainchild of Alexander Hamilton and the first great American corporation, brought the first corporate rights case to the Supreme Court in 1809; the Southern Pacific Railroad pushed to win rights of equal protection and due process in Roscoe Conkling's case; tobacco companies sued to gain the Constitution's protections for criminal defendants; and First National Bank fought to win political speech rights for corporations three decades before *Citizens United*. Standard Oil, Ford Motor Company, General Motors, the New York Times Company, and U.S. Steel all played roles in the story of corporate rights—along with insurance companies, brewing companies, mining companies, newspapers, and national chains. Political scientists have shown that large companies tend to be more politically active and show greater sophistication in their political activity than smaller firms, and the pursuit of corporate constitutional rights may be understood as another illustration of the phenomenon.[8]

Although the focus of this book is on business corporations, we will see that several of the Supreme Court's most important corporate rights cases involved other types of organizations that nonetheless took the corporate form: Dartmouth College, the National Association for the Advancement of Colored People, and even Citizens United, a non-profit advocacy group, were all "corporations" that fought to establish their own rights. Yet because the Supreme Court has rarely differentiated among the various types of corporations, even these cases resulted in greater constitutional protections for business.*

Corporations have a straightforward motivation to seek constitu-

---

* Throughout this book, "corporation" is used primarily to refer to a business corporation. Other types of corporations typically include a modifier, such as "nonprofit corporation" or "educational corporation." On occasion, where the context makes it clear, "corporation" is also used to refer to the entire category of organizations that take the corporate form.

tional rights: to fight laws and regulations that restrict business autonomy and interfere with the pursuit of profit. The profit motive has
long made corporations formidable political actors who exert a strong
influence on lawmaking, and indeed the vast majority of lobbyists in
Washington work for companies and business-oriented trade associations. Yet as the story of corporate constitutional rights reminds us,
business influence is not restricted to the elected branches. Corporate
interests have also exerted themselves aggressively in the courts of law,
using the Constitution to expand their power. When popular pres-
sures have succeeded in winning laws to restrict corporations—be it
in the name of consumers, investors, the environment, or the public
at large—constitutional litigation has provided business with another
chance to manipulate public policy to increase its own profits. Even if
the companies lose in the end, the costs of litigation might still serve to
discourage lawmakers from adopting future regulations.[9]

Corporations are all but compelled to seek constitutional rights by
American corporate law—the body of legal rules that dictate how corporations are formed and managed. Corporations are required by long-
standing corporate law principles to maximize profit for shareholders,
at least in the long term. When government regulations impose significant costs on a corporation, this legal requirement directs companies
to pursue any lawful, cost-effective means of reducing the cost of compliance. For corporations, filing lawsuits to establish their rights and
overturn unwanted regulations is just another cost of doing business.[10]

In gaining the protective coverage of the Constitution, corporations have been assisted by the brightest, most able lawyers of the day.
Just as the civil rights movement had Thurgood Marshall and the
women's rights movement Ruth Bader Ginsburg, corporate rights had
Daniel Webster, widely considered the greatest advocate in the history
of the Supreme Court, who argued 223 cases before the justices, many
on behalf of the nation's largest corporations; Horace Binney, a young
and creative lawyer who won the first corporate rights cases in the
Supreme Court by employing an ingenious argument designed to hide
the fact that a corporation was involved; and Theodore Olson, the lawyer who argued *Citizens United* and the dean of an emergent school of

Supreme Court specialists that bolstered the clout of business in the nation's highest tribunal. Even Thurgood Marshall argued for constitutional rights for corporations during the height of the civil rights era, when corporate rights became entangled with issues of race.

As Marshall's example suggests, the fight for corporate rights weaves through some of the most important controversies and turning points in American history: Alexander Hamilton and Thomas Jefferson's battle over the national bank; the fight over slavery before the Civil War; the trust-busting crusades of Theodore Roosevelt and the demagoguery of Huey Long; the civil rights revolution; and the emergence of the Tea Party. The nature and growth of corporate constitutional rights were shaped by those debates. And in turn, we will see, those debates were influenced by the struggle for corporate rights.

The history of corporate rights reveals that corporations are both adept *constitutional leveragers* and creative *constitutional first movers*. As constitutional leveragers, corporations have successfully exploited constitutional reforms originally designed for progressive causes, transforming them to serve the ends of capital. The Fourteenth Amendment, for example, was designed to protect the rights of the freedmen, but Conkling and the Southern Pacific Railroad pushed the Supreme Court to use it to protect the rights of corporations. In the 1970s, Ralph Nader won a landmark case on behalf of consumers that established a First Amendment right to advertise—a right that corporations, including tobacco and gaming companies, used to overturn laws designed to help consumers.

Yet corporations are also constitutional first movers, and historically have often been innovators at the cutting edge of constitutional litigation. They have not always piggybacked on the rights already held by individuals. In fact, numerous individual rights Americans hold dear today were first secured in lawsuits involving corporations. Businesses often have an unusual appetite for pursuing novel and risky legal claims, stirred by the desire to increase profits and untangle themselves from regulation. They also often have the resources to justify the costs of litigation. As a result, the earliest Supreme Court cases to strike down laws for violating the First Amendment, for example, were spearheaded by corporations, as were some of the earliest search-and-seizure cases under the Fourth Amendment. Corporations were behind the preponderance of early cases that breathed life into the equal protection and due process guarantees of the Fourteenth Amendment—rights that in subsequent years became the basis for *Brown v. Board of Education*, outlawing racial segregation in schools; *Roe v. Wade*, guaranteeing the right to choose abortion; and *Obergefell v. Hodges*, recognizing the right to same-sex marriage. It is not fanciful to say that on more than one occasion, corporations have been among the unsung heroes of civil rights.

To say that corporations have had a civil rights movement of their own should not trivialize the historic struggles by racial minorities, women, the LGBT community, and others to gain equal citizenship. The people involved in those fights for constitutional protections overcame violence and terror to establish their rights, and some lost their lives in the effort. There is no moral equivalency between the civil rights, women's rights, and gay rights movements on the one hand, and the corporate rights movement on the other. Nor should the recounting of the history of corporate rights be taken as an endorsement of broad protections for corporations—or, for that matter, as an attack on corporate rights. The goal here is simply to show how corporations have pursued a long-standing, strategic effort to establish and expand their constitutional protections, often employing many of the same strategies as other well-known movements: civil disobedience, test cases, and the pursuit of innovative legal claims in a purposeful effort to reshape the law. For better or worse, the corporate rights movement, like its more famous cousins, has also transformed America.

We the Corporations uncovers this lost history of the corporate rights movement and tells the dramatic, surprising, and even shocking stories behind the landmark Supreme Court cases that extended the Constitution's most fundamental protections to corporations.

PART ONE

CORPORATE ORIGINS

—

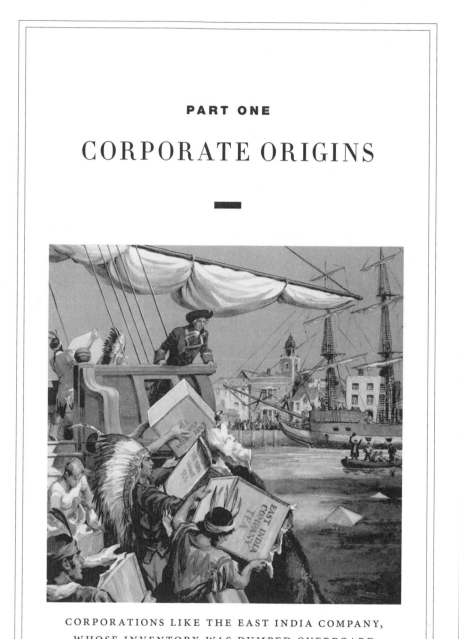

CORPORATIONS LIKE THE EAST INDIA COMPANY,
WHOSE INVENTORY WAS DUMPED OVERBOARD
DURING THE BOSTON TEA PARTY, PROFOUNDLY
INFLUENCED THE REVOLUTION AND THE
CONSTITUTION.

—

CHAPTER 1

In the Beginning,
America Was a Corporation

THERE IS NOTHING IN THE TEXT OF THE CONSTITUTION
that explicitly recognizes corporations or grants them individual
rights. In fact, the word *corporation* appears nowhere in the Constitution. Nor do the records of the Constitutional Convention provide
any hint that the Founders ever thought about whether the Constitution should extend its protections to corporations. When the Founders met in Philadelphia in the summer of 1787, the only discussion of
corporations was a proposal by James Madison to give Congress the
power to charter them, which was ultimately defeated. Corporations
and their place in the constitutional structure were not debated in
the state conventions that ratified the Constitution, nor mentioned
in the famed *Federalist Papers*, the series of essays written by Madison, Alexander Hamilton, and John Jay to defend the proposed charter of liberty. As best we can tell, the people who wrote and ratified
the Constitution simply never considered whether the Constitution
applied to corporations.[1]

One reason the Founders overlooked corporations might be the
paucity of business corporations at the time. In 1917, Joseph Stancliffe

Davis, an economic historian at Stanford, systematically examined the records of all thirteen of the original states to determine the number of corporations created in early America. Davis knew that, prior to the Revolution, there had been a few colleges in the colonies that were technically corporations, including Yale, Dartmouth, and Harvard. Though not for-profit businesses, all were formed as corporations. Ordinary business corporations, however, were quite rare. Davis found that, in the years immediately preceding the Constitutional Convention, only a small handful of business corporations had been chartered: two banks, two insurance companies, six canal companies, and two toll bridge operators. It is a sign of the Founders' failure of imagination in Philadelphia that two of these early American corporations would eventually end up in the Supreme Court claiming constitutional protections.[2]

Some have argued that the Founders were strongly opposed to corporations. According to one scholar, the Founders believed corporations were "dangerous organizations that, if not heavily regulated, would threaten the very freedom of their fledgling nation." There is surely a kernel of truth in this: the Founders worried about all sorts of concentrations of power, including the concentration of wealth. Thomas Jefferson condemned "the aristocracy of our monied corporations which dare already to challenge our government to a trial of strength and bid defiance to the laws of our country." Madison, too, worried that "the indefinite accumulation of property" was "an evil which ought to be guarded against" and that the "power of all corporations, ought to be limited in this respect." Influential Founder George Mason refused to sign the Constitution because it did not do enough to prevent commercial monopolies, and James Wilson, the Pennsylvanian who would go on to become one of the original six Supreme Court justices, warned that corporations "should be erected with caution, and inspected with care" lest "monopoly, superstition, and ignorance" be their "unnatural offspring."[3]

Yet it is easy to exaggerate the founding generation's hostility to corporations. The men who wrote the Constitution were among the wealthiest in America, and many held corporate stock as an investment. Gouverneur Morris, the peg-legged New Yorker who spoke more than anyone else at the Constitutional Convention, was a stockholder in the Bank of North America. So was Robert Morris (no relation), one of only two Founders to score the Revolutionary Era hat trick of signing the Declaration of Independence, the Articles of Confederation, and the Constitution. George Washington was a major investor in the Potomac Company, which built canals along the river north of Georgetown. Benjamin Franklin, Oliver Ellsworth, Elbridge Gerry, and Rufus King were all stockholders; even the wary James Wilson owned shares. There may not have been many corporations, but those that did exist could count a Founder among their investors.[4]

Moreover, although the men who gathered in Philadelphia never considered whether corporations should have the rights of individuals, the corporation nonetheless profoundly affected their handiwork. For while ordinary business corporations were few in number, extraordinary and exceptional corporations were very much part of the Founders' world—and heavily influenced their understanding of limited government, individual rights, and constitutionalism. As we will see, the Constitution the Founders wrote reflected the legacy of three corporations in particular: the Virginia Company of London, which brought the first taste of democracy to America; the Massachusetts Bay Company, which provided the Founders with a model for limited government based on a written constitution; and the East India Company, which helped inspire the Revolution that made the Constitution possible. The Founders did not build from scratch, nor did they model their government exclusively on the political institutions of England. Several of the Constitution's most distinctive and significant features can be traced to America's colonial experience with the corporation. Indeed, in the beginning, America was a corporation—and the demands of business have shaped the nation and its governmental structures from the start. Centuries before *Citizens United*, the corporation in many ways had already been bred into the very genes of the American democracy.

* * *

AMERICANS BELIEVE THEIR NATION was born a land of liberty. The origin myths taught to schoolchildren center on the Pilgrims, religious outcasts who landed at Plymouth Rock in 1620. We are told these black-and-white-hatted refugees came to the New World to escape persecution by the king of England and practice their religion freely. In the romanticized stories of America's beginning, the Pilgrims are potent symbols of the identity and fundamental values of the nation to come: freedom from tyranny, individual rights, and self-government.

The tale of the Pilgrims, however, easily obscures the truth about America's beginning. This land was first colonized not by religious dissenters but by a business corporation. Thirteen years before the *Mayflower* brought the Pilgrims to Plymouth, the Virginia Company of London founded England's first permanent New World colony in Jamestown, on the banks of the Chesapeake. Arriving in 1607, the colonists sent by the Virginia Company were not seeking to exercise their fundamental rights or live free of the monarchy. They were primarily employees of, and investors in, the business, and they came with King James's blessing (hence the colony's name). The purpose of their journey was to make money—for themselves, for the stockholders, and for James, who planned to take a cut of everything they made. Even before the Pilgrims brought the idea of personal liberty to colonial America, the profit-seeking business corporation was already established on its shores.[5]

Founded originally in 1606, the Virginia Company of London was one of the earliest business corporations in England. Started by a group of wealthy investors who sought new business opportunities in overseas trade, it was soon granted a corporate charter by King James. Along with a short-lived sister firm, the Virigina Company of Plymouth, the corporation enjoyed exclusive trading rights for the area stretching roughly from modern-day North Carolina to Maine. The company's charter specified that one-fifth of the revenue from trade was to be delivered to the Crown. Indeed, James, who ruled England from 1603 to 1625, was desperate for the money.

England at the turn of the seventeenth century was a weak international power, an island nation with few resources. The era was one of intense competition between England and Spain, which was then the most successful colonial power in the New World. By the late 1500s, Spain had conquered Mexico and Peru, where mines abundant in gold and silver supplied the riches that transformed Spain from a poor, divided country into the strongest nation in Europe if not the world. Every year, fleets of up to seventy ships were transporting hundreds of tons of precious metals back to Spain. In England, meanwhile, the government could barely afford to maintain the Royal Navy, the most important tool for exercising international influence. English sea power had to be outsourced. The Crown granted ship owners and groups of merchants "letters of marque and reprisal," which authorized them to attack Spanish vessels, capture the ships, and take their cargo in the name of England. The government would receive one-fifth of the bounty.[6]

Privateering, as a result, became an integral part of the English economy, accounting for 10 percent of imports in the 1590s. In 1603, however, the flow of money abruptly stopped. That was the year James ascended to the throne and, in an effort to reconcile with Spain, he put an end to the practice. Nonetheless, the experience provided a model for how England could compete with the other colonial powers, especially Spain, without significant government spending: have private citizens, driven by the profit motive, do it instead. That lesson would help inspire the formation of the Virginia Company, which was also funded by private citizens and promised to generate revenue for the Crown.

To raise the funds necessary to organize an expedition, the Virginia Company did exactly what corporations do today: turn to the capital markets. The company sold shares of stock to investors, who were lured by the promise of dividends expected to come from exploitation of New World resources and trade. Offered at a face value of 12 pounds, 10 shillings, the shares attracted more than 700 "adventurers," as they were then called. Anything but persecuted dissenters, the stockholders included 96 knights, 21 lords, and numerous doctors, ministers, lawyers, and merchants. Sir Francis Bacon, the philosopher who popularized the scientific method, held shares, as did eventually Sir Thomas Hobbes, the father of modern political philosophy. A bit like the similarly named venture capitalists of the future, these investors were willing to gamble on a highly risky startup.[7]

The largest stockholder was Sir Thomas West, an English nobleman whose lineage could be traced back to a signer of the Magna Carta, adopted in 1215 as England's first constitution limiting the power of the Crown. Said to be a "man of the highest social position and character," West served in Parliament, was a member of the powerful Privy Council, and was knighted by Queen Elizabeth, James's immediate predecessor, in 1599. Although few Americans know him today, West,

ONE OF AMERICA'S FORGOTTEN FOUNDERS,
SIR THOMAS WEST, THE LORD DE LA WARR.

whose aristocratic title was Lord De La Warr, had such an influence on the colonial era that one of the original thirteen states, Delaware, was named after him.[8]

West was still back home in England when the *Discovery*, the *Godspeed*, and the *Susan Constant*, the first trio of ships sent by the Virginia Company's "council"—its board of directors—landed in the New World in April of 1607 with more than one hundred colonists. From the council's perspective, the colonists were mostly employees. Other than a handful of gentlemen sent to maintain order, most of these voyagers were servants indentured to the company or to individual investors for periods of four to seven years. All were under the direction of the company and the council in London, which sent with the colonists detailed work instructions. The settlers were directed to establish camp on "some navigable river . . . such as one as runneth furthest into the land." Most importantly, they were to expeditiously organize a team to begin searching for precious metals, such as gold and silver, or a passage to the South Seas. (The directors were certain America was just a thin isthmus like present-day Panama and expected to find an easy route to the Pacific Ocean.) Because such discoveries were the company's best hope to make money, the board commanded a full third of the settlers to begin searching immediately.[9]

The colonists dutifully followed orders, to their considerable misfortune. They selected a site for the settlement that satisfied the company's demands but that turned out to be a deathtrap. They set up amidst bogs and marshes with stagnant water and, as a result, the colonists unknowingly drank water polluted with their own waste; disease—typhoid, scurvy, dysentery, pellagra, beriberi—ran rampant. Because the company had sent such a large contingent of men out to explore for valuable commodities or a passage to the Pacific, the land was not cleared in time for planting. Moreover, the colonists did not have enough supplies to make it through a winter that would be more brutally cold than any of them had previously experienced in England.[10]

The Virginia Company was a first mover, with all the unforeseen risks that typically confront a pioneering firm opening up a new market. One risk the company had not considered was drought. According to historical archeologists, who have studied tree rings to determine rainfall in the area at the time of the first settlement, the seven years beginning in 1606 brought the worst drought to that region since the 1200s. Conditions were so bad that when the Virginia Company's first supply ships arrived in January of 1608, nine months after the initial landing, only 38 of the original 108 colonists had survived.[11]

In the vast expanse of North America, there was but one lone corporation, and it was barely holding on. The company sent several hundred additional settlers, but they too suffered from the harsh conditions—and from the company's unreliable supply chain. In 1609, one of the company's supply ships, the *Sea Venture*, encountered a tempest and was shipwrecked on Bermuda. The council in London did not discover what had happened for months, so the company had not sent additional supplies. The *Sea Venture*'s fate, once publicized in England, inspired an aging writer to author one of his last plays, a story about a group of sailors caught in a storm and marooned on a faraway island in the New World. Shakespeare called his play *The Tempest*.[12]

If the first few years were not difficult enough, the bitter winter of 1609–1610 nearly put the Virginia Company out of business. Relations with the local native tribe, the Paspahegh, had already turned violent, largely due to competition for the supplies of food diminished by the drought. The colonists refused to leave their small fort out of fear of ambush; inside, however, they had not nearly enough food. The colonists reported having to eat "dogs, cats, rats, and mice," and some boiled and ate their own shoes. Eventually, we know now, they turned to cannibalism. Archaeologists studying a trash deposit at the Jamestown site discovered a human skull with scores of knife marks from where the meat was cut away. ("They were clearly interested in cheek meat, muscles of the face, tongue, and brain," reported a researcher who examined the remains.) This period, referred to as the "starving time," saw only sixty—of the more than five hundred settlers who by then had come to Virginia—survive.[13]

In early 1610, after supply ships returned to London with reports on the "sick and miserable estate" of the colonists, Sir Thomas West decided it was time for him to come to America. With a considerable portion of his wealth invested in the venture, he thought it necessary to become more personally involved in the day-to-day operations of the colonial enterprise. Leaving behind his wife, young children, and all the comforts of his aristocratic life, West was not only motivated by money. He was seeking personal redemption. Although a nobleman, West had been imprisoned in 1601 on suspicion of conspiring to overthrow Elizabeth, the queen who had knighted him. He was exonerated, but his reputation was nonetheless unavoidably tarnished. If he could save Jamestown, he would impress his peers and prove his loyalty to the Crown. Like many who would come to America after him, West was seeking a second chance.[14]

West was determined that Jamestown would avoid the fate of previous efforts to colonize North America. The first European attempt had occurred fifty years earlier, when the Spanish conquistador Tristan de Luna y Arellano landed in what is now Pensacola, Florida, only to have his nascent settlement destroyed by a hurricane. Spain had more success with a base further east in St. Augustine. However, all the previous English efforts had ended in failure. The explorer Sir Walter Raleigh, for example, organized an expedition that left over one hundred settlers on Roanoke Island off North Carolina in 1587. Due to hostilities with Spain, however, the first resupply ship did not return for three years. By then, the settlement was deserted; none of the colonists were ever seen again and their fate remains a mystery to this day.[15]

In the spring of 1610, West set sail in a fleet of three ships with four hundred new colonists and a year's worth of supplies. He also came with new powers. The board believed the colony had suffered from a lack of clear authority. In Jamestown, "no man would acknowledge a superior," the company admitted, "nor could from this headless and unbridled multitude, be anything expected but disorder and riot." The settlers needed a boss. West was appointed "Lord Governor and Captain General" of the colony, with "full and absolute power and authority to correct, punish, pardon, govern, and rule." The company expected that the mere presence of an all-powerful boss who hailed from the aristocracy would make the settlers fall into line. Should that fail, however, West brought with him a contingent of military men to enforce discipline. He came to Jamestown to bring order, not liberty.[16]

During his two-month voyage, conditions in Jamestown continued to deteriorate. Desperate, the surviving settlers decided to disregard the Virginia Company's orders and return home. They packed up the ships and were about to set fire to the fort until someone objected that it was not really theirs to destroy. The fort and the other structures were the rightful property of the corporation. Leaving behind the Virginia Company's fixed assets, the settlers departed for England. Jamestown was abandoned.[17]

England's colonial enterprise might have ended right there had it not been for West's uncanny timing. As the ships carrying the settlers who had quit Jamestown made their way down the James River on June 7, 1610, they encountered a longboat from West's fleet coming in the opposite direction. West immediately ordered the settlers to turn around and return to Jamestown. Had West left England a few

ON JUNE 7, 1610, THE JAMESTOWN COLONY WAS SAVED
BY THE ARRIVAL OF SIR THOMAS WEST, A LEADING
STOCKHOLDER IN THE VIRGINIA COMPANY.

days later or been delayed even just a bit longer at sea, the ships would have missed each other. West would have landed at Jamestown to find a fort but no one left there for him to govern. Instead, the colony and the company, and perhaps even the American experiment itself, were saved.

Under West's rigid system of discipline in the colony, settlers were to rise at 6 a.m. and attend morning services at the church. Failure meant the loss of a week's food allowance for the first offense; for the third, the punishment was death. Indeed, capital punishment was threatened for a variety of misdeeds, including profaning God's Word, unauthorized trading with the Indians, and fleeing the colony. If someone robbed the common store of food, they would be bound to a tree to starve. All the settlers' guns were gathered up and declared to be part of the common arsenal. This was ostensibly to make them available if needed to fight the Indians but had the added benefit of making it harder for any colonists who chafed at West's harsh rule to revolt.[18]

West's reign in Jamestown finally put the colony on a stable footing. Although he returned to England before long due to illness, contemporaries credited him with rescuing the colony. As Richard Martin, a lawyer for the Virginia Company, reportedly told the House of Commons in 1614, "Since Lord De la Warr became Governor, Virginia had become a settled plantation, and all it now needed was the fostering care of England." According to Alexander Brown, an influential nineteenth-century historian, West "planted an English nation, where none before had stood." Indeed, Brown went so far as to say that if "any one man can be called the founder of . . . this country," Sir Thomas West "is that man."[19]

While Brown's view has much to commend it, the story of Jamestown points to another contender for the honorific title of America's founder: a legal person, a corporation, known as the Virginia Company.

* * *

ALTHOUGH THE STRICT SYSTEM of discipline instituted by West stabilized the fledgling colony at its most precarious moment, within a few years those same rules became a hindrance to recruiting settlers from England, which in turn scared away investors. To make James-town more attractive to both groups, the Virginia Company board instituted major changes in land ownership and governance begin-ning in 1616. These corporate reforms, designed to maximize the com-pany's profits, brought the earliest measures of democracy to America.

During its first decade, the Virginia Company hemorrhaged money. The colony was stable, but the company had yet to find any precious metals or a passage to the South Seas. There had been no profit to dis-tribute to investors, who the company admitted were rewarded so far with only "fairy tales and hopes." Seeking to turn things around, the board used the one asset it had in abundance: land. Every stockholder was offered 100 acres of land in the colony for each share held, plus additional acres for each settler the stockholder sent to Jamestown. Land was an intriguing lure to successful English merchants who, given the paucity and historical control of land in England by the aris-tocracy, could never expect to own real property at home. The catch was that the stockholders would also have to finance the development of their parcels themselves—just as someone who buys land today has to build on it herself. Instead of the Virginia Company financing the colonists, the stockholders were to be individually responsible for finding settlers, paying for their transportation, and furnishing their supplies.[20]

This new system of land ownership fundamentally changed the colony. Instead of everyone working company land on company orders for company profits, landowners now worked primarily for themselves, with the Virginia Company only taking a cut. Almost exclusively, landowners chose to grow tobacco, America's first mar-ketable crop. Developed for commercial trade by John Rolfe in 1614, tobacco would have an enormous influence on the course of American history, fueling demand for slave labor until the Civil War and shap-ing cultural attitudes ever since. Tobacco, we will see, would also play a starring role in the history of corporate rights, as tobacco companies and their allies would prove to be among the most ardent proponents of constitutional protections for corporations. Back in the Jamestown era, however, commercial tobacco was in its infancy and the colonists' choice to focus on this crop displeased the Virginia Company board, which had wanted the development of even more profitable commodities. Still, the land reform was an unquestioned success, encouraging new settlers to come and enticing new investors for subsequent rounds of financing.[21]

One of the instigators of the company's reforms was Sir Edwin Sandys. The son of the archbishop of York and a leading member of King James's opposition in Parliament, Sandys had been an investor in the Virginia Company from early on and an active member of the board of directors. He had an independent streak that rubbed off on the corporation, which became a bit of a radical. In 1619, when Sandys was nominated for the chief executive job, James reportedly

THE VIRGINIA COMPANY'S CHIEF EXECUTIVE,
SIR EDWIN SANDYS, INSTITUTED REFORMS THAT
INCREASED PROFITS AND ALSO BROUGHT THE FIRST
ELEMENTS OF REPRESENTATIVE DEMOCRACY TO AMERICA.

sent a message to the stockholders meeting: "Choose the Devil if you will, but not Sir Edwin Sandys." Feeling Sandys's renegade influence, however, the stockholders did not bow. Reading the company's charter out loud at the stockholders meeting, with emphasis on the provisions giving them the right to freely elect corporate officers, they chose Sandys.[22]

Under Sandys's leadership, the Virginia Company decided to give the settlers a similar measure of autonomy over their affairs. The company authorized the creation of a "General Assembly" in Jamestown, comprised of representatives of the various plantations, to promulgate rules to govern the colony. The first representative assembly in America met in July of 1619 in the Jamestown Church. Constructed of timbers, with a cobblestone foundation, the church was small—and, in the humidity of a Virginia summer, suffocatingly so; one man died during the convening. Faring better were attendees such as Rolfe, the tobacco innovator; Francis West, the younger brother of Thomas; and John Jefferson, reputed to be an ancestor of the famous Founding Father. Another was Nathaniel Powell, who came over with the first company ships. Generations later, his descendant Lewis Powell would sit on the Supreme Court and became one of the most forceful voices ever in American law for expanding the constitutional rights of corporations.[23]

The emergence of the first measures of self-government in Jamestown was not a reflection of Sandys's liberal leanings. It was a corporate necessity, essential to entice men of character, disciplined and public-spirited, to move to the Chesapeake. Such men would not want to live under martial law, even if that had been necessary in the colony's first years. Settlers would want to have some say over their day-to-day lives. As a result of Sandys's reforms, the company recruited nearly 4,000 new colonists to come to the New World, including the Pilgrims.

Sandys had begun corresponding with the Pilgrims as early as 1617 because they were precisely the kind of dedicated, devout, and hard-working people needed to make a successful colony. Unlike the original Jamestown settlers, the Pilgrims, who were bound together by religious and kinship ties, could largely be trusted to work unselfishly. By happenstance, the *Mayflower* landed far to the north of its intended destination, and the Pilgrims decided to make their home in Plymouth.²⁴

According to legend, the Pilgrims celebrated their first successful harvest with a day of thanksgiving in 1621. Yet the first official Thanksgiving in America was actually two years earlier, and it was a corporate initiative. The Virginia Company had authorized a group of settlers, known as the Berkeley Hundred, to move to the colony. The company ordered them to establish an annual holiday to thank the almighty upon landing: "We ordain that the day of our ships arrival at the place assigned for plantation in the land of Virginia shall be yearly and perpetually kept holy as a day of thanksgiving to Almighty god." On December 4, 1619, when the Berkeley Hundred's ship dropped anchor in the James River, the settlers followed the company's instructions and Thanksgiving in the New World was born.²⁵

The corporation that brought democracy and Thanksgiving to America also brought more nefarious practices, including human trafficking, even before the first African slaves arrived. The Virginia Company board was concerned that men did not want to stay long in Virginia because of the lack of women—or what the company called "the comforts without which God saw that man could not live contentedly, no not [even] in Paradise." To rectify this problem, Sandys launched an extraordinary program to recruit women to emigrate to the colony. Investors in London put together a special fund to subsidize the shipping of young women to Jamestown. Upon arrival in the New World, the women were bartered off by the company to the highest bidder. According to Pulitzer Prize–winning historian Bernard Bailyn, "The women were snapped up by the more affluent planters, bought at such high rates, it was said, that poor men never got near them."²⁶

Sandys's elaborate reorganization of the colony and recruitment of the Pilgrims and women was still not enough to make the Virginia Company profitable. Sandys himself encountered trouble just a few years after taking the company's reins, tripped up by an issue that continues to bedevil corporate executives to this day: executive compensation. After it was publicized that Sandys had awarded himself an extravagant fee to manage the company's tobacco dealings, inves-

THE FIRST MEETING OF THE JAMESTOWN ASSEMBLY, JULY 1619.

tors were outraged. The Privy Council launched an investigation that humiliated Sandys, much to King James's pleasure. Faith in the Virginia Company dissolved further when, in 1622, Indians launched a surprise attack on the settlers, killing about a third of them in what came to be known as the Virginia Massacre. The company tried to blame the settlers, but regardless of fault there was no denying the numbers: nearly 8,000 people had moved to Virginia over the first 15 years and approximately 6,800 of them had died. In 1624, Jamestown took one more life, so to speak, when the Virginia Company itself was finally shut down. With the corporation out of business, the colony was turned over to the Crown.[27]

Although the Virginia Company failed to turn a profit, it nevertheless provided a template for future English colonies—if not for the United States itself. Jamestown revealed what one historian called the "ingredients for success," including "widespread ownership of land," "the institution of a normal society through the inclusion of women," and, in tobacco, the "development of a product that could be marketed profitably to sustain the economy." The corporation's most historic innovation, however, was the representative assembly instituted at Sandys's urging. No idea would be more formative of the nation to come. Democracy had come to America in the same way as the nation's earliest settlers—sent by the Virginia Company in search of profit.[28]

* * *

SEVERAL OF THE ENGLISH COLONIES that followed Jamestown were also formed as corporations. In the years after the arrival of the Pilgrims in 1620, what would become New England was largely settled by the Massachusetts Bay Company, Roger Williams's Rhode Island and Providence Plantations, and the Connecticut Colony, each of which operated under corporate charters. Much of present-day Canada was controlled by the Hudson's Bay Company, which, although founded in 1670 as a trading company, remains in business today as a global retail giant. As corporations, these colonies followed commonplace corporate norms and practices. Yet because they were also governments, responsible for overseeing the people who lived there, they exerted a considerable influence on American attitudes and understandings about governance. Indeed, while the Founders did not self-consciously invoke the corporation as a model at the Constitutional Convention, the Constitution exhibited telltale signs of America's corporate origins. After all, the Constitution was designed in part to do what corporate charters had long done in the colonies: establish government offices, set out the procedures for lawmaking, and impose limits on what the government could do.[29]

The similarities between the Constitution and the original 1629 charter of the Massachusetts Bay Company, for example, are striking. Just as the Constitution begins with a description of who were the sovereigns who did "ordain and establish" that charter of liberty—*We the People*—the company's charter, written over 150 years earlier, begins by identifying that it was "given and granted" by the then-sovereign, King Charles. The company's charter then sets out, very much like the Constitution, a framework for government, complete with a representative assembly, an elected chief executive, and guarantees of individual rights. The assembly mandated by the charter had the power to enact "orders, laws, statutes, and ordinances" necessary for the colo-

THE CHARTERS OF COLONIAL CORPORATIONS, LIKE THE
MASSACHUSETTS BAY COMPANY CHARTER OF 1629, INFLUENCED
THE DESIGN OF THE US CONSTITUTION.

ny's governance. The company had a "governor," a chief executive who
was elected by the residents of the colony and served as commander-
in-chief, responsible for repelling "by force of arms" threats to the colony. This corporate officeholder also had the power to issue pardons,
was required by oath to "take care" that the laws be properly enforced,
and could be impeached for "any misdemeanor or defect." In the event
the governor was unable to serve, the "deputy governor," like the vice
president today, stepped in.[30]

The Massachusetts Bay Company's charter also recognized individual rights. Anyone who moved to the colony or was born there "shall
have and enjoy all liberties and immunities of free and natural subjects." Although the charter did not list what all of those rights were in
detail, it did identify a few, including one far more controversial today

than back in the 1600s, the right to bear arms. Residents were guaranteed the right "to take, lead, carry, and transport . . . armor, weapons, . . . munitions, powder, [and] shot." While that right would be reflected in the Constitution as the Second Amendment, other rights specified in the Massachusetts Bay Company's charter were more attuned to its earlier era, such as "the full and free power and liberty to [engage in the] trade of fishing." Regardless of the substance of the particular rights, these fundamental liberties functioned similarly to constitutional rights in that they were understood to be limits on the power of those holding office under the charter.

Although the Constitution would bear resemblance, the Massachusetts Bay Company's charter was fundamentally a corporate document. Many of the charter's features that reappear in the Constitution were common among the era's business corporations. The legislative power vested in the assembly was just the ordinary power of a corporation to enact bylaws, and the popular assembly was a meeting of the stockholders. The governor and the deputy governor were elected because corporate executives were traditionally chosen by the corporation's members. The duty of the governor to ensure the faithful execution of the colony's laws represented one of the standard fiduciary duties that corporate officers owe to their companies.[31]

Like the Virginia Company, the Massachusetts Bay Company was a business venture pursuing profit. The charter was designed to organize, manage, and govern the business enterprise. Shares were priced at 50 pounds each and came with 200 acres of land, with an additional 50 acres for every laborer sent to the colony. While many stockholders were London investors who planned to send indentured servants to the New World, some, like the Puritan John Winthrop, took their shares and crossed the ocean themselves.[32]

Winthrop emigrated because he *was* seeking religious freedom. The Puritans were being persecuted in England, and to finance their escape Winthrop sold the entire estate he inherited from his father and invested in Massachusetts Bay Company stock. Soon after Winthrop arrived in the New World, he was elected to serve as governor by the stockholders. Once in office, however, Winthrop adopted reforms that made the Massachusetts Bay Company look less like a business corporation and more like a nascent democracy. Early English corporations gave the right to vote for directors to stockholders, typically on a one-stockholder, one-vote basis (compared to modern corporations that usually afford one vote for each share). Winthrop encouraged the company to allow all resident adult male church members to vote in the assembly. Reflecting what today would be considered a capacious understanding of who should have a voice in corporate decision-making, Winthrop believed that all stakeholders, regardless of whether they owned shares, should be enfranchised. In place of a stockholders meeting, Winthrop said his goal was to remake the general assembly "rather in the nature of a parliament."[33]

Another of Winthrop's innovations would transform elections in both democracies and corporations: proxy voting. Although Winthrop had expanded the franchise, many colonists were still unable to attend the assembly due to winter snow, dispersed settlements, and the threat of Indian attacks. Population growth also made the meetings increasingly unwieldy. Winthrop urged the company to allow the voters of a town to meet in advance of the assembly to select representatives who could attend in their place and vote on their behalf. Today, of course, corporations often employ a similar approach to corporate elections, allowing stockholders to cast their votes for a "proxy" who attends the stockholder meeting in their place. And although American elections do not allow for the exact same sort of proxy voting, they follow a similar principle: voters in a particular district elect a representative who is responsible for attending legislative sessions and voting on behalf of her constituents.[34]

As with the popular assembly first instituted in Jamestown by Sir Edwin Sandys, the adoption of proxy voting was not intended to be a progressive step in the advance of democratic ideals. It was instead a more convenient way of managing the affairs of the corporation. Yet proxy voting marked a major difference between American assemblies and the English Parliament. Although Parliament was also made up of delegates sent from towns, the prevailing understanding of the delegates' role was to represent the entirety of the English people, not the residents of their local communities. As English prime minister

George Grenville explained in the run-up to the Revolution, "every Member of Parliament sits in the House, not as a Representative of his own Constituents, but as one of that august Assembly by which all the Commons of Great Britain are represented." That is why the English thought it perfectly acceptable for populous cities like Birmingham and Manchester—much less Philadelphia and Boston—to not have any formal representatives in the House of Commons.[35]

Winthrop could not have known how significant his way of understanding representation would turn out to be. Over the next century and a half, the idea that representatives were the voice of their particular constituents would feed the American urge for independence. "No taxation without representation," the rallying cry of the Revolution, was not primarily a grievance about British tax policy. It was a complaint about not having a proxy in Parliament who was fighting for the colonists' interests.

Another reform adopted by the Massachusetts Bay Company that would influence the Constitution was the enactment in 1641 of the "Body of Liberties." A precursor to the Constitution's Bill of Rights, this corporate bylaw contained explicit, written guarantees of fundamental rights that colonial officials were bound to respect. It provided for due process (punishment must be "by virtue . . . of some express law of the country warranting the same"); equal protection of the laws ("Every person within this jurisdiction, whether inhabitant or foreigner, shall enjoy the same justice and law"); just compensation for the taking of property ("No man's cattle or goods . . . shall be pressed or taken for any public use or service . . . without such reasonable prices"); the right to a speedy trial for criminal defendants ("his cause shall be heard and determined at the next court"); the right against double jeopardy ("No man shall be twice sentenced by civil justice for one and the same crime, offense, or trespass"); and the right against cruel and unusual punishments ("For bodily punishments we allow amongst us none that are inhumane, barbarous, or cruel"). In some ways, the Body of Liberties was more progressive than the Bill of Rights that would mimic it over a century later. For example, the Massachusetts Bay Company prohibited certain forms of spousal abuse and protected children from punishments of "unnatural severity." (In other ways, however, it was more regressive, allowing, for instance, the torture of witches.)[36]

The Body of Liberties was at the time the most extensive listing of explicit individual rights in Anglo-American law. It preceded by forty years the similar English Bill of Rights and offered more detailed individual protections than the Magna Carta. Other colonies followed suit and either by law or by charter guaranteed a broad range of personal liberties. Rhode Island's charter of 1663 granted protection for religious liberty and freedom of conscience. New York adopted a Charter of Liberties in 1683 that included a right to trial by jury, a right to bail, and a prohibition on quartering of troops in private homes. New Jersey's 1677 bill of rights explicitly provided that the general assembly could not repeal it, making that colony's guarantees more durable. Pennsylvania's Charter of Privileges, adopted in 1701, added protections for the right to counsel and the right of the accused to call witnesses on his own behalf. (The famous Liberty Bell was cast to celebrate the fiftieth anniversary of that document.) As a result of these reforms, American colonists enjoyed a broader set of rights than did their fellow countrymen back in England. They referred to their "charter rights" much as people today refer to their "constitutional rights."[37]

In 1639, some settlers broke off from the Massachusetts Bay Company and set up their own colony in Connecticut. Lacking a charter from the Crown, they wrote their own. What they called the Fundamental Orders established a general assembly authorized to enact laws for the "good of the Commonwealth," provided for an elected governor, and guaranteed the right of inhabitants of the various towns to choose deputies to represent them in the assembly. According to historians, the Fundamental Orders were "a conscious imitation" of the Massachusetts Bay Company charter. The main difference was the identity of the sovereign. Whereas Massachusetts's charter was ordained by the king, Connecticut's charter was established by "we the Inhabitants and Residents" of Connecticut. The Fundamental Orders were America's first written constitution formally adopted by the people themselves.[38]

The budding democratic ethos bred by the colonial charters was matched by a growing spirit of independence, much to the displeasure of Charles II. After being exiled by Oliver Cromwell in 1651, Charles, once restored to the throne seven years later, had little appetite for dissent. In the 1680s, he began to convert most of the American colonial corporations into royal colonies governed by the Crown rather than by the company's members. The Massachusetts Bay Company's charter was revoked in 1684, a half-century after it was issued, and royal administrators were appointed to serve in the executive positions from then on. Nevertheless, the Massachusetts Bay Company's corporate structure—along with its corporate reforms, such as proxy voting and the Body of Liberties—continued to impact the shape of colonial government up and down the eastern seaboard.

During the colonial era, Americans came to see their colonial charters as legal documents that provided a model for government and established limits on what the government could do. That is to say, in the years after John Winthrop and the Massachusetts Bay Company immigrated to the New World, Americans began to regard their corporate charters as constitutions.

* * *

IN THE YEARS LEADING UP to the Revolution, the colonists came to believe that the rights guaranteed to them by their charters were under attack. The British Parliament, seeking to pay down war debts and assert authority over the increasingly independent-minded colonists, imposed taxes on a number of staples in the colonies: glass, paper, lead, paint, tea, and even printed materials. Claiming these tax laws violated their colonial charters, the colonists responded angrily. The most dramatic manifestation of their passionate objection took place in December of 1773, when scores of Bostonians boarded ships docked in the local harbor and dumped 342 crates of tea overboard. The tea belonged to a corporation, the East India Company. And what became known as the Boston Tea Party occurred because the East India Company, as they would later say about American financial institutions in the Great Recession of 2008, was "too big to fail."

Founded several years before the Virginia Company, the East India Company by the mid-eighteenth century had grown into the most powerful corporation in the world. In 1757, the company effectively took control of India, which it ruled for the next century. Although the Scottish economic philosopher Adam Smith called this exercise of sovereign power by a joint-stock company a "strange absurdity," it was similar to what had happened in Virginia, Massachusetts, and several other American colonies, just on a far grander scale. The corporation had become a government, with all the power that entails. Exporting silk, salt, tea, and cotton, the East India Company was immensely profitable at first. One of its governors, Elihu Yale, made such a fortune that he thought little of the £500 he donated to endow a college in Connecticut; leaders of the college, however, were so overwhelmed by his abundant generosity they renamed the school in Yale's honor.[39]

Soon after the takeover of India, the company ran into serious financial trouble. Fueled by investors' expectations of windfall profits, the company's stock price had risen dramatically in a flurry of frenzied speculation. Yet 50 percent of the company's income came from tea, and it was stuck with an oversupply of inventory. Because the tea was subject to numerous levies and duties in England, a black market had emerged; smugglers were importing tea illegally into England from Holland and selling it at a significant discount. The company was left with a glut of inventory, with tons of tea wasting away in warehouses. This, coupled with military setbacks in the Bengal region, caused the stock bubble to burst in 1769. A recession spread like a contagion across Europe, where banks had overconfidently purchased far more stock in the East India Company than they could afford—again, not unlike the banks that overinvested in mortgage-backed securities and triggered the 2008 financial crisis. When the East India Company's stock price tumbled, it "threw an entire network of heavily leveraged banks into ruin."[40]

The East India Company, like many business corporations, was dependent upon regular infusions of working capital. Yet in the economic downturn, the banks stopped loaning money. With over £1 million in payments due to the government, the company sought a loan from the Bank of England, which refused. The company was so desperate for revenue that it took to smuggling itself, importing valuable opium illegally into China—planting the seeds of two future wars between Britain and China. It was not nearly enough to save the company, which was forced to go to Parliament for a bailout. Lord North, the British prime minister, thought he had little choice but to rescue the teetering company. The English economy, too, was on the brink of disaster. As one contemporary warned, the East India Company was a "great money engine of state" whose credit was "inseparably connected with government and the Bank of England." Indeed, the company had become so important to the English economy that, one historian wrote, "No minister could ever let the East India Company go to the wall."[41]

North engineered a bailout package of legislation to loan the company over £1.4 million (roughly $270 million in 2017 dollars). So that the company could unload its crippling surplus of tea, North also won passage of the Tea Act of 1773, which allowed the company to sell directly to the colonies instead of, as before, shipping the tea to England and selling it to middlemen in the London tea auctions who alone were authorized to import the tea into the colonies. The Tea Act also provided for a rebate on duties imposed on tea intended for sale abroad. Although the colonists still continued to have to pay a small tax on tea, as they had for years, the overall effect of the Tea Act was to *reduce* the price of tea in the colonies.[42]

Despite the lower tea prices, taxes more generally had become a source of conflict in the colonies, especially as the economy suffered under the weight of the East India Company's financial struggles. Since the mid-1760s, colonists like Samuel Adams in Massachusetts and Patrick Henry in Virginia had been organizing protests against taxes imposed by Parliament, arguing that Parliament lacked the authority to tax the colonists. It was not just that colonists did not have any representation in Parliament; Adams, Henry, and other patriots also framed their objections in corporate terms. By taxing the colonies, Parliament was infringing the colonists' fundamental right of self-government—the right to pass bylaws and legislation as specified in their colonial charters.[43]

This corporate frame was visible in the vigorous public debate over the Stamp Act of 1765, the law that imposed a tax on printed materials. Newspapers, pamphlets, deeds, court documents, and even playing cards had to be printed on paper affixed with a special stamp. Colonists argued that the law violated their charter provisions, like that in Connecticut which gave that colonial corporation the right to "Make, Ordain, and Establish all manner of wholesome, and reasonable Laws, Statutes, [and] Ordinances." The town of Rowley declared the tax "an invasion upon our charter rights and privileges." Throguout Massachusetts, the tax was said to be "universally esteemed here as arbitrary and unconstitutional, and as a breach of charter and compact between K[ing] and subject."[44]

This notion of colonial corporate charters as contracts between the colonists and the Crown made concrete the idea that Parliament was overstepping its bounds by interfering with colonial governance. In the years before the Declaration of Independence announced that all men were "endowed by their Creator with certain unalienable rights," the colonists insisted that their right to enact bylaws for their colonies could not be denied because it had been freely bargained for with the king. According to Sir William Meredith, a British supporter of the colonists who weighed in on the issue in the House of Commons in 1778, "the foundation of every unalienable right is this; when he who is competent to convey, *conveys*; and he who is competent to receive, *accepts*; such conveyance on one hand, and acceptance on the other . . . constitute a right, which, by the law and constitution of England, is *unalienable*; and, unless by consent or forfeiture, cannot be taken away."[45]

Meredith's view, however, was in the minority in Parliament, where most members took the view that colonial charters were subject to revision by Parliament just like the charters of any other corporation. Lord Mansfield insisted that Parliament could regulate the colonies "all on the same footing as our great corporations in London." Soame Jenyns, who wrote an influential defense of colonial taxes, argued that colonial charters "are undoubtedly no more than those of all corporations, which empower them to make bylaws and raise duties for the purposes of their own police . . . they can have no more pretense to plead an exemption from this parliamentary authority, than any other corporation in England." "All charters granted by our Kings," wrote one tax supporter, "are subject to be revised or annihilated by the legislature whenever they operate against the general interest of the British nation."[46]

Whatever the niceties of English corporate law, the proponents of colonial taxes had all the power, leaving the colonists little option but to protest. After the Stamp Act was passed, the outcry in the colonies took increasingly violent form. After rioters in Massachusetts ransacked the houses of Andrew Oliver, a tax collector, and Thomas Hutchinson, the deputy governor, it was reported that men of the army "who have seen towns sacked by the enemy, declared they never before saw an instance of such fury." Soon not a single tax collector for the Stamp Act could be found in the colonies. A more peaceful form of protest was the boycott of products subject to taxes, such as tea. Housewives gave up the brew, even though it was at the center of their social lives, and began drinking coffee. Students at Harvard College—incorporated in 1650 as the "President and Fellows of Harvard College" and today the oldest nonbusiness corporation in America—promised to forsake tea for the duration of their studies.[47]

Paradoxically, one of the main reasons the colonists objected to the Tea Act was that, by lowering the price of tea, it threatened to undermine the tea boycott. Cheaper tea was more likely to attract purchasers. The Tea Act also threatened local merchants, who had made a good business out of purchasing tea in the London auctions and selling it back home in the colonies. Many of the middlemen whom the East India Company was now allowed to cut out were colonists. Fear spread that Parliament might adopt similar rules for other products, harming any number of local businesses and further deepening the economic downturn in the colonies. Even if the tax on tea was small, it continued to represent the assertion of Parliament's power to tax the colonies, which was the essence of Adams and Henry's complaint.[48]

So when the *Dartmouth*, a ship carrying 114 chests of the East India Company's tea, arrived in Boston harbor in November of 1773, Adams determined to prevent that tea from ever being sold in the colony. The Sons of Liberty, an informal organization of patriots of which

Adams was a leader, posted notices around Boston: "Friends, breth-ren, countrymen—The worst of plagues, the detested tea shipped for this port by the East India Company, is now arrived in the harbor. The hour of destruction, or manly opposition to the machinations of tyr-anny, stares you in the face." At a meeting of the townspeople at the Old South Meeting House, it was decided that armed guards would be sent to the wharf and the tea would not be allowed off the ship. The ship would be forced to return to England. When the king's men dis-covered the plan, the royal governor of Massachusetts forbade the ship from leaving port. A stalemate ensued, soon ensnaring two more ships that arrived carrying East India Company tea.[49]

The ship owners, who were American colonists, had no choice but to keep the ships docked and the tea unloaded. This was not a viable long-term solution, however, as English law only permitted ships to remain in port for twenty days without unloading their cargo; after that, the ships' goods were subject to seizure by customs officials. Town meetings were held throughout early December as the colonists debated what to do. Finally, the deadline came. December 16 marked the *Dartmouth*'s twentieth day in port. If the tea was still on board at midnight, a confrontation between the Sons of Liberty's armed guards and royal troops, who were sure to come to collect the tea, was inevitable.[50]

After a final meeting at the Old South Meeting House, a group of men, many dressed as natives, set out for the wharf at dusk. They were disciplined; there was no rioting or collateral violence. They boarded the three ships, hoisted up the tea, broke open the chests, and dumped the leaves overboard. With quiet efficiency, they destroyed more than £18,000 (over $3 million today) worth of the East India Company's tea in just a few hours. The locally owned ships were left unharmed, with some reports suggesting that after the tea was dumped, the men even swept the decks clean. The targets of the protest were the East India Company and its tea.[51]

It would be another fifty years before the incident came to be known as the "Boston Tea Party," but the impact of the event in the colonies was felt right away. All up and down the coast, colonists refused to allow tea ships to unload their cargo. Parliament responded by ordering the closure of Boston harbor until the colonists repaid the East India Company for all the tea it had lost. Parliament also enacted new legislation abrogating Massachusetts's charter. Assemblies were forbidden without the consent of the royally appointed governor, and the power to choose members of the executive council (what had once been the company's board of directors) was transferred to the Crown. To many colonists, Parliament had lawlessly overridden their sacred charters and it was finally time to take up arms.

Although we rightly call it the Revolution, there were clear lines of continuity with America's corporate past. After Independence, the Framers would eventually adopt the Constitution, the most potent symbol of the new nation—and one that preserved many of the features of the colonial corporate charters. Just as the colonial corporations were bound by written charters that specified limits on the power of officeholders and guaranteed the rights of members, so was the new nation. The Constitution was America's charter, its founding document, and the Constitution's shape and scope reflected the Framers' experience with corporate governance.

Indeed, as we have seen, democracy and constitutionalism were intimately tied up with the corporation from the very beginning. America was founded by the Virginia Company, fundamentally shaped by the colonists' experience with the Massachusetts Bay Company, and inspired to Independence by the East India Company. Although the Founders at the Constitutional Convention never considered whether corporations should be afforded individual rights under the Constitution, the idea of the corporation nonetheless influenced the constitutional system they established.

Once the Constitution was ratified, it would not be long before corporations would invoke it to secure their own rights in an effort to win greater freedom from business regulation. In a harbinger of what was to come, the first corporate rights case was brought to the Supreme Court by what was then the nation's most politically powerful corporation, the Bank of the United States. The Bank's lawsuit would be the beginning of another revolution, this one in favor of constitutional protections for corporations.

PART TWO

THE BIRTH OF CORPORATE RIGHTS

—

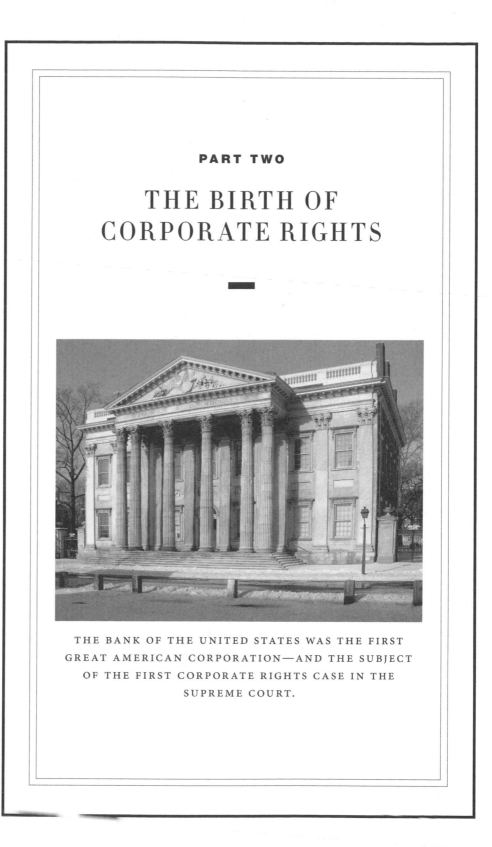

THE BANK OF THE UNITED STATES WAS THE FIRST
GREAT AMERICAN CORPORATION—AND THE SUBJECT
OF THE FIRST CORPORATE RIGHTS CASE IN THE
SUPREME COURT.

CHAPTER 2

The First Corporate Rights Case

THE CONSTITUTION OF THE UNITED STATES WENT INTO effect in 1789, but it took nearly seventy years before the Supreme Court heard its first case explicitly addressing the constitutional rights of African Americans, *Dred Scott v. Sandford*, in 1857. The court in that case held that African Americans had "no rights which the white man was bound to respect." The first women's rights case, *Bradwell v. Illinois*, on whether women had a right to practice law, was not heard until 1873, and the Supreme Court ruled against the woman. Conversely, the first corporate rights case in the Supreme Court was decided decades earlier, in 1809, and the corporation won.

That 1809 case is one of the buried landmarks of American constitutional law, and the company behind it was the nation's first great corporation, the Bank of the United States. The brainchild of Alexander Hamilton, the Bank was chartered by the first Congress in 1791 and carried the name of the new nation, yet was what Americans today would think of as a private business. It was a for-profit corporation with publicly traded stock, managed by executives who were accountable to stockholders. At a time when the handful of existing American corporations were local concerns—operating, say, a toll bridge across the Charles River—the Bank was the first truly national enterprise, with headquarters in Philadelphia and branches from Boston to New Orleans.[1]

Like so many of the giant corporations that feature in the history of the corporate rights movement—the Southern Pacific Railroad, Standard Oil, Philip Morris—the Bank of the United States provoked considerable controversy in its day. Opponents accused the Bank of having too much political and economic power. Today's critics of *Citizens United* who worry about corporate corruption of American democracy would have found an ally in fiery Kentucky Whig Henry Clay, who complained of the Bank that "our liberties" were in the hands of "a body, who, in derogation of the great principle of all our institutions, responsibility to the people, is amenable only to a few stockholders." When Georgia passed a law to limit the Bank's influence in that state, the nation's most powerful corporation simply refused to comply. The Bank's civil disobedience led to the earliest Supreme Court case on whether corporations had constitutional protections, two centuries before *Citizens United*.[2]

The Supreme Court's decision in *Bank of the United States v. Deveaux* has been largely lost to modern memory. Although occasionally cited by courts, the case is not featured in modern constitutional law books or even in very many of the tomes on American legal history. Yet back in the first decade of the nineteenth century, the drama surrounding the case was well known. It pitted the legacies of two Founding Fathers, Alexander Hamilton and Thomas Jefferson, against each other. Their split over the Bank is already justly famous for giving birth to the two-party system. Less well known, however, is how their conflict spilled over into the struggle over constitutional protections for corporations. On this issue, Hamiltonians were *corporationalists*—proponents of corporate enterprise who advocated for expansive constitutional rights for business. Jeffersonians, meanwhile, were *populists*—opponents of corporate power who sought to limit corporate rights in the name of the people. The competing views of Hamiltonian corporationalists and Jeffersonian populists would set the terms of debate over constitutional protections for business for much of the next two centuries. Over the course of that history, the corporationalists would prove to be far more successful.

Another issue on which corporationalists and populists disagreed was corporate personhood. From the start, the Supreme Court has wrestled with whether corporations should be considered "people" under the Constitution and what exactly that might mean. Some critics of *Citizens United* argue that the reason corporations have constitutional rights today is that the Supreme Court has said that corporations are people. Indeed, one proposed response to *Citizens United* has been a constitutional amendment to clarify that corporations are not people under the language of the Constitution and do not have the rights of people. Yet, as we will see, corporate personhood has played only a small role in the expansion of constitutional rights to corporations. While the Supreme Court has said from time to time that corporations are people, the justices have more frequently offered other reasons to justify constitutional protections for corporations—often obscuring and hiding the corporate person rather than exalting it.

Beginning with *Bank of the United States v. Deveaux*, and for most of American history, corporate personhood has been deployed in precisely the opposite way from how today's critics of *Citizens United* imagine. Counterintuitively, it has usually been populist opponents of corporations who have argued in favor of corporate personhood. For them, treating corporations as people was a way to *limit* the rights of corporations. And many of the most important Supreme Court decisions extending rights to corporations did not rely on corporate personhood at all. More commonly, the Supreme Court rejected the idea that a corporation was an independent, legal person with rights and duties all its own, and instead allowed the corporation to claim the rights of its members.

To understand the role of corporate personhood in American constitutional law requires a careful examination of the *Bank of the United States* case, which was the first Supreme Court case on the constitutional rights of corporations and laid the foundation for the many corporate rights cases to come. Oddly enough, the justices would preside over the case not in the usual Supreme Court courtroom but in a working pub, and the charismatic group of lawyers who participated in this mostly forgotten yet profoundly important case included a future president of the United States, a founder of Harvard's Hasty Pudding social club, and a British Loyalist who fought against Independence in the Revolutionary War. They would argue over what might appear to be an esoteric issue: Did corporations have a constitutionally guaranteed right to sue in federal court? For the Bank, however, it was a matter of life or death. If forced to litigate the lawfulness of the Georgia tax in the Georgia courts, the Bank was sure to lose. For the nation, the case was even more significant. *Bank of the United States v. Deveaux* would graft onto the Constitution the first of many constitutional rights for corporations.

* * *

THE MISSION OF THE BANK of the United States was nothing less than to save America. Hamilton, George Washington's first secretary of the treasury, was the Founding Father most preoccupied with stabilizing the nascent nation's precarious economy. At the time, there was no national currency; each bank issued its own notes. Yet the notes at the existing state-created banks were unreliable. A federal bank, backed by Congress, would have the resources to guarantee its notes. Hamilton also thought the Bank would be a more secure place for the federal government to stash deposits. Indeed, once established the Bank was a tremendous success and, according to historians, helped "to place American finance on a sound footing." Within five years of the Bank's creation, the United States had the highest credit rating in the world. Hamilton, then, was also the Founding Father of surely one of the most important corporations in American history.[3]

Hamilton had been inspired by the success of an earlier bank, the Bank of North America, founded during the Revolutionary War. Washington's army was short on rations and pay, soldiers were on the verge of mutiny, and the war had depreciated American currency to near worthlessness. The Bank of North America was proposed, like the later Bank of the United States, to create more reliable notes and insure liquidity. The plan worked to the benefit of both the nation and investors, who received annual dividends of 13–14 percent. The Bank of North America was transformed into a private state bank in 1786, and today, after more than two centuries of mergers and reorganizations, remains a tiny part of Wells Fargo.[4]

Hamilton faced a significant hurdle in setting up his bank: the text of the Constitution. Did Congress have the power to create a corporation under the Constitution? In the vigorous debate over Hamilton's proposal for a bank in 1791, James Madison and Thomas Jefferson argued that Congress did not have that authority. No one would know better than Madison, one of the Constitution's primary authors. During the Constitutional Convention, Madison had proposed to give Congress the authority to charter corporations, but his proposal was rejected. As a result, Madison said Congress could not charter Hamilton's bank. Fortunately for Hamilton, the men who populated Congress at the time did not believe the only appropriate way to interpret the Constitution was by reference to the original intent of the Framers. With strong advocacy by northern commercial interests, which mobilized in favor of the Bank, Hamilton's bill was passed. President George Washington signed the law over the objections of Jefferson, his secretary of state. The law, along with spurring the creation of two separate political parties where once there was none, also breathed life into a uniquely powerful and influential corporation. The Bank of the United States would live only a short life, but its impact on the nation, the economy, and the Constitution was prodigious.[5]

In the early years, the Bank was quite conservative. It showed more interest in public service than in maximizing profit. Hamilton in his original proposal had advised, "Public utility is more truly the object of public banks than private profit." The Bank adhered to this wisdom, forsaking opportunities to make money for stockholders in order to maintain the stability of the nation's finances. "Arguments in favor of a Safe & Prudent Administration are paramount to all considerations of pecuniary interest," the board of directors instructed branch managers. In that spirit, the Bank in the 1790s and early 1800s was cautious in extending loans and maintained a large cash reserve. The Bank was nonetheless quite profitable, earning stockholders 8–10 percent annually.[6]

Still the Bank stoked passions. To Jefferson, the Bank was not just a financial institution; it was a threat to his vision of America. A populist who believed in the cause of the common man over the privileged interests of capital and wealth, Jefferson aspired for America to be a decentralized, agrarian society built upon a foundation of independent, yeoman farmers. The Bank, by contrast, represented the concentration of power in the hands of an unaccountable corporation based in the North, one that used its effective control over lending to pursue a nationalist agenda. Moreover, its lending policies favored loans to commercial interests, like manufacturing and infrastructure, which threatened to pull more people from the farm. Increasingly, the borrowers on the receiving end of the Bank's loans were corporations—threatening to multiply the very entities Jefferson feared.[7]

The Bank also offended Jeffersonians' notion of states' rights. Jefferson and his emergent opposition party, the Democratic-Republicans, thought states should have broad authority to regulate business within their borders to promote the public interest. Yet the Bank, the nation's largest and most powerful corporation, was seemingly immune to state regulation because of the Constitution's supremacy clause. The Bank was created by Congress, and under Article VI of the Constitution, "the Laws of the United States . . . shall be the supreme law of the land." That meant that state lawmakers, who were used to complete control over the businesses in their states, had no say over the operations of the Bank. Despite stabilizing the economy, the Bank became "the target of every possible derogatory charge, of every species of vituperation." After Jefferson won the presidency in the bitterly disputed election of 1800, he promptly ordered the sale of all of the government's shares of the company stock. Yet even Jefferson, the archenemy of the Bank, found he could not live without it; when he left the presidency, he was deeply in debt and went to the Bank for a personal loan.[8]

Jefferson, however, was still in office wracking up those debts in 1805 when his allies in Georgia made a daring move against the Bank. Shortly after the Bank opened a new branch in Savannah, lawmakers, frustrated they could not prohibit the federal institution outright, instead imposed a tax on the Bank's locally held capital and notes. If the Bank wanted to do business in Georgia, it would have to pay dearly for the privilege. And if the tax were not enough to persuade the Bank to close up and go home, Georgia could always impose additional taxes.[9]

The usually conservative Bank responded with uncharacteristic brashness. Headquarters in Philadelphia instructed the Savannah branch officials to ignore the law and refuse to pay the tax. A century and a half before African American protestors sat in at lunch counters to force the nation to confront civil rights, the Bank of the United States similarly chose to engage in an act of civil disobedience to defend its rights. Not unlike the civil rights protestors, the Bank frankly admitted that it hoped the refusal to comply with the law would "bring the question before the Supreme Court of the United States."[10]

* * *

ANGRY AT THE BANK'S failure to pay the taxes, Peter Deveaux, a Georgia tax collector, decided to force the issue. Deveaux was known for his confident assertiveness, which had served him well before. As a soldier in the Revolutionary War, Deveaux once happened upon a group of American soldiers vengefully preparing to hang two ragged-looking spies captured after an American defeat. Deveaux risked his own life to intervene—and saved the lives of the two men, who turned out to be two American soldiers. One of the two, John Milledge, went on to become a US senator, governor of Georgia, and founder of the University of Georgia. In April 1807, amidst the controversy over the Bank, Deveaux once again stuck his neck out for what he thought was right. With "force and arms," the tax collector barged into the Savannah branch of the Bank and carted off two boxes of silver coins.[11]

The Bank wanted to turn to the courts for help. Yet filing a lawsuit in Georgia state court to contest the Georgia tax and the actions of a Georgia tax collector was not an appealing option. State judges were widely perceived at the time to be biased in favor of their home states and local residents. For a controversial out-of-state corporation like the Bank, justice was not likely to be found in the Georgia courts. So the Bank filed suit instead in federal court. It was not so much that the

Bank was opposed to biased judges; it just wanted ones more likely to lean in the Bank's favor.

The federal courts might do just that, at least if the case made it up to the Supreme Court. By 1807, the high court was beginning to reflect the strong nationalist imprint of Chief Justice John Marshall. Like Hamilton, Marshall was a Federalist and a supporter of the Bank. Under his leadership, the Supreme Court would become known for its rulings enhancing federal power and minimizing states' rights. Georgia's tax on the Bank was a reaction against federal power and a manifestation of the Jeffersonians' robust view of states' rights. The Bank, created by Congress and operating nationwide, could fairly expect that Marshall's Supreme Court would naturally sympathize with it.

One potential pitfall for the Bank, however, was the text of the Constitution. Under Article III, section 2, the jurisdiction of the federal courts is limited; they can hear only certain types of cases. One type of case they are authorized to hear is a lawsuit "between Citizens of different States." The Founders had the same worry as the Bank about biased state court judges. If both parties to a lawsuit were from the same state, neither would be disadvantaged by a judge's parochial allegiances and there was little need for a federal forum. If, however, the parties were from different states, the federal courts should be available to protect the "foreigner" from unfair treatment. This constitutional doctrine is known as diversity jurisdiction, and it effectively creates a right of access to the federal courts when disputes involve citizens that are diverse—that is, from distinct states. One of the first laws passed by Congress was the Judiciary Act of 1789, which established the lower federal courts and, borrowing the language of Article III, provided explicit statutory authority for federal courts to hear disputes between diverse citizens. Given that Deveaux was a citizen of Georgia and the Bank was headquartered in Pennsylvania, the two parties to the Bank's lawsuit were from different states and thus could be seen as diverse. The question facing the Bank was whether corporations counted as "Citizens" under the Judiciary Act and Article III of the Constitution—the exact same question *Dred Scott* posed a half-century later about African Americans.

The Framers at the Constitutional Convention who drafted Article III never paused to consider whether corporations, like ordinary people, should be guaranteed any rights under the Constitution, much less whether they enjoyed a right to sue in federal court. This was due in part to the fact that, during the colonial era, England had significantly curtailed the formation of ordinary business corporations after the South Sea Bubble of 1720. Foreshadowing what would happen with the East India Company half a century later, stock prices for the South Sea Company, which held a monopoly on trade with South America, soared in a speculative buying binge, only to tumble precipitously. It was the first international stock market collapse and it led Parliament to adopt the Bubble Act, which prohibited any unincorporated entity from having transferable shares. Coupled with an uncompromising refusal by successive English monarchs to grant charters to any business that had stock, the new law prevented any significant growth in the population of ordinary business corporations. That tradition of hostility to the stock corporation is why the industrial revolution in England was led primarily by businesses organized as partnerships, not by corporations as in the United States.[12]

In the years after the Constitution was ratified, the founding generation, liberated from English control, enthusiastically embraced the corporate form. Joseph Stancliffe Davis, the Stanford historian who discovered there were only a handful of corporations formed in the decade prior to the Constitutional Convention, found over three hundred business corporations chartered in the United States in the decade following ratification of the Constitution. It was a spurt of corporate growth without precedent. Americans formed corporations to produce silk, cotton, iron, and maps; to construct aqueducts, dig mines, and run waterworks; and to operate ferries, banks, and insurance companies. Most of all, corporations were created to build the scores of turnpikes, bridges, and canals that began to stitch together the independent colonies into one nation with a single, national economy. John Adams, the second president of the United States—and, as we will see, the father of one of the earliest advocates for constitutional rights for corporations—was led to ask, "Are there not more legal corporations,—literary, . . . mercantile, manufactural, marine insurance, fire, bridge, canal, turnpike, &c. &c. &c.,—than are to be found in any known country of the whole world?"[13]

Hamilton's faith in corporations was such that he was willing to rest the weight of the unsteady American financial system on the shoulders of one. Yet the Bank now faced a serious legal problem. It could not win in state court, yet how could it claim a right to sue in federal court in the absence of any evidence that the Framers intended to protect corporations? Moreover, the text of the Constitution seemed to go against the Bank too. Article III said that "Citizens" could sue in federal court, and citizens are generally thought to be natural people who belong by law to one country. They are members of a political community who owe their allegiance and support to a particular polity. If that was what the Constitution meant by the "Citizens" in Article III, then corporations like the Bank of the United States would not have any right to sue in federal court. And absent this fundamental right, the Bank would find itself, quite literally, regulated to death by Jeffersonians eager to shut it down.

* * *

THE IDEA THAT A CORPORATION could have legal rights similar to those of ordinary people might seem absurd. Corporations are fictional entities, created by people primarily for economic reasons. Nevertheless, the very reason the corporation was invented was to enable the establishment of a durable, legal entity that could exercise at least some legal rights. To understand why requires turning from the early United States to ancient Rome—and to the celebrated English scholar who first detailed the legal rights of corporations.

The earliest version of the corporation was created in Rome three centuries before the birth of Christ. Called a *societas publicoranum*, this prototype was Rome's answer to a pressing problem: how could a group of people hold property together and make contracts for their common enterprise? The Romans already had business partnerships, called *societas*, but they could be unreliable. The *societas*'s property, like that of a partnership today, was owned by the partners in the partners' own names; there was no legal separation between the partnership and the partners. Moreover, Roman law required partnerships to be dissolved in any number of circumstances, such as when any one partner became insolvent or died. (Today, by contrast, partners can contractually agree to maintain the business in the event of one partner's departure.) In a time when life spans were short, the Roman partnership was useful as a way of aggregating capital but also created an unwelcome yet constant state of chaos for the businesspeople who tried to use it.[14]

The *societas publicoranum* offered much greater stability. It was authorized to own property and form contracts in its own name and did not have to be dissolved if a member died or went bankrupt. Because of these special privileges, the *societas publicoranum* had to be authorized by a decree of the Senate or the emperor. Individuals could form partnerships on their own, but only the sovereign had the authority to create a corporation. From the very beginning, sovereigns believed that corporations needed to be strictly controlled and limited.

Nonetheless, the corporation became quite successful in Rome. *Societas publicoranum* were created for shipbuilding, mining, public works projects, temple construction, and tax collection. Even some of these earliest corporations had a global impact. A 1997 study of ice core samples from Greenland found "unequivocal evidence of early large-scale atmospheric pollution" caused by Roman silver and lead mining corporations operating in southern Spain between 366 BC and AD 36.[15]

In the centuries to follow, the corporate form became popular for other sorts of organizations that also had the need to own property or form contracts in their own names, regardless of the shifting identity of their members. For example, beginning in the fourth century, the Catholic Church claimed to be a corporation so that it could receive gifts of land and hold that property in the Church's own name for perpetuity. Oxford University, which was founded sometime in the eleventh century—the precise date has been lost to history—was a corporation, as were the English guilds and even the City of London.[16]

IN HIS COMPREHENSIVE TREATISE ON THE LAW OF
ENGLAND, SIR WILLIAM BLACKSTONE IDENTIFIED
CORPORATIONS AS "ARTIFICIAL PERSONS" WITH
LEGALLY RECOGNIZED RIGHTS.

In 1758, an English lawyer and Oxford professor named William
Blackstone sought to bring some order to English law and, in particular, the legal status of the corporation. Blackstone's first love was not
the law but architecture, and while still a teenager he wrote a much-
praised treatise on "the art of building." As a lawyer, however, his
practice was notable mostly for its lack of distinction. A priggish, ill-
tempered man, Blackstone could not keep clients. He may have just
been a lousy lawyer; when he was appointed to the bench later in life,
his rulings were reportedly overturned on appeal more than those of
any other judge in London. Yet, as a scholar and chronicler of English
law, Blackstone was without peer. His scholarly effort to detail, organize, and explain English law, published under the title *Commentaries*

on the Law of England, would come to be hailed as the "most influential law book in Anglo-American history."[17]

That influence was immediate, and not just in England. Thousands of copies were sold in the American colonies before the Revolution. Thomas Jefferson called Blackstone's *Commentaries* "the most elegant and best digested of our law catalogue." Years later, Abraham Lincoln advised anyone who wanted to be a lawyer to start by reading the *Commentaries*. For decades, lawyers would include Blackstone's volumes in the background of their portraits. One historian said that "no other book—except the Bible—has played so great a role" in shaping American institutions. Even today, Blackstone's *Commentaries* is cited about ten times a year by the Supreme Court of the United States.

The corporation was one of the topics that Blackstone tackled in the *Commentaries*: how it was formed, how it operated, and what legal rights and duties it had. He began his explanation by describing the corporation as an "artificial person." By this Blackstone meant two things. First, the corporation was an independent legal entity in the eyes of the law, separate and distinct from the people who formed it. Second, as an independent legal entity, it had certain legally enforceable rights similar to those of a natural person.

An individual's "personal rights die with the person," Blackstone wrote. So "it has been found necessary, when it is for the advantage of the public to have any particular rights kept on foot and continued, to constitute artificial persons." Called "bodies corporate, or corporations," these artificial persons "may maintain a perpetual succession, and enjoy a kind of legal immortality." There were, Blackstone noted, "a great variety" of corporations used for such things as "the advancement of religion, of learning, and of commerce."[18]

Blackstone analogized the corporation to a person because the individual human being was the paradigmatic legal actor in the minds of lawyers. Only people, not objects like tables or shrubs, had standing to make a claim in court seeking the law's protections; only people had rights. Indeed, this remains a common frame of mind today. When proponents of animal rights go to court seeking legal protections for chimpanzees, for example, they claim the animals are "legal persons." They do not necessarily mean that chimpanzees are exactly the same as human beings, or that they have all the same rights as people, including the right to free speech, freedom of religion, or the right to bear arms. They mean only that chimpanzees should have standing before the law, that they have some rights entitling them to the court's attention.[19]

Because the corporation was its own independent, identifiable legal person, Blackstone wrote, it had to have a name. "When a corporation is erected, a name must be given to it; and by that name alone it must sue, and be sued, and do all legal acts." The name of the corporation was not just a nicety. The name was "the very being of its constitution" and was essential to enable the entity to "perform its corporate functions." English courts took the corporation's name very seriously, voiding contracts for failing to state a corporation's formal name precisely. The name was so important for corporations for the exact same reason it was important for individuals: it was the signifier of the unique identity of that person. Acts taken in the corporate name were, in the eyes of the law, acts of the corporation—not acts of the members.

Today, corporations are typically thought of as private enterprises, created by private citizens to pursue profit for themselves. In Blackstone's day, however, corporations more clearly straddled the divide between public and private. They had unambiguously private aspects, in that they were financed and managed by private parties. Yet they were also inherently public. They could only be formed by charter granted by the government, and the government would not grant one unless the corporation had a public purpose. "The king's consent is absolutely necessary to the erection of any corporation," Blackstone noted. To be a separate, legally recognized entity required special governmental approval, and it would not be forthcoming if a corporation's mission were not "for the advantage of the public." Corporations had to serve the commonweal, whether it was by building a road, maintaining a bridge, or providing insurance. Individual investors took home profits, but the ultimate mission of the corporations had to be in the service of the public. Corporations, in other words, were both public and private enterprises at the same time.

Corporations were also strictly regulated in Blackstone's day. Today businesses are controlled through labor laws, consumer protection laws, environmental laws, workplace safety laws, and alike, but corporations in the 1700s were regulated primarily though their charters. The charter was both the corporation's birth certificate and the corporation's rulebook. It was the visible manifestation of the king's consent—and a tool for the king to control his creations. Charters were often detailed documents that set forth the corporation's mission, powers, and duties. They might dictate how much the corporation could charge for goods or services, how much capital it could raise, and how corporate decisions were to be made. A corporation had a measure of autonomy, to be sure; Blackstone recognized that one of the fundamental attributes of the corporation was the power "to make by-laws or private statutes for the better government of the corporation." Nevertheless, a corporation could only lawfully act in ways permitted by the government-issued charter. Anything else was beyond the power of the corporation—what the law would later term *ultra vires*—and unenforceable. Blackstone also identified another limit: corporate bylaws were "binding . . . unless contrary to the laws of the land, and then they are void."[20]

Under English law, corporations nonetheless always possessed certain rights. "After a corporation is so formed and named," Blackstone wrote, the law gives it "many powers, rights, capacities, and incapacities." These rights are "necessarily and inseparably incident to every corporation." As a separate legal entity, the corporation typically enjoyed the right to "purchase lands, and hold them"—in other words, the right of property. This was why the corporate form had been developed in ancient Rome, so that groups of people could own property together without the hassles and inefficiencies of partnerships. Corporations were designed to pull together the property interests of a diverse group of people for consolidated control. Without property rights, corporations could not function.

Another right of corporations was the right to form contracts. They had the legal power to make agreements with others—employees, suppliers, lenders—that would "bind the corporation." Consistent with the legal requirements of his day, Blackstone noted that corporations could only form binding contracts with the use of a "common seal." The seal, like the corporation's name, served to differentiate the entity from the people who composed it. "For though the particular members may express their private consent to any acts, by words, or signing their names, yet this does not bind the corporation," he wrote. The corporation as a distinct legal person "acts and speaks only by its common seal."

Blackstone also recognized that corporations had a third right: the right to "sue or be sued . . . by its corporate name." Although Americans today may not always think of the right to sue and be sued as a fundamental right, it may in fact be the most vital because it is preservative of all the others. If someone takes your property or restricts your religious freedom, the right to sue enables you to defend your rights and obtain a lawful remedy. Without access to the courts, rights would be just words on paper with little practical significance. Of course, a corporation cannot appear in court like an ordinary person. It must, Blackstone recognized, "always appear by attorney," a representative of the corporation. The people who formed or ran the corporation could not appear in their own names. The suit had to be by or against the corporation itself.

These were the three core rights of any corporation: the right to own property, the right to make contracts, and the right of access to the courts. Each of these rights, Blackstone explained, was exercised by the corporation in its own name. The members of the corporation did not own the corporation's property, the corporation did. The members of the corporation were not personally bound by the corporation's contracts, the corporation was. The members of the corporation could not sue or be sued for legal controversies involving the corporation, only the corporation could. Corporations were their own independent entities under the law, separate and distinct from their members and with certain rights deserving of protection.

Although corporations were legal persons and had some legal rights, they did not have the exact same rights as individuals. Blackstone highlighted the differences between real people and corporations. "A corporation cannot commit treason, or felony, or other crime, in its corporate capacity: though its members may, in their distinct individual capacities." With no physical body, the corporation could not "be committed to prison" or "be beaten." Nor could the corporation swear an oath. Blackstone also wrote that corporations had special duties that individuals did not have. For example, corporations could be "visited" by authorities, who were allowed to "inquire into, and correct all irregularities that arise" should the corporations "deviate from the end of their institution." Because of the unique features and characteristics of the corporation, the rights and duties of this artificial person were distinct from the rights and duties of ordinary individuals.

Blackstone's understanding of the corporation is old but hardly outdated. Open any law book on corporations and one of the first things discussed is likely to be the strict separation between the corporate entity and its members. As George Field wrote on the first page of *A Treatise on the Law of Corporations*, published in 1877, a corporation is a "legal person" whose acts "are considered those of the body, and not those of the members composing it." More than a century later, Harvard Law School dean Robert Charles Clark wrote in the opening pages of his own corporate law treatise, "One of the law's most economically significant contributions to business life . . . has been the creation of fictional but legally recognized entities or 'persons' that are treated as having some of the attributes of natural persons." And because the "law conceives corporations to be legal persons with certain powers and purposes," the rights and obligations of corporations do not transfer to their members, and vice versa. Due to this legal separation, the stockholders of a corporation are not liable for its debts; corporations have their own independent legal standing. According to the Supreme Court, the "basic purpose" of incorporation is "to create a legal entity distinct from those natural individuals who created the corporation, who own it, or whom it employs." This idea—that a corporation is in the eyes of the law its own, separate legal person—remains "a general principle of corporate law deeply ingrained in our economic and legal systems." It would not, however, be as successful in shaping American constitutional law.[21]

* * *

BLACKSTONE'S *COMMENTARIES* WOULD BE among the sources Horace Binney, the young lawyer for the Bank of the United States, would use to argue for constitutional rights for corporations. Although the Framers had not set out to protect corporations, Binney was blessed with a creative mind. A precocious child from Philadelphia who grew up surrounded by power—President Washington's residence was across the street and Hamilton lived next door—he went to Harvard College at the age of 14. To make friends and build cama-

HORACE BINNEY, THE CREATIVE YOUNG LAWYER
FOR THE BANK OF THE UNITED STATES.

raderie there, he founded a group he called the "Hasty Pudding Club," which remains in existence today as the oldest collegiate social club in America. As a budding young lawyer, Binney's innovative arguments quickly earned him the respect of the Pennsylvania bar, and he was still only in his twenties when he was hired in 1808 to represent the nation's most preeminent corporation in the fight for its life.[22]

Binney and the Bank filed suit in the federal court in Georgia to recover the money taken by Peter Deveaux. Binney was hopeful the Bank could receive a more fair hearing there than in the state courts—and, even if not, the Bank would be prepared to appeal to the Supreme Court, whose justices were sure to lean in the Bank's direction. The two judges who first heard the Bank's case in the lower federal court in Georgia, however, were William Johnson, a sitting Supreme Court justice who hailed from South Carolina, and William Stephens, the local federal judge. Both had been appointed to the bench by Jefferson after his election to the presidency in 1800, and both shared the Sage of Monticello's populist opposition to corporations like the Bank. If the philosophical leanings of the presiding judges were not enough of an obstacle, Binney also faced the daunting task of persuading them to extend to corporations the right of "Citizens" to sue in federal court.[23]

Binney could possibly have argued that corporations were citizens because they enjoyed many of the characteristic features of citizenship. A corporation, like a citizen, could have a nationality, a country to which it belonged. Today, for example, it is commonplace to ascribe a nationality to a corporation—to call General Motors an American company and Renault a French one—and the same was true in Binney's era. In an 1814 case, Supreme Court justice Joseph Story explained that "where a corporation is established in a foreign country, by a foreign government, it is undoubtedly an alien corporation." Nor would it have been completely outrageous for Binney to argue that a corporation was a citizen of a particular state—the type of citizenship at issue in diversity cases under the Judiciary Act and Article III. Then and now, a corporation is incorporated in one state and must follow that state's laws on issues of corporate governance, such as the

fiduciary duties of officers and the voting rights of stockholders. As in
Binney's day, Americans today might speak of a Delaware corporation
or a New York corporation.[24]

Even if corporations could arguably be seen as citizens for legal
purposes, Binney understood how difficult it would be for him to win
with this argument. As a student of rhetoric and persuasion, he knew
that even the most compelling logic falters if it defies common sense.
Saying that corporations were "Citizens" under the Constitution was
precisely such an argument, because citizenship was a status usually
thought to be reserved for actual human beings. Binney nonetheless
came up with a clever, even fateful, solution. If he could not persuade
the courts that corporations were citizens, perhaps he could persuade
the courts that his case was not really about a corporation.

Binney focused the court's attention on the people behind the corporation. The Bank itself might not be a citizen under the Constitution, but what Binney called the Bank's "members" were. The people
who formed, ran, and financed the corporation were ordinary human
beings entitled to all the rights provided in the Constitution. They
undeniably were citizens, and Article III was written to protect their
rights. To decide his case, the court should look to the rights of the
corporation's members.

"A corporation is composed of natural persons," Binney argued.
Although the Bank was the formal party to the lawsuit, the "real parties" were the Bank's members. If they were citizens of states other
than Georgia, where Deveaux was a citizen, then they should have
access to federal court to protect them "against fraudulent laws and
local prejudices." The purpose of the constitutional right to access federal court for diverse citizens was to reduce the possibility of local bias,
and that same concern was present in the Bank's case. The members
of the locally reviled Bank were not likely to find an impartial judge in
Georgia state court.[25]

Binney's solution was to make the corporation invisible, to make it
transparent, and, in effect, to hide its corporate-ness. He did not deny
that a corporation was involved, yet he sought to make the corporate
form irrelevant. He sought to collapse the distinction between the cor-

poration and its members, suggesting the courts see right through the corporation and focus instead on the people who compose it.

Corporate lawyers today have a name for this way of thinking about corporations. They call it "piercing the corporate veil." The ordinary rule, ever since the days of Blackstone, is that there is a strict separation between the corporation and the people behind it. That is why the corporation, not the stockholders, is liable if someone is injured using the company's products. In a small number of highly unusual cases, however, the courts will pierce the corporate veil, ignoring the separate legal status of the corporation and imposing liability on the stockholders personally. Piercing the corporate veil in business law cases is very rare, and courts typically only do it when someone uses the corporate form to perpetuate a fraud or commit wrongdoing.[26]

Binney wanted the courts to approach the corporation in a similar way. They should pierce the corporate veil, even though there was no fraud or wrongdoing by the Bank. According to Binney, corporations and their members were not separate and distinct entities when it came to the Constitution. Instead, Binney argued, corporations were associations of individuals, and corporations should be able to assert the same rights as the people who come together within them. Unlike veil piercing in corporate law, which is used to extend the liability of the corporation to its members, Binney's version sought to extend the rights of the members to the corporation. Binney's way of thinking about corporations would be repeated often by corporationalists throughout American history and ultimately prove to be profoundly influential in shaping constitutional rights for corporations.

Binney's influence, unlike Blackstone's, was not immediate. Judges Johnson and Stephens ruled against him and the Bank. Johnson authored the court's opinion. First, he rejected the idea that a corporation could be a citizen under Article III of the Constitution. "A corporation cannot with propriety be denominated a citizen of any state, so that the right to sue in this court under the Constitution can only be extended to corporate bodies by a liberality of construction, which we do not feel ourselves at liberty to exercise." Then Johnson rebuffed Binney's creative argument about piercing the corporate veil. "As a suit in right of a corporation can never be maintained by the individuals who compose it, either in their individual capacity or by their individual names, how is the citizenship of the individuals of the corporate body ever to be brought into question by the pleadings?"[27]

From Johnson's perspective, the law was clear. It was the Bank's money that was taken, not the money of the Bank's members. The Bank's stockholders were not parties to the case. If any of them had tried to sue Peter Deveaux in their own names, Johnson would have dismissed the case. Similarly, if Deveaux had sued the Bank's stockholders for some wrongdoing committed by the Bank, the corporation's members would have urged dismissal on the very same ground—that there was a strict separation between the rights of the corporation and the rights of those who form, own, or manage it. Johnson recognized, in other words, the same long-standing principle of law that Blackstone had explained in his *Commentaries*: corporations were their own independent legal entities, separate and apart from their members.

For Johnson, however, corporate personhood did not mean that corporations had the same constitutional rights as individuals. It meant the opposite. Corporations only had those rights appropriate for such a unique, specialized type of legal entity. So while corporations might have a right to own property or form contracts as appropriate for a business, they still had *fewer* rights than natural people: individuals had the right to sue in federal court on diversity grounds but corporations did not.

* * *

IN 1790, WHEN THE JUSTICES of the Supreme Court convened for the very first time, they met not in Washington but in New York City, at the Royal Exchange Building. Located on Broad Street, near the current home of the New York Stock Exchange, the commercial building, which also housed an open-air market, was nonetheless an appropriate locale for the court. Over the following two centuries, the Supreme Court would frequently side with business interests. One measure of the court's business-friendly attitude was the gradual expansion of numerous constitutional rights to corporations—a phenomenon that began with Horace Binney's case on behalf of the Bank of the United States.[28]

Oral argument in *Bank of the United States v. Deveaux* took place in February of 1809, and the justices were no longer holding court in the Royal Exchange but in, of all places, a pub. When the court first moved to Washington, the justices were given a committee room in the Capitol Building to hear cases. Beginning in 1808, however, renovations were undertaken on the building and the justices were forced to move into a drafty, frigid library on the second floor. The justices decided to hear their cases instead across the street in the cozier confines of Long's Tavern. Although one envisions the justices hearing cases while tipsy on port, this location too was appropriate in its own way: Long's Tavern was apparently located on the same plot of land where the majestic neoclassical Cass Gilbert–designed Supreme Court Building sits today.[29]

Binney told the justices they should pierce the corporate veil. To decide this case, they ought to look right through the corporate form and allow the Bank to sue in federal court because the Bank's members were "Citizens." "A corporation is a mere collection of men," Binney insisted. The "residence and inhabitancy [of] the particular members" ought to determine whether a corporation can sue or be sued in federal court. The Farmers guaranteed the right of access to the federal courts to protect people from the biases of local judges, and denying the corporation's members such access "would be a result clearly contrary to the intention and spirit of the constitution."[30]

Another lawyer who appeared before the Supreme Court at the same time as Binney was John Quincy Adams. At 44, the son of the second president of the United States had already been a US senator and a professor at Harvard, and was about to be named minister to Prussia. Just months after the Bank case, Adams would be nominated and confirmed to the nation's highest court himself. He declined, thinking the Supreme Court position somewhat of an insult; after all, he was by then busy negotiating the fate of the world with the tsar. Yet back in February, Adams was still practicing law, which was what brought one of the most legendary figures in American history to Long's Tavern at the same time as Binney. Adams's case, *Hope Insurance v. Boardman*, would be his last appearance in the Supreme Court for thirty-two years, when he returned in 1841 as the former president to argue in the famous *Amistad* case for the rights of African slaves caught at sea.[31]

Historians have written off the *Hope Insurance* case as "of little consequence." Yet, along with the *Bank of the United States* case, it was part of the first set of corporate rights cases. And much as he would later argue for the rights of slaves, Adams argued here for the constitutional rights of corporations. Adams was representing two Boston men whose case against the Hope Insurance Company, a Rhode Island insurance corporation, raised the same issue of corporate citizenship under the Judiciary Act and Article III. Adams, however, was seeking

FUTURE PRESIDENT JOHN QUINCY ADAMS ARGUED THAT
CORPORATIONS, LIKE CITIZENS, HAD THE RIGHT TO SUE
AND BE SUED IN FEDERAL COURT.

to vindicate the other side of the corporation's right to sue: the right to *be* sued. Recall that Blackstone described the corporation as typically having the right to sue and to be sued. The corporation's legal standing could be used by the corporation when it sued someone, as in the Bank's case, or by others when they sued the corporation. The latter was the type of case Adams had. His clients wanted to sue in federal court because they thought the judiciary of Rhode Island, where Hope Insurance was located, would be biased in favor of the company. Although Binney and Adams were coming at the problem from different angles, they ended in the same place: corporations, both argued, should have the right to sue and be sued in federal court.[32]

Rounding out the all-star cast of lawyers were Jared Ingersoll, a former member of the Constitutional Convention of 1787 who was appearing on behalf of Hope Insurance, and Philip Barton Key, who represented Peter Deveaux, the Georgia tax collector. Key, the uncle of "The Star-Spangled Banner" lyricist Francis Scott Key, was perhaps in some ways the most extraordinary of the remarkable figures who gathered in Long's Tavern. Key had fought in the Revolutionary War on the side of the British, but he became the rare Loyalist welcomed back into the upper echelons of American society after Independence. He was elected to Congress, served for a short time as a federal judge, and then returned to private practice, where he represented powerful clients. In 1805, for instance, four years before the Bank case, Key successfully defended Supreme Court justice Samuel Chase in his impeachment trial, establishing a precedent—still adhered to today— that federal judges should not be impeached for political reasons. So when Key appeared before the justices in the corporate rights case, he could count on the personal gratitude of one justice and the warm appreciation of all the others.[33]

Key's argument for limiting corporate rights was centered on corporate personhood. "But it is said that you may raise the veil which the corporate name interposes, and see who stand behind it," said Key, in response to Binney. The Bank's lawsuit, however, "is brought in the corporate name." The members "expressly averred themselves to be a body corporate, and to sue in that capacity." The Bank itself, "not the indi-

IN THE FIRST CORPORATE RIGHTS CASE, PHILIP BARTON KEY
ARGUED FOR LIMITING THE RIGHTS OF CORPORATIONS BY
RECOGNIZING THEIR UNIQUE LEGAL PERSONHOOD.

vidual stockholders," was the plaintiff. Using an argument that populists would make often in the two hundred–plus years of corporate
rights cases, Key insisted that the corporation and its members must
be deemed separate and distinct under the law. "No corporation . . .
can derive aid from the personal character of its members; nor does it
incur any disability from [their] disabilities," Key told the justices. The
purpose of the corporation was to be an independent legal actor, separate and apart from the people who create it. The court, Key argued,
was without the "power to examine the character of the individuals to
ascertain whether the corporation has a right to sue in a certain court."
The question was whether *corporations* were "Citizens" under the Judiciary Act and Article III, not whether their members were.

When Adams rose to address the justices, he was forced to admit Key's point, that under the law a corporation was traditionally deemed a person with its own separate legal identity. A corporation's "powers, its duties and capacities are different from those of the individuals of whom it is composed," Adams recognized. "It can neither derive benefit from the privileges, nor suffer injury by the capacities, of any of those individuals." Nonetheless, he argued, the court should still ignore the corporate form. The justices, he advised, should rule that corporations were citizens under Article III because that would serve the basic purposes of diversity jurisdiction—perhaps even more so in the case of a corporation than in one involving an individual. "If there was a probability that an individual citizen of a state could influence the state courts in his favor, how much stronger is the probability that [the courts] could be influenced in favor of a powerful moneyed institution which might be composed of the most influential characters in the state?" In determining whether corporations had constitutional rights, Adams argued, the justices should not be "limited by the letter of the constitution" but should instead promote the broad purposes of the document.

Bank of the United States v. Deveaux and its companion case, *Hope Insurance*, thus presented the Supreme Court with two different ways of thinking about the constitutional rights of corporations. Like the populist Justice Johnson, Key argued that corporations were people—independent entities with legal rights and obligations separate and apart from the people who make them up. Due to that legal separation, the rights and duties of the members did not transfer to the corporation, or vice versa. The question facing the court was whether corporations, as such, were citizens guaranteed the right to sue in federal court. Horace Binney and John Quincy Adams argued conversely that corporations were associations—collectivities that enjoyed the same rights and obligations as their members. According to this more corporationalist perspective, the court should pierce the corporate veil and ask whether the corporation's members were citizens guaranteed the right to sue in federal court.[34]

These two contrasting ways of thinking about corporations were first introduced to American law in the *Bank of the United States* and *Hope Insurance* cases. Ever since, the history of corporate rights has largely been a struggle between the disparate poles of personhood and piercing, between populists and corporationalists. Today's critics of *Citizens United* often blame corporate personhood for the Supreme Court's expansive protection of corporate rights. Yet historically, the logic of personhood has usually been employed by populists seeking to narrow or limit the rights of corporations. By contrast, expansive constitutional rights for corporations have frequently been a product of the corporationalist logic of piercing. When the Supreme Court has ignored the corporate form and looked to the rights of the individuals who made up the corporation, the rulings naturally tended to give corporations nearly all the same rights as individuals. Expansive constitutional rights for corporations were built into the logic of piercing.

After the hearing, Adams confided in his diary that his presentation to the justices had not gone well. "The ground which I was obliged to take appeared to the court untenable, and I shortened my argument, from the manifest inefficacy of all that I said to produce conviction upon the minds of any of the Judges." He need not have been so worried. For despite Jefferson's appointment of justices like Johnson to the Supreme Court, Hamiltonian justices like Chief Justice John Marshall and Samuel Chase, who favored corporate rights, remained in control.[35]

* * *

IN THE *BANK OF THE UNITED STATES* case, Hoarce Binney was asking the Surpeme Court to exercise its fundmental power of judicial review—the authority to determine the constitutionality of laws and strike them down. Binney and the Bank ultimately hoped to have Georgia's tax on the Bank declared unconstitutional and void. The origins of this power of courts to invalidate duly passed laws have long been obscure. At the time of the Revolution, English courts did not have this ability to review acts of Parliament. For many years, Chief Justice Marshall was credited with inventing judicial review "out of the constitutional vapors" (in one historian's memorable description) in the celebrated 1803 case of *Marbury v. Madison*. In truth, however, judicial review is another of the distinctive features of American constitutionalism that can be traced back to the corporation.[36]

Recall that Blackstone wrote that corporate bylaws "contrary to the laws of the land . . . are void." As an earlier treaty from 1659 phrased it, bylaws must not be "repugnant to the Laws of the Nation." In England, where there was no written constitution, the "laws of the land" were those adopted by Parliament. Colonial corporate charters explicitly referenced this principle of repugnancy. The Virginia Company's revised charter of 1611, for example, provided that the corporation could enact bylaws for its own governance if they "be not contrary to the laws and statutes of this our realm of England." The principle of repugnancy grew to serve as a restriction on colonial legislatures, the bodies empowered by the charters to adopt bylaws for the colonies. The Privy Council in England reviewed over 8,500 acts of the colonial legislatures for repugnancy before the Revolution. That practice of repugnancy review was gradually transformed from a limit on English corporations into a limit on colonial lawmaking.[37]

In England, the laws passed by Parliament were the supreme law of the land. In nascent America, however, the supreme law of the land was found in the Constitution of the United States. Hamilton referred to this in *Federalist 78*, where he famously described the duty of the judicial branch "to declare all acts contrary to the manifest tenor of the Constitution void." The repugnancy principle also appeared in the Judiciary Act of 1789, which authorized the Supreme Court to review state laws alleged to be "repugnant to the constitution, treaties or laws of the United States." Marshall's opinion in *Marbury* referred to this key principle that grew out of corporate law too. The question in that case, Marshall wrote, was "whether an act, repugnant to the Constitution, can become the law of the land." A "law repugnant to the Constitution is void," Marshall explained, and therefore the courts were obliged to invalidate it.[38]

Over the course of American history, the power of judicial review would be used by the Supreme Court to transform the nation. Most famously, the court would employ this authority in the civil rights era to tear down Jim Crow in cases like *Brown v. Board of Education*, voiding laws requiring racially segregated schools, and *Loving v. Virginia*, holding prohibitions on interracial marriage contrary to the Constitution. The court used the power of judicial review to vindicate the rights of women in the 1970s, the rights of the disabled in the 1980s, and the rights of gays and lesbians at the turn of the twenty-first century. For most of American history, though, the Supreme Court used judicial review to benefit business. And one of the earliest examples was the Bank case of 1809, in which Chief Justice Marshall and the Supreme Court established the first constitutional right for corporations.

* * *

LIKE ALEXANDER HAMILTON, John Marshall favored the growth of corporate enterprise and supported the Bank of the United States in particular. In his opinion for the court in *Bank of the United States v. Deveaux*, Marshall enthusiastically embraced Horace Binney and John Quincy Adams's theory about how to think about corporations under the Constitution. (Despite Adams's poor performance, the future president won his case, too. Although there was no separate opinion in *Hope Insurance*, the Supreme Court reporter directed readers to see the opinion in *Bank of the United States*, which decided the same issue, "the right of a corporation to litigate in the courts of the United States.")[39]

Marshall's opinion admitted that the question involved in the case was "one of much . . . difficulty." First he examined the Bank's charter of incorporation to see if Congress, in creating the Bank, had explicitly conferred upon it the right to sue and be sued in federal court. Although the charter did explicitly grant the Bank "a capacity to make contracts and acquire property, and enables it 'to sue and be sued'"— the three core rights identified by Blackstone—Marshall said that was insufficient. Congress could have meant only to grant the Bank the right to sue and be sued in *state* court. To extend to corporations the right of access to *federal* court, however, would have required Congress to say so explicitly.[40]

CHIEF JUSTICE JOHN MARSHALL WROTE THE OPINION
IN *BANK OF THE UNITED STATES V. DEVEAUX* (1809),
THE FIRST SUPREME COURT DECISION RECOGNIZING
CORPORATE RIGHTS.

The question, then, turned not on the meaning of the Bank's charter but on the meaning of the Constitution. Although Marshall recognized that the law often deemed a corporation to be a legal person—"for the general purposes and objects of a law," the corporation was often "included within terms of description appropriated to real persons"—a corporation was "certainly not a citizen." That title was reserved to human beings, and there was no evidence from the founding period that the citizens referred to in Article III included corporations.

Yet that still did not answer the question conclusively, Marshall explained, because constitutions were to be read expansively. "A Constitution, from its nature, deals in generals, not in detail. Its framers cannot perceive minute distinctions which arise in the progress of the nation, and therefore confine it to the establishment of broad and general principles." The purpose of diversity jurisdiction under Article III was to protect people against potentially parochial and biased state courts. The court was obliged to read Article III to fulfill that promise, which in Marshall's view meant extending the right to sue and be sued in federal court to corporations—regardless of the fact that corporations were not citizens.

While Marshall embraced John Qunicy Adams's argument about broadly reading the Constitution, he also pierced the corporate veil as Horace Binney had suggested. Corporations might not be citizens, but their members were. Marshall described the corporation as an "invisible, intangible, and artificial being," employing a phrase he would use again in another corporate rights case, *Dartmouth College v. Woodward*, decided a decade later. Although some have mistakenly interpreted that language in *Dartmouth College* to mean that Marshall embraced corporate personhood, in fact he meant the opposite. Marshall was saying that corporations were too ethereal to be the basis for constitutional rights and that, instead, the court should focus on the corporation's members. "Substantially and essentially, the parties in such a case" are the "members of the corporation." The corporation was just a stand-in for a group of "individuals who, in transacting their joint concerns, may use a legal name." Because the people who associated together within the corporation were the real parties to the case, Marshall held, *their* citizenship should control. According to Elizabeth Pollman and Margaret Blair, two of the few scholars to have carefully studied the *Bank of the United States* case, Marshall "looked to the natural persons composing a corporation." As Marshall himself stated in the opinion, the court was obliged to "look beyond the corporate name and notice the character of the individual."[41]

An astute legal craftsman, Marshall knew that his reasoning ran counter to the traditional way the law had treated corporations—as independent legal entities with rights and obligations separate and distinct from those of their members. His opinion surveyed a series of English cases dealing with the ability of corporations to sue and be sued more generally, admitting sheepishly that they provided "more strong" support for treating a corporation as its own legal person rather than "to consider the character of the individuals who compose it." Nevertheless, Marshall insisted, "this technical definition of a corporation" should be set aside to protect the rights of the corporation's members, who undoubtedly were citizens.

Although Marshall based a corporation's ability to sue in federal court on the citizenship of its members, the esteemed jurist never identified who exactly counted as a member of a corporation. Was it the stockholders? The employees? The directors? *Bank of the United States v. Deveaux* offered no answer, even though the logic of piercing made this question vitally important. In 1806, three years prior to the *Bank of the United States* case, the Supreme Court held in another case involving diversity jurisdiction that the parties must be completely diverse; all of the plaintiffs must be from different states than all of the defendants. Even today, the requirement of complete diversity remains the law of the land. Yet because Marshall did not specify who counted as a member of the corporation, he never bothered to ask whether, in fact, all of the Bank's members were diverse from Peter Deveaux. Given the Bank's relatively large class of stockholders, it was likely that at least one hailed from Deveaux's home state of Georgia, which meant there would not be complete diversity. Marshall skipped right over this key issue and declared that the Bank had the right to sue the tax collector in federal court. He declared the rights of the members paramount, but the actual membership remained abstract, undefined, and unexamined. This would become a common theme in the corporate rights cases to come; the courts would base corporate constitutional protections on the rights of the members without ever seriously questioning who the members were or what the members wanted.

Chief Justice Marshall's embrace of piercing was nevertheless so complete that *Bank of the United States*, although mostly overlooked today as a constitutional law case, is from time to time still cited for establishing the business law doctrine of veil piercing. As previously noted, however, piercing the veil in business law cases is limited to rare cases involving fraud or abuse; it is the exception, not the rule. In constitutional law, by contrast, the exception would become the rule. And although modern corporate rights cases like *Citizens United* do not cite *Bank of the United States*, the court's approach in that ancient case nonetheless features prominently throughout the two centuries of corporate rights jurisprudence that followed in its wake. Piercing the veil, and allowing a corporation to claim the rights of its members, would be the conceptual tool the court would use to justify the extension of a wide variety of constitutional rights to corporations.

* * *

THE BANK OF THE UNITED STATES was a constitutional first mover. Although the text of the Constitution did not explicitly grant any protections to corporations, the Bank set out to secure an authoritative ruling by the Supreme Court recognizing the Bank's rights. In time, other movements would follow a similar pathway to secure their civil rights. Yet the Bank's victory was both long-lasting and short-lived. It was durable in that the general principle established by the decision—that corporations have constitutional protections—remains firmly embedded in American law. The triumph was temporary in that the Bank would not survive long enough to exercise its newfound constitutional freedom.

When Chief Justice Marshall handed down the court's ruling in March of 1809, the Bank of the United States faced the threat of imminent closure. While modern corporations typically enjoy perpetual life, Congress had only chartered the Bank for twenty years as a compromise to attract the votes necessary to pass Hamilton's controversial law. That meant the Bank would need to obtain a new charter from Congress in 1811 if it were to carry on. Hamiltonian backers of the Bank had already begun lobbying Congress to renew the charter when *Bank of the United States v. Deveaux* was argued before the Supreme Court. Jeffersonians remained firmly opposed, and the bitter partisanship of the earlier Bank debate manifested itself once again.

That larger context explains why an important question in the *Bank of the United States* case was left unanswered by the court. Marshall's opinion said nothing about the legal issue that led the Bank to sue in the first place: Did the Constitution permit a state like Georgia to tax a federal corporation like the Bank? Students of constitutional law will recognize that to be the same question at issue in *McCulloch v. Maryland*, a landmark Supreme Court case from 1819 that held states could *not* impose such taxes on federal entities. *McCulloch* remained to be decided only because Marshall had ducked that same question a decade earlier in the first corporate rights case. Marshall's opinion avoided the issue entirely, returning the case to the lower court for consideration instead. It was not an oversight. Marshall was trying to protect the Bank. A Supreme Court ruling prohibiting states from taxing the Bank would only inflame populists opposed to reissuing the Bank's charter.[42]

In the congressional deliberations over extending the charter, the Bank's prospects appeared at first quite dim. Then the Bank received unexpected support from two of its most vociferous and abiding critics, James Madison and Thomas Jefferson. Although both men had opposed the original creation of the Bank, their views ultimately changed, likely due to having subsequently seen the issue from the vantage point of the White House. Madison, who was president during the debate over renewal of the charter, and Jefferson, who had just finished his two terms in office, came to recognize how the Bank strengthened the economy, stabilized the nation's finances, and eased credit—everything Hamilton, the father of the Bank, had said it would. By endorsing the renewal of the Bank's charter, Madison, who had once insisted that the Framers never gave Congress the power to create corporations, revealed that not even the author of the Constitution believed it truly necessary to adhere to the original understanding. Jefferson, meanwhile, simply abandoned his Jeffersonianism.[43]

Madison and Jefferson's support buoyed the northern commercial interests who favored extending the life of the Bank, but it was not enough. In Congress, the Bank's renewal lost by a single vote and the charter expired. The Bank of the United States was shut down. The Bank died an early death, but its impact on the Constitution and corporate rights would be profound. The Bank had fought and won the first case affording corporations rights under the Constitution, and many corporations to come would build on that foundation in seeking additional protections. Frequently, those cases would present the court with the same choice between two different ways of conceptualizing the corporation—as a person or as an association. Is a corporation, as Blackstone said, a legal person with rights of its own? Or is a corporation, as Binney and Marshall said in *Bank of the United States*, best understood to be an association of people whose rights are derived from its members?

One of the corporations to carry on the Bank's fight would be its younger sibling, the Second Bank of the United States. In 1812, a year after the first Bank's renewal vote, America went to war with Britain, and the absence of a national bank made financing the military effort difficult. President Madison finally succeeded in pushing Congress to charter a new bank in 1816. Like the original Bank, the Second Bank would also pursue constitutional rights in the Supreme Court. And the Second Bank would be represented by perhaps the most famous lawyer ever to practice before the high court, Daniel Webster. Corporate rights would help make Webster's name legendary—but would also lead, in his own lifetime, to despair.

CHAPTER 3

The Corporation's Lawyer

DANIEL WEBSTER IS FREQUENTLY RECOGNIZED AS ONE OF the most influential lawyers ever to argue before the Supreme Court of the United States. Webster distinguished himself in numerous positions of prominence over the course of his career: secretary of state (twice), US senator (twice), presidential candidate (thrice), and longtime leader of the Whig Party, the pro-business successor to Hamilton's Federalist Party. Yet his advocacy before the nation's highest court remains his greatest achievement. Known as "the leading lawyer of his generation" and "one of the most important in the nation's history," he was indisputably a magnificent orator. It was said Webster was so persuasive that when he went fishing, the trout jumped straight into his pocket, knowing there was no sense fighting him. He argued an extraordinary 223 Supreme Court cases between 1814 and 1852, a time when the scope and meaning of many provisions of the Constitution were being interpreted for the first time. No lawyer argued as many important cases or equaled his influence on such a wide variety of constitutional doctrines. Webster came to be known as the "Defender of the Constitution."[1]

With equal accuracy, Webster could also have been called the Defender of the Corporation. Throughout his career, Webster's clients were among the wealthiest businesses in the nation. They included manufacturers, mercantile companies, insurance companies, railroads, banks, and shipping houses; "businessmen of every type engaged his services." Webster was the Corporation's Lawyer, and in many of the cases that made him famous he argued for broad protections for corporations under the Constitution. In one of those cases, Webster's client was not even a business corporation, yet he was still able to establish a landmark precedent that benefited businesses by imposing new constitutional limits on the ability of states to regulate corporations of any type.[2]

Lawyers like Webster played an unusually profound role in the expansion of corporate constitutional rights. Of course, lawyers have

DANIEL WEBSTER, KNOWN AS THE GREATEST ADVOCATE IN THE HISTORY OF THE SUPREME COURT, ARGUED FOR EXPANSIVE CONSTITUTIONAL PROTECTIONS FOR BUSINESS.

starred in all the great constitutional struggles; think of Thurgood Marshall in civil rights and Ruth Bader Ginsburg in women's rights. To obtain judicial recognition of constitutional rights, there must be lawyers to bring the cases, write the briefs, and persuade the justices. Litigation in other rights movements, however, has usually been coupled with broad-based, political mobilization of the masses. Corporations never paraded with placards demanding their rights, nor did they always engage in public advocacy to gain constitutional protections. Corporate rights have largely been won in the courts, not in the streets, and have developed largely without much public scrutiny— even though many of the lawsuits leading to corporate rights were highly publicized in their time.

To gain these rights, corporations employed the most elite lawyers in the nation. Certainly Webster fit that description. Not only was he the most illustrious lawyer of his time, he was also reportedly the highest paid. His corporate clients were more than willing to pay his inordinately high fees because, for business, hiring the best lawyers to defeat regulation is often well worth the investment. In contrast to dispossessed and subjugated people, who often cannot afford to pay for the best representation, corporations have long used their deep pockets to finance legal challenges to laws burdening their rights. One reason corporations have been so effective in obtaining an ever-greater share of individual rights under the Constitution is that they have the financial means to hire the best lawyers to pursue cutting-edge, push-the-boundaries lawsuits.

Webster charged his clients so much because he desperately needed the money. With extravagant tastes and a notorious inability to manage his finances, Webster lived nearly all his life in debt. Indeed, it is no exaggeration to say that one reason Webster had such an enormous influence on the Constitution over the course of so many years was that he never had enough money to retire. So he could pay his bills, he was forced to try cases right up until his death, at the age of 70, in 1852.[3]

The trajectory of Webster's career maps the rise and fall of corporate rights in the early years of the United States. Between 1809 and

1835, the years immediately after *Bank of the United States v. Deveaux*, Webster succeeded in expanding constitutional rights for corporations. The Supreme Court under the leadership of Chief Justice John Marshall was receptive to Webster's corporationalist arguments about the need to protect business from excessive state regulation. Yet the court changed with Marshall's death in 1835, and with it so did Webster's fortunes. Marshall's successor, Roger Taney, was a populist who thought corporate rights should be strictly circumscribed.

Although he presided over thousands of cases in his nearly thirty years as chief justice of the United States, Taney's historical reputation is defined by one: *Dred Scott v. Sandford*. His opinion in that 1857 case, which held that blacks were not "Citizens" under the same provision of Article III at issue in *Bank of the United States*, is deservedly condemned for its racism and shortsightedness. *Dred Scott*, however, obscures other aspects of Taney's wide-ranging jurisprudence, including one that many opponents of *Citizens United* might nonetheless appreciate. Taney was a corporate reformer who, unlike Marshall and Webster, believed states should have broad regulatory authority over business. As a result, Taney thought corporations had only limited rights under the Constitution. The Taney court was one of the few in American history to rule against expansive constitutional protections for corporations, which did not bode well for Webster. Taney was no trout.

The Taney court's corporate rights cases hold other surprises too. It was the Taney court, not the Marshall court, that first embraced the concept of corporate personhood. The Taney court justices treated the corporation as if it were a person—that is, as an independent legal entity with rights and responsibilities distinct from those of the people who form it. Whereas Webster and the Marshall court followed Horace Binney's way of thinking about corporations—piercing the corporate veil to look past the corporate entity and allow companies to exercise the same rights as their members—the Taney court saw corporate personhood as a way to limit the rights of corporations. Moreover, as we will see, the Taney court's approach to corporate rights would eventually be challenged and influenced by the same issues that have defined Taney in history's memory: race and slavery.

Webster and his relationships with Marshall and Taney offer a revealing window into the early years of corporate rights in the Supreme Court. From Webster's first corporate rights cases in the Marshall court to his final ones in the Taney court, Webster's career illustrates how constitutional protections for corporations became more firmly embedded in American law—and how the first limits on corporate rights were justified. His example also highlights the vital role that lawyers played throughout the more than two-centuries-long struggle over corporate rights. Webster, however, also reminds us that a lawyer's influence is inevitably a function of the judges who preside over the cases. Moreover, for those today who wish to see the Supreme Court restrict the constitutional rights of corporations, looking back to Webster's era reveals a potential model. By embracing corporate personhood, rather than piercing the corporate veil, the Taney court imposed boundaries on the rights of corporations.

* * *

"IT WAS IN THE YEAR 1818 that an occasion occurred, which is as memorable as any in the professional life of Mr. Webster, and brought him before the nation, if not in a new light, at least in a more striking light than any in which he had hitherto been seen," recalled Joseph Story, the Supreme Court justice. Story, whose influence on early American constitutional law was second only to that of John Marshall, was referring to Webster's magnificent argument in *Dartmouth College v. Woodward*:

> He began by unfolding the facts in that brief but exact manner, for which he is so remarkable. . . . As he went on he kindled into more energetic action, and if one may say so, he scintillated at every step. . . . And when he came to his peroration, there was in his whole air and manner, in the fiery flashings of his eye, the darkness of his contracted brow, the sudden and flying flushes of his cheeks, the quivering and scarcely manageable movement of his lips, in the deep guttural tones of his voice, in the struggle to suppress his own emotions, in the almost convulsive clench-

ings of his hands without a seeming consciousness of the act, there was in these things what gave to his oratory an almost superhuman influence.[4]

Not many lawyers have enraptured the justices of the Supreme Court as Webster did in the *Dartmouth College* case. Of course, Webster was no ordinary lawyer and *Dartmouth College* was no ordinary case. "Few Supreme Court decisions have had more influence through American history," wrote historian Francis Stites. *Dartmouth College* has been called "one of the most important precedents in the history of the Supreme Court." The decision "played a key role in the rise of the American business corporation" and helped pave the way for modern corporate rights cases like *Citizens United* and *Hobby Lobby.*[5]

Dartmouth College, Webster's client, was not a business corporation but a school, run as a nonprofit (or, in the terminology of the day, "eleemosynary") institution. Dartmouth was, however, formed as a corporation, and the central question in the college's case had a direct bearing on all corporations, business or otherwise: Are corporations public or private? Are they public entities subject to broad governmental control? Or are they private entities over which the state has only limited regulatory authority? Today, we take for granted that corporations are private entities. In the early 1800s, however, the question of whether corporations were public or private remained unsettled. Webster's *Dartmouth College* case would largely settle it.

Like all corporations of its day, Dartmouth College had both public and private parentage. On the private side was Eleazar Wheelock, a Puritan minister who ran Moor's Indian Charity School in Connecticut in the 1760s. Short on students and funds, Wheelock solicited financial support back in England from a number of notables, including the Earl of Dartmouth, after whom the school would be renamed. Wheelock also solicited a royal charter from the governor of New Hampshire—Dartmouth's public progenitor—who issued one in 1769 on condition the school relocate to that colony. The charter afforded Dartmouth the basic rights typically enjoyed by all corporations: the right to own property, to form contracts, and to sue and be sued in courts of law "as a natural person, or other body politic or corporate, is able to do." The charter also recognized a new mission for the school. In addition to teaching Indians, the college was to be "enlarged and improved to promote learning among the English."[6]

Daniel Webster, Class of 1801, was among those who benefited from Dartmouth's new calling. As a student there, he honed the rhetorical skills for which he later gained fame. After graduation, Webster started a thriving law practice in Boston, where a booming factory sector was fueling economic growth. When Dartmouth came seeking representation for its impending legal battle, Webster, as a loyal alumnus, readily agreed. The goal was to have the courts declare that Dartmouth College was a private, not public, corporation, with rights secure from state interference.[7]

The controversy arose out of a struggle for control of Dartmouth in the years after Wheelock died in 1779. His son, John, assumed his father's executive position at the college, to the displeasure of some members of the board of trustees, who complained about the "family dynasty." Eventually, the younger Wheelock's opponents gained enough seats on the board to marginalize him. John Wheelock fought back by appealing to the press and enlisting the state legislature to investigate the board. This only angered the other trustees, who fired him from the presidency and voted him off the board. New Hampshire lawmakers, with John Wheelock's backing, responded by enacting legislation to take control of the college from the trustees. The new laws revised Dartmouth's corporate charter to expand the board from twelve to twenty-one people; created a new board of overseers to review the trustees' decisions; vested the state's governor with the power to appoint trustees; and changed the name of the educational corporation to "Dartmouth University."[8]

Represented by Webster, the original Dartmouth College trustees filed suit against William H. Woodward, the man who had been appointed the secretary-treasurer of the reformed school. Webster argued that New Hampshire's reorganization of the college's charter violated Article I, section 10 of the Constitution, which provided that "No State shall . . . pass any . . . Law impairing the Obligation of

Contracts." Webster claimed that the college's charter was a contract immune from alteration by the state. To make that argument work, however, he had to convince the courts that corporations were private entities. Public entities were, by their nature, subject to public control. If Dartmouth was a kind of government agency, serving a government purpose, then it could not claim any immunity from government control. New Hampshire could alter it, reorganize it, or even abolish it at will. The contract clause only protected private parties, like individuals, from having their existing contracts interfered with by the government.

The challenge for Webster was that, as Blackstone recognized in his *Commentaries*, corporations had both private *and* public features. Individuals could form partnerships on their own but if they wanted the benefits of the corporate form—special rules enabling the accumulation of capital and a separate legal identity (that is, personhood)—they had to petition the legislature or the Crown for a charter of incorporation. And the charter was only to be granted if the corporation served to further some public end, such as building a road, operating a bridge, or, as in the Bank of the United States, handling the government's loans and deposits. The individuals who financed the corporation could make money but the public, too, had to profit.[9]

Legislatures exerted public control over corporations through the chartering process. The charter of the Bank of the United States, for example, only allowed the Bank to exist for twenty years, limited the Bank's ability to purchase land, prohibited the Bank from trading in "goods, wares, merchandise, or commodities," and capped the amount the Bank could lend to the federal or state governments. Corporations that strayed from these restrictions were subject to *quo warranto* suits by the government, which could result in the loss of their charters. Despite private investors, a corporation was so controlled by the state of incorporation that it was, in the words of historians Oscar and Mary Handlin, an "agency of government . . . designed to serve a social function for the state."[10]

Perhaps, then, Webster was not surprised when the New Hampshire Superior Court ruled against him and the college in 1817. The state court, in a populist turn, held that corporations were public institutions subject to broad public control within the state of their incorporation. Moreover, the school had been founded to promote the public-spirited ends of advancing Christianity and literacy: "These great purposes are surely, if anything can be, matters of public concern." The trustees who ran Dartmouth, were, in that role, not private citizens; they were public servants carrying out a public duty. The Constitution's contract clause was designed to protect private contracts from state interference. It was never intended, the New Hampshire court explained, "to limit the power of the states, in relation to their own public officers and servants, or to their own civil institutions." Corporations, in other words, were public entities subject to public control.[11]

The New Hampshire court's ruling did not spell the end of the lawsuit. Dartmouth's plan, like that of the Bank of the United States nearly a decade earlier, was to have the relevant laws "reexamined and reversed by writ of error in the Sup. Court of the United States." Only a definitive ruling from the highest court in the land could establish the principle that corporations were private entities under the Constitution.[12]

* * *

THE SUPREME COURT of the United States met in March of 1818 to hear arguments in Daniel Webster's *Dartmouth College* case. According to Justice Story, the controversy over New Hampshire's takeover of Dartmouth College "attracted . . . intense attention" because it dealt with an issue of "paramount" importance: "the extent to which a claim to exercise legislation over literary and other corporations on the part of state sovereignty could be maintained." As a result, the courtroom was filled with interested spectators—only, once again, the room was not really a court. Although the Supreme Court had moved from Long's Tavern back into the Capitol after the *Bank of the United States* case, the British had destroyed much of the latter building in the War of 1812. Chauncey Allen Goodrich, a Yale professor who observed the *Dartmouth College* proceedings, recalled that the court met "in a mean apartment of moderate size" and the audience was made up "chiefly of legal men, the elite of the profession throughout the country." Those who gathered there would witness what has since been called "one of the most eloquent performances in the court's history."[13]

Webster needed to be very persuasive if he was to win the case on behalf of the college. Momentum was on the side of New Hampshire, and Webster's goal was to convince the justices to accept a principle the law had never previously recognized explicitly: that corporations were private entities immunized by the Constitution's contract clause from a state takeover.

As Webster stood before the justices, whatever disadvantage he may have had in his legal position was overcome by his edge in oratory and preparation. The two lawyers arguing on behalf of New Hampshire, John Holmes and William Wirt, were both accomplished advocates, yet neither did an effective job in this case. Holmes, according to one account, "made a noisy rhetorical, political speech, which pleased his opponents and disgusted his clients and their friends." Wirt was

"THIS, SIR, IS MY CASE! IT IS THE CASE NOT MERE-LY OF THAT HUMBLE INSTITUTION, IT IS THE CASE OF EVERY COLLEGE IN OUR LAND!...IT IS, SIR, AS I HAVE SAID, A SMALL COLLEGE. AND YET..."

DANIEL WEBSTER ARGUING *DARTMOUTH COLLEGE V. WOODWARD*
BEFORE THE SUPREME COURT.

too busy with his primary job—he was then the attorney general of the United States—to adequately prepare for the Supreme Court hearing in this matter arising out of his on-the-side practice. Given the nature of Supreme Court argument at the time, the deficiencies of Webster's opponents opened wide the door of opportunity.[14]

In the early 1800s, oral argument in the Supreme Court was far more important than today. In Webster's era, many cases were decided without the benefit of written briefs, which were not required until 1821, after the *Dartmouth College* case. Today, Supreme Court hearings typically last an hour, whereas Webster's case was argued over the course of three days. The justices back then did not often interrupt the advocates as they do now, allowing the lawyers instead to give long, florid orations. Today, oral argument is widely disparaged by "attitudinalist" scholars, who believe judges vote their preexisting policy preferences, and often by the justices themselves, who say oral argument usually has little influence on their decisions. Early America, however, was known for its legendary advocates of the spoken word: William Pinckney, Horace Binney, and, after the *Dartmouth College* case, Daniel Webster.[15]

The arguments of these lawyers were not transcribed by a stenographer as they would be now. Yet some of the lawyers, including Webster, later set down on paper from recall their Supreme Court presentations. These can give us the flavor of the advocates' reasoning but not of the advocates' presence. Justice Story, upon reading Webster's written account of his argument in *Dartmouth College* years later, said that it could not capture Webster's "form and impress, the manner and the expression, glowing zeal, the brilliant terms of diction, . . . the ever moving tones of the voice." It gave "no adequate idea of the eloquence, or sudden blazes of thought with which it abounded."[16]

Nor do the written accounts reveal Webster's charisma, which augmented his persuasive power. When he entered a room, Webster "drew all eyes to himself and hushed the murmur of conversation." He was handsome, his own eyes black and penetrating, with broad shoulders that gave him an "imposing physical appearance." His voice was said to be "deep, dark, with a roll of thunder in it." One contemporary who was acquainted with many kings and princes said that none of them "approached Mr. Webster in the commanding power of their personal presence."[17]

Webster began by reciting the facts of the case, "in the calm tone of easy and dignified conversation," recalled Professor Goodrich. Dr. Eleazar Wheelock had obtained a charter of incorporation that vested the twelve trustees with control over Dartmouth College. New Hampshire lawmakers decided years later to take over the college, giving the power of the trustees to a larger and different group of men. "The general question is," Webster told the justices, "whether the acts of the legislature of New Hampshire . . . are valid and binding on the plaintiffs, without their acceptance or assent." The court had to decide if those laws were "repugnant to the Constitution of the United States," Webster said, using the language traditionally associated with corporate bylaws but now integrated into the American practice of judicial review.[18]

Dartmouth's original charter of incorporation was, Webster argued, a contract between the government and the private individuals who formed the college. As such, the charter was protected by the Constitution's contracts clause from revision by the state legislature. The contract clause had no application to the charters of what he called "public corporations," such as "towns, cities, and so forth," which "the legislature may, under proper limitations, have a right to change, modify, enlarge, or restrain." Lawmakers, however, had no such liberty with regard to "private corporations"—those "founded by private persons," "on private property," and financed not by "the money of the public, but of the private persons." For this type of corporate entity, a "grant of corporate powers and privileges is as much a contract as a grant of land." And just as a grant of land would give the new landowner a property right that lawmakers could not lawfully snatch away, a charter gave the corporation's members property rights similarly immune from deprivation.

An effective lawyer knows his audience, and Webster shaped his argument to appeal specifically to Chief Justice Marshall, who had embraced Horace Binney's piercing-the-corporate-veil argument in

Bank of the United States v. Deveaux. The New Hampshire legislation, Webster said, affected "the rights of the individuals who compose" the corporation. "The twelve trustees were the sole legal owners of all the property acquired under the charter," he told the justices. That was not quite accurate; the corporation itself was the sole legal owner of the property. The twelve trustees had no authority, say, to divvy up Dartmouth's assets amongst themselves and sell them for personal gain, as if those assets were truly their own property. Yet Webster was correct that the charter gave the trustees the authority "to appoint and remove all officers at their discretion; to fix their salaries, and assign their duties; and to make all ordinances, orders, and laws for the government of the students." These are, he told the justices, "the legal rights, privileges, and immunities which belong to them, as individual members of the corporation." Such rights "are holden by the trustees expressly against the State for ever."

"When he had finished his argument, he stood silent for some moments, until every eye was fixed upon him," Goodrich remembered. Marshall leaned in "as if to catch the slightest whisper" and Webster looked straight at him. "Sir, you may destroy this little institution," Webster began. "It is weak; it is in your hands! I know it is one of the lesser lights in the literary horizon of our country. You may put it out. But if you do you must carry through your work! You must extinguish, one after another, all those greater lights of science which for more than a century have thrown their radiance over our land," he thundered. Then Webster turned quiet again. "It is, sir, as I have said, a small college. And yet there are those who love it." Goodrich recounted how Webster's "voice chocked" and his "tones seemed filled with the memories of home and boyhood; of early affections and youthful privations and struggles." The chief justice's "eyes suffused with tears."

Then Webster, who like any good courtroom lawyer was skilled at acting, glared at opposing counsel and steeled himself. "Sir, I know not how others may feel but for myself, when I see my alma mater surrounded, like Caesar in the senate-house, by those who are reiterating stab after stab, I would not, for this right hand, have her turn to me and say, *Et tu quoque, mi fili!* And you too, my son!" Webster sat and there was, according to Goodrich, "a deathlike stillness throughout the room for some moments; everyone seemed to be slowly recovering himself, and coming back to his ordinary range of thought and feeling." "When Mr. Webster ceased to speak," Justice Story recalled, "it was some minutes before any one seemed inclined to break the silence. The whole seemed but an agonizing dream, from which the audience was slowly and almost unconsciously awakening."[19]

* * *

CHIEF JUSTICE JOHN MARSHALL handed down his opinion for the Supreme Court in *Dartmouth College v. Woodward* in February of 1819. The court ruled in Webster's favor—and established that the corporation was, in the eyes of the Constitution, a private entity, which like an individual person had rights. The court held that Dartmouth College's corporate charter was a binding contract between the state and the incorporators and, therefore, New Hampshire's reorganization of the college was unconstitutional under the Constitution's contracts clause. To reach that conclusion, Marshall, the corporationalist, insisted that the corporation's rights were exactly the same as they were prior to the Revolution. "It is too clear to require the support of argument that all contracts and rights respecting property, remained unchanged by the revolution," he wrote. "Circumstances have not changed [the charter]. In reason, in justice, and in law, it is now what it was in 1769."[20]

Despite Marshall's claims of continuity, his *Dartmouth College* opinion was itself revolutionary. While the property rights of Dartmouth's members may have been the same, the rights of the other party to the contract, the government, were radically different. In 1769, when Dartmouth received its charter, Parliament had the right to alter, amend, or vacate a corporate charter—as British lawmakers had repeatedly argued in the run-up to the Revolution. Marshall admitted as much: "According to the theory of the British Constitution, their Parliament is omnipotent. To annul corporate rights might give a shock to public opinion, which that government has chosen to avoid, but its power is not questioned." Yet while Marshall recognized that "by the revolution, the duties as well as the powers, of government devolved on the people of New Hampshire," the state did not retain Parliament's power to alter corporate charters. The Constitution has "imposed this additional limitation—that the legislature of a State shall pass no act 'impairing the obligation of contracts.'" Circumstances *had* changed since 1769, and drastically so. The Revolution, in Marshall's view, had significantly reduced the government's power over existing corporations.[21]

Marshall's opinion also reflected adaptation and change with regard to the nature of the corporation. While Blackstone emphasized the corporation's public aspects—only the sovereign could create one, and only if there was a public purpose—Marshall viewed the corporation as a private entity. Dartmouth was not created by the government; it was, the chief justice wrote, "really endowed by private individuals, who have bestowed their funds for the propagation of the Christian religion among the Indians and for the promotion of piety and learning generally." The government, Marshall claimed, had not given any money or assets to fund the college. Although Marshall placed the emphasis on Dartmouth's source of financing, this hardly distinguished Dartmouth College from the Virginia Company, the Massachusetts Bay Company, or any of the corporations Blackstone had written about; all were privately financed. Nonetheless, Marshall declared Dartmouth College to be for this reason "a private corporation."[22]

Marshall also downplayed Dartmouth College's public purposes. Although the promotion of religion and education were "beneficial to the country," that did not make the corporation public in nature. Corporations served their public ends by fulfilling their missions, not by being controlled or regulated by the state. "The objects for which a corporation is created are universally such as the government wishes to promote," Marshall wrote. Yet the "benefit to the public is considered as an ample compensation for the faculty [incorporation] confers."

Marshall's opinion fundamentally reconceived the nature of the American corporation. The government did not create corporations, people did. And they did so to pursue private purposes, not public ones. The *Dartmouth College* case, says scholar David Ciepley, transformed the corporation into "a pure creature of the market rather than a creature of government, exempting it from any duty to the public, or accountability to the public." Yet Marshall's view, however incongruous from the perspective of traditional corporate law, nonetheless resonated with the claims colonists made about the limits on parliamentary power during the debates over independence. Colonists had insisted back then that charter rights had been bargained for and were subsequently secure from legislative overreach. *Dartmouth College* broke from the traditions of corporate law but in this sense at least adhered to the rhetoric of the Revolution.[23]

Marshall's opinion flirted with corporate personhood, and it has occasionally been misunderstood to support the idea that corporations are people in the eyes of the law. Corporations, he wrote, were a means "by which a perpetual succession of many persons are considered as the same, and may act as a single individual." A corporation was a legal person. At the same time, Marshall explained, the corporation "possesses only those properties which the charter of its creation confers upon it either expressly or as incidental to its very existence." As legal persons, corporations had rights—but *only* those granted by charter or inherent in that type of corporation.

Yet Marshall then abruptly reversed course and, as in the *Bank of the United States* case, pierced the corporate veil. He embraced Webster's argument that this was a case about the property rights of the corporation's members. The "corporation is the assignee of [the donors'] rights" and "stands in their place." The trustees were responsible for carrying out the corporation's mission and, according to Marshall, the charter gave those trustees a property right to manage the corporation's affairs. The rights of the corporation were defined by the rights of the indivudal members—here, the trustees. So when Marshall echoed his line from *Bank of the United States* and described the corporation in *Dartmouth College* as "an artificial being, invisible, intangible, and existing only in contemplation of law," he was offering a justification for once again rejecting corporate personhood. The artificiality and invisibility of the corporation made it appropriate to look right through the corporation to focus instead on the members.[24]

The impact of the *Dartmouth College* case was felt well beyond New Hampshire. The decision established the principle that corporations were creatures of private initiative formed in the marketplace over which states had only limited regulatory authority. They were accountable to their members but not necessarily to the larger public. Although Parliament had the power to alter corporate charters, the American states did not. And while an educational corporation may have been the instigator, the diminished regulatory authority of states over corporations had the greatest impact on business. Because the ruling applied to all types of corporations, *Dartmouth College* made business investment more secure by limiting the government's power to interfere with corporate property. The decade following the decision saw astonishing growth in the number of corporations, which were quickly becoming the preferred form of business enterprise in the American economy. Equally significant, the decision became, according to historian R. Kent Newmyer, "a potent legal and ideological weapon for corporations who sought to defeat regulation and establish the ideological primacy of laissez-faire capitalism."[25]

Dartmouth College did not mean that corporations were completely immune from all regulation, of course. In his concurring opinion in the case, Justice Story observed that the logic of Marshall's ruling might still allow states to require *future* charters to include a "reservation clause," reserving the state's authority to alter or amend charters. Nevertheless, the contract clause became "the primary constitutional protection for property rights during the first half of the nineteenth century." Courts used it to strike down bankruptcy laws forgiving debts, laws repealing tax exemptions, and laws reorganizing bond payments. The burden on lawmakers was nonetheless such that the normally levelheaded jurist Thomas Cooley bemoaned more than a half-century after *Dartmouth College* the consequences of Marshall's decision: "The most enormous and threatening powers in our country have been created; some of the great and wealthy corporations actually having greater influence in the country and upon the legislation of the country than the states to which they owed their corporate existence."[26]

While Dartmouth's original trustees celebrated the Supreme Court's landmark ruling, the school was nevertheless on the verge of bankruptcy. Webster's fees were enormous, and the school's revenue had fallen precipitously during the course of the legal battle. In time, of course, Dartmouth would prosper to become a world-class institution of higher education, with Webster receiving his fair share of credit. In 1901, the school installed a bronze plaque on a building named in Webster's honor which read, "Founded by Eleazar Wheelock, Refounded by Daniel Webster."[27]

* * *

IN 1839, TWENTY YEARS after the *Dartmouth College* case and just a few weeks after his 57th birthday, the Corporation's Lawyer was once again standing before the justices of the Supreme Court arguing for expansive constitutional protections for corporations—though this time for business corporations. Much had changed in those two decades. Webster was now a US senator, a former presidential candidate, and one of the nation's leading advocates for a strong national government in the face of growing demands for states' rights. The once strapping young man had been transformed by age and perhaps even more so by his two populist rivals, President Andrew Jackson and Chief Justice Roger Taney. Webster's penetrating black eyes had become severe and unwelcoming, flashing suspicion and anger rather than charm and authority.

The corporations seeking constitutional protections in Webster's later case, *Bank of Augusta v. Earle*, were a railroad and two banks, including one with a familiar name. Like the corporation involved in the first corporate rights case, the Second Bank of the United States was also a political and financial powerhouse, at least in its youth. It used the financial leverage gained from holding the federal government's deposits to control the nation's credit and money supply. And like the first Bank, the Second Bank would become the victim of partisan disputes. By 1839, when Webster appeared on the Second Bank's behalf in the Supreme Court, the once mighty corporation

THE CORPORATION'S LAWYER || 89

A CHECK FROM THE SECOND BANK OF THE UNITED STATES,
SIGNED BY DANIEL WEBSTER AND DATED JULY 24, 1824.

was but a shell of its former self—like Webster, a victim of Jackson and Taney.[28]

With Webster as its attorney, the Second Bank had once enjoyed great success in the Supreme Court. Back in 1819, the same year he rescued Dartmouth College, Webster also came to the defense of the Second Bank in the famed case of *McCulloch v. Maryland*. As mentioned earlier, the facts were similar to those of *Bank of the United States v. Deveaux*. After the Second Bank was founded, Maryland opponents of the new corporation imposed a tax on it. While the Supreme Court in the first Bank case only addressed whether corporations have a constitutional right to sue in federal court, the court in *McCulloch* went further and clarified that federally chartered corporations were indeed protected against state taxes. It was another Hamiltonian victory for business, and Marshall's opinion relied heavily on Webster's arguments, repeating them almost verbatim.[29]

During Marshall's tenure on the Supreme Court, Webster enjoyed an impressive track record of success for his corporate clients. The Marshall court consistently promoted the powers of Congress and the rights of corporations. Yet by the time of Marshall's death in 1835, the nation's political tide had turned against him and his Hamiltonian allies. The Federalist Party had folded (largely replaced by Webster's Whig Party), and populists like Jackson, the intellectual heir to Jefferson, were now in power. President when Marshall died, Jackson selected Roger Taney to replace him.

Taney, both before and after his Supreme Court appointment in 1836, was a populist and a corporate reformer. The Marylander bolted the Federalist Party out of disgust when northern business interests in the party refused to support the War of 1812. He was drawn instead to the Jacksonian movement, which condemned corporate monopolies and advocated for broad state control over business. This put him directly at odds with Webster, whom Taney knew well. The two men had worked together on Taney's first case as a lawyer before the Supreme Court. Yet by the time of Taney's confirmation as chief justice, the two men had come to despise each other. Taney, guided by his populism and fueled by his hatred of Webster, would move the court toward a more restrictive approach to corporate rights under the Constitution.[30]

* * *

THE PERSONAL ANIMOSITY BETWEEN Taney and Webster grew out of disagreements about the very client Webster was representing in the *Bank of Augusta v. Earle* case, the Second Bank of the United States. To Jackson and Taney, the Second Bank was the most egregious example of how corporations corrupted politics and the economy.

At the heart of the Jacksonian complaint about corporations was the chartering process. Corporations, in Jackson's view, were too often a way by which politically connected insiders obtained special economic privileges unavailable to others. Corporate charters usually gave a business a monopoly: the Virginia Company had exclusive rights to trade in the northern hemisphere of the New World, for example, and the first Bank of the United States alone had the right to print federal notes. The impetus for monopoly was to encourage capital investment, but the effect was also to reduce competition, closing off economic opportunities for new businesses that wanted to compete in the same space. Corporate monopolies not only corrupted the marketplace, they soiled democratic politics. The special privileges of a corporate charter were so valuable that some people were more than willing to pay to persuade lawmakers, creating a political culture of bribery and extortion. Jackson won the presidency in 1828 with the anticorporate slogan, "Equal rights for all. Special privileges for none."[31]

Jacksonsonians argued that special corporate chartering was also fundamentally at odds with democratic principles. Chartered corporations "take away from the people, their common rights, and give them to a few," argued Pennsylvania's populist governor Francis Rawn Shunk. The *Dartmouth College* decision exacerbated the democratic defect of corporations by limiting the ability of the community to regulate and control them once created. "Whatever power is given to a corporation, is just so much power taken away from the State, in derogation of the original power of the mass of the community," concluded the delegates at the 1837–1838 Pennsylvania constitutional convention. Because of the chartering process, Jacksonians argued that

PRESIDENT ANDREW JACKSON, A POPULIST, ARGUED FOR LIMITING THE SPECIAL PRIVILEGES OF CORPORATIONS.

wealth was determined by one's political connections, not hard work and industry. Their answer, however, was not to destroy the corporation. Instead, populists sought to democratize the corporation to better serve the public welfare.[32]

Indeed, Jacksonians expanded access to the corporate form—but theirs was a more democratic version. Jacksonians pushed for laws allowing "general incorporation," permitting anyone to form certain types of corporations once a set of legally specified conditions were met, without the need for a special act of the legislature. In the 1830s, states increasingly adopted general incorporation statutes for specific industries like manufacturing, banking, or infrastructure construction to make the corporate form more accessible to businessmen. Newcomers were better able to compete with wealthy, established entrepreneurs. General incorporation was not, however, intended to end legislative supervision and regulation of corporations, which had traditionally been achieved through the charting process. Jacksonians were strong proponents of the idea that corporations had to be disciplined and controlled by the people. Even general incorporation laws typically set floors and ceilings on capitalization, imposed obligations on directors to protect investors, vested stockholders with voting rights, and required the filing of annual disclosures as ways of protecting investors and the public.[33]

The Second Bank was not created under a general incorporation law. It was chartered by a special act of Congress and exercised effective monopoly power over the nation's credit—much to the anger of Jackson. Jacksonians blamed the Second Bank's lending practices for the devastating financial panic of 1819, whose effects reverberated throughout the economy of the 1820s. Moreover, because the Second Bank was a stock corporation accountable to investors, the "Eastern Monster," as Jackson said, was just a means by which "the rich and powerful too often bend the acts of government to their own selfish purposes." Sounding like Jefferson, Jackson complained about "powers and privileges" of the national bank—special benefits that were "unauthorized by the Constitution, subversive of the rights of the States, and dangerous to the liberties of the people."[34]

Nelson Biddle, the Second Bank's forceful chief executive, had been a longtime Federalist and ardently opposed Jackson. Biddle believed his corporation was more powerful than the president of the United States, and he challenged Jackson to a uniquely Washington game of chicken. The Second Bank's charter, like that of the original Bank of the United States, was for only a limited duration, and was due to expire in 1836. In 1832, Biddle, with Webster's support, pushed the Second Bank's allies in Congress to pass a bill four years early to extend the bank's charter. Biddle was betting that Jackson, facing reelection, would not want to risk the public backlash and economic disruption that might come from undermining the bank. Jackson, however, held steady and vetoed the bill. The Second Bank was forced to reorganize under Pennsylvania law, becoming a Pennsylvania corporation. Jackson also ordered the withdrawal of all federal deposits held in the Second Bank, depriving Biddle of the one thing most responsible for his corporation's outsized influence on the national economy.[35]

Biddle used all of his corporation's amassed resources to fight back. The Second Bank called in loans, restricted access to credit, and reduced the nation's money supply. Biddle set out to humiliate Jackson and saddle his presidency with the hard times. It worked in part, successfully putting the brakes on what had been a period of rapid economic expansion. Yet Jackson, who appeared strong in the face of the corporation's onslaught, won reelection nonetheless. Rather than break Jackson's resolve, Biddle's aggressive response proved to many the accuracy of Jackson's accusation that the Second Bank was an irresponsible, untrustworthy, and all-too-powerful corporation.[36]

Both Webster and Taney played leading roles in the bank controversy. In 1833, Jackson's first treasury secretary, Louis McLane, a former Federalist who thought the Second Bank was a benefit to the national economy, refused to follow Jackson's order to withdraw all the federal government's funds from the institution. Jackson shipped McLane off to the State Department, only to find that his replacement at Treasury, William Duane, a Pennsylvanian who also favored the national bank, similarly refused to comply. Jackson then fired Duane and nominated Taney, who had been Jackson's attorney general and was known to be fiercely loyal to the president. Taney's new position, however, required confirmation by the Senate, and Webster, one of Massachusetts's two senators, led the opposition to Taney's nomination. Webster was on retainer for the Second Bank and his loyalties were to his financial patron. Fighting the Second Bank's fight, Webster was able to defeat the nomination, humiliating Taney, who became the first cabinet nominee in American history rejected by the Senate.[37]

It is tempting to believe that Washington today suffers from unprecedented rancor and partisanship, especially when it comes to the judicial confirmation process. Critics often point to the Senate's 1987 rejection of Robert Bork, an outspoken conservative nominated by President Ronald Reagan, as the turning point. Yet politics in the 1830s was equally divisive, if not more so, and Webster was one of the most aggressive partisan warriors. Unsatisfied with merely embarrassing Taney by defeating his cabinet nomination, Webster in 1834 organized a Senate censure of both Taney and Jackson. Nonetheless, when a seat opened up on the Supreme Court, Jackson submitted Taney's name again. Webster once again led the opposition, publicly questioning Taney's integrity and calling him "a pliant instrument" of the president. Taney returned the charge in a public address, saying that "it is well known that [Webster] has found the bank a profitable client, . . . he has become its 'pliant instrument,' and is prepared on all occasions to do its bidding, whenever and wherever it may choose to require him." Webster, however, still had the upper hand in the Senate, and Taney's nomination to the Supreme Court was rejected largely on partisan grounds—a hundred fifty years before Bork.[38]

Jackson, upon learning that Webster had frustrated Taney's Supreme Court nomination, stormed out of the Capitol swearing revenge on the "gang of scoundrels." After midterm elections brought a wave of populist Democrats to Washington, the president in 1836 nominated Taney to the Supreme Court once again, this time to replace the recently deceased Marshall as chief justice. Despite newspaper editorials calling for rejection of "the elevation of any man who is not perfectly sound in regard to the fundamental principles of the

Constitution as expounded by Daniel Webster," Taney easily won confirmation in a Senate now controlled by Jackson's allies. In a note to
Jackson hinting at Webster, Taney thanked the president for sticking
with him "in spite of the opposition of the men who have so long and
so perseveringly sought to destroy me."[39]

With Taney the corporate reformer ensconced as chief justice of a
court quickly being filled with Jackson appointees, a gloomy Webster
groaned, "the Supreme Court is *gone*." Webster was referring to how
the new justices would transform constitutional law, but he could just
as easily have been referring to how the new justices would react to
him personally. No more could Webster count on dazzling the justices
with his soaring, emotional oratory; no longer could he bring tears
of sympathy to the eyes of the chief justice. Webster's troubles were
apparent from his very first argument before the Taney court in 1837,
just a year after Taney had won confirmation, in *Charles River Bridge
Company v. Warren Bridge Company*.[40]

Webster was representing the Charles River Bridge Company,
which operated a toll bridge over the waterway separating Boston and
Charlestown. For nearly sixty years, the company had the only bridge
for miles and, as a result, was immensely profitable. Yet those profits,
and the high tolls charged to the public to earn them, eventually turned
local residents against the company. Responding to public pressure,
the Massachusetts legislature awarded a charter to the Warren Bridge
Company to build a competing, toll-free bridge nearby. The Charles
River Bridge Company hired Webster to defend its monopoly, which
it claimed was part of its constitutionally protected property rights.
Under the rule of *Dartmouth College*, the company's long-standing
charter was an inviolable contract which the state government was not
free to revise.[41]

Taney wrote the majority opinion against Webster and the Charles
River Bridge Company. Taney explained that the company's original
charter said nothing about a monopoly. Although some people back
in 1785, when the company was first chartered, might have assumed
otherwise because monopolies were so commonplace, in fact the charter was silent on the question. Although the Marshall court would

A CORPORATE REFORMER, CHIEF JUSTICE ROGER TANEY
EMPLOYED THE PRINCIPLES OF CORPORATE PERSONHOOD TO
LIMIT THE RIGHTS OF CORPORATIONS.

likely have read the charter broadly in favor of the existing corporation, as it did in *Dartmouth College*, the Taney court thought it necessary to strictly construe charters to limit corporate power and enhance
the regulatory authority of the state. Taney, an opponent of monopoly
generally, was not about to read monopoly privileges into an otherwise
ambiguous charter—especially not if it meant helping out a client of
Webster. Without overturning *Dartmouth College*, the Taney court nevertheless imposed new limits on the reach of the Marshall court's decision. Even if a charter were a contract, it would be read narrowly and
not presumed to include an implicit guarantee of monopoly privileges.

Taney warned that one "must not forget that the community also have rights, and that the happiness and well being of every citizen depends on their faithful preservation."

Taney's decision in *Charles River Bridge Company* would eventually be recognized as a historic ruling that expanded competition at the expense of exclusive corporate privileges. Historians credit the decision as a boon for the economy, unsettling the rights of some older corporations but spurring the creation of many new ones, which were more apt to innovate. For Webster, however, the decision was a sign of difficult times ahead.[42]

* * *

TWO YEARS AFTER HIS DEFEAT in the *Charles River Bridge Company* case, Daniel Webster was back before the Taney court, representing the Second Bank of the United States in *Bank of Augusta v. Earle*. Webster faced a bench that was hostile to his worldview and a chief justice that was hostile to him. A sign of how much the court had changed from when he could enchant the justices with his oratory, Webster in one appearance before the Taney court was left to joke awkwardly, "It has been my duty to pass upon the question of the confirmation of every member of the Bench, and I may say that I treated your honors with entire impartiality—for I voted against every one of you."[43]

Webster was still representing the Second Bank and still arguing for expansive rights for corporations. The constitutional provision at issue in the *Earle* case was the comity clause of Article IV, section 2 of the Constitution: "The Citizens of each State shall be entitled to all Privileges and Immunities of Citizens in the several States." This was essentially an antidiscrimination rule prohibiting states from treating out-of-state (or "foreign") citizens who move into the state differently from their own native citizens. If a Pennsylvanian moved to Alabama, for example, he would be entitled to all the same legal rights and privileges that a native Alabaman would have. This constitutional principle helped glue together the many states into one nation by encouraging the mobility of people across state borders. Webster in *Earle* claimed

EVEN AS THE SUPREME COURT UNDER ROGER TANEY
TURNED AGAINST HIM, DANIEL WEBSTER CONTINUED
TO ARGUE FOR THE RIGHTS OF CORPORATIONS.

that corporations should have the same constitutional protection against discrimination.[44]

The Second Bank was not the first litigant to bring a case under the comity clause. In fact, by 1839, there was already a well-developed jurisprudence on the privileges and immunities of state citizens under Article IV. In this instance, the corporation was a constitutional lever-ager, adapting previously decided cases involving individual rights to promote the rights of business. Yet, in Webster's hands, the Second Bank was pursuing an innovative take on an older argument. Individuals sought the right to be free from discrimination when they packed up their belongings and moved into a state, but the Second Bank was asking for something quite different. The Second Bank wanted to come into any state and do business there without having to move at all. Corporations, Webster argued, should be able to come into a state and operate under the same terms and conditions as any local corporations, even if headquartered elsewhere. What Webster was seeking, in essence, was to give corporations a constitutional right to do business nationwide without state interference.

The issue arose largely due to the growing interstate marketplace of the 1830s, coupled with a long tradition of state control over corporations and other businesses operating within their borders. With a few exceptions (like the Bank of the United States), corporations in early America did most of their business in their home states, with suppliers and customers being primarily local. By the 1830s, business corporations were increasingly operating across state lines, assisted by millions of federal dollars going to internal improvements—highways, railroads, canals—that spurred trade. State lawmakers enacted numerous restrictions on out-of-state corporations, such as taxes, license fees, cash bond requirements, and outright prohibitions on their ability to engage in certain business activities altogether. Some of these restrictions were sheer protectionism, designed to preserve local businesses from competition. Oftentimes, however, the restrictions were populist measures to protect state residents from special dangers presented by out-of-state corporations. During that time, the primary way to regulate corporations was through charters and conditions on incorporation—unlike today, when states use other types of laws, such as labor laws, workplace safety laws, and consumer protection laws, to accomplish that goal. Because foreign corporations were by definition incorporated elsewhere, they were hard for state lawmakers to regulate and supervise. *Bank of Augusta v. Earle* presented the question of whether these state laws imposing special conditions on foreign corporations were constitutional under the comity clause. It was but the first of several innovative constitutional arguments corporations would make in a nearly century-long battle to defeat these types of state laws.[45]

Joseph B. Earle and W. D. Primrose, a pair of hard-up businessmen from Mobile, claimed Alabama law prohibited out-of-state banks like the Second Bank, now chartered in Pennsylvania, from operating in the state. It was a convenient argument given that Earle and Primrose had eagerly borrowed money from the Second Bank and a number of other out-of-state banks. In the midst of the Biddle-induced panic of 1837, however, the two men sought desperately for a way out of their agreements. They seized upon a provision of the Alabama constitution that barred the state legislature from chartering any bank in which the state did not own stock. Because Alabama was not a stockholder in the Second Bank, Earle and Primrose argued, the bank was not authorized to conduct business there. The argument was not a strong one—Alabama law only spoke to the legislature's power to charter a bank and said nothing about an already chartered, foreign corporation conducting business in the state—but the two men won in the lower court.[46]

When the Supreme Court heard the case in 1839, the controversy was headline news and stirred up "much excitement in the mercantile community." The prospect that Earle and Primrose would be excused from their obligations, it was said, "frightened half the lawyers and all the corporations of the country out of their properties." Webster, on behalf of the Second Bank, argued that corporations, like individuals, have a right to do business in any state they wish. States could regulate them like any other similarly situated business, but could not discriminate against out-of-state corporations through higher taxes and special rules. Although the text of the comity clause only said that states could not discriminate against foreign "Citizens," Webster relied on the logic of *Bank of the United States v. Deveaux.*[47]

The first corporate rights case also presented the question of whether corporations were "Citizens." And while the earlier precedent was construing a different provision of the Constitution—Article III in *Deveaux* and Article IV in *Earle*—Webster argued that the court should once again pierce the corporate veil. Corporations might not be citizens but their members were. Corporations, Webster insisted, "may do in their corporate character, in Alabama, all such acts, authorized by their charter, as the members thereof would have a right to perform as individuals." The members of the Second Bank were citizens of other states entitled to do business in Alabama. The corporation, which was just a stand-in for its members, should enjoy the same rights.[48]

Arguing on behalf of Earle and Primrose was Charles Ingersoll, whose father Jared argued against corporate rights in *Bank of the United States v. Deveaux*. The son was a populist lawyer and politician whose name was said to be "a rallying standard for the enemies of large corporations, money powers, and other unpopular causes." Playing upon the Taney court's sympathy for states' rights and hostility to corporate privilege, Ingersoll claimed that states, as sovereigns, had the inherent right to determine which, if any, corporations could do business within their borders. Citizens of foreign states could do business anywhere under the comity clause, but corporations were entities separate and distinct from their members; the citizenship of the latter did not attach to the former. Corporations, moreover, were subject to much broader state control than ordinary individuals. Webster's argument, Ingersoll warned, turned democracy upside down by creating "sovereign corporations and subject states."[49]

Ingersoll's populist arguments had appeal, no doubt, to Taney and his brethren. Indeed, over the course of Taney's tenure, the Supreme Court would expand the power of the federal courts over commercial matters, enabling federal judges to play a larger role in overseeing the interstate businesses of the emergent national economy. While Taney believed in the authority of states to regulate corporations, the new, large interstate businesses posed an obvious challenge to the small, localized state courts of the mid-nineteenth century. Federal courts, by contrast, applying federal common law, could better supervise corporations operating across multiple state lines.[50]

The Supreme Court's decision in *Bank of Augusta v. Earle*, handed down in March of 1839, announced a new approach to corporate rights. The court rejected Webster's argument that, as Taney's majority opinion characterized it, "the court should look behind the act of incorporation and see who are the members of it." Instead, Taney held, the corporation "is a person for certain purposes in contemplation of law," "Whenever a corporation makes a contract, it is the contract of the legal entity—of the artificial being created by the charter—and not the contract of the individual members. The only rights it can claim are the rights which are given to it in that charter, and not the rights which belong to its members as citizens of a state." In Taney's view, corporate personhood required a strict separation between the rights of the corporation and the rights of its members.[51]

To Taney, the corporate person had more limited rights than an ordinary person because of the way corporations were organized. In *Earle*, Taney made reference to a recent development in the organization of corporations gradually taking hold by the late 1830s: limited liability. Stockholders could lose the money they invested in stock if a corporation went bankrupt, but their personal assets were completely shielded from that corporation's creditors. Limited liability, then, was a function of corporate personhood. The corporation was its own, independent person in the eyes of the law, and it had legal rights—or, in this instance, legal obligations—wholly separate and distinct from those of its members. Taney suggested that stockholders should not be able to take advantage of personhood to shield their assets, only to turn around and argue for piercing the corporate veil when it came to corporate rights.

Taney's opinion in *Bank of Augusta v. Earle* was the first time the Supreme Court ruled explicitly against extending a constitutional right to corporations. And unlike the Marshall court's corporate rights cases, *Earle* embraced corporate personhood. Because a corporation was its own legal person, its rights and duties were separate and distinct from those of its members. Corporations had only those rights appropriate for this unique and special type of legal entity, one that already enjoyed special legal privileges, such as limited liability. Corporate personhood served as a limit on the rights of corporations and a basis for distinguishing corporations from ordinary people.

The decision was not all bad news for Webster and the Second Bank. While refusing to pierce the corporate veil and give corporations the rights of their members, Taney also rejected Earle and Primrose's baseless argument that Alabama law prohibited out-of-state banks from doing business there. While Taney made clear that states had the authority to prohibit out-of-state corporations if they liked, Alabama had never enacted any law excluding the Second Bank or the other corporations involved in the case. As a result, those companies were entitled to do business in Alabama absent legislation to the contrary, and the two men could not renege on their notes. Corporate rights in general had lost, but Webster and the Second Bank eked out a victory.[52]

Nonetheless, Taney's opinion articulated in decisive terms a principle both the Second Bank and Webster abhorred: states had the inherent power to exclude out-of-state corporations from their borders. Indeed, shortly after the Supreme Court's ruling in *Bank of Augusta v. Earle* was handed down in 1839, Alabama put this principle into practice and prohibited the Second Bank from doing business in the state. In the Taney court, even Webster's victories turned into defeats.[53]

* * *

IN THE YEARS after *Earle*, the Taney court set out to scale back the reach of *Bank of the United States v. Deveaux*. In a series of cases decided between 1844 and 1853, the Taney court narrowed, refocused, and finally rejected *Bank of the United States*'s rule that, for access to federal court, the citizenship of a corporation was defined by the citizenship of its members. The court held that a corporation's citizenship was determined instead by the corporation's own state of incorporation. The corporation was a separate, independent legal actor under the law. Moreover, for the Taney court, treating corporations as people was a way to limit corporate power. Although the court continued to hold that corporations could sue and be sued in federal court, the court revamped the rule so that the federal courts, now largely in the hands of Jacksonian judges, could use it to supervise the growing number of interstate businesses that states were finding increasingly difficult to control.

Alexander Marshall—no relation to the late chief justice—was the plaintiff in the most colorful of the Taney court cases on the issue. A self-described "lobby member," Marshall was hired in 1846 by the

Baltimore & Ohio Railroad Company to bribe Virginia lawmakers to approve a right-of-way through the state to the Ohio River. "The mass of the members in our legislature are a thoughtless, careless, light-hearted body of men, who came here for the 'per diem,'" Marshall explained in a letter to the B&O's president. All it would take was "a contingent fund of at least $50,000" to turn the legislators into "wax, to be molded by the most pressing influences." Marshall, however, was clearly not as skilled at the art of persuasion as Daniel Webster. Although a route was eventually approved by the legislature, it was not the one originally sought by the B&O, which then reneged on its agreement to pay Marshall.[54]

That Marshall felt no embarrassment about bringing a lawsuit to enforce such an agreement reveals much about the nature of politics in the antebellum era. Unlike today, there were no campaign finance laws or lobbying restrictions. Yet corporations, even after the adoption of Jacksonian general incorporation laws, still had ample reason to try to corrupt lawmakers. This was especially true of a railroad like the B&O. Established in 1827 to compete with New York's Erie Canal, the B&O was the nation's first passenger line. The corporation was celebrated—earning a place on the game board of Monopoly in 1935— and, when it came to politics, widely mimicked. Many of the railroads that followed would similarly use cash or stock to sway elected officials to approve railroad measures. Graft was treated as a cost of doing business. Over the second half of the nineteenth century, bribery of public officials would become as commonplace as the leaden smoke billowing from the engines of the B&O's imitators.[55]

Marshall's lawsuit against the B&O raised the same issues as the *Bank of the United States* case: Do corporations have a constitutional right to sue in federal court on diversity grounds? And, if so, how should courts determine the citizenship of a corporation? Back in 1809, the Supreme Court sought to protect corporations from the anticorporate bias of state courts by broadly reading the Constitution to give them access to friendlier federal tribunals. Corporations, the court ruled, had the right to sue in federal court based on the rights of their members. So long as a corporation's members were from states

ADVERTISEMENT FOR THE BALTIMORE &
OHIO RAILROAD, 1864.

different from the opposing party's, then the parties were diverse and entitled to sue or be sued in federal court.

By the 1840s and 1850s, however, *Bank of the United States*'s rule was being undermined by changes in both the economy and the corporation, many of them attributable to the rise of the railroads. With over 3,000 miles of track, the railroads were reshaping the nation. Lines like the B&O dramatically reduced the cost of shipping and increased the mobility of both goods and people. The impact was to begin to transform an agrarian society where people rarely saw anything more than thirty miles from their home to an industrial one with far broader horizons. Even more than the canals of the early 1800s, the railroad lines were essential to creating an increasingly integrated economy. Other businesses, too, were innovating in ways that would further that process. In 1844, Samuel Morse established the first telegraph line, making long distance communication immediate and, hence, more powerful. Surprisingly, Morse's first long distance message was sent from the Supreme Court—he was demonstrating the technology before lawmakers, and the court's chambers were in the basement of the Capitol—and the telegraph arrived successfully at its intended destination, the Baltimore depot of the B&O railroad.[56]

The railroads also transformed the stock market. The capital demands of buying land, grading and laying tracks, and operating the lines could not be met by the personal wealth of a handful of partners. Banks, scared by the cutthroat competition that often led to new railway lines being sited right next to existing ones, saw the roads as risky investments. To raise money, railroad corporations turned instead to the stock market. In 1830, before the exponential growth of the railroads, the New York Stock Exchange had days when fewer than fifty shares were traded. By the outbreak of the Civil War in 1861, however, when railroad stocks were pervasive, tens of thousands of shares were traded daily.[57]

Railroad corporations were easily able to manipulate the rule of *Bank of the United States*. Courts would often look to a corporation's directors in determining the state of citizenship of that corporation's members. So when railroads wanted to escape federal court they would add a director from the same state as the plaintiff, thus destroying the necessary diversity of citizenship. The logic of piercing the corporate veil meant that corporations could often choose for themselves whether they would be subject to suit in federal court.[58]

Like many of the emergent interstate businesses, the B&O wanted Alexander Marshall's case about the broken lobbying contract to be heard in state court—preferably in Maryland, where the B&O was among the most influential businesses in the state. If the original Bank of the United States fretted about anticorporate bias in the state courts, the B&O was counting on the state court to be biased in its favor. The federal courts, by contrast, were filled with populist judges less likely to lean in favor of corporate interests. So while the Taney court agreed that corporations should have some access to federal court, Taney's vision of that right was different. He objected to the easy manipulability of *Bank of the United States*'s piercing rationale and sought to establish a rule that would make corporations more easily and reliably amenable to suits in federal court by those who sought to hold the emergent insterstate businesses accountable.

The Taney court first made that clear in another railroad case of the era, *Louisville, Cincinnati & Charleston Railroad Company v. Letson*. Decided in 1844, the same year as Morse's telegram, *Letson* was the first Taney court case to suggest that a corporation could not use the citizenship of its members to keep itself out of federal court. Observing that *Bank of the United States* had "never been satisfactory to the bar" and suggesting, improbably, that John Marshall himself later thought the case wrongly decided, the Taney court insisted that the citizenship of "the members, who cannot be sued," was irrelevant. "The corporators, as individuals, are not defendants in the suit," the court explained. The suit was against the railroad itself, so "nothing must be looked at but the legal entity." The Louisville was incorporated in South Carolina, its home state, and that, not the citizenship of the Louisville's members, should control. The court explicitly relied on corporate personhood: a corporation "seems to us to be a person, though an artificial one, inhabiting and belonging to that state, and therefore entitled for the purposes of suing and being sued to be deemed a citizen of that state."[59]

In *Marshall v. Baltimore & Ohio Railroad Company*, the court continued to divorce itself from the corporationalist logic and reasoning of *Bank of the United States*. The court's 1853 decision refused to allow the B&O to remove its case to state court. For purposes of federal court jurisdiction, the railroad's state of incorporation was determinative, regardless of the citizenship of the directors, stockholders, or any other members. The corporation had a right to sue and be sued in federal court, but that right was not based on the rights of members. It was based on the rights appropriate for a corporate person created and established under the laws of a particular state. The court held that no inquiry into the citizenship of the members would even be allowed. The corporation was, the court said, a "juridical person"—an independent legal actor in the eyes of the law whose rights were separate from the rights of its members.[60]

To this day, when corporations are sued in federal court on diversity grounds, the Taney court's decisions remain the law of the land. Corporations can sue and be sued in federal court, but their citizenship is determined by their state of incorporation or by their principal place of business. The courts do not look to the citizenship of the corporation's directors or stockholders. Corporations continue to enjoy the basic constitutional right to sue and be sued in federal court first extended to them in *Bank of the United States*, yet because of the Taney court's interventions the right today is different in scope and effect than it was under Marshall. Here, at least, corporations were people, with their own independent legal identity and rights.

* * *

DESPITE THEIR HEATED BATTLES over the rights of corporations, Daniel Webster and Roger Taney would both have their legacies deeply impacted by another great American fight over equal rights. Slavery would stamp the historical memories of both men with a measure of dishonor. Taney, of course, would forever be associated with *Dred Scott v. Sandford*, the Supreme Court's 1857 decision holding that blacks were not citizens under the Constitution. The "peculiar institution" took its toll on Webster too when, in 1850, at the end of his career and desperate to save the Union from being torn apart, the longtime opponent of slavery endorsed the Compromise of 1850, which allowed slavery in the southern territories. Webster's constituents in Massachusetts, the hub of abolitionism, were outraged. After four months of withering attacks, Webster was forced to resign from the Senate in humiliation.

America in the 1850s was roiled by debates over slavery. After decades of avoiding direct confrontation, elected officials in Washington were forced by westward expansion to confront, once and for all, the future of involuntary servitude in America. The results were bloody, from the plains of Kansas, where a small-scale civil war foreshadowed a larger one, to the floor of Congress, where Senator Charles Sumner was caned nearly to death after making an antislavery speech. The Constitution only exacerbated the growing sectional tensions. Because the Constitution guaranteed each state two votes in the Senate, a representative in the House, and votes in the Electoral College, each side in the slavery debate fought to win the admission of more and more states sympathetic to it.

Slavery tainted Taney's legacy, Webster's memory, and nearly everything else in the years before the Civil War—including the rights of corporations. Indeed, when the Supreme Court decided *Marshall v. Baltimore & Ohio Railroad Company*, slavery was foremost on the minds of several of the justices. Peter Daniel, John Campbell, and John Catron were three southern justices and strong defenders of slavery. Although they agreed with Taney that corporations should not have expansive rights, they went even further than the chief justice on the issue of the corporation's right of access to federal court. They argued that *Bank of the United States* should be overturned in its entirety, and that corporations should have no right whatsoever to sue in federal court. Race was their reason. A definition of "Citizens" loose enough to include a purely legal person like a corporation might also be broad enough to include slaves, who were after all real, living human beings. And if slaves were citizens, they too would have constitutional rights.[61]

Whether blacks were "Citizens" under Article III was the precise question at issue in *Dred Scott*. Dred Scott claimed to have been liberated when he was taken through "free" territory, and he sued in federal court to clarify his legal status. Just like the Bank of the United States before him, Dred Scott argued that he was a citizen entitled to sue in the federal courts. Justices Daniel, Campbell, and Catron need not have worried that expansive rights for corporations would translate into expansive rights for the racially oppressed. Taney's majority opinion in *Dred Scott* dismissed Scott's claim of constitutional citizenship. The Framers of the Constitution did not intend for blacks to be citizens, Taney argued, and the Constitution "must be construed now as it was understood at the time of its adoption." It was a principle of constitutional interpretation the Taney court did not apply in the context of corporations; there was no evidence the Framers understood Article III to include corporations. Taney, who wrote the infamous line about African Americans having "no rights which the white man was bound to respect," thought blacks were not legal persons but corporations were.[62]

Taney's decision in *Dred Scott* would go down as one of the worst decisions in Supreme Court history. Taney imagined it would have precisely the opposite legacy, that it would calm the growing tensions over slavery and put the country on a sound foundation going forward. If anything, it hastened the resort to arms and a conflict that would take the lives of over 600,000 Americans. The Civil War, however, also led to broad new protections being added to the Constitution to protect the rights of racial minorities. Yet for several decades, the intended beneficiaries would have little to show for their newfound constitutional guarantees. Corporations, by contrast, would use those same provisions to greatly expand the civil rights of business. And the story of how they did is one of the most bizarre and disturbing in the history of the Supreme Court.

PART THREE

PROPERTY RIGHTS, NOT LIBERTY RIGHTS

—

KNOWN AS THE "OCTOPUS" FOR ITS GRIP
ON POLITICS IN THE WEST, THE SOUTHERN
PACIFIC RAILROAD COMPANY ALSO FOUGHT
IN COURT TO SECURE CONSTITUTIONAL
PROTECTIONS FOR CORPORATIONS.

—

CHAPTER 4

The Conspiracy for
Corporate Rights

The FOURTEENTH AMENDMENT TO THE CONSTITUTION, adopted after the Civil War, is one of the brightest stars in the constellation of liberty. As everyone knew when it was ratified in 1868, the amendment's guarantees of equal protection and due process were designed to secure the rights of the newly freed slaves and protect them from discrimination by the states. Nearly a decade and a half later, however, in December of 1882, the esteemed Roscoe Conkling told the justices the Fourteenth Amendment was also written to protect the rights of corporations like his client, the Southern Pacific Railroad Company.

Although no lawyer could approach Webster's soaring rhetoric, Conkling was also known as a master orator and had the respect of the justices, as well as their ear. "No man ever came into our court who was listened to with more undivided attention than Roscoe Conkling," said Chief Justice Morrison Waite, who presided over the Southern Pacific's case. Justice Samuel Miller, whose previous opinions seemed to foreclose Conkling's argument that the Fourteenth Amendment applied with equal force to corporations, nonetheless agreed that "for the discussion of the law and the facts of the case Mr. Conkling is the best lawyer who comes into our court."[1]

Conkling was the leader of the Republicans in Congress for nearly two decades immediately after the Civil War, when Republicans dominated Washington. A member of the House and then the Senate, Conkling was often rumored to be a presidential candidate. Although he never became his party's presidential nominee, he was twice nominated to the Supreme Court. The second time was just months before he made his argument on behalf of the Southern Pacific. Even though the Senate voted to confirm him, Conkling declined, pleading poverty. Like Webster, Conkling, who spent his career in public service, needed the money—especially the kind a lawyer could make representing the Southern Pacific, one of the largest, most politically powerful corporations of the late nineteenth century.[2]

Conkling was especially persuasive when it came to the meaning of the Fourteenth Amendment. He had, after all, helped write it. Back in 1866, Conkling served on Congress's Joint Committee on Reconstruction, which drafted the Fourteenth Amendment. Now, a decade and a half later, who would know more than Conkling about what was on the mind of the drafters when they wrote it? By 1882, Conkling was the last surviving member of the Joint Committee. With no one to refute him, Conkling told the justices that he and the other drafters intended to protect business corporations in addition to the freed slaves. The amendment was designed to protect not just the weakest and most subjugated people in the nation but also the most powerful and wealthy corporations. Even the Southern Pacific, whose grip on politics in the West earned it the nickname "the Octopus," was entitled to the protections of the Fourteenth Amendment—and could use those protections to overturn laws burdening the railroads.

Like Webster, Conkling had a flair for showmanship, and he backed up his claim with a surprising piece of evidence: a journal that included the never-before-published record of the deliberations of the Joint Committee as it drafted the Fourteenth Amendment. The journal, Conkling told the justices, supported his recollection about the intent of the drafters. While obviously the freedmen were the primary concern of the committee, Conkling pointed to passages of the journal which showed, he said, that the wording of the amendment had been purposefully changed during the drafting process to include corporations. The amendment as finally ratified provided in relevant part, "No State shall . . . deprive any *person* of life, liberty, or property without due process of law; nor deny to any *person* within its jurisdiction the equal protection of the laws." Conkling told the justices that an early version had used the word "citizen" instead of "person." The latter was ultimately chosen, however, because the drafting committee had received many complaints from businesses about discriminatory state laws, such as the types of restrictions on interstate commerce endorsed by the Taney court in *Bank of Augusta v. Earle*. To protect those businesses, the drafters used the word *person* because corporations, according to Blackstone, had been recognized to be legal persons.

Conkling's extraordinary argument was an admission of a conspiracy of constitutional dimensions. He was saying that there had been a concerted effort by the men who drafted the Fourteenth Amendment, working at the highest levels of the government, to protect corporations under the guise of protecting the freedmen. The drafters had inserted the word *persons* instead of *citizens* with the goal of covering corporations but never told anyone of their purpose or of the effect of the word choice. As a result, the constitutional rights of corporations were not mentioned in any of the ratification debates over the amendment. Nevertheless, corporations now had rights of equal protection and due process.[3]

Conkling's account of the drafting history was fanciful. There was no conspiracy by the drafters of the Fourteenth Amendment to sneak broad new protections for corporations into the Constitution. Congress had not hoodwinked the American people. Rather, the fraud was Conkling, who purposefully misled the justices about the original meaning and intent of the Fourteenth Amendment.

If there was any conspiracy, it was not in the drafting of the Fourteenth Amendment back in the 1860s but involved instead a quartet of corporationalists more than a decade later who doggedly sought a rul-

THE PUSH TO EXTEND FOURTEENTH AMENDMENT RIGHTS TO
CORPORATIONS WAS LED BY ROSCOE CONKLING (TOP LEFT), JUSTICE
STEPHEN J. FIELD (TOP RIGHT), J. C. BANCROFT DAVIS (BOTTOM LEFT),
AND THE SOUTHERN PACIFIC RAILROAD (BOTTOM RIGHT).

ing by the Supreme Court extending Fourteenth Amendment rights to corporations. They included Conkling, who in a moment of personal and financial crisis was willing to say anything to win his case; Justice Stephen J. Field, an influential pro-business jurist with questionable scruples who was once arrested for murder; and J. C. Bancroft Davis, a self-aggrandizing court reporter who sought to write his own views about the rights of corporations into the law books. The fourth "person" in the quartet was one only by the lights of the law: the Southern Pacific Railroad Company, whose fight for constitutional protections would lead it to employ some of the same affirmative, strategic litigation tactics that would later be used by civil rights activists in the 1940s and 1950s.

We do not know if these four ever explicitly agreed to work together to expand the rights of corporations. Yet there was significant interaction among them, and as a result of their combined, if perhaps not coordinated, efforts the Fourteenth Amendment was converted from a shield for the rights of racial minorities—who found little protection from the Supreme Court for the next half-century—into a weapon for corporations to use against state laws regulating business activity.

* * *

WHEN ROSCOE CONKLING ADDRESSED the justices of the Supreme Court on December 20, 1882, the courtroom was packed. The justices were now holding court in the former Senate Chamber, off what journalist E. V. Smalley described as a "rather dingy and ill-lighted passage" in the United States Capitol. The entryway, said Smalley, looked like a "closet door." Inside there were rows of benches covered with red velvet cushions, where a coterie of Washington's society women could often be found. They were not necessarily there for the love of the law. Smalley noted that the Supreme Court had "the only really comfortable seats for public use to be found in the Capitol."[4]

In fact, the spectators in the plush benches had a plethora of entertainment options, a by-product of the Gilded Age. After the Civil War, the American economy, fueled by industrialization and urbanization, experienced unprecedented growth, nearly doubling in size between

1877 and 1893. American workers moved from farms to factories, and their increasing employment by corporations meant fewer working hours, more leisure time, and more dependable—and disposable— income than could be found in agriculture. Leisure activities, once the exclusive province of the wealthy, were now beginning to become available to the emerging middle class, which eagerly embraced spectator sports, like baseball and boxing; amusement parks, circuses, and dime museums; and the ribald comedy of burlesque shows. The novel forms of entertainment were all born of, or quickly transformed into, commercial enterprises. Entertainment became a product to sell to the masses.

Literacy, propelled by compulsory education laws, also boomed in the Gilded Age, and anyone who read the *New-York Daily Tribune* the day of Conkling's appearance before the Supreme Court would have learned from an editorial that "constitutional questions of the gravest interest" were at issue in the case. On the surface, *San Mateo County v. Southern Pacific Railroad Company* was just a simple tax dispute. The railroad was challenging a California law that prohibited railroads, but not individuals, from deducting mortgages when calculating the value

"CIVIL RIGHTS OF CORPORATIONS," *NEW-YORK DAILY TRIBUNE*, DECEMBER 19, 1882.

of their land for tax purposes. The title of the *Daily Tribune* editorial, however, told readers what the case was really about: "Civil Rights of Corporations."[5]

Conkling was claiming that California's ban on railroads deducting mortgages, which did not apply to other landowners, including individuals and other businesses, was a violation of the Southern Pacific's right to equal protection and due process under the Fourteenth Amendment. San Mateo County admitted that the law treated railroads differently but insisted there was good reason for the disparity. By necessity, the railroads owned enormous amounts of real estate, much of it mortgaged for more than the market value of the land itself. If the Southern Pacific and its sister line, the Central Pacific, were allowed to deduct their mortgages like other landowners, the companies—the state's most high-profile and profitable big businesses—would pay no real estate taxes. Californians thought the special tax rule was necessary to avoid such profound unfairness. In the eyes of the Southern Pacific and Central Pacific railroads, however, the tax discriminated against railroad corporations.

California's two leading railroads were both founded by the robber barons Leland Stanford and Collis P. Huntington, who together with their partners dominated transportation in the West—and gained a stranglehold on politics in the West too, as the Southern Pacific's nickname reminded. Yet even an Octopus loses its grip sometimes, and in 1879, with California temporarily in the hands of populist reformers—intellectual heirs of the Jeffersonian and Jacksonian opponents of concentrated corporate power—a new state constitution put the railroad tax in place. The companies' tax bills soared.[6]

To fight the tax increase, the Southern Pacific and the Central Pacific undertook a litigation campaign that could have served as a template for future civil rights movements. First, the railroads engaged in civil disobedience. They simply refused to pay the taxes and launched a public relations campaign in the newspapers against the law. The counties, which were responsible for collecting the tax, were forced to go to court seeking redress. The courts, however, were exactly where the railroads wanted the controversy to be decided. Judges, especially the ones in federal court, were not likely to share the anticorporate populism of California voters.

The railroad corporations were constitutional first movers who employed innovative tactics to secure new rights. They envisioned the lawsuits as a form of strategic litigation, or what their lawyers called "test cases," to determine whether corporations had the same rights as ordinary people to equal protection and due process under the Fourteenth Amendment. The railroads did not want merely to lower their tax bills in California. They wanted to establish broad new protections against burdensome regulations of all sorts. Their remarkable series of cases—more than sixty in all—would become "landmarks in American constitutional history," wrote historian Howard Jay Graham, a leading expert on the Fourteenth Amendment, and "an important turning point in our social and economic development." Graham was referring primarily to the outcome of these cases, which expanded corporate constitutional rights, but he also could have been describing the railroads' strategy of civil disobedience backed by strategic test cases as a method for pursuing equal rights.[7]

Conkling's case, coming out of California's San Mateo County, was the first of the test cases to reach the Supreme Court. Assisting Conkling was a team of well-known lawyers: S.W. Sanderson, former chief justice of the California Supreme Court; George Edmonds, a US senator from Vermont and former presidential candidate; and John Norton Pomeroy, one of the nation's most influential law professors. The Southern Pacific, like so many corporations before and since, was willing and able to hire the best lawyers in the country, the kind that could implement a novel but potentially rewarding strategy of test cases to expand, as the *Tribune* said, the civil rights of corporations.[8]

* * *

THE SOCIETY WOMEN WHO sat in on the Supreme Court the morning of the Southern Pacific's test case would have been impressed by the dashing Conkling. Standing six foot three, the handsome lawyer, who favored boxing for exercise, was described as "erect and muscular, with wavy sandy-blond hair, a full pointed beard, and, falling across his broad forehead, a golden Hyperion curl." He was a well-known ladies' man, and his confident dress, often an elegant vest worn with a black tailcoat and a brightly colored tie, attracted ample attention.[9]

He was also, as one of his rivals was forced to concede, a "great master of language." Conkling had begun the study of oratory at the age of thirteen under the tutelage of an English professor who himself had learned the art from the Corporation's Lawyer himself, Daniel Webster. With a powerful, almost musical voice, Conkling peppered his speeches with precise quotations of Shakespeare, Edmund Burke, and the Bible, all from memory. Conkling, it was said, much like Webster, did not merely persuade juries, "he overpowered them and made his will theirs." As a young lawyer, Conkling once won a startling $18,000 verdict against one of Cornelius Vanderbilt's railroads; when the losing lawyer suggested an appeal, Vanderbilt scolded, "Pay it! If Conkling tries this case again, he may get fifty thousand!"[10]

For most of his adult life, Conkling employed his oratorical skills on behalf of the Republican Party while serving in Congress, first as a congressman from Utica, New York, and then as a senator. He was, like Webster, an unabashed partisan at a time of truly unparalleled partisanship. Americans today consider the current partisan rancor in Washington unprecedented, but when Conkling arrived in the nation's capital in 1858, on the eve of the Civil War, even the galleries in Congress were politically segregated. Northern spectators sat on one side and southern spectators sat on the other. And, of course, the divide back then led to a bloody armed conflict. After the Civil War, Conkling became a leader of his party, helping to usher in Reconstruction and securing civil rights legislation to aid the newly freed slaves. He was closely allied with the Union general turned president, Hiram Grant, who preferred to be called by his more heroic-sounding middle name, Ulysses. It was Grant who first nominated Conkling to the Supreme Court, to be chief justice no less. That was in 1873 and Conkling, at the height of his power in the Senate, declined the post. Later, Grant expressed hope that Conkling would succeed him in the White House.[11]

Conkling remained in the Senate until 1881, when he returned to New York and the practice of law. He sought out wealthy clients, and his very first was Jay Gould, the notorious speculator who years later would be named by *Fortune* as one of the fifteen richest people of all time. Soon after, Conkling was hired by successful inventor and entrepreneur Thomas Edison, who had already gained fame for the phonograph and was then undertaking the first effort to illuminate lower Manhattan with electric lighting. Conkling charged clients like these more than four times the typical lawyer's fee. Not too many lawyers could say they had once been nominated to be chief justice of the United States.[12]

The Southern Pacific had no difficulty paying Conkling's hefty retainer. The railroads were the largest and most politically powerful corporations of the day. They had to be. The capital required to lay tracks through the wilderness and across mountains like the Appalachians and Rockies was without precedent, as were the challenges of managing such dispersed operations. As we saw earlier, the railroads began to significantly change the American economy in the 1840s and 1850s, and along the way expanded the stock market. Railroad innovations in the Gilded Age would also transform the corporation's internal organization and size, giving rise to the first modern business corporations.

With some exceptions, traditional business enterprises of early nineteenth-century America tended to be owned by an individual, a family, or a small number of partners. Businesses were specialized to focus on one aspect of commerce, such as production, sale, or distribution of particular types of goods, and they were largely local. They hired, sold to, and served primarily people in the vicinity, and the owners supervised a relatively small number of employees. The railroads created a new model. Employees were far more numerous and scattered along the lines. Business functions were separated into multiple divisions or units, and a hierarchical organizational structure was created to control them. Within each unit, managers managed not only laborers but also other managers. This was the beginning of what economic historian Alfred Chandler called "managerial capitalism." Prior to 1840, no American corporation had these features. By 1920, this kind of corporation, with layers of hierarchical organization ruling over multiple divisions, had become the dominant type of business firm in major sectors of the American economy.[13]

Railroads, which had already experienced explosive growth before the Civil War, built more than 100,000 miles of additional tracks in the two decades following it. As before the war, graft remained popular with politicans and the railroads seeking to persuade them for rights of way, eminent domain power, and other privileges. When Congress was deciding whether to subsidize the building of the first transcontinental railroad in 1861, Leland Stanford sent one of his men to Washington with a suitcase full of Central Pacific stock certificates to dole out liberally to lawmakers. According to the best estimates, the Central Pacific Railroad alone distributed to lawmakers and lobbyists $500,000 annually—equal to roughly $13 million today. As congressional leader James G. Blaine explained the political reality in postbellum America, "to make the wheels revolve we must have grease."[14]

When bribes were not enough to prevent unfavorable legislation, railroads like the Southern Pacific hired the nation's top lawyers—men like Roscoe Conkling—and mounted their attack in the courts.

* * *

IN THE *SAN MATEO* CASE, Conkling's argument on behalf of the Southern Pacific focused on the Fourteenth Amendment, which from the beginning had been controversial. For decades after ratification, southerners insisted that the amendment had never been properly ratified. This may have been mostly proverbial sour grapes, but that is not the entire story. In fact, the ratification of the Fourteenth Amendment, one of the Constitution's most important and influential provisions, has always been a little bit suspect.

Article V provides two ways of amending the Constitution. The first, never yet used, is through a constitutional convention, which Congress is obligated to call upon the application of two-thirds of the state legislatures. The second way is for Congress to propose an amendment for the states to approve. This latter method, which has been used for all twenty-seven amendments, requires a favorable vote by two-thirds of each house and then ratification by three-fourths of the states. It was this last requirement that raised questions about the Fourteenth Amendment.

In 1866, after Congress approved the proposed amendment Conkling had helped to write, many state legislatures acted quickly. Connecticut and New Hampshire voted in favor, followed shortly after by New Jersey, Oregon, Vermont, and Ohio. Ten southern states, including North Carolina, South Carolina, and Louisiana, predictably voted against it; Tennessee was the sole Confederate state to approve the amendment—and only then because opponents miscalculated and boycotted the vote in a vain attempt to prevent the legislature from having a quorum. The amendment, which was controversial, stalled in several Union states, including California, Maryland, and Delaware. By March of 1867, it was clear that the amendment would not obtain the three-fourths of the states necessary.

The Republicans who controlled Congress, including Conkling, responded by passing the Reconstruction Acts, which effectively disbanded the governments of all the former Confederate states, save Tennessee. The Reconstruction Acts created new, multiracial Reconstruction governments for these recalcitrant states and required the exclusion from office of anyone who served in the Confederacy. Congress also warned the southern states that they would not be fully admitted back into the Union until they ratified the Fourteenth Amendment.[15]

This bit of congressional hardball only made the proposed amendment more dubious in the eyes of some. In the next elections, the amendment was a major issue, and Democrats opposed to ratification won control of several statehouses in the North. With the amendment still short of the necessary three-fourths of the states, legislators in New Jersey and Ohio voted again, this time rescinding their earlier approval. Nevertheless, in July of 1868, after new Reconstruction governments in North Carolina, South Carolina, and Louisiana voted to approve the amendment, Congress passed a resolution declaring the Fourteenth Amendment ratified. The three-fourths threshold was only met with the inclusion of the two states that had rescinded their earlier endorsements, New Jersey and Ohio.

Defenders of Congress's actions insisted that states like New Jersey and Ohio could not change their minds about ratification, even though the larger ratification process was still under way. There was certainly merit to that view, although there were questions about whether the principle had been applied evenhandedly. Congress had eagerly recognized the second, subsequent votes of North Carolina, South Carolina, and Louisiana, southern states that had originally voted against the amendment.

While other southerners sought to undermine the legitimacy of the Fourteenth Amendment, John Archibald Campbell decided the wiser strategy was to use the amendment to serve southern ends instead. An ardent segregationist, Campbell was also a former Supreme Court justice. He had been one of the three Taney court justices who voted to overturn *Bank of the United States v. Deveaux* because he feared an expansive definition of "Citizens" might include slaves. Campbell had resigned from the court in 1861, two weeks after South Carolina militiamen attacked Fort Sumter. He became a leader in the Confederate government, and, after the war, returned to private practice as a lawyer. Campbell understood how Washington worked, especially the Supreme Court, and knew the Fourteenth Amendment was not about to be declared invalid. Instead of trying to overturn the amendment, Campbell would seek to exploit it in an attempt to defang Reconstruction.

By all accounts brilliant, Campbell graduated from the University of Georgia at the precocious age of 14 and, thanks to a special act of the state legislature, was admitted to the bar at 18. He moved to Alabama and made such a quick impression there that by the age of 25 he had been twice offered appointment to that state's supreme court. Campbell, who loved the practice of law, declined both times. In 1851, after the 40-year-old Campbell argued six cases in the Supreme Court of the United States in one term, the impressed justices lobbied President Franklin Pierce to appoint him to the high court when the next vacancy arose. Campbell served as an associate justice from 1853 until the outbreak of the Civil War. Although he thought secession a mistake, he was forever loyal to the South.[16]

AFTER RESIGNING FROM THE SUPREME COURT TO JOIN
THE CONFEDERACY, JOHN CAMPBELL SOUGHT TO USE
THE FOURTEENTH AMENDMENT TO PROTECT ECONOMIC
RIGHTS IN HIS FIGHT AGAINST RECONSTRUCTION.

After the Civil War, Campbell became a leader of the movement to fight Reconstruction and reassert white supremacy. In Louisiana, where Campbell then resided, a popular saying among reactionaries was, "Leave it to God and Mr. Campbell." In a series of cases in the early 1870s, he represented a group of New Orleans butchers who sought to overturn a law enacted by Louisiana's Reconstruction government requiring the city's butchers to slaughter their meat in a centralized facility. Previously, local butchers carved up livestock anywhere they liked and dumped the entrails and waste from more than 300,000 animals slaughtered annually into the Mississippi River, which was also the city's main source of drinking water. The result was repeated epidemics of yellow fever and cholera. An outbreak in 1853 took the lives of 40,000 residents—twenty times more than were lost in the devastation of Hurricane Katrina in 2005. The new law gave a monopoly to a single slaughterhouse downriver, on the outskirts of the town, and mandated that it provide equal access to all butchers at a reasonable rate. Given the public health hazards of the old slaughtering practice, one might have expected the new law to win broad popular support among New Orleans residents. Instead, the law was seen through the filters of race and Reconstruction, and public opinion sided with the butchers.[17]

Campbell challenged the Louisiana law as an infringement of the butchers' constitutional right under the Fourteenth Amendment to the "unrestricted exercise of the business of butchering." Although the Massachusetts Bay Company's charter included the right to fish, the right to be a butcher was nowhere mentioned in the Fourteenth Amendment. Instead, Campbell relied on a provision of the amendment that required states to respect the "privileges or immunities" of citizens. One of those privileges, Campbell claimed, was the right to ply one's trade, free from undue government interference.

Campbell's suits came before the Supreme Court in what were together called the *Slaughter-House Cases* of 1873. The court ruled against Campbell and the butchers in an opinion by Justice Samuel Miller. In many ways the dominant figure on the court in the years immediately after the Civil War, Miller, an associate justice, was called in some circles "the real chief." Over the course of his twenty-eight-year tenure, he wrote 616 majority opinions, more than any other previous justice. (For comparison, the influential Antonin Scalia, who served for thirty years before he passed away in 2016, wrote 270 majority opinions.) A common thread in Miller's best-known rulings was a narrow view of the Fourteenth Amendment—and he certainly was not going to read it broadly to help Campbell. As much as Roger Taney had disliked Daniel Webster, Samuel Miller loathed John Campbell. Miller, a Lincoln appointee, said of Campbell, "I think no man that has survived the rebellion is more saturated today with its spirit." He "deserves all the punishment he . . . can receive, not so much for joining the rebellion as for the persistency with which he continues the fight."[18]

Although Justice Miller's opinion in the *Slaughter-House Cases* had nothing directly to do with corporate personhood, the question raised by the case was related: Did the Fourteenth Amendment create a barrier to laws regulating economic activity? Miller answered in the negative, insisting that the Fourteenth Amendment was designed with "one pervading purpose": "the protection of the newly made freeman and citizen from the oppressions of those who had formerly exercised unlimited dominion over him." Quoting the legendary early nineteenth-century jurist James Kent of New York, Miller reminded Campbell that, when it came to economic matters, "private interests must be made subservient to the general interests of the community." The Fourteenth Amendment was not intended to protect white butchers unhappy with economic regulation. It was designed to protect African Americans.

"We doubt very much," Miller predicted with startling inaccuracy, "whether any action of a State not directed by way of discrimination against the negroes as a class, on account of their race, will ever be held to come within the purview of this provision."[19]

* * *

IF ANYONE COULD PERSUADE Justice Miller and the other members of the court to read the Fourteenth Amendment more broadly, it was Roscoe Conkling. He spoke from his own experience about what was on the mind of the drafters—what was on *his* mind—when the amendment was written.

By the time *San Mateo County v. Southern Pacific Railroad* came before the justices in 1882, the law was changing in ways that would help Conkling's argument for expansive corporate rights. Reconstruction had ended, and Congress's decision to turn a blind eye to southern racial discrimination after the disputed election of 1876 was matched by crimped readings of the Fourteenth Amendment by the Supreme Court. Although Samuel Miller's court was not willing in the 1870s to broadly read the amendment to give rights to businessmen like the New Orleans butchers, it also refused to read it broadly to protect the rights of racial minorities in cases like 1876's *United States v. Cruikshank* and *United States v. Reese*. The same year Conkling appeared before the justices, the court struck down the Civil Rights Act of 1875, which like the Civil Rights Act of 1965 outlawed racial discrimination in theaters, restaurants, and other places of public accommodation. With race minimized in the emerging jurisprudence of the Fourteenth Amendment, the time was ripe for another effort to establish protections for economic rights.[20]

The stakes in the Southern Pacific case were high for Conkling personally, despite his renown. The year before his Supreme Court argument, Conkling suffered an embarrassing public humiliation when he resigned from the Senate to protest President James Garfield's appointment of one of Conkling's rivals to run the New York Custom House, a spoils appointment that Conkling thought he should control. Garfield and Conkling, however, were in a titanic power struggle over control of the Republican Party, and the president made the appointment over Conkling's objections in order to make a statement. Conkling promptly resigned, although he intended it only as a symbolic gesture. At the time, before the adoption of the Seventeenth Amendment, senators were chosen by the state legislatures. Conkling, for decades the most powerful politician in New York, expected state lawmakers to quickly return him to the Senate. Yet Conkling's political influence was already on the wane, and the New York legislature selected someone else. Garfield heard the news on his deathbed, the victim of an assassin's bullet, but was nonetheless able to summon the strength to whisper, "Thank God."[21]

Conkling's appearance before the Supreme Court was his return to the halls of power, a chance to show that he was still a man of influence. He still garnered ample respect in many circles; President Chester Arthur, one of Conkling's protégés, had offered him a seat on the Supreme Court earlier that year. He had been forced by his finances to turn down the Supreme Court appointment but he could nevertheless still exert his power over the law. According to one of Conkling's biographers, the Southern Pacific case would be "the most important case he ever argued."[22]

Judicial review, Conkling once remarked, made "the Constitution, the institutions of the country, nothing but wax in the hands of judges; it amounts to a running power of amendment." Conkling's concerns about judicial activism were widely shared among Republicans of the time, for whom the Supreme Court was associated with *Dred Scott v. Sandford* and the series of postwar decisions that minimized the Fourteenth Amendment's protections for racial minorities. Yet now Conkling, sloughing off his hesitancy about activist judges, sought to persuade the Supreme Court to mold the wax again, in the shape of a corporate person.[23]

"May it please your Honors," Conkling began. "I come now to say that the Southern Pacific Railroad Company and its creditors and stockholders are among the 'persons' protected by the Fourteenth Amendment of the Constitution of the United States." In the law, the word *person*, Conkling told the justices, "has by long and constant acceptance, and by multiplied judicial construction, been held to embrace artificial persons as well as natural persons."[24]

The drafting history of the amendment offered proof. The Joint Committee's first version was changed on what Conkling implied was his own recommendation. He had suggested the committee strike "the words 'citizens of the United States'" and replace them with "'persons in each State'" in order to provide broader protections, whose reach would extend to artificial persons like corporations.

A skilled lawyer, however, recognizes the weakness of his own argument, and Conkling's had a few. The Fourteenth Amendment used the word *person* or *persons* five times, and most of those references were unambiguously to human beings. The first sentence guaranteed citizenship to "all persons born or naturalized in the United States"; corporations were neither born nor naturalized. Section two of the amendment, which established how representatives would be apportioned among the states, required a "counting" of "the whole number of persons in each State, excluding Indians not taxed." No one, either then or since, has claimed that business corporations should be counted in determining the number of seats a state has in Congress. Section three of the Fourteenth Amendment prohibited any "person" from serving in federal office who had previously violated an oath to support the Constitution by joining the Confederacy. Conkling was asking the justices to read the same word *person*, used in multiple provisions added to the Constitution at the same time, to mean different things.

Conkling's was an argument that had been made—and rejected— once before. In 1871, the Continental Insurance Company of New York sued to invalidate a New Orleans ordinance that required out-of-state insurers to pay license fees double that of in-state insurers. It

THE FOURTEENTH AMENDMENT WAS DRAFTED BY THE JOINT COMMITTEE ON RECONSTRUCTION, WHICH INCLUDED AMONG ITS MEMBERS ROSCOE CONKLING.

was one of the many nineteenth-century cases in which corporations challenged state laws burdening foreign companies, similar to Daniel Webster's case on behalf of the Second Bank of the United States in *Bank of Augusta v. Earle.* Two decades after the Taney court rejected Webster's challenge, which had been based on the Constitution's comity clause, the Continental Insurance Company based its claim on the brand new Fourteenth Amendment and its guarantee of equal protection of the laws. New Orleans was not treating the out-of-state insurance company equally to in-state insurance companies, the corporation argued. Federal judge William Burnham Woods, a veteran of the Civil War with a populist view of corporations, disagreed. Noting that the Fourteenth Amendment's use of the word *person* clearly meant human beings in several of its clauses, Woods, who would join the Supreme Court in 1880, found it hard to believe, as the insurance company suggested, "that the word 'person' . . . has a wider and more comprehensive meaning" in the equal protection clause. "This would be a construction for which we find no warrant in the rules of interpretation."[25]

In the Supreme Court, Conkling had to have a response to Woods's point, not least because Woods was among the justices on the bench before him. Conkling's answer was one only a drafter of the amendment could plausibly offer. He told the justices the various provisions of the Fourteenth Amendment did not have "a single inspiration or design." Rather, "the different parts of what now stands as a whole" were, he said, "separately and independently conceived" by the committee over the course of months. The meaning of the word *person* in one sentence was not necessarily the same as the meaning of the word in another. The several provisions "came to be collected in one proposal of the amendment—put together in sections for the convenience and simplicity of submission to the States."

What about the *Slaughter-House Cases*, which had suggested that the Fourteenth Amendment was about equal rights for the former slaves? "It may be true, as Mr. Justice Miller has observed, that but for these considerations this amendment never would have been suggested," Conkling acknowledged. Yet while the "rights and wrongs of the freedmen were the chief spur and incentive" of the amendment, Conkling's committee had intended to do far more, he said. Invoking the American Revolution, Conkling, a well-versed student of American history, reminded the justices that "a tax by way of a paltry stamp on paper sundered the relations of the colonies and Great Britain. But what then?" The Revolution did not confine itself to overturning the Stamp Act, it was not limited "to the little cause, the particular instance" that gave rise to the conflict. "A particular grievance, some startling illustration of a grievance, is commonly the spur of agitation, and of popular or legislative action—sometimes of revolution."

Of course there was still the most glaring problem with Conkling's corporationalist argument: no one in the public debate over the ratification of the Fourteenth Amendment had ever mentioned business corporations. Conkling's response was to point to the text. It referred to persons, not African Americans. "The American people," he said, "in giving it their imprimatur understood what they were doing, and meant to decree what has, in fact, been decreed." In other words, it did not matter that no one talked about protecting corporations. All that mattered were the words that the sovereign people added to the text, which should be read expansively to protect everyone, including corporations, from discriminatory laws. Paraphrasing a Ralph Waldo Emerson poem well known at the time, Conkling shrugged off the people's ignorance of their deed by suggesting they "may have builded better than they knew."

For additional support for what might have been seen as a scurrilous argument, Conkling also had his musty old journal. It had been compiled contemporaneously "by an experienced recorder" to capture the Joint Committee's deliberations over the Fourteenth Amendment. Conkling's surprising revelation must have stirred the fine ladies watching from the court's red velvet benches. It may have had an even more profound effect on his intended audience, the justices. After Conkling sat down, his cocounsel S. W. Sanderson rose to the lectern to add to the Southern Pacific's argument, only to be quickly interrupted by Justice Miller. The author of the *Slaughter-House Cases* unexpectedly offered a more nuanced view of the Fourteenth Amendment: "I have never heard it said in this Court, or by any judge of it, that these articles were supposed to be limited to the negro race."

* * *

CHARLES A. BEARD, A PROFESSOR at Columbia University in the early decades of the twentieth century, was among the first to suggest that Conkling's argument revealed a profoundly troubling conspiracy behind the adoption of the Fourteenth Amendment. Beard, perhaps the most influential historian of the Progressive era, was best known for his 1913 book, *An Economic Interpretation of the Constitution of the United States*, which argued that the Founding Fathers were men of wealth who crafted the Constitution largely to protect their own economic interests. His blasphemous accusation sparked tremendous controversy. Some, like Harvard historian Alfred Bushnell Hart, called the claim "little short of indecent," while populist reformers praised it as proof that our constitutional system was rigged to favor the rich—that ours was a government "of the capitalists, by the capitalists, and for the capitalists."[26]

In Beard's view, political actors were almost always motivated not by high principle but by economic and class concerns. This applied both to the Founding Fathers who wrote the Constitution and to the Roscoe Conklings who so attempted to radically revise the document after the Civil War. Beard's 1927 book, *The Rise of American Civilization*, coauthored with his wife Mary Beard, argued that there were two factions in the Reconstruction Congress, "one bent on establishing the rights of the Negroes; the other determined to take in the whole range of the national economy." Conkling and Representative John A. Bingham, a leading drafter of the Fourteenth Amendment, belonged to the latter faction. Bingham, the Beards noted, was a lawyer for the railroads, and they accused him of manipulating the wording of the amendment "by including among the safeguards devised for Negroes a broad provision for the rights of all 'persons,' natural and artificial, individual and corporate." Conkling's argument to the Supreme Court in the *San Mateo* case was the culmination of the plot, the fruit of the seeds planted by the drafters years earlier. Yale law professor Walton

H. Hamilton labeled the Beards' story the "conspiracy theory" of the Fourteenth Amendment.[27]

In later years, however, other historians reexamined the evidence and found much to disagree with in the Beards' analysis. No one looked more closely than Howard Jay Graham, a deaf librarian who became the nation's leading expert on the Fourteenth Amendment. In the 1950s, Graham played an influential role as an advisor to the NAACP in the drafting of its briefs in *Brown v. Board of Education*, the school desegregation case. Back in 1938, however, Graham published a two-part series of articles in the *Yale Law Journal* refuting the Beards' charges. The Beards, Graham argued, badly misconstrued Bingham's speeches and were too easily swayed by Conkling's misleading argument in *San Mateo*. Graham's reconstruction of the history of the Fourteenth Amendment's drafting led him to conclude that the Joint Committee had not engaged in a secret, purposeful effort to mislead the public and protect corporations.[28]

Conkling was another story altogether. It was true, as Conkling said, that business corporations were petitioning Congress for protection against oppressive state laws during the drafting of the Fourteenth Amendment. Graham studied the *Congressional Globe*, however, and found that the petitions were seeking protective legislation, not a constitutional amendment. Their efforts failed to produce even the legislation, much less the harder-to-enact amendment. Indeed, when the amendment was submitted to the states for ratification, business newspapers and journals ignored it, suggesting that business interests did not expect it to have any relevance to them. And none of the men who drafted the Fourteenth Amendment, many of whom were practicing lawyers representing businesses, invoked their handiwork when opportunities arose in challenges to regulation the years immediately after the amendment was ratified. Graham noted "astute draftsmen and smooth operators do not choose to wait a decade and a half to divulge intentions and reap contemplated gains."[29]

Conkling's journal, Graham discovered, was legitimate; it was in fact a previously unpublished record of the deliberations of the Joint Committee that drafted the Fourteenth Amendment. Yet, when

Graham looked at the journal closely, he quickly realized that it did not support Conkling's arguments at all. In particular, the journal refuted Conkling's claim that the committee had changed the wording of the amendment from *citizen* to *person*. Examining all the proposed drafts and Conkling's journal, Graham concluded that "neither the sub-committee, nor anyone, at any time or under any circumstances, so far as the historical record indicates, ever used the word 'citizen' in any draft of the equal protection or due process clauses." Contrary to Conkling's suggestion, the language of the amendment was never revised to cover business corporations.[30]

Conkling, Graham concluded, "suppressed pertinent facts and misrepresented others," "resorted to misquotation and unfair arrangements of the facts," "made free use of inference and conjecture, and above all he imposed upon the good faith of listeners who undoubtedly had a high regard for his veracity." "Whether, and to what extent, his gains were the result of deliberate plan and artifice can never be known with certainty," Graham admitted. Yet "it is almost impossible to believe that he did not do this intentionally." In the end, the only reasonable conclusion was that Conkling's argument was "a deliberate, brazen forgery."[31]

There was no conspiracy by the drafters of the Fourteenth Amendment to sneak protections for business corporations into the Constitution. Graham's analysis, however, suggested that there was a secret, purposeful effort to mislead the justices in the *San Mateo* case.

* * *

WITH A BALD CROWN offset by a thick tangle of curly hair in the back and a beard so long it concealed his bow ties, Stephen J. Field was among the justices presiding the day Conkling made his argument to the Supreme Court. Although Field was not convinced by Conkling's claims about the drafting of the Fourteenth Amendment, he was a corporationalist who, like Conkling, was determined to see business gain the protections of the Fourteenth Amendment.

Field had a forceful personality that provoked strong feelings—including, in some, a desire to kill. Field came close to being murdered twice. The first time, in 1853, when Field was still a lawyer in California, a man he had defeated in a case snuck up behind him and put a gun to his head. The man demanded Field, who was known to carry a gun, draw his own weapon to defend himself. When Field refused, the man walked away, following a code of honor not always adhered to in the Wild West.[32]

The second time Field was targeted, the sitting justice ended up in jail for murder. Field's arrest was itself a testament to the passions he aroused. In the nineteenth century, Supreme Court justices were required to "ride circuit." Each would travel to a particular region of the country and hear cases, a grueling part of the job for men in the later stages of life traveling in harsh conditions. Justices were often assigned to cover circuits with which they had some geographical connection. Field was assigned to the new western Ninth Circuit, which included California, Field's home state prior to joining the bench. He had been born in Connecticut but moved west when gold was discovered in 1849. Within a year of his arrival in California, he was elected to the state legislature and, a few years later, to the state supreme court. One of the other judges on the California court was David Terry, and the two men shared an intense, mutual animosity for one another. Years later Terry would become the second person to threaten Field's life.

Riding circuit in 1888, Field presided over a case involving Terry, who was then no longer a judge, and his new young wife, Sarah Althea Hill. The couple sought a share of the estate of a wealthy former senator to whom Hill claimed to have been secretly married. As proof, Hill produced a marriage contract purportedly signed by the deceased. Field's court, however, deemed the contract to be a forgery, and Field from the bench questioned Hill's virtue, the lack of which stood out even in as rough and ready a state as California in the late nineteenth century. Soon after, Terry swore publicly that he would exact revenge if Field dared to return to California. The threats were sufficiently serious—Terry was reputed to have killed two other men—that the attorney general of the United States ordered extra security for Field.[33]

On the justice's next trip to California, Field and his bodyguard,

Deputy Marshal David Neagle, were having breakfast at a train stop in Lathrop, about 70 miles due east of San Francisco, when Terry snuck up behind the justice and struck him. Neagle jumped up and shot Terry twice, once in the head and once in the heart, killing the former judge instantly. It was then discovered, however, that Terry was unarmed, and California authorities arrested both Neagle and Field for murder. To this day, Field remains the only justice ever arrested while serving on the Supreme Court, much less for a crime as serious as murder.

On account of his position, Field was quickly released, but California prosecutors charged the hapless Neagle with murder. Before trial, Neagle sought relief from the federal courts and his writ went to the Supreme Court. Writing for the court, Justice Samuel Miller held that California could not hold a federal officer in custody for acts the officer was authorized to take under federal law. Because Neagle was appointed to guard Field against an attack by Terry or Hill, he could not be prosecuted under California law for performing his duties. The Supreme Court's decision *In re Neagle* remains a landmark precedent on federal/state relations still studied by law students today.[34]

Although Field's run-ins made headlines, he was best known among lawyers for his bold and influential rulings from the bench. John Norton Pomeroy, the law professor who also was one of Southern Pacific's lawyers in the *San Mateo* case, wrote that Field "impressed his own conceptions upon the jurisprudence of the country—as much so, perhaps, as any living jurist in America." When Field was on the California Supreme Court, he had authored groundbreaking opinions on property rights and mining claims, reorganized the state judiciary, drafted ethical guidelines for lawyers, and written comprehensive rules of procedure for both criminal and civil cases. His influence "upon the people and material prosperity has been simply immeasurable," gushed Pomeroy. Even more levelheaded analysts would acknowledge that the California Supreme Court under Field's leadership gained national renown—a stature it retains to this day.[35]

It is tempting to believe that Field was born for such success. His ancestors were among America's first settlers, arriving as early as the 1630s. Both of his grandfathers fought in the Revolutionary War. His siblings were also an accomplished lot. His brother Cyrus laid the first transatlantic telegraph cable and was mentioned by name in Jules Verne's 1870 classic, *20,000 Leagues Under the Sea*. Another brother, David, was "known throughout the world" for spearheading the codification movement, which brought order and clarity to what was a morass of judge-made common law rules by incorporating them into written statutes. Henry, Field's youngest brother, humbly chose to become a Presbyterian minister, only to end up the influential editor of one of the nation's leading religious newspapers.[36]

Stephen Field was said to possess an "iron character" marked by "intensity, and persistent force." He was, one biographer wrote, "self-confident, almost to the point of being offensive; and he was sometimes hot-tempered and vindictive." His confidence was reflected in his opinions. Field did not believe the role of a judge was, as John Roberts would famously say in his confirmation hearings more than a century later, to be a passive umpire calling balls and strikes. Field believed, like most elites in the bar at the time, that the law was to be shaped for the betterment of society. As Pomeroy described him— using language that would be unheard of today—Field's most distinctive trait as a judge was "his *creative power*," "his ability in developing, enlarging, and improving the law." Field's jurisprudence was one of "constant rejection of ancient common-law dogmas, no matter how firmly settled," to be replaced by "more just, consistent, and practical doctrines adapted to the needs of our own country and people." In the late nineteenth century, the mark of a good judge was not how well he adhered to the Framers' original understanding but how much his innovations bettered society.[37]

Field, moreover, had the will to make other justices go along. When Chicagoan Melville Fuller was appointed chief justice in 1888, Wirt Dexter, a lawyer familiar with both men, reportedly said, "Field will eat him in one bite."[38]

* * *

THE MOST POWERFUL CORPORATIONS of the Gilded Age were the railroads, and Stephen Field was a vote they could usually count on. Field had well-known and controversial ties with the railroads, especially the Southern Pacific and its president, Leland Stanford. Field and Stanford were close friends, and when Stanford established Leland Stanford Junior University near Palo Alto in 1891, he asked Field to be one of its founding trustees. Stanford was even said to be behind Field's nomination to the Supreme Court. Throughout his time on the bench, Field ruled consistently in Stanford's favor. Even when he was not assigned to the case, Field was known to lobby the presiding judges to help them see the merits of Stanford's positions.[39]

Field's allegiance to Stanford and his railroad corporations did not go unrecognized by his colleagues. When Field tried to convince Chief Justice Waite to assign him the majority opinion in one case decided on behalf of another Stanford railroad, the Central Pacific, Waite refused, citing Field's "intimate personal relations with the managers." Waite explained that it was "specially important that the opinion come from one who would not be known as the personal friend of the parties representing these railroad interests."[40]

For Field, however, ruling in favor of the railroads and against burdensome state regulation was not just a matter of personal ties; it was a manifestation of his forcefully pro-business worldview. A subscriber to the emergent theory of social Darwinism, Field thought meddling in the marketplace stagnated and distorted economic evolution, enabling the government to pick winners and losers. Like modern-day libertarians, Field generally believed that leaving markets alone would produce a higher standard of living for more Americans. His faith in the free market was buttressed by the enormous growth in the American economy in the last half of the nineteenth century, much of it fueled by corporations.[41]

The Gilded Age was also known as the "Age of Enterprise." Almost daily, incredible new products were being introduced: telephones, phonographs, cable cars, ready-to-wear clothing, soft drinks,

LELAND STANFORD OF THE SOUTHERN PACIFIC
RAILROAD HAD A CLOSE RELATIONSHIP WITH
JUSTICE STEPHEN FIELD.

and canned fruits. Kerosene, marketed by Rockefeller's Standard
Oil, became a cheap and widely available substitute for whale oil and
candles to illuminate homes, only to be challenged soon after by the
advent of electrical lighting. The Home Insurance Building in Chicago, the nation's first skyscraper, was completed in 1885, and at ten
stories it became the tallest man-made structure in the world. Homes
were being outfitted with running water and cooled by electric fans,
the first home appliance. By the time Justice Field was asked to decide
whether corporations had rights under the Fourteenth Amendment,
technological development promoted by commercial enterprises of
the post–Civil War era had radically transformed the daily lives of
most Americans.

The railroads could plausibly claim to have improved society as much as any other corporations. In 1869, the transcontinental railroad was completed when Stanford drove in the famous Golden Spike, engraved with Stanford's name, at Promontory Summit. Not only did the transcontinental railroad enable people to cross the country with ease—something that could be appreciated by Field, whose first journey to California more than twenty years earlier had taken six weeks on a boat packed with cholera-infected passengers—but goods moved easily too. Railroads transported more than 350 million tons of freight each year and employed upwards of 1.5 million people. The new refrigerated railroad cars brought fresh fruits and vegetables grown in Florida and California to markets across the nation, a sign of the truly national economy.[42]

Field thus had little sympathy for the populist heirs to Jefferson, Jackson, and Taney who enacted laws subjecting successful businesses like the railroads to special, disadvantageous rules and taxes. When Stanford and the railroad corporations decided to mount their test cases against California's tax, Field recommended the Southern Pacific hire Professor Pomeroy, who would write so glowingly about Field's creative approach to judging.[43]

There was nothing inappropriate about a judge recommending a good lawyer to a friend involved in a lawsuit. Yet by modern-day standards of judicial ethics, Field crossed the line by then participating as a judge in that case. Indeed, Field presided over the case multiple times. Before Conkling made his argument in the Supreme Court, the case was heard by the federal circuit court in California, presided over by Field. Rather than recuse himself for the obvious conflict of interest, Field took the lead role among the judges, writing a strong opinion in favor of the Southern Pacific and endorsing the arguments made by the lawyer he had recommended. Field also traversed ethical boundaries when, during the litigation, he shared with the Southern Pacific's lawyers confidential memoranda about the case written by other justices.[44]

Field's luck ran only so far, however, and he was denied his opportunity to deliver a victory for Stanford and the Southern Pacific in Roscoe Conkling's case. Although Field wrote to a friend that the oral argument went "great," the case, he explained, "will be held under advisement until next term." In fact, the justices never issued a final decision on the merits in *San Mateo County v. Southern Pacific Railroad*. Two years later, the court having yet to rule, the case was suddenly settled. The Southern Pacific surprisingly agreed to pay the taxes owed to San Mateo County.[45]

Why Stanford agreed to settle the *San Mateo* case remains something of a mystery, but it may have had something to do with Conkling's deception. Test cases do not typically settle. The lawsuit had been designed solely to spur a Supreme Court decision. Graham, the librarian who rebutted Conkling's conspiracy theory of the Fourteenth Amendment, speculated that the justices might have been troubled by certain factual discrepancies in the record and, with other test cases challenging the California tax law wending their way up through the courts, Stanford cut his losses. Yet the supposed discrepancies were exceedingly minor, and hardly enough to prevent the justices from ruling on the case had they so desired. One is left to wonder whether the justices had, in fact, realized the larger discrepancy in Conkling's account of the drafting of the Fourteenth Amendment. Or perhaps the other lawyers on the Southern Pacific's legal team, who were all men of public repute, uncovered their colleague's deception and made it known that the case should be dropped.

Another of Stanford's test cases made its way to the Supreme Court shortly after, and the actions of the lawyers in that case suggest Conkling's deceit had been discovered. The case came out of Santa Clara County and challenged the same California railroad tax rules. Southern Pacific had the same legal team, save for Conkling, who was no longer involved. Tellingly, none of the Southern Pacific's briefs in the Santa Clara County case made mention of Conkling's journal or his statements about the drafters' intentions. Given that Conkling, a drafter himself, had offered direct testimony about the intended meaning of the Fourteenth Amendment, such an omission was glaring. If the lawyers believed Conkling had been telling the truth, omitting his argument would have been malpractice. In any event, the test cases were about to take another unexpected turn.[46]

* * *

THE JUSTICES WOULD HEAR arguments in the Southern Pacific's second test case, *Santa Clara County v. Southern Pacific Railroad*, in January of 1886. The issues were exactly the same as in the *San Mateo* case: Did corporations have rights under the Fourteenth Amendment? And, if so, did California's tax rules prohibiting railroads from deducting mortgages that other landowners were allowed to deduct amount to an unconstitutional denial of the corporations' right to equal protection of the laws? The procedural posture of the case was also the same. In both cases, the circuit court had ruled in the Southern Pacific's favor before the appeal to the Supreme Court. And, in both cases, Justice Field had written the circuit court opinion holding that corporations were protected by the Fourteenth Amendment. In fact, the *only* significant difference between the *San Mateo* case and the *Santa Clara* case was the absence of Conkling and of any discussion of his journal.

In Field's ruling for the circuit court in *Santa Clara*, he made clear that corporations should have Fourteenth Amendment rights of equal protection and due process in order to protect the property rights of the stockholders. He explained that "whenever a provision of the constitution or of a law guaranties to persons protection in their property, . . . the benefits of the provision or law are extended to corporations." Treating the property of corporations differently was unconstitutional, in Field's view, not because the drafters intended that result but because such disparate treatment was "the very essence of tyranny." "Strangely, indeed, would the law sound in case it read that in the assessment and taxation of property a deduction should be made for mortgages thereon if the property be owned by white men or by old men, and not deducted if owned by black men or young men; deducted if owned by landsmen, not deducted if owned by sailors." Field was saying that just as a person's racial identity was an inappropriate basis for singling someone out, so too was the Southern Pacific's corporate identity.[47]

For Field, any other interpretation of the Fourteenth Amendment would empower the enemies of capitalism and threaten the nation's economic well-being. "Indeed, the aggregate wealth of all the trading, commercial, manufacturing, mining, shipping, transportation, and other companies engaged in business," he warned in his circuit court opinion, "amounts to billions upon billions of dollars; and yet all this vast property which keeps our industries flourishing, and furnishes employment, comforts, and luxuries to all classes, and thus promotes civilization and progress, is lifted, according to the argument of counsel, out of the protection of the constitutional guaranties, by reason of the incorporation of the companies." Such a result would be absurd. "How petty and narrow would provisions thus limited appear in the fundamental law of a great people!"

Field supported broad constitutional protections for corporations, but he did not embrace corporate personhood—at least in anything more than a superficial way. While his circuit court opinion insisted that a corporation does count as a "person" under the equal protection and due process guarantees of the Fourteenth Amendment, Field's logic and reasoning were based on piercing the corporate veil and allowing the corporation to claim the rights of other people, namely, its members. As legal historians Morton Horwitz and Greg Mark have recognized, Field treated the corporation like an association of people. The corporation's "members do not, because of such association, lose their rights to protection," wrote Field. The court should look not to "the name under which different persons are united, but to the individuals composing the union." While Field did say that corporations were people, he did not treat corporations as independent legal actors, with rights separate and distinct from the rights of members. Like Horace Binney, John Marshall, and Daniel Webster, Field treated the corporation as an association of people, not as a person itself.[48]

Field had not always conceptualized the corporation as an association whose interests were reducible to those of stockholders. Years earlier, in 1869, he had authored an opinion for the Supreme Court that did rest on corporate personhood. *Paul v. Virginia* was a rehash of *Bank of Augusta v. Earle*, the Taney court decision holding that corporations were not protected by the comity clause of the Constitution. And just like the Taney court, the court in *Paul* affirmed that states could impose special rules on out-of-state corporations. Field's opinion explicitly rejected the corporation's argument that the justices should "look beyond the act of incorporation and see who were its members for the purpose of affording them" the protections of the comity clause. Field reaffirmed the Taney court's reasoning that when "a corporation makes a contract it is the contract of the legal entity, the artificial being created by the charter, and not the contract of the individual members."[49]

Nearly two decades later, however, Field reasoned from very different premises in the Southern Pacific cases, where he looked to the rights of the corporation's members. Perhaps he only used the reasoning of corporate personhood in *Paul* because he was repeating the arguments found in the Taney court precedent. Or perhaps it was that Field's views about corporate rights changed over the course of the 1870s, when he became increasingly hostile to government regulation of the economy. According to Field's biographer, Carl B. Swisher, the justice had generally been open-minded about state regulation of private property prior to 1870. The violence brought on by the Paris Commune of 1871, however, highlighted the dramatic rise of communist and radical agitation in Europe and deeply affected Field. Indeed, in 1876 Field himself wrote an opinion that scaled back the rule of *Bank of Augusta v. Earle* and *Paul v. Virginia* by allowing companies to challenge state foreign corporation fees under the commerce clause. (It is a sign of how determined corporations were to invalidate these state laws that they repeatedly challenged them, first under the comity clause, then the Fourteenth Amendment, and then under the commerce clause.) Whatever the cause of Field's transformation, one thing is clear: by the time the justices heard arguments in the *Santa Clara* case in 1886, Field was restless to establish new protections for corporations under the Fourteenth Amendment.[50]

Chief Justice Morrison Waite, who had a long-running feud with Field, did not share the commitment to corporate rights. Although Waite was the chief justice, he was not a natural leader. When Waite was nominated to the post by President Grant in 1874—after Ros-

CHIEF JUSTICE MORRISON WAITE DISAGREED WITH
JUSTICE STEPHEN FIELD ON ISSUES RELATING TO
BUSINESS AND ETHICS.

coe Conkling declined the position—he had little support from the
other justices. Lacking any judicial experience and never even having
argued a case at the high court, Waite seemed like the underwhelm-
ing type so often appointed by Grant, who was said to have "a peculiar
talent for elevating incompetent or corrupt individuals to important
federal posts." Of Waite, Justice Miller opined that one "can't make a
great chief justice out of a small man." With a strong work ethic and
even temperament, however, Waite overcame the resistance of Miller,
who eventually would praise Waite's leadership. Field, however, was
never swayed.[51]

Certainly part of the acrimony between Field and Waite stemmed
from their conflicting views on the economy and business. Although
Waite had been a railroad lawyer prior to joining the court, his rulings

in business cases often favored state regulators. In *Munn v. Illinois*, for example, a landmark decision of 1877 allowing states broad leeway to regulate private property when it is "affected with a public interest," Waite wrote the majority opinion over Field's vigorous dissent. "The legislation in question," a state law setting rates for grain warehouses, "is nothing less than a bold assertion of absolute power by the State to control at its discretion the property and business of the citizen, and fix the compensation he shall receive," Field warned, and violated "the fundamental maxims of a free government."[52]

Another difference between the two men was that Waite, unlike Field, had an abiding commitment to judicial integrity. When Field and Waite were asked to serve on the commission to settle the bitterly contested Tilden-Hayes presidential election of 1876, Field readily agreed but Waite refused, fearing his participation might embroil the court in partisan politics. Waite also chafed at Field's informal, ethically questionable association with Stanford and the Southern Pacific. Perhaps that was one reason that when the Supreme Court hearing in the *Santa Clara* case began, Waite informed the lawyers that the justices did not want to hear arguments on corporate rights, the issue Field had devoted so much attention to in his circuit court opinion. Waite thought the case could be decided on narrower grounds, without addressing the rights of corporations.[53]

When the ruling in the *Santa Clara* case was issued three months later in 1886, it was decided on narrower grounds. The court sided with the Southern Pacific, although without saying anything about corporate rights. The tax assessments imposed on the Southern Pacific were invalid, the court explained, because the county had factored into the railroad's tax bills the value of fences running alongside the tracks, which was not allowed by California law. In essence, the court said the tax assessments were improperly calculated. Because the case could be decided "upon this ground," the court's opinion explained, "it is not necessary to consider any other questions," including the "grave questions of constitutional law upon which the case was determined below."[54]

In a companion case handed down the same day, an unhappy

Field filed a concurring opinion voicing his displeasure with the court for avoiding the question of corporate rights under the Fourteenth Amendment. "At the present day, nearly all great enterprises are conducted by corporations," he noted. "Hardly an industry can be named that is not in some way promoted by them, and a vast portion of the wealth of the country is in their hands." America's corporations deserved to know if they enjoyed the rights guaranteed by "the great constitutional amendment which insures to every person, whatever his position or association, the equal protection of the laws." "But I regret that it has not been deemed consistent with [the court's] duty to decide the important constitutional questions involved, and particularly the one which was so fully considered in the circuit court," he complained.[55]

Once again, Field was foiled. Yet he was not about to concede in his quest to expand the rights of business corporations, and he soon found an unlikely ally in the Supreme Court reporter, J. C. Bancroft Davis.

* * *

NOT TO BE CONFUSED with a journalist, the Supreme Court's Reporter of Decisions is the government officer responsible for publishing the official opinions of the justices. Today one expects the reporter to be a functionary who dutifully proofreads, typesets, and distributes the justices' handiwork. In 1883, however, when J. C. Bancroft Davis became the reporter, it was a prestigious and profitable post that attracted men of public stature. The reporter prior to Davis, William Tod Otto, was assistant secretary of the interior and a close confidant of Lincoln who was present at the president's deathbed. Two reporters before him was Jeremiah Sullivan Black, who had served as secretary of state and attorney general of the United States.[56]

Davis came from an influential Massachusetts family. His father, John Davis, was a US senator and former governor of the state. The son was related by marriage to Rufus King, a Massachusetts delegate at the Philadelphia Convention and signer of the Constitution. Educated at Harvard, J. C. Bancroft Davis had been the US ambassador to Germany and an assistant secretary of state twice. He resigned his position as a federal judge on the United States Court of Claims to become the Supreme Court reporter. Money was a major draw. Still in the era of the spoils system, the reporter was given the exclusive right to sell the *United States Reports*, the official bound versions of the court's opinions.[57]

When Davis took the post, demand for the volumes was soaring. A movement to create publicly accessible libraries had been sweeping the nation, especially in urban areas swelling with an increasingly literate middle class. Between 1850 and 1875, over two thousand new libraries were founded. Scores of them were dedicated specifically to the law, especially in the newly emergent law schools that were replacing the old sytem of legal training through apprenticeships. As the reporter, Davis's income would likely exceed the salaries of the justices.[58]

The problem with staffing the reporter's post with accomplished men like Davis was that they often had grandiose egos to match their bloated resumes. Davis himself was known to be patronizing to the justices and, according to one historian, "never established a good working relationship with the members of the court." Davis often refused justices' requests to make corrections to published opinions, believing his own understanding of what they meant was better than theirs. Davis's views, moreover, were idiosyncratic. In one volume of the *United States Reports*, he included an appendix purporting to list every Supreme Court decision invalidating a state or federal law for violating the Constitution. But strangely, he omitted *Dred Scott*—undoubtedly the most momentous of such decisions in the history of the Supreme Court to date—while including other cases that were not decided on constitutional grounds at all.[59]

By tradition, the reporter includes a summary or "syllabus" of each decision along with concise headnotes describing the court's reasoning in a given case. The syllabus and headnotes, which are written by the reporter, appear in the published volume at the front of the relevant case. Although they are not official statements of the court, they serve the bar by making legal research easier. A lawyer can look over the syllabus and headnotes and quickly understand what the court decided before delving into the opinion itself. A headnote for *Brown v. Board of Education*, for example, tells us, "Segregation of children in public schools solely on the basis of race deprives children of the minority group of equal educational opportunities, even though the physical and other 'tangible' factors may be equal."

Over the course of his tenure, Davis's syllabi and headnotes became an unending source of tension between him and the justices. In one case, Justice John M. Harlan, the "Great Dissenter" who refused to join the court's opinion endorsing racial segregation in *Plessy v. Ferguson*, complained to the chief justice, "I have read the head-notes in the Bank case. They are awful and are enough to make you . . . sick. There is time to correct them." When a lawyer in one case relied on one of Davis's headnotes to support an argument, Justice David Brewer, who was also Stephen Field's nephew, rebuked, "The headnotes to the opinions of this Court are not the work of the Court, but are simply the work of the Reporter, giving his understanding of the decision, prepared for the convenience of the profession." In this particular instance, wrote Brewer, Davis's headnote was "a misinterpretation of the scope of the decision." Eventually the justices would actively lobby for Davis to be replaced.[60]

Davis, however, was still relatively new in his job and had not yet earned the complete enmity of the justices in 1886, when *Santa Clara* was decided. Yet his syllabi and headnotes in *United States Reports* for the *Santa Clara* case reflect his penchant for error, if not outright deception. According to Davis's headnotes, the holding of the case was: "The defendant Corporations are persons within the intent of the clause in section 1 of the Fourteenth Amendment to the Constitution of the United States, which forbids a state to deny to any person within its jurisdiction the equal protection of the laws." Then, just before the first lines of the court's opinion itself, Davis added:

One of the points made and discussed at length in the brief of counsel for defendants in error was that "corporations are persons within the meaning of the Fourteenth Amendment to the Constitution of the United States." Before argument, Mr.

CHIEF JUSTICE WAITE said: "The Court does not wish to hear argument on the question whether the provision in the Fourteenth Amendment to the Constitution which forbids a state to deny to any person within its jurisdiction the equal protection of the laws applies to these corporations. We are all of the opinion that it does."

Anyone who read the syllabus and headnotes without carefully reading the opinion itself would mistakenly conclude that the court in *Santa Clara* decided that corporations were people entitled to the protections of the Fourteenth Amendment. The court, of course, had not ruled on that question at all, prompting Field's angry rebuke. Although the chief justice had instructed the lawyers not to focus on corporate rights, his purpose was likely to focus their attention on the other issues in the case, not to suggest that all the justices were persuaded that corporations had Fourteenth Amendment rights. One of the justices then serving on the court was William Burnham Woods, who earlier had written the *Continental Insurance* decision specifically rejecting that view. It would also be a surprise if all the other justices, several of whom had ruled against commercial interests repeatedly over the previous terms, simply reversed course to favor broad new Fourteenth Amendment rights for corporations.

"Nowhere in the United States Reports are there to be found words more momentous or more baffling than these," wrote Howard Jay Graham, the Fourteenth Amendment expert. While Davis never explained why he added such misleading language to the published version of the opinion, speculation since has focused on whether Davis might have had some personal interest in expanding the rights of corporations like the Southern Pacific. Davis, it turns out, had once served as president of the Newburgh and New York Railway Company.[61]

While Davis was prone to error, his inaccurate syllabus and headnote in *Santa Clara County v. Southern Pacific Railroad* were not thoughtless mistakes. Before the decision was published, Davis sent to Waite a note indicating that he would include what he recalled to be the chief justice's statement to the lawyers at the beginning of oral argument. Waite replied, "I leave it with you to determine whether anything need be said about it in the report inasmuch as we avoided the constitutional question in the decision." Davis, in other words, had been explicitly reminded by the chief justice that the Supreme Court in the Southern Pacific's case had not decided the corporate rights question. Yet there it was in the official *United States Reports*: in *Santa Clara County v. Southern Pacific Railroad*, the Supreme Court had ruled that corporations were entitled to the protections of the Fourteenth Amendment.[62]

* * *

STEPHEN FIELD QUICKLY SAW the opportunity presented by J. C. Bancroft Davis's misleading syllabus and headnote. Even if they did not faithfully describe the Supreme Court's decision, they could be used to advance the cause of corporate rights.

The headstrong justice had previously shown his willingness to deviate from controlling Supreme Court precedent when he disagreed with it. In the 1870s, Field was responsible for what came to be known as the special "Ninth Circuit Law" that departed from the Supreme Court's decision in the *Slaughter-House Cases*. The Ninth Circuit was the western region of federal courts, including those in California, over which Field presided when riding circuit. In a series of opinions for the Ninth Circuit, Field struck down several California laws that restricted the ability of Chinese immigrants to work. He was not motivated by concerns for racial justice; Field's personal letters reveal a deep-seated racism, and as a justice he would author the notorious *Chinese Exclusion Case* of 1889, which employed racist assumptions to uphold a ban on immigration from China. In the Ninth Circuit cases, Field ruled in favor of the Chinese laborers not because they were *Chinese* but because they were *laborers*. Like the butchers in the *Slaughter-House Cases*, the laborers had economic rights under the Constitution and were entitled to pursue their calling. Due to a technicality in federal law at the time, however, the Chinese laborer cases were not appealable to the Supreme Court. As a result, Field's rulings striking down California's labor laws for violating economic rights under the Fourteenth

Amendment were final. For the western region of the United States, Field's opinions became their own, unique "constitutional law of the Ninth Circuit" in which Field's dissent in the *Slaughter-House Cases*, rather than the court's majority opinion, controlled.[63]

Field's rulings in the Chinese laborer cases also became incubators of what would develop into one of the most significant pro-business constitutional doctrines of the early twentieth century, the liberty of contract. Although this right sounds a bit like the contractual protections at issue in Daniel Webster's *Dartmouth College* case, it was different. While Webster had argued that the state could not revise previously formed contractual arrangements, Field's "liberty of contract" protected an individual's right to practice the trade or profession of one's choice without undue state interference. That is what Field had advocated for in his *Slaughter-House Cases* dissent. Beginning in 1897, the Supreme Court would embrace Field's understanding of economic liberty and read this unenumerated principle of laissez-faire into the due process clause of the Fourteenth Amendment. A 1905 decision striking down a New York law that prohibited employees of bakeries from working more than sixty hours a week, *Lochner v. New York*, would give the jurisprudential period its name. Although Field had retired from the Supreme Court by the time of the *Lochner* era, the justice would nonetheless be credited as the intellectual "pioneer and prophet" of the court's jurisprudence. His thirty-year battle to expand economic rights had proven victorious, and the Supreme Court in the *Lochner* era would become known for striking down dozens of laws regulating business activities.[64]

In Field's view, corporate rights were a necessary component of economic liberty—and, by March of 1888, the ranks of Field's opponents on the court were thinning. Justice Woods, who wrote the lower court opinion rejecting corporate rights in the *Continental Insurance* case, had passed away the year before. Field's nemesis, Chief Justice Waite, was on his deathbed from pneumonia. Field took advantage of the lack of oversight to insert into a Supreme Court majority opinion an affirmation that corporations had Fourteenth Amendment rights.

The case, *Pembina Consolidated Silver Mining Company v. Pennsylvania*, involved another of the seemingly endless lawsuits by out-of-state companies seeking to escape foreign corporation fees and other requirements. Field was assigned to write the court's opinion upholding the fees. Although Field believed small foreign corporation fees were no real barrier to interstate businesses and were constitutionally permissible, he slipped into his majority opinion broad, affirmative assertions—wholly irrelevant to the case—about the constitutional rights of corporations. "Under the designation of 'person' there is no doubt that a private corporation is included," he wrote. "Such corporations are merely associations of individuals united for a special purpose and permitted to do business under a particular name and have succession of members without dissolution." Denying corporations constitutional rights would enable the government to infringe on the rights of members.[65]

Four days after the court issued its opinion in *Pembina Consolidated Mining Company*, Waite passed away. He was replaced by Melville Fuller, who would quickly prove an ally of Field in the struggle to define the Fourteenth Amendment. In appearance, Fuller was the spitting image of Mark Twain; the humorist was once mistakenly asked for his autograph by a fan of the new chief justice, leading Twain to write, "It is delicious to be full, but it is heavenly to be Fuller." Both Twain and Fuller had unusual relationships to the corporation. Late in life, Twain decided to become one. Anxious to keep the earnings from his writings in his own family, he formed the Mark Twain Company of New York, with the stock to go to his two daughters upon his death. He was one of the first celebrities to form a corporation to keep control over their artistic output, and the practice would eventually become commonplace. Fuller, for his part, became a consistent vote on the high court for expansive constitutional protections for corporations. It was under Fuller's leadership that the court finally adopted Field's "liberty of contract" and pursued the largely pro-business agenda of the *Lochner* era.[66]

In 1889, with Fuller as chief justice, the court decided another Fourteenth Amendment case involving a corporation, *Minneapolis &*

St. Louis Railway Company v. Beckwith, and Field seized the chance to promote corporate rights once again. A railroad corporation objected to an Iowa law that made railroads doubly liable for any damage caused to livestock. The law was designed to encourage railroads to fence in their tracks and to protect neighboring ranchers. When one of the railroad's trains killed three hogs, the company was ordered to pay $24 in damages. Instead of paying the miniscule fine, the railroad spent tens of thousands of dollars litigating the case up to the Supreme Court. The money would be worth it if the corporation could gain stronger legal protections from future laws of this sort.

Field, in his opinion for the court, upheld the law—yet managed at the same time to transform J. C. Bancroft Davis's misleading head-note into binding Supreme Court precedent. To Field, Iowa's law was a justifiable regulation. Although it imposed a burden on the railroad, it served the interests of another group of businessmen: ranchers, who raised pigs, cattle, and other livestock for market. And although the railroad in this case would be disappointed with the immediate results, Field embedded in his majority opinion language that would go far to serve the interests of railroads and other corporations for generations to come. "It is contended by counsel as the basis of his argument, and we admit the soundness of his position, that corporations are persons within the meaning of the clause in question," Field wrote. Then the fearless justice stated, "It was so held in *Santa Clara County v. Southern Pacific Railroad*."[67]

Of course, that statement was patently false—but it could not have been inadvertent. Field, who three years earlier had written an opinion in the companion case to *Santa Clara* excoriating the other justices for failing to address the constitutional rights of corporations, surely had not forgotten. Field, like Roscoe Conkling, was willing to resort to deception when it came to the cause of corporate rights, and was able to get away with this sleight of hand in part because of the publication process of Supreme Court opinions back then. Today, all the justices see drafts of the opinions before they are released, but in the 1880s the justices typically did not. The justice authoring an opinion was given the latitude to write up the opinion as he felt best captured the justices' decision, and the other justices often did not view the opinion until after it was published. Field was thus able to secure Fourteenth Amendment protections for corporations, possibly without any of the other justices knowing about it beforehand.[68]

Even though the other justices may not have known in advance about Field's expansion of corporate rights in *Minneapolis & St. Louis Railway Company v. Beckwith*, Field nonetheless captured the tenor of a court that was entering the *Lochner* era. More surprising, however, is that the justices would follow Field's lead and rely on *Santa Clara* as a binding precedent. Over the next two decades, *Santa Clara* would take on sweeping importance as the justices repeatedly cited and relied on that case for authoritatively deciding that corporations were entitled to the Fourteenth Amendment's guarantees of equal protection and due process—legal principles never endorsed by the decision itself.[69]

By 1890, just as the nation was entering the era of the trusts, in which corporations would gain more political and economic power over the lives of ordinary Americans than ever before, corporations had secured new constitutional tools to use in their fight against unwanted regulation. Corporate rights under the Fourteenth Amendment were no longer just a headnote.

* * *

THE TRANSFORMATION OF THE Fourteenth Amendment from a guarantee of equal rights for racial minorities into a tool for corporations to strike down business regulation was the subject of one of the first quantitative studies of the Supreme Court, conducted in 1912. Charles Wallace Collins, a lawyer who also served for a time as the law librarian for Congress and the Supreme Court, collected and analyzed every Fourteenth Amendment case decided by the justices in the nearly half-century since the provision's unorthodox ratification. The court, he found, had heard 604 Fourteenth Amendment cases between 1868 and 1912. A mere twenty-eight of those cases (less than 5 percent) involved African Americans, the group whose plight motivated the adoption of the amendment, and in nearly all of those cases the racial minorities lost. More than half of all the Fourteenth Amendment cases decided by the Supreme Court—312 in total—involved corporations, which succeeded in striking down numerous laws regulating business, including minimum wage laws, zoning laws, and child labor laws.[70]

Those results would likely have pleased Justice Field, even if Collins bemoaned them. Collins hailed from Alabama and later in life became the "most influential intellectual and strategist" of the Dixiecrat Revolt of 1948, when southern white Democrats bolted to form their own, pro-segregation party. (Collins's 1947 book, *Whither the Solid South? A Study in Politics and Race Relations,* which presciently argued for a political realignment joining white southerners and economic conservatives to create a new, powerful, right-wing voting bloc, was heralded as "both a manifesto and blueprint for the states' rights" movement.) Yet Collins, following in the footsteps of Roger Taney, was a populist critic of corporate power who believed in states' rights—among them, the states' right to regulate business. Echoing the economist Arthur Twining Hadley, who asked "whether a single one of the members of Congress who voted for [the Fourteenth Amendment] had any conception that it would touch the question of corporate regulation at all," Collins, a loyal southerner, suggested the best thing to do was simply repeal the Fourteenth Amendment in its entirety.[71]

The Southern Pacific and the powerful corporations that would arise at the end of the nineteenth century, by contrast, would find much to celebrate in the new and, in their view, improved version of the Fourteenth Amendment. To be sure, corporations lost plenty of cases too—a fact often ignored in histories of the *Lochner* era. The guarantees of the Fourteenth Amendment did not prevent the court from upholding what the justices saw as minimal or necessary restrictions on business activity. Although corporations brought the overwhelming majority of Fourteenth Amendment cases to the Supreme Court in the years covered by Collins's study, they lost many of them.

Even when the court ruled against corporations, however, the companies could often count their lawsuits as small victories. Their never-ending string of Fourteenth Amendment lawsuits delayed for years the implementation of countless laws that, like California's railroad tax, threatened to reduce their profits. Corporate lawsuits also imposed huge costs on government. California's counties spent untold hours and money fighting off the Southern Pacific's groundbreaking series of test cases, which dragged on for years. Perhaps the most revealing thing about Collins's study was that, regardless of the losses, corporations kept litigating case after case after case.[72]

Meanwhile, African Americans found little protection in the courts. The years just before and immediately after *Santa Clara* was decided saw a striking rise in racially discriminatory laws. In the South, slavery was replaced with a system of racial segregation and white supremacy, in which blacks were told where they could live, whom they could marry, which jobs they could have, and which schools they could attend. Despite the Fourteenth Amendment and its companions, the Thirteenth (outlawing slavery and involuntary servitude), and the Fifteenth (outlawing denials of the right to vote on the basis of race), blacks found themselves disenfranchised by literacy tests and poll taxes. These laws—named after "Jump Jim Crow," a popular song and dance routine performed by T. D. Rice, a white comedian in blackface—were upheld in nearly every case.

The most notorious of the Supreme Court's cases upholding Jim Crow laws was *Plessy v. Ferguson*, decided in 1896, which established that "separate but equal" government facilities were not prohibited by the Fourteenth Amendment. Justice Field joined the majority's decision, and it would be one of his final votes as a Supreme Court justice. He retired the next year, battling senility but having served for longer than any previous justice in American history. Certainly no other justice left as big a mark on the emerging jurisprudence of the Fourteenth Amendment. He led the charge for judicial recognition of unwritten rights of economic liberty under the due process clause, which would come to define the Supreme Court's jurisprudence for half a century. Even after the court abandoned Field's liberty of contract, the justices would continue his practice of reading unenumerated rights into the Fourteenth Amendment's due process clause, including rights of privacy, abortion, and marriage. Field also spearheaded the recognition of corporate rights to equal protection and due process, although for him corporate personhood was merely a textual hook. Corporations were not really people in the sense of having rights of their own. They had rights merely as a way of protecting the property of the stockholders.

In upholding Louisiana's "Separate Car Act," the court in *Plessy* explained that the issue in the case "reduces itself to the question whether the statute of Louisiana is a reasonable regulation, and, with respect to this, there must necessarily be a large discretion on the part of the legislature." The triumph of corporate rights under the Fourteenth Amendment meant that legislatures had considerably less discretion in regulating business. Stephen Field, Roscoe Conkling, J. C. Bancroft Davis, and the Southern Pacific Railroad had overhauled the Fourteenth Amendment to make it what Charles Wallace Collins called "the Magna Charta of accumulated and organized capital."[73]

CHAPTER 5

—

The Corporate Criminal

ONE MORNING IN MAY OF 1905, EDWIN F. HALE, A MID-level executive at a company that imported licorice, arrived at the federal courthouse in lower Manhattan to testify before a grand jury. The youthful Kentuckian, who had only recently moved to New York in search of career opportunities, was accompanied by his attorney, DeLancey Nicoll. Called one of "the great lawyers of the city," Nicoll was ranked by contemporaries alongside Clarence Darrow, the legendary defender of unpopular causes, as masters of the courtroom. Nicoll came from one of the oldest families in New York—Sir Richard Nicoll had arrived in the New World in 1664—and the esteemed lawyer counted among his clients railroad magnate Cornelius Vanderbilt and financier Thomas Ryan. He was, in other words, not the type of lawyer one would expect to represent a plebeian fellow like Edwin Hale. In fact, Nicoll was only at Hale's side as a service to another, far more important client: the American Tobacco Company, the ringleader of the powerful Tobacco Trust.[1]

Hale, the secretary and treasurer of MacAndrews & Forbes Licorice Company, walked into the grand-jury room with trepidation. He knew why he had been called to testify. The subpoena he received required him to bring any and all correspondence, contracts, and other documents relating to the business dealings of his company and nearly a dozen other companies, all of which were involved in some way with the Tobacco Trust. The administration of President Theodore Roosevelt had recently launched a wide-ranging and high-profile investigation into potential violations of the Sherman Antitrust Act by the tobacco companies.[2]

Nicoll had given Hale a plan for making sure he did not reveal any secrets about his employer's anticompetitive dealings. Nonetheless, this was a federal investigation conducted by the Department of Justice. The inquiry would surely be exhaustive, proverbially turning every stone. As a result, Hale had cause to be nervous. The investigation might well uncover Hale's own personal crimes. And to make matters worse, he walked into the grand-jury room alone, without Nicoll to protect him. No lawyers but the prosecutors are allowed in the grand-jury room. Even though Nicoll was left out in the hallway, the illustrious lawyer had every intention of controlling what happened inside.

Waiting inside for Hale was Henry Waters Taft, the special prosecutor who was heading the Department of Justice's investigation into

TOBACCO TRUST LAWYER DELANCEY NICOLL ARGUED THAT CORPORATIONS HAD THE FOURTH AMENDMENT RIGHT AGAINST UNREASONABLE SEARCHES AND THE FIFTH AMENDMENT RIGHT AGAINST SELF-INCRIMINATION.

the American Tobacco Company and the Tobacco Trust. Taft was the younger brother of William Howard Taft, who was then secretary of state and would go on to serve as president of the United States and chief justice of the Supreme Court. Like his older brother and Nicoll, Henry Taft was well respected in legal circles. He was a partner in the Cadwalader law firm of New York, which was founded in 1792 and remains an elite firm more than two centuries later. Taft, an antitrust specialist who typically defended businesses fighting against regulation, took a leave of absence from the firm to serve as a special prosecutor for the Roosevelt administration with the specific purpose of bringing down the Tobacco Trust.[3]

No development impacted the economy of the United States at the turn of the twentieth century more than the rise of the trusts. The trusts were big business on steroids, monopolistic entities that controlled all of the major firms within an industry in order to reduce competition and dictate prices, output, and profits. These were not the same type of monopolies earlier opposed by Roger Taney and Andrew Jackson, who criticized exclusive privileges granted by the state legislatures. These modern monopolies were national enterprises that controlled whole industries, often winning that influence through market manipulation rather than legislative grace. Yet the trusts had still been made possible by lawmakers, who at the end of the nineteenth century adopted extensive reforms of corporate law that enabled the formation of the trusts. Corporations rushed to take advantage of the law's new permissiveness to form huge companies through reorganizations and acquisitions in what historians have called the "Great Merger Movement."[4]

Breaking up the trusts was a priority for Roosevelt, who assumed the presidency in 1901 after the assassination of the decidedly pro-business Republican William McKinley. Attuned to the prevailing political winds, Roosevelt recast himself as a populist corporate reformer in the mold of Jefferson and Jackson. In his first State of the Union speech, Roosevelt recognized the "widespread conviction" that "the great corporations known as trusts are in certain of their features and tendencies hurtful to the general welfare." He said that "artificial bodies, such as corporations" ought to be "subject to proper governmental supervision." Yet unlike Jefferson and Jackson, Roosevelt was not burdened by the baggage of states' rights and slavery. In fact, Roosevelt believed the way to curtail excessive corporate growth and power was to expand the power of the *federal* government. National corporations of such size and power as the trusts needed national regulation. To that end, Roosevelt called for a host of new federal regulations on business: maximum-hour laws, workplace safety laws, railroad laws—and, for the first time, vigorous enforcement of the federal antitrust law.[5]

Many of these laws, including the antitrust law with which Henry Taft was concerned, included an important legal innovation: they held corporations criminally liable for wrongdoing. Writing a century and a half earlier, Blackstone in his *Commentaries* had recognized the long-standing notion that "a corporation cannot commit treason, or felony, or other crime, in its corporate capacity." The corporation itself was deemed to have no authority to break the law, so any criminal act by the company was attributed to the officers of the company personally. The Progressive era push to regulate the trusts led not only to a wave of new federal laws but also to the imposition for the first time of widespread criminal liability on corporations. That, in turn, led to new questions about the scope of corporate rights under the Constitution.[6]

It is easy to forget how much of the Bill of Rights was designed to protect criminals and people suspected of crime. While Americans today might first associate the Constitution with rights of personal conscience, such as freedom of speech and religious liberty, the Founding Fathers were largely focused on the investigation, prosecution, and punishment of criminals. The Fourth Amendment protects against unreasonable searches and seizures in investigations. The Fifth Amendment provides that a person cannot be compelled to incriminate himself. The Sixth Amendment promises a "speedy and public" trial, the right to confront witnesses, and the right to counsel for accused criminals, while the Eighth Amendment outlaws cruel and unusual punishment for those convicted. The new wave of turn-of-the-century regulation that imposed criminal penalties on corporations would force the Supreme Court to decide whether corporations, like individuals, enjoyed those same constitutional protections.

The issue would be first brought to the Supreme Court as a result of the battle between DeLancey Nicoll and Henry Taft over Edwin Hale's testimony in the grand-jury room that May morning. Their fight, of course, was just a skirmish in a larger struggle between the populist Roosevelt and the huge corporations, like American Tobacco, that dominated the economy. The Supreme Court at the time was in the early years of the *Lochner* era, yet its decisions on corporate criminal rights were not nearly as expansive as one might expect given the court's notoriously pro-business reputation. The justices would say that, when it comes to the Constitution's protection of the rights of criminals, corporations were fundamentally different from individuals. Although corporations had some criminal rights protections, they were not the exact same as those enjoyed by individuals. The *Lochner* court drew a new boundary on the scope of corporate rights, ruling that corporations were entitled to rights of *property* but not rights of *liberty*.

* * *

AFTER THE DOOR TO the grand-jury room closed to shut DeLancey Nicoll outside, Edwin Hale was ushered into a seat before the gathered panel of jurors and Henry Taft administered the oath. Hale's swearing of the oath was, on the one hand, banal and routine; witnesses have sworn "to tell the truth, the whole truth, and nothing but the truth" countless times since that language was first adopted by the courts of fourteenth-century England. Nonetheless, the oath in this instance was notable for two reasons. The first was that Hale had absolutely no intention of living up to that promise. The whole truth might include admitting to illegal gambling, embezzling funds, and conspiring to steal from his employer. No, he could not tell the whole truth—nor would he have to if he stuck to Nicoll's plan.[7]

The second reason the oath was significant on this day was that it was a corporation taking it. Hale was not appearing in his personal

SPECIAL ANTITRUST PROSECUTOR HENRY TAFT ARGUED
AGAINST EXTENDING TO CORPORATIONS THE CONSTITUTION'S
RIGHTS FOR CRIMINAL SUSPECTS.

capacity but as an officer of MacAndrews & Forbes, the licorice company. By subpoenaing Hale, Taft was seeking to make the corporation, MacAndrews & Forbes, reveal the secrets about its business dealings. Because a corporation cannot take the stand and can only testify through an officer, as Blackstone had noted, when Hale appeared before Taft's grand jury he was there to testify in his capacity as an officer of the corporation.

Taft began his inquisition with a series of standard questions. He asked Hale to state his name, his hometown, and his current place of residence. To the last question, Hale responded vaguely, "New York City," omitting any mention of the Hotel Earlington on West 27th Street, where he lived in a bachelor apartment next door to Harry Smock, another employee of MacAndrews & Forbes; in addition to an address and an employer, the two men also shared a love of gambling and, when that did not work out, a willingness to steal.[8]

"What is your business?" asked Taft.

"I am secretary and treasurer of MacAndrews & Forbes Company," replied Hale. Although Hale did not elaborate, MacAndrews & Forbes was the nation's leading importer of licorice root. Business for the corporation was booming. Almost since the dawn of human history, licorice has been revered for its medicinal properties—prescribed for ailments ranging from athlete's foot to emphysema—as well as for its more spiritual benefits. The malodorous plant was, for example, placed in Tutankhamen's tomb to shepherd the child pharaoh's soul safely to the afterlife. MacAndrews & Forbes favored instead licorice's commercial qualities. The commodity had become especially valuable once tobacco companies like James Duke's American Tobacco developed an insatiable demand for it. The company bathed tobacco leaves in licorice to sweeten and mellow their flavor.⁹

If James "Buck" Duke was not the father of the American tobacco industry—an honor appropriately reserved for John Rolfe, the Virginia Company colonist who first developed tobacco into a marketable crop in 1614—he was at least the savvy son-in-law who doubled the family fortune. The modern era of American tobacco, in which large, profitable tobacco corporations marketed mass-produced, branded products on a national scale, began with Duke. In 1884, his North Carolina tobacco company was the first to adopt automated rolling machines, which dramatically increased production, lowered costs, and expanded the consumer market for cigarettes. His company was also the first in the industry to spend lavishly on advertising, promoting his brands in the new magazines, newspapers, and weeklies that coincided with the late nineteenth century's growing literacy rates. Duke, like many of the most successful executives before and since, understood the value of innovation.¹⁰

It was Duke's leveraging of one innovation in particular that led more or less directly to Edwin Hale's appearance before the grand jury: the trust. The first trust was John D. Rockefeller's Standard Oil Company, formed in 1879. The idea was the brainchild of a lawyer named Samuel Dodd. Rockefeller had wanted to expand his regional, Ohio-based company by buying up other oil companies, but Ohio corporate law prohibited one corporation from owning stock in another corporation. Rockefeller hired Dodd to find a way around that bar. Dodd, much like his fellow Pennsylvanian Horace Binney, who devised the novel argument about piercing the corporate veil to win the first corporate rights case, was nothing if not creative. He came up with an ingenious plan based on an ancient practice dating from the Middle Ages.[11]

During the Crusades, English knights would be abroad for years at a time fighting for Christendom. Men of property, knights needed someone to take care of their affairs during their long absences. Because their wives had an inferior legal status, knights could not leave the decision-making to them. Instead, a knight would select a kinsman to manage his property and see to his family. Yet the rules were strict: the kinsman was not allowed to use the knight's money or assets for his own personal gain. He was obligated to manage the property in the interests of the absent knight. This medieval practice evolved into a legally authorized device, the trust, which today still allows one person to hold and manage property exclusively for the benefit of another.[12]

Dodd realized that, like the knights of old, the major stockholders of the different oil companies could tender their property (i.e., their stock) to a modern group of "kinsmen" (the trustees), who would manage the assets on the stockholders' behalf. The stockholders became beneficiaries of the trust, entitled to a share of the trust's income and the right to vote for trustees. And the trustees would control multiple companies. Because the trust was not incorporated, it was not technically a corporation—and, as a result, would not be governed by Ohio's restrictive corporate law rules. Implementing Dodd's plan, Rockefeller soon controlled 80 percent of the country's oil refining and 90 percent of the nation's oil pipelines. Standard Oil became the largest business enterprise in the world.[13]

The justices on the Ohio Supreme Court reacted with alarm to Standard Oil's end-run around the state's corporate law code, ruling in 1892 that the trust was illegal and ordering that it be dissolved. Dodd, a wellspring of corporate law innovations, came up with another: reincorporate Standard Oil in New Jersey, where the rules of corporate law were being overhauled—under the watchful supervision of a lawyer for the cotton oil trust—to loosen the traditional restrictions on corporate management. Beginning in 1888, New Jersey became the first state to allow one corporation to own stock in another, which was precisely what Rockefeller was looking to do. Over the course of the next decade, New Jersey would also allow corporations to freely form for any business purpose whatsoever and eliminate traditional limits on the size of firms. Corporations were not required to base their operations in New Jersey to take advantage of the new corporate laws, so long as they paid the state's mandatory corporation fees. Other states soon followed, and the wave of reform was said to have "turned corporate law inside out"; after hundreds of years, no longer would the body of rules governing the formation and governance of corporations be used in any significant way to regulate corporations.[14]

Dodd shifted all the oil trust's assets to a New Jersey corporation, Standard Oil of New Jersey, keeping the same management structure and same market control. The practice quickly accelerated in the succeeding years, with nearly all of the nation's big corporations and trusts following Standard Oil's blueprint and reincorporating in New Jersey, including Buck Duke's American Tobacco Company. Speaking

STANDARD OIL FORMED AN IMMENSELY SUCCESSFUL TRUST, AND EFFORTS TO BREAK UP THE TRUSTS WOULD LEAD TO THE EXPANSION OF CORPORATE RIGHTS.

to the New York State Bar Association in 1899, just a decade after the new corporate code was enacted, attorney Charles F. Bostwick noted that "so many trusts and big corporations were paying tribute to the State of New Jersey that the authorities had become greatly perplexed as to what should be done with the surplus revenue."[15]

Decades later, long after the trusts had been defeated, some corporate law scholars would argue that New Jersey's reforms were the beginning of a "race to the bottom." States seeking the revenue from incorporation fees continually made corporate law more permissive, which attracted corporate executives freed up by the new rules. Over time, the traditional corporate law doctrines limiting the power of corporate officers were rendered largely meaningless; corporate law became mainly a template that private parties could use to organize their affairs. After New Jersey's windfall, Delaware was one of several states to follow suit. Although populists in New Jersey would eventually strengthen that state's corporate code, Delaware continued to make its laws more permissive. Today, the tiny state named after one of America's forgotten founders is home to less than 1 percent of the American population but more than 60 percent of Fortune 500 companies.[16]

* * *

BACK IN 1905, when Edwin Hale was called by Henry Taft to testify before the grand jury investigating the Tobacco Trust, American consumers bought most of their staples from a handful of trusts: sugar, whiskey, cotton, linseed oil, cookies, crackers, and fruit. In the last decade before electricity became common in urban areas, Americans at night enjoyed these items under the glow of gas lamps fueled by Standard Oil. Buck Duke's American Tobacco Company, meanwhile, was responsible for production of over 75 percent of the smoking tobacco, 90 percent of the snuff, and 80 percent of the chewing tobacco sold in America.[17]

As part of the Tobacco Trust, Duke took over the American licorice industry too. Seeking vertical integration, Duke bought up two-thirds of MacAndrews & Forbes stock, and then took control of all the other major American licorice root importers. He then fixed the price

THE AMERICAN TOBACCO COMPANY WAS BEHIND THE FIRST
SUPREME COURT CASE ON THE RIGHTS OF CORPORATIONS
UNDER THE FOURTH AND FIFTH AMENDMENTS.

of licorice, divvied up customers among the companies, limited production, and refused to sell to customers unwilling to sign long-term
contracts at an inflated cost. The result was that American Tobacco
controlled 95 percent of the licorice trade and used that market power
to raise prices nearly 50 percent.[18]

Did these agreements among American Tobacco, MacAndrews,
and the other licorice companies amount to an unlawful restraint of
trade in violation of the Sherman Antitrust Act? That was the question the special prosecutor Taft was charged with answering. The antitrust law, enacted in 1890, outlawed any "contract, combination . . . or
conspiracy" that restrained trade and prohibited attempts "to monop-
olize any part of the trade or commerce among the several States."
The Sherman Act was inspired by the rise of muckraking journalism
in the late 1800s. The Muckrakers, who borrowed their name from
a seventeenth-century Christian allegory about people who refused
salvation to live instead in filth, were reform-minded journalists who
investigated corporate corruption and other social ills. Among their
favorite targets were the trusts, especially Standard Oil. Henry Demarest Lloyd's exposé of that company, "The Story of a Great Monopoly,"
published in *The Atlantic* in 1881, was one of the earliest and most

influential pieces of muckraking journalism. It revealed how Rocke-feller had come to dominate not only the national petroleum market—making Standard Oil "the meanest monopoly known to history"—but also politics. "The Standard," Lloyd wrote, "has done everything with the Pennsylvania legislature, except refine it."[19]

For the first ten years after it was enacted, the Sherman Act was ignored by both corporate America and the Department of Justice. Although many states actively enforced their own state antitrust laws during this time, the federal government remained on the sidelines until Roosevelt's 1902 suit to dissolve financier J. P. Morgan's railroad trust, the Northern Securities Company, the first major prosecution under the law. When Roosevelt assumed the presidency, few would have predicted his historical reputation would be so intimately tied to trust busting. Born into wealth, Roosevelt had been vice president in a McKinley administration well known to favor business interests. Indeed, as we will see, McKinley won the 1896 and 1900 elections with an unprecedented amount of corporate funding for his campaign—a real occurrence of the kind of corporate takeover of the electoral process that worries *Citizens United*'s critics. While Roosevelt was not opposed to big business—and would even come to rely on corporate money to fund his own reelection campaign—he believed that numerous trusts gained their success by wrongful means.[20]

Because the Sherman Act had not previously been seriously enforced, the Department of Justice had little experience with anti-trust cases, and private lawyers like Henry Taft, who had defended corporations in antitrust cases brought under state law, were hired to conduct the prosecutions. In the grand-jury room, prosecutors have enormous, unchecked power. Mandated by the Fifth Amend-ment, grand juries are the vehicle by which the federal government brings criminal charges against someone. Distinct from the more familiar trial jury, which presides over public trials to render final verdicts of guilt, the grand jury's role is to determine if charges should be brought in the first place. The Framers saw the grand jury as a check on governmental power, yet given the prosecutor's nearly complete authority over the proceedings, it has not worked out that way. The grand jury meets in secret, hearing evidence and testimony brought to the jurors' attention by the prosecutor alone. There is no judge, and the normal rules of evidence that limit what jurors see in an ordinary trial do not apply. According to an old courthouse saying, the grand jury would indict a ham sandwich if the prosecutor asked it to.[21]

Yet Taft was as unfamiliar with the grand-jury room as his witness, Hale. Indeed, Hale was the very first witness Taft called to testify in his first case as a prosecutor. Nevertheless, the grand-jury room was certainly a more comfortable environment for Taft than for Hale. Unlike Taft, Hale had to worry someone might discover that he had embezzled from MacAndrews & Forbes $50,000—or roughly $1.3 million in 2017 dollars.

Taft, however, was focused on antitrust issues, and he had called Hale to testify in the hope that the executive would prove a wellspring of information on MacAndrews & Forbes's anticompetitive practices. He knew nothing of Hale's own crimes; his aim instead was the Tobacco Trust. MacAndrews & Forbes was just the tool Taft would use to gain incriminating information on the American Tobacco Company and its business dealings. In the same way that a prosecutor might file charges against a small-time street dealer in the hopes of bringing down the drug kingpin, Taft was going after MacAndrews & Forbes to get Buck Duke.

For DeLancey Nicoll, waiting outside of the grand-jury room, MacAndrews & Forbes was also just a tool. As Taft sought to use Hale's appearance to open the spigot of incriminating evidence on the Tobacco Trust, so was Nicoll determined to use Hale to gum up the inquiry on behalf of the tobacco companies. Chances are Nicoll, a chain smoker, passed some of the time out in the hallway enjoying an American Tobacco cigarette. Or perhaps he spent the time reflecting on the inequities of the criminal justice system, as the former district attorney—who first won election as a reform candidate—was known to do. Nicoll had once complained that "the rich can go practically unpunished, unless their crime is so glaring . . . while the poor have to receive the penalty of their offense in every instance." Whatever

his general sensitivities about equal justice, however, Nicoll was determined to see that in this case at least his very wealthy client, American
Tobacco, went unpunished.²²

* * *

INSIDE THE GRAND-JURY ROOM, Taft continued to question Hale
about MacAndrews & Forbes. "That company is engaged in what business?" Taft asked.

The answer was hardly a secret but Hale paused nonetheless. This
was the question for which he and Nicoll had prepared. Nicoll had
told Hale what to say and how to say it. Nicoll's strategy, designed
to protect American Tobacco's interests, would also protect him. "I
shall have to respectfully decline to answer further questions," Hale
responded to Taft. His explanation of why he could not answer any
more questions was obviously rehearsed: "first, that there is no legal
warrant or authority for my examination as a witness, and second,"
he said, invoking the Fifth Amendment, "that my answers may tend
to criminate me."

"Who is the president of the MacAndrews & Forbes Company?"
Taft asked. "I shall only have to repeat what I said before," Hale replied.
The special prosecutor tried to return to Hale's past, about which the
witness had already offered some superficial answers. Perhaps Hale
would continue to talk about that. "What business were you in before
you came to New York City?" Taft asked. Hale was not fooled and
tartly responded, "I shall have to decline to answer further questions
on the same grounds."

Taft persisted in rattling off questions. "Is there any agreement,
or understanding, or arrangement, between the American Tobacco
Company and MacAndrews & Forbes Company, in relation to the
trade or business in licorice, licorice paste, or licorice mass, affecting the business between several states of the United States?" Hale
declined to reply.

This fruitless back-and-forth continued for several minutes before
Taft turned to the documents Hale had been ordered to bring in the

subpoena. MacAndrews & Forbes's company records and correspondence were likely to have plenty of useful information. "Have you brought any of the papers called for by that subpoena?" Taft must have known the answer to that question before he even asked it. Given the breadth of the subpoena, which requested all contracts, correspondence, and any other documents MacAndrews & Forbes had ever created or received from over a dozen different companies, Hale would have to have brought with him boxes and boxes of papers.

"I have not," answered Hale.

It was futile for Taft to allow himself to become frustrated. He could not force Hale to answer or produce the documents. A judge, however, could. A week later, Taft hauled Hale before Emile Henry Lacombe, a law-and-order federal judge with little tolerance for troublemakers. The issues in the case revolved around the Fourth and Fifth Amendments to the Constitution. When Hale refused to turn over the enormous quantity of documents subpoenaed by Taft, he was asserting the Fourth Amendment "right of the people to be secure in their persons, houses, papers, and effects, against unreasonable searches and seizures." When he refused to testify about MacAndrews & Forbes and the Tobacco Trust, he was asserting rights under the Fifth Amendment, which provided, "No person shall be . . . compelled in any criminal case to be a witness against himself." The unusual twist was that Hale was not asserting these rights on behalf of himself—at least not so far as anyone else involved in the tobacco investigation knew. He was asserting those rights explicitly on behalf of MacAndrews & Forbes, a corporation. The subpoena and grand jury questions, Nicoll told Judge Lacombe, violated the *corporation's* constitutional rights.[23]

Judge Lacombe was not convinced and ordered Hale to answer Taft's questions nonetheless. Without offering a detailed rebuttal to Nicoll's argument, the judge simply issued an order requiring Hale to testify and produce the requested documents or go to jail. On Nicoll's advice, Hale refused once again. With so much to lose personally, he had little choice but to do as he was told. Hale was remanded to the custody of the local US marshal, William Henkel. Nicoll then appealed

Lacombe's decision and, pending resolution of the appeal, Hale was released into his lawyer's custody.[24]

The reprieve was temporary. Four months later, in September of 1905, MacAndrews & Forbes found out about the money Hale and his neighbor and gambling partner Harry Smock had stolen. The theft was reported to New York's district attorney, William Travers Jerome, who had run for office promising to combat corruption. On an otherwise ordinary Thursday at the company's corporate offices on lower Fifth Avenue, Jerome had police march in and arrest the two men as coworkers looked on. The *New York Times* headline the next day announced, "TRUSTED MEN IN JAIL FOR LARGE DEFALCATION," above a story connecting Hale to the antitrust investigation, Roosevelt, and American Tobacco.[25]

Although Hale's personal fate was sealed, the dispute over his refusal to testify and turn over documents continued on to the Supreme Court. The issue in the case was one of first impression: Do corporations like MacAndrews & Forbes have the rights guaranteed to criminal suspects under the Fourth and Fifth Amendments?

* * *

TODAY, THE FOURTH AND FIFTH Amendments are the most frequently litigated provisions of the Constitution. Anytime police search a home, they are required to follow strict rules on warrants required by the Fourth Amendment. When they arrest someone, they must read the *Miranda* warnings informing the criminal suspect of the right to remain silent under the Fifth Amendment. If a suspect can show these rights were violated, often the evidence uncovered as a result of the constitutional infringement will be suppressed, supplying ample incentive to suspects to raise such claims. Courts deal with Fourth and Fifth Amendment cases daily, and law students' casebooks are filled with a detailed and rich body of cases concerning these constitutional provisions.[26]

When DeLancey Nicoll brought MacAndrews & Forbes's case to the Supreme Court in 1905, however, the jurisprudence of those two amendments was still in its infancy. Crime control was traditionally the province of the state governments, which under the original Constitution were not required to follow the Fourth and Fifth Amendments. Nor were they required to respect the freedom of speech, religious liberty, the right to keep and bear arms, or any other right listed in the Bill of Rights. For the first hundred-plus years of US history, the Supreme Court held that the Bill of Rights was only a limitation on the federal government, not on state and local governments. Over the course of the twentieth century, the Supreme Court would reverse course and gradually extend most of the provisions of the Bill of Rights to the state and local governments, but that was still years away when Nicoll appealed Judge Lacombe's ruling.

Another reason there had been so few Fourth and Fifth Amendment cases was that the federal government had few criminal laws to enforce, at least until the late nineteenth century. The Gilded Age saw the rise of huge, national corporations like the railroads and the trusts that were beyond the power of any one state to control. Beginning in 1887, Congress increasingly began to fill the regulatory void, starting with the Interstate Commerce Act—the first comprehensive federal regulation of a national industry, the railroads. The law required railroad rates to be "reasonable and just," prohibited railroad companies from certain forms of rate discrimination, and established the first modern regulatory agency, the Interstate Commerce Commission, to oversee the industry. The Sherman Act was passed three years later, followed after the turn of the century by the Meat Inspection Act of 1906 and the Food and Drug Act of 1907, two additional laws inspired by muckraking journalism.

This wave of federal regulation backed by criminal penalties inevitably brought Fourth and Fifth Amendment cases to the Supreme Court's docket—pushing businesses to become once again constitutional first movers. Indeed, businesses being investigated or prosecuted for wrongdoing brought the earliest Supreme Court cases on the Fourth and Fifth Amendments, including *Boyd v. United States* and, ultimately, Nicoll's case. The *Boyd* case was decided in 1886, the same year as the *Santa Clara* case with the misleading headnote, and is considered the first significant Supreme Court decision on

GOVERNMENT REGULATION AND INSPECTION OF BUSINESS
GREW IN THE EARLY TWENTIETH CENTURY.

the criminal rights protected by the Fourth and Fifth Amendments. The case did not involve a corporation but a business partnership, which was accused of failing to pay customs duties on imported glass. The government seized the glass and obtained a court order requiring the partnership to turn over all the relevant invoices. The Supreme Court, however, ruled for the partnership. The justices held that the compelled disclosure of a company's papers was an unreasonable search and seizure under the Fourth Amendment. Moreover, the court held the use of those papers as evidence against their owner was forced self-incrimination under the Fifth Amendment. Although the court would water down these principles considerably in the decades to come, *Boyd* was nevertheless the case that first breathed life into the Fourth and Fifth Amendments, and it involved a business.[27]

The new federal laws of the era were part of that wave of laws, including many at the state level, that for the first time expressly specified that corporations could be prosecuted criminally. The Sherman Act, for example, set penalties of up to $350,000 for an individual and up to $10 million for "a corporation." Of course, unlike individuals, corporations could not be sentenced to prison. Traditionally, as Blackstone recognized, corporations were not subject to criminal prosecution at all. Corporations, one nineteenth-century court explained, had "no soul" and so were incapable of having the "actual wicked intent" that criminal law usually requires for conviction. Yet as business corporations became more commonplace and economically influential in the Gilded Age and Progressive era, the notion that they were incapable of criminal intent waned and prosecutions of corporations for crime waxed. Writing in 1892, criminal law expert Joel Prentiss Bishop captured the shifting mood when he wrote that if corporations can set out, as they had, to "level mountains, fill up valleys, lay down iron tracks, and run railroad cars on them," they could do so "as well viciously as virtuously."[28]

Philosophers, both at home and abroad, engaged in a lively debate about the nature of the corporation around the turn of the century. Was the corporation a state-created fiction? Or was it a real entity with a will of its own? American pragmatist John Dewey dismissed the various "theories" of the corporation as inherently indeterminate. Indeed, the shift toward corporate criminal liability had little to do with philosophy. Criminal law came to be applied to corporations because it was a valuable tool to discipline the emerging corporate giants of the era. As the Supreme Court would explain in a 1909 case, "the great majority of business transactions in modern times are conducted through these bodies, and . . . to give them immunity from all punishment because of the old and exploded doctrine that a corporation cannot commit a crime would virtually take away the only means of effectually controlling" business activity.[29]

In his briefs filed with the Supreme Court, DeLancey Nicoll took a corporationalist tack and argued that MacAndrews & Forbes, the corporation, should be protected in the same way as the partnership in the *Boyd* case. Yet Nicoll was forced to address the question the justices skirted in *Boyd*: whether business entities, as such, even had Fourth and Fifth Amendment rights at all. For Nicoll, the answer was straightforward—if corporations could face penalties similar to those faced by individuals, they should have similar protections: "For if corporations may suffer the judgment of death by dissolution, if they may be condemned to forfeit the corporate property, if they may be indicted, convicted and sentenced to pay a fine as individuals may, what excuse can be made for denying to them the beneficent protection of these amendments?" Nicoll cited for support *Santa Clara County v. Southern Pacific Railroad.*[30]

Corporations were once again on the cutting edge of constitutional law. The Bank of the United States had been an early pioneer of the right to sue in federal court. Dartmouth College's case breathed life into the contract clause. The Southern Pacific Railroad brought the lawsuits that transformed the Fourteenth Amendment into a vibrant guarantee of equality and due process for business. Now it was businesses like the partnership in *Boyd* and the MacAndrews & Forbes corporation that fought the first cases in the Supreme Court to establish Fourth and Fifth Amendment rights. It was only subsequent to these cases involving businesses that individuals would obtain judicial protection for those rights. Rather than corporations building on the established rights of individuals, individuals would instead build on the rights established by businesses.

* * *

IN APRIL OF 1905, when DeLancey Nicoll was preparing for the Supreme Court, the justices decided an important case that gave him reason to be confident in MacAndrews & Forbes's chances. *Lochner v. New York* held unconstitutional a New York law that capped the number of hours bakers could work at ten per day, sixty per week. Although the case did not involve corporate rights directly, the decision proved a boon for business. The ruling made it harder for states to regulate workplace conditions, and did so in the name of empowering employees: maximum hours and minimum wage laws, the court held, interfered with the employee's right to agree to work even longer for less money.[31]

More importantly, from Nicoll's perspective, was what the *Lochner* decision said about the court's relative embrace of business interests. Indeed, *Lochner* would give its name to a forty-year period in Supreme Court history, lasting from 1897 to 1936, in which the justices gained notoriety for striking down labor laws, minimum-wage laws, banking reform, and other efforts to regulate business. What Nicoll could not have known, however, was that the *Lochner* court, like the Taney court, would also impose new limits on corporate rights.

Although the *Lochner* era took its name from the 1905 case involving the bakers, as we have already seen, Justice Stephen Field was the intellectual godfather of the era's jurisprudence. One of the last cases decided by the Supreme Court before the colorful Field was forced by senility to retire was *E. Allgeyer & Company v. Louisiana*, in 1897, which is often thought to be the beginning of the *Lochner* era. E. Allgeyer & Company was a partnership, not a corporation, but like Daniel Webster and the Second Bank of the United States in *Bank of Augusta v. Earle*, the company claimed to have a right to do business across state lines. The Taney court declined to extend that right to corporations, but as we have seen, businessmen persistently continued to bring new cases, raising essentially the same claim under any provision of the Constitution that might sound plausible: the comity clause, the commerce clause, and, in *Allgeyer*, the Fourteenth Amendment's due process clause. The *Lochner* court ruled in favor of the partnership, holding that unduly protectionist state laws violated the "liberty of contract."[32]

The liberty of contract, as such, appears nowhere in the text of the due process clause—which is partly why Justice Rufus Wheeler Peckham Jr.'s opinion in *Allgeyer* became one of the most important in the history of the Supreme Court. Peckham's opinion established a groundbreaking precedent for reading the promise of "liberty" in the due process clause broadly to protect unwritten rights. For Peckham, a confidant of Gould, Vanderbilt, and Morgan, those rights were largely economic, including the right to form contracts and pursue

THE JUSTICES OF THE SUPREME COURT IN THE *LOCHNER*
ERA. STANDING, LEFT TO RIGHT: RUFUS PECKHAM, GEORGE
SHIRAS, EDWARD WHITE, JOSEPH McKENNA. SITTING,
LEFT TO RIGHT: DAVID BREWER, JOHN HARLAN, MELVILLE
FULLER, HORACE GRAY, HENRY BROWN.

any lawful calling free from undue government interference. Yet *All-geyer* was such an important precedent because, long after the *Lochner* era had ended, the Supreme Court continued to read the due process clause to protect unwritten rights, including the right to privacy, the right to choose abortion, and the right to same-sex marriage. Not only did *Allgeyer* launch the *Lochner* era, the decision—another landmark case in constitutional history brought and argued by a business— fundamentally reshaped American constitutional law.[33]

For years, critics of the *Lochner* era Supreme Court condemned the justices for making it nearly impossible for the government to regulate business. In recent years, however, scholars have gone back and reexamined the court's *Lochner* era jurisprudence and found that the court, while certainly favorable to business interests, allowed many regulations to stand. And rather than simply making up a novel right of liberty of contract, the court was in many ways trying to preserve an older notion, traceable to the Framers, that understood the Constitution largely in terms of protecting private property and private economic relationships from majority rule. To the justices, individual liberty was being threatened by the unprecedented growth of the regulatory state in the late nineteenth century. The *Lochner* era saw many business regulations struck down, but the Supreme Court's jurisprudence was far more complicated and nuanced than often portrayed.[34]

A similar nuance ran though the Supreme Court's treatment of corporate rights at the turn of the century. The first decades of the twentieth century witnessed an onslaught of corporate rights cases, as corporate litigants were encouraged by the court's business-friendly reputation to bring numerous cases to the Supreme Court seeking expanded constitutional protections. The *Lochner* court did grant corporations some new constitutional protections. Yet the *Lochner* court also articulated new limits on the scope of corporate rights. The *Lochner* court held that corporations had *property* rights but not *liberty* rights.[35]

That line was formally drawn in *Northwestern National Life Insurance Company v. Riggs*, a case decided in 1906—the same year the justices ruled on Nicoll's case for MacAndrews & Forbes. An insurance company had challenged a Missouri law requiring insurers to pay out on life insurance policies even if the insured had violated the policy by lying on the application. The corporation claimed the law infringed the liberty of contract under *Allgeyer* and *Lochner*, but a majority of justices disagreed. "It is true that this Court has said that the liberty guaranteed by the Fourteenth Amendment against deprivation otherwise than by due process of law embraces the right to pursue a lawful calling and enter into all contracts proper, necessary, and essential to the carrying out of the purposes of such calling." Nonetheless, the court held, the "liberty referred to in that Amendment is the liberty of natural, not artificial, persons." In the spirit of the Taney court, which first rejected expansive claims of corporate rights, the *Lochner* court identified a new boundary to the scope of corporate constitutional protections.[36]

What the *Lochner* court never did, however, was to offer a thoughtful justification of the distinction between property rights and liberty rights—or even bother to define the respective terms. The *Riggs* case provided no discussion beyond the brief statement quoted above. The differential treatment of property rights and liberty rights was not obviously required by the text of the Constitution. The due process clause of the Fourteenth Amendment, for example, joins both types of rights together in its guarantee that no state shall "deprive any person of life, liberty, or property, without due process of law." Of course, the notion that corporations had property rights was relatively simple to understand. Since their earliest days in ancient Rome, corporations were recognized to have the ability to own property, like real estate or financial assets, in their own names. That was, indeed, the original motivation for creating the corporate form. The right of corporations to own property had been firmly established in American law ever since the *Dartmouth College* case, when Daniel Webster's victory prevented New Hampshire's attempted takeover of the incorporated school.

Yet what exactly were liberty rights? The justices never offered a clear answer. Some years later, in a case called *Meyer v. Nebraska*, the court admitted that it had never "attempted to define with exactness" which rights fell under the rubric of liberty rights. At its core, the notion of liberty is associated with "freedom from bodily restraint." Yet, the court explained, liberty must include "also the right of the individual to contract, to engage in any of the common occupations of life, to acquire useful knowledge, to marry, establish a home and bring up children, to worship God according to the dictates of his own conscience." The court was describing an array of fundamentally personal freedoms closely tied to control over your body, your conscience, and your family. With the exception of the right to contract, none of these liberty rights had anything to do with traditional business entities. Corporations did not have bodies, consciences, or families over which to exercise personal autonomy. And the law had long imposed limits on the types of business activity in which corporations could engage—even if, as the *Lochner* era began, many of the reins were being loosened by the new, permissive corporate laws of states like New Jersey.[37]

The Supreme Court recognized corporations to have property rights because the companies could not function without them. Liberty rights, however, which oriented around physical and spiritual freedom, had no application to corporations. Corporations had constitutional rights but not the same constitutional rights as individuals.

* * *

WHEN THE SUPREME COURT issued its decision in MacAndrews & Forbes's case, *Hale v. Henkel*, the *New York Times* announced that American Tobacco and the Tobacco Trust had been "beaten" in a "sweeping" decision. On "every issue they have lost," the paper reported, "and apparently there is no refuge for a trust." In fact, however, the court's opinion, written by Justice Henry Billings Brown, was, like the *Lochner* court jurisprudence itself, more complicated than it might initially have appeared. By and large, the newspaper was correct that DeLancey Nicoll and MacAndrews & Forbes had lost; Brown's decision ruled against the company on its Fifth Amendment claim, for example, holding that corporations do not have a right against self-incrimination and that Edwin Hale would have to testify. Nonetheless, the court at the same time held that corporations did have the Fourth Amendment right to be free from unreasonable searches and seizures. Moreover, the court held that Henry Taft's subpoena for documents was an overbroad infringement of that right.[38]

In fairness to the *New York Times*, Brown's opinion was hardly a model of clarity and has confused readers ever since. Brown himself had an undistinguished tenure—or, rather, a tenure of only undesired distinction, as he remains known today solely as the author of *Plessy v. Ferguson*, the discredited decision establishing separate but equal. He was unpredictable when it came to business regulation, voting in the *Lochner* case to strike down ten-hour workday limits for bakers but then voting in another case to uphold eight-hour workday limits for miners. Even Brown's own biographer wrote that the justice's career showed "how a man without perhaps extraordinary abilities" could rise to "the highest judicial position by industry, by good character, pleasant manners and some aid from fortune." Brown's opinion in the *Hale* case has never prompted anyone to argue he was underrated.[39]

When viewed in light of the distinction drawn that same year in the *Riggs* case between property rights and liberty rights, however, Brown's opinion begins to make more sense. By denying corporations the right against self-incrimination, the court was excluding them from a right associated with personal liberty and bodily autonomy, or what Brown called "a purely personal privilege." Henry Taft had argued in his brief that the right against self-incrimination was designed to protect people from being tortured; "the mischief" the Framers sought to prevent

JUSTICE HENRY BILLINGS BROWN WROTE THE SUPREME COURT OPINION RECOGNIZING CORPORATIONS TO HAVE SOME, THOUGH NOT ALL, OF THE CONSTITUTION'S PROTECTIONS FOR CRIMINAL SUSPECTS.

was "the demoralizing effect on the administration of justice of a possible resort to brow-beating and abuse." Corporations, however, unlike people, were not subject to torture or physical abuse.[40]

The Fourth Amendment, however, was more like a property right. It protected "persons, houses, papers, and effects" from being unreasonably searched or seized by the government. This was largely protection for tangible property, and corporations had long enjoyed the same property rights as individuals. Taft's subpoena illustrated why corporations needed this type of protection, according to Brown. Taft had not required "the production of a single contract, or of contracts with a particular corporation, or a limited number of documents, but all understandings, contracts, or correspondence" between MacAndrews & Forbes and all its major business partners—"as well as all letters received by that company since its organization from more than a dozen different companies." In an era before photocopying, complying with such a subpoena was more than a minor inconvenience. "Indeed, it is difficult to say how its business could be carried on after it had been denuded" of all the documents Taft requested, Brown wrote. Without some constitutional protection for corporate property, the government could, under the guise of a mere investigation, "completely put a stop to the business."[41]

Although *Hale* reached different outcomes with regard to corporations' Fourth and Fifth Amendment rights, Brown's reasoning in both instances relied on a similar understanding of the nature of the corporation. Again, however, Brown's opinion was opaque. Brown began by stating that the "question of whether a corporation is a 'person' . . . really does not arise," and then repeated the language of Horace Binney, Daniel Webster, and Stephen Field by referring to corporations as "associations of people." Amidst his confusing and inconsistent language, however, Brown's logic rested on corporate personhood; that is, like the Taney court, he approached the corporation as an independent legal actor, separate and distinct from the members who composed it. Edwin Hale, for instance, was not able to assert the privilege against self-incrimination because, Brown explained, his testimony would not incriminate *him* but might instead incriminate someone else: MacAndrews & Forbes. Although Hale was called as an agent of the corporation, Brown saw a strict separation between the corporate entity and its members—including, in this case, its employees.

Hale v. Henkel also reflected the view that corporations were fundamentally different from ordinary individuals in ways that mattered to constitutional law. There was, Brown wrote for the majority, a "clear distinction" between "an individual and a corporation." Unlike an individual, who "owes no duty to the State or to his neighbors to divulge his business," the corporation was "a creature of the State" who "receives certain special privileges and franchises."[42]

Although the court held that corporations enjoyed the Fourth Amendment right against unreasonable searches and seizures, corporate rights in this regard were more limited than those of individuals. Brown recognized that, when it came to government investigation of corporations, there was "a reserved right in the legislature to investigate [a corporation's] contracts and find out whether it has exceeded its powers." Brown was referring to what Blackstone in his *Commentaries* had called the "visitatorial power," which authorized the government to inspect the books and records of corporations to ferret out wrongdoing. As the court explained a few years after *Hale*, "The reserved power of visitation would seriously be embarrassed, if not wholly defeated in its effective exercise, if guilty officers could refuse inspection of the records and papers of the corporation."[43]

Although the visitatorial power meant that corporations had a diminished expectation of privacy, the *Hale* court nonetheless held that corporations had a right against *unreasonable* searches and seizures. The government could not, as Henry Taft had attempted to do, seize so many of a company's documents that the business could no longer function. Such a blunderbuss approach to a criminal investigation violated MacAndrews & Forbes's Fourth Amendment rights.

* * *

ALTHOUGH THE *NEW YORK TIMES* failed to notice that DeLancey Nicoll and MacAndrews & Forbes had won an important victory for corporate rights in *Hale v. Henkel*, the newspaper's exaggerated claims of the government's sweeping victory were nonetheless prescient. The case was returned to the lower courts, where Henry Taft immediately continued the Roosevelt administration's aggressive push to break up the Tobacco Trust. MacAndrews & Forbes's corporate officers could now be forced to testify about the company's business dealings. And Taft followed the Supreme Court's guidance and issued more narrow, targeted demands for specific documents. In June of 1906, a mere three months after *Hale* was decided, American Tobacco, MacAndrews & Forbes, and over sixty affiliated companies were indicted for violating the Sherman Act.[44]

Although Taft had wasted no time bringing his case, the prosecution would bog down in the federal courts for years. The litigation finally came to an end in 1911 when the justices of the *Lochner* era Supreme Court upheld the breakup of American Tobacco and James Duke's trust. Duke, said to be left "morose and drinking heavily," found some solace in gifting a substantial portion of his wealth to a small college near his birthplace in Durham, North Carolina, that was subsequently renamed in his honor. His pain would also be felt by John D. Rockefeller, the father of the trusts. In 1911, the Supreme Court upheld the breakup of Standard Oil too. Duke's and Rockefeller's trusts, which had been created with the help of New Jersey's corporate law reforms, were finally defeated.[45]

The Supreme Court has not as of this writing reconsidered its holding in *Hale* that corporations do not have the Fifth Amendment right against self-incrimination. And while corporations continue to enjoy Fourth Amendment rights, the scope of those rights remains more limited than for individuals. In a series of cases in the 1970s, the court held that the Fourth Amendment permits the government far more leeway to search corporate workplaces than to search the homes of individuals. Because of the historical tradition of close governmental supervision over the sale of alcohol and guns, for example, the government does not need a warrant at all to search businesses involving those areas of commerce. While warrants are generally required for inspections of ordinary workplaces, even here corporations have less protection than individuals. For an individual, the government must show probable cause to obtain a warrant; for corporations, the government need only show that the inspection was part of a regular policy of inspections, with no individualized suspicion of wrongdoing required. As the court explained, "corporations can claim no equality with individuals in the enjoyment" of Fourth Amendment rights.[46]

In the context of criminal rights, corporations have been recognized to have some but not all of the same rights the Constitution guarantees to individuals. And even the rights they do have are somewhat narrower than those rights are for individuals. Corporate rights in the criminal context are not the same as the rights of the people who make up the corporation; they are the corporation's rights, separate and distinct from the rights of members. Here, at least, the court has approached the corporation as if it were a person—but one with more limited rights than real people.

As corporations would soon discover, one of the rights they did not enjoy was the right to influence elections. Although they would gain that right a century later in *Citizens United*, when the first cases arose in the early twentieth century, even the business-friendly courts of the *Lochner* era would rule against the corporations.

CHAPTER 6

Property, Not Politics

FOUR MONTHS AFTER EDWIN HALE WALKED INTO THE GRAND jury room as part of the investigation of the Tobacco Trust, George W. Perkins walked into New York City Hall in lower Manhattan, just blocks from where Hale had testified, to offer testimony of his own. Perkins, too, had been asked to testify as part of a high-profile investigation into corporate wrongdoing. Unlike Hale, the scheming gambler from Kentucky, Perkins was an influential member of New York's business and social elite. His titular position was vice president of the successful New York Life Insurance Company, but he was also known to be the right-hand man of financier J. P. Morgan and a confidant of President Theodore Roosevelt. In contrast to the secrecy of the grand-jury room, this hearing was open to the public. Indeed, the ornate and cavernous Aldermanic Chamber in City Hall, with its rich mahogany paneling and forty-foot-high ceilings, was packed with hundreds of reporters, spectators, and elected officials eager to hear what Perkins had to say.[1]

Although Perkins was entitled to have with him a lawyer, he chose to appear without one. Perkins was sure he had done nothing improper and, unlike the nervous Hale, who hoped to say as little as possible on the stand, Perkins, with the supreme confidence of an upstanding member of New York society, planned to speak frankly. But just like Hale, Perkins did have a secret, and once it was revealed, Perkins too would find himself facing criminal charges.

Perkins's revelations would dramatically impact the careers of three of the most important men of the era: Teddy Roosevelt, Louis Brandeis, and Charles Evans Hughes. Each man's reputation would be catapulted, shaped, or challenged by what eventually would be called the Great Wall Street Scandal of 1905. Perkins's testimony would also transform how Americans understood the emerging corporations of the modern era—especially the growing number of large, publicly held companies of the sort that would come to dominate the US economy in the twentieth century—and the potential they posed for corrupting democracy. The result would be a wave of reform that, for the first time in American history, explicitly limited corporate money in politics.

Those reforms, which heralded the birth of campaign finance law, were challenged in the first decades of the twentieth century by corporations. Foreshadowing *Citizens United* by nearly a hundred years, corporations argued that they enjoyed the same right as individuals to try to influence elections. Back then, however, the corporations lost. Adhering to the distinction drawn in corporate rights cases like *Hale v. Henkel* and *Northwestern National Life Insurance Company v. Riggs*, which held that corporations had rights of property but not rights more closely associated with personal liberty, courts refused to extend political speech rights to corporations. Once again, the courts of the *Lochner* era, so well known for ruling in favor of business, drew a firm boundary on the rights of corporations.

* * *

AS HE TOOK THE STAND in the Aldermanic Chamber of City Hall, the slender George Perkins, with his youthful, innocent face and hair neatly parted in the middle like a schoolboy, appeared no match for the tall, broad-shouldered, stern-looking lead investigator for the Armstrong Committee, Charles Evans Hughes. A future governor of New York, two-time Supreme Court justice, Republican presidential nominee, and secretary of state for two presidents, Hughes was

GEORGE PERKINS (LEFT) OF NEW YORK LIFE INSURANCE
AND CHARLES EVANS HUGHES (RIGHT), LEAD
INVESTIGATOR FOR THE ARMSTRONG COMMITTEE.

destined to have one of the most distinguished careers of any American in history. Back in September of 1905, however, when Perkins appeared before the committee, the insurance man was by far the more influential of the two. Yet reputations can change in an instant, and here they would.

The Armstrong Committee was charged by the New York state legislature to investigate financial mismanagement in the life insurance industry, and the 43-year-old Hughes was a surprising choice to head up the inquiry. A "scarcely known" corporate lawyer and part-time law professor, Hughes's only prosecutorial experience had come earlier that same year when he served as counsel to a legislative investigation into gas utility rates. Although Hughes had impressed lawmakers in that earlier investigation with his methodical questioning, it was paradoxically his then-middling career that proved decisive in his appointment to lead the life insurance hearings. Unlike the more successful corporate lawyers of the city, Hughes was unaffiliated with any of the major law firms and investment banks that regularly did business with the insurance companies. Hughes's unexceptional practice meant he could lead the inquiry without any conflicted interests.[2]

Hughes certainly was not fooled by Perkins's diminutive appearance. Perkins had begun at New York Life Insurance as an office boy but worked his way up to become the company's vice president. His work there earned him wide respect in business circles and in 1898, J. P. Morgan, the nation's leading investment banker, asked Perkins to join his firm as a partner. Satisfied with his current position, Perkins did what few men ever did and turned Morgan down. That, of course, only made Morgan want him more. The next year, when Perkins was named by then-governor of New York Theodore Roosevelt to head up a commission to save the majestic palisades of the Hudson River, Morgan offered to pay for the entire project on one condition: that Perkins join his firm. This time Perkins agreed but on a condition of his own. He insisted on continuing his job at the New York Life, working in the mornings there and the afternoons at Morgan's firm. That the legendary financier agreed to this half a loaf told Hughes everything he needed to know about how shrewd and capable Perkins really was.[3]

Hughes sought Perkins's testimony on a number of matters, but one ambiguous entry in the New York Life's accounts was especially curious. It was an expenditure paid out to Morgan's investment firm in the amount of $48,000 (about $1.2 million in 2017 dollars). Was this a payment for services rendered—and, if so, what services? Was it an investment—and, if so, why was it not listed on the company's balance sheet? There seemed to be no other mention of this expense anywhere else in New York Life's accounts.

Neither Hughes nor Perkins would have been in this situation had it not been for a lavish Versailles-themed costume ball. The party was thrown by James Hazen Hyde, the vice president and son of the founder of the Equitable Life Insurance Company. The 29-year-old Hyde was known as a "spectacular dilettante," a socialite whose exploits were often covered in the gossip rags of the day. In January of 1905, he threw a coming out costume party for his niece at the swank Sherry's Hotel on Fifth Avenue. While most newspapers gushed over the outré decorations and glamorous celebrities on the guest list, Joseph Pulitzer's *New York World* turned its readers' attention to the cost of the party. Who, the *World* asked, had paid the estimated $200,000 (or approximately $5 million in 2017 dollars) to host this ball?[4]

Pulitzer, the Hungarian-born newspaper publisher who perfected the art of yellow journalism, often ran eye-catching headlines atop reports of supposed scandals that, in the end, had little truth to them. His insurance stories, however, had substance. Tipped off by one of Hyde's opponents in an ongoing battle for control of the insurance giant, Pulitzer claimed the bill for the costume party had been paid for by the insurance company. Throughout the spring and summer of 1905, Pulitzer's papers relentlessly went after Hyde and his company, publishing stories daily under the banner "Equitable Corruption." Pulitzer sought to expose the many other ways beyond the party that the executives were enriching themselves at the expense of the company's policyholders. Charges of self-dealing included startlingly high salaries for executives and speculative investments certain only to benefit company insiders. Hyde's expensive, and alledgedly expensed, party was just the most egregious example of how the company's policyholders—the "widows and orphans," according to the World— were taken advantage of by unscrupulous management.

Prompted by Pulitzer's exposés, the New York legislature recruited Hughes to investigate the management practices at Equitable and the other major life insurance companies, including Perkins's New York Life. Over the first few weeks of the investigative hearings, according to one report, there were "a few minor sensations but nothing very shocking had been brought to light." Then Perkins took the stand.[5]

Full of energy, Perkins literally stood—refusing to sit in the witness box and remaining on his feet for the better part of four days of testimony. He was eager to talk not just about company finances; he wanted to defend his honor. Pulitzer's stories on Hyde and Equitable had sullied the image of everyone in the insurance business, and Perkins wanted the world to know he was no flamboyant, self-dealing playboy like Hyde. He offered lengthy answers to Hughes's questions, filled with excessive detail about his upright character, outstanding job performance, and pure motives. Everything he had done was for the benefit of New York Life Insurance and its policyholders, he insisted, and the company had consistently profited from his decisions.[6]

Presenting himself as a man with nothing to hide, Perkins answered all of Hughes's questions without hesitation. There was, however, one thing about which Perkins thought Hughes ought not inquire. On the first day of his appearance, Perkins requested a private audience with Hughes at the luncheon break. Once they were behind closed doors, Perkins advised Hughes not to dig any deeper into that ambiguous $48,000 entry in the New York Life's books. "You're handling dynamite," Perkins warned.[7]

* * *

OFTEN REPRODUCED IN TEXTBOOKS, Joseph Keppler's "The Bosses of the Senate" is a famous political cartoon that captured the way many Americans in the late nineteenth century understood how corporations corrupted democracy. First published in *Puck* magazine

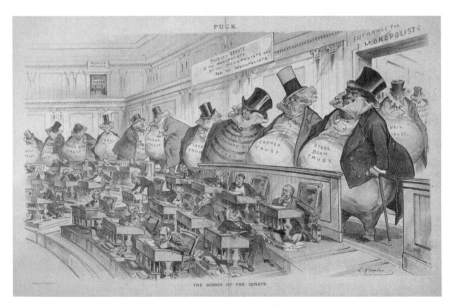

JOSEPH KEPPLER'S 1889 CARTOON "THE BOSSES OF THE SENATE" REFLECTED THE PUBLIC'S FEAR ABOUT THE POWER OF THE TRUSTS.

in 1889, it shows twelve colossal businessmen, clad in the signature top hat, ruffled collar, and tails of the Gilded Age, filing into the United States Senate through a doorway marked "Entrance for Monopolists." More than ten times the size of the Lilliputian senators, the titans of industry, each with a dollar sign and a label scrawled across his corpulent belly—"Standard Oil Trust," "Copper Trust," "Sugar Trust"—dominate the chamber. In the age of the trusts, political corruption came from huge corporations that were stronger and more powerful than any government. Those businesses used their amassed wealth to overwhelm and control legislators, securing laws to bloat corporate profits.[8]

This vision of corporate corruption was a product of the burgeoning industrial revolution, which swept the American economy in the decades after the Civil War. To win favorable legislation in this changing environment, corporations turned to lobbying, special favors, and, when that failed, flat out bribery. That was the approach taken by the B&O Railroad back in Roger Taney's day and by the Central Pacific around the time of the Civil War. With money and stock certificates to dish out, large corporations like the railroads became politically influential, sometimes immensely so. Yet one area of politics that corporations had not previously been involved with was financing election campaigns. Up until the 1890s, candidates drew their funds from family wealth, local machines, or patronage, but not from corporations.

The end of the nineteenth century, however, saw "politics' own industrial revolution," as the American electoral process went through a radical transformation similar to what was happening in the American economy more generally. The unprecedented corruption of the Grant administrations of the 1870s, along with growing frustration with machine politics, helped spur a series of reforms to clean up elections and government bureaucracy. In 1883, Congress passed the landmark Pendleton Act, which curtailed patronage and reduced partisan appointments to federal office. Civil service reform at the federal level was coupled with ballot reform in the states. In the past, voters had brought to the polls their own ballots, often in bright colors so that partisan poll watchers could be sure they were voting correctly. In the 1880s, however, laws requiring an official, government-printed ballot that could be cast in secret, behind the curtains of the polling place, swept the nation. The result of these and other election reforms reduced the ability of political machines to control who won on Election Day. Increasingly, candidates needed to earn their support in the marketplace of public opinion, much like a business selling a product.[9]

No one understood the implications of this transformation better than Marcus Alonzo Hanna. The Karl Rove of his day, Hanna, with a round face, loose jowls, and sloping, shiny forehead, resembled more than a bit the man who would shepherd George W. Bush's two successful presidential campaigns. Hanna was also the political mastermind behind a twice-successful Republican presidential candidate, William McKinley, who took the White House in 1896 and was reelected in 1900. Hanna was raised in Cleveland, where he was a high school classmate of John D. Rockefeller, and enjoyed a successful career in the coal and steel industries. His true passion, however, was politics. In 1895, he handed off his company to his brother and turned his full attention to electing McKinley, a fellow Ohioan. He used his businessman's instinct for innovation and marketing to revolutionize how election campaigns raised and spent money—and, for the first time, brought significant amounts of corporate cash into the electoral process.[10]

As chairman of the Republican National Committee in 1896, Hanna felt a pressing need to raise more money than any previous presidential campaign. The Democrats had nominated the fiery William Jennings Bryan, a Jeffersonian populist opponent of corporate power who drew broad support from farmers and the working class. These were the people hardest hit by the financial panic of 1893, the worst economic depression in US history to date. As with the historic Crash of 1929, blame was placed squarely on the bankers and moneymen of Wall Street. In his celebrated speech at the 1896 Democratic convention, Bryan accused the leaders of corporate America of trying to "crucify mankind upon a cross of gold."[11]

Early in the campaign, one of the most significant in presidential history, Bryan had all the momentum. Bryan's broad appeal meant

MARCUS ALONZO HANNA REVOLUTIONIZED THE
FINANCING OF ELECTION CAMPAIGNS AND SOLICITED
MONEY FROM CORPORATIONS.

that even traditionally safe Republican strongholds were in play. To counter Bryan, Hanna decided to undertake an exhaustive and systematic publicity campaign to educate voters. The effort would be expensive, but it would require more than just money. It would require overhauling how presidential campaigns were run. Hanna sought to conform the national committee's methods to the standards of corporate America—and, in the process, created the first modern political campaign.

Although state committees had traditionally managed the local campaigns, even for presidential candidates, Hanna centralized them all under his authority in order to be "the general staff of the whole army." He reorganized the RNC's executive offices and introduced an improved system of bookkeeping. He opened a branch headquarters in Chicago, closer to the midwestern voters whose support McKinley would need. He created the first nationwide advertising campaign to market a presidential candidate and produced over 100 million pieces of campaign literature printed in German, Spanish, French, Italian, Danish, Swedish, Norwegian, and Hebrew to appeal to immigrants. Buttons, cartoons, placards, posters, billboards, and leaflets were manufactured "by the carload." The

RNC hired 1,400 people to go out and promote McKinley in every competitive district. When a canvass in Iowa revealed a probable majority for Bryan, Hanna sent speakers and distributed campaign material "into every town and village" until public opinion turned. Theodore Roosevelt, the vice-presidential candidate on the McKinley ticket, remarked that Hanna "advertised McKinley as though he were a patent medicine."[12]

Hanna's new methods of electioneering required far more money than campaigns of old—and corporations would be willing to supply it. More than most, Hanna recognized the value of money in electoral politics. Even before he became the Republican Party's chief fundraiser, he had been a generous contributor. One morning back in 1887, he had happened upon a meeting of glum campaign operatives from Cuyahoga County. "It looks pretty blue here," said Hanna. "What's the matter?" After they complained about their campaign being more than a thousand dollars in debt, Hanna sat down and wrote out a check for the entire amount. "There," he said. "Pay your debts and look cheerful." Hanna, whose own giving made him credible with donors, once famously (and perhaps apocryphally) quipped, "There are two things that are important in politics. The first is money, and I can't remember what the second one is."[13]

More than a century before *Citizens United* opened the floodgates to corporate money in elections, Hanna sought to make corporations both a model for organizing modern political campaigns and also a source of financing for them. The amassed capital of the late-nineteenth-century corporate giants meant they had the wealth to spend on electoral politics—just as they had the means to afford the best lawyers to pursue corporate rights.

Business leaders were fearful of the economic consequences of a Bryan presidency, but at first Hanna had few connections to eastern money or Wall Street. His early efforts in 1896 to raise funds from big business had been a failure, so much so that Hanna contemplated quitting the campaign, as he explained to James J. Hill, an old friend he bumped into one day on the street. Hill, a railroad magnate, offered to introduce Hanna to the right people. The two men went on a five-day tour of New York firms, and soon Wall Street money was flowing generously into McKinley's coffers.[14]

Once his campaign fund-raising was under way, Hanna approached it like a businessman, not a beggar. He told the leaders of America's biggest corporations that McKinley was good for their bottom lines, and they should contribute according to their ability and their stake in American prosperity. Banks should give one-quarter of one percent of their capital; large industrial corporations were recommended to give five- and six-figure amounts. Standard Oil, the economic giant run by Hanna's schoolmate, was asked to donate $250,000. Hanna "systematized fundraising as no political operative had done before." At the same time, he made clear he was not selling favors. When one Wall Street firm sent in $10,000 along with a suggestion of some service in return, Hanna promptly returned the check. He had a different and seemingly more benign vision: if businesses placed their money in McKinley's campaign, they would profit from his wise economic polices.[15]

Hanna's fund-raising efforts generated $7 million for McKinley, more than ten times the amount spent by Bryan and the most ever at the time for a presidential candidate. While election campaign costs tend to increase steadily every cycle, Hanna's haul in 1896 was so huge that no presidential campaign would equal it for nearly half a century. "Dollar Mark," as he came to be known, revolutionized political campaigns by adopting the methods of business and by relying for the first time on significant amounts of corporate money. When McKinley took the oath of office, the leaders of America's richest corporations knew they had made his victory possible.[16]

Most other Americans, however, did not know it. While many people today worry that gaps in campaign disclosure laws permit too much "dark money," or funds from unidentified donors, the 1896 election took place with no disclosure laws whatsoever. The first federal law requiring any campaigns to disclose their funders was not enacted until 1910—in part a reaction to Dollar Mark's voracious fund-raising. Before then, candidates raised and spent their money in secret. Hanna, of course, chose not to advertise his methods for fear of fueling Bryan's claims about big corporations dominating politics. Nonetheless, in December of 1896, after stories began to circulate of corporate donations to McKinley, Texas governor Charles A. Culberson asked New York Life Insurance, George Perkins's company, to submit a sworn affidavit specifying "the amount, if any, paid by or on behalf of the company for political purposes" during the presidential campaign. The company's treasurer complied, insisting that New York Life had made no contributions, either "directly or indirectly."[17]

Rumors of corporate money flowing into the Republican presidential campaigns continued to swirl around the 1900 and 1904 elections. During the 1904 campaign, Democratic presidential nominee Alton Parker charged Roosevelt, the incumbent president after McKinley's assassination in 1901, with taking contributions from big business in exchange for promises of political favoritism. "Political contributions by corporations and trusts mean corruption," Parker said. "A corporation will subscribe to a political party only because the corporation expects that party . . . to do something for the benefit of the corporation or to refrain from doing something to its injury. No other motive can be imagined."[18]

Roosevelt bristled at the charges. Parker had impugned his integrity by suggesting he could be bought, and also threatened to undermine Roosevelt's carefully constructed public image as a trustbuster. Although the McKinley administration was strongly pro-business, Roosevelt cast himself as a populist once he assumed the White House. From his first State of the Union address, in which he promised to break up the large corporations that were crushing competition, to his unprecedented prosecutions of trusts like Standard Oil and American Tobacco under the Sherman Act, Roosevelt sought to harness the growing public sentiment for reform. Roosevelt's transformation prompted steel magnate Henry C. Frick to complain, "We bought the son of a bitch and he didn't stay bought."[19]

Roosevelt, however, cared more about what the public thought of him. More than any previous president, Roosevelt purposefully managed his public image. Back when he was governor of New York, he had learned that meeting with reporters regularly helped to promote his agenda. As president, Roosevelt brought his press secretary into his cabinet and created the White House press corps, establishing the first formal press room in the West Wing and issuing credentials to reporters. Seeking to stem the public relations damage from Parker's accusations, Roosevelt issued what the *New York Times* called a "direct and fierce" denial.[20]

* * *

"YOU'RE HANDLING DYNAMITE," George Perkins warned Charles Evans Hughes when the two men met privately during the lunch break of the insurance hearings. Hughes, Perkins advised, should not ask for an explanation of the ambiguous entry in the New York Life's books. "That $48,000 was a contribution to President Roosevelt's campaign fund."

Hughes was surely taken aback. New York Life officials had previously sworn under penalty of perjury that the company had made no political contributions, and Roosevelt had publicly denied receiving any inappropriate corporate gifts. Yet here was Perkins, an associate of the president, admitting that his company had made contributions to Roosevelt's campaign. The situation was fraught for Hughes, himself a Republican. Hughes had been active in party politics at least since 1887—when he campaigned for a reform-minded candidate for district attorney, DeLancey Nicoll—and had inchoate political ambitions of his own. If he let Perkins's secret out, Hughes might be blacklisted from the party, and any dreams of elected office might be dashed. "You want to think very carefully before you put that into the evidence," Perkins advised Hughes. "You can't tell what may come of it."[21]

Hughes, who prized his integrity more than anything, did not have to think about it for long. "After lunch, I'm going to ask you what was done with that $48,000," Hughes told Perkins. "And I expect a candid answer."

When the hearing resumed, Hughes asked Perkins about the money. Perkins admitted the expenditure had been made to J. P. Morgan & Company to reimburse Perkins for making a contribution of the same amount to Roosevelt's campaign. The Aldermanic Chamber erupted. Hughes recalled that reporters jumped out of their seats and "ran to the nearest telephones"—taking advantage of the novel communication device appearing more and more in America's cities. Spurred by Perkins's admission, Hughes burrowed deeper into the account books of the life insurance companies to find additional political contributions. The investigation eventually revealed that New York Life had contributed substantial sums to the Republican National Committee in each of the previous three presidential elections. Like many corporations who fell in line with Mark Hanna's practices, New York Life had become an active player in financing Republican presidential campaigns, including in 1896, when officials had issued a sworn denial.[22]

New York Life's contributions were just the initial strike of what was called the "gushing oil well of insurance sensations tapped by the Investigating Committee's drill." Each of the other major insurance companies had also secretly contributed to political campaigns, mostly to Republicans. Equitable Life had given even more than Perkins's company to Roosevelt's 1904 reelection fund, alongside large annual

THE ARMSTRONG COMMITTEE OF THE NEW YORK
STATE LEGISLATURE AND ITS LEAD INVESTIGATOR,
CHARLES EVANS HUGHES.

payments to Senator Chauncey Depew (R-NY). Mutual Life Insurance had also contributed to Roosevelt. All told, insurance companies had contributed nearly $5 million (in 2017 dollars) to recent campaigns. Despite the president's denials, his 1904 campaign had raised more than 70 percent of its financing from corporations.[23]

Relative to the total assets of the wealthy insurance companies, the amounts contributed to Roosevelt and other politicians were small. Yet the public outcry they provoked in this era of muckraking journalism was enormous. The Great Wall Street Scandal would prompt 115 front-page stories in the *New York Times*; between August 1905 and January 1906, the influential weekly *Collier's* published an article on the scandal in every issue, save for the special Christmas edition. The uproar was not simply over how politics had been corrupted. As the investigation continued, it would become increasingly clear that the modern corporation had been corrupted too.

* * *

UNDOUBTEDLY THE MOST INFLUENTIAL book ever written about the corporation in America was Adolf Berle Jr. and Gardiner Means's *The Modern Corporation and Private Property*, published in 1932. Berle and Means, two Columbia professors who would go on to become key advisors to Franklin D. Roosevelt, detailed the changing nature of corporate business around the turn of the century. The distinctive feature of the modern, publicly traded corporation, they argued, was "the separation of ownership and control." In contrast to the corporations of early America, which were typically owned and managed by a single family or small group of investors, modern corporations of the early twentieth century were more likely to have a dispersed class of passive stockholders who could not exert much control over management decision-making. A quarter of a century before Berle and Means's book, however, the American public was first introduced to the separation of ownership and control by the Great Wall Street Scandal of 1905. The evidence adduced in Charles Evans Hughes's highly publicized investigation made it clear that executives in the modern corporation had access to a tremendous amount of other people's money—and that the law did little to stop executives from misusing it for their own purposes.[24]

One reason Hughes's investigation garnered so much public attention was the special place that insurance played in the American economy at the turn of the century. Insurance companies "were among the lustiest of American corporations," according to historian Morton Keller, and only the railroads and a handful of trusts rivaled them in terms of accumulated capital. More than 10 million people had life insurance policies and, if beneficiaries are factored in, about half the nation's population of 76 million had a stake in the companies. In an era before pensions, life insurance was the preferred retirement plan of most Americans who could afford it. If the policyholder died, life insurance would provide for the policyholder's family. If the policyholder survived to retire, the policy would provide cash value. As *Collier's* reported, "there is not a county or town in which somebody is not insured. No other business, therefore, can compare with insurance in the extent of the raw nerve surface exposed to every breath of scandal."[25]

That nerve was especially sensitive because insurance companies were understood as fiduciaries to the policyholders—holding, it was said, "the widows and orphans' money" in trust. Richard A. McCurdy, the president of Mutual Life, promoted that view in his testimony before Hughes's committee, calling his corporation "a great beneficent missionary institution." Hughes, who responded, "the question comes back to the salaries of the missionaries," revealed that while Mutual Life's dividends to policyholders had dropped by 20 percent, McCurdy's annual compensation had increased five-fold. All told, the McCurdy family had drawn a startling $15 million from the company (or $375 million in 2017 dollars).[26]

Such excessive self-dealing was possible, Hughes discovered, because the policyholders had no effective way to control corporate management. Even where policyholders had a right to vote in the corporate elections, few ever did; in George Perkins's company, with more than three-quarters of a million policyholders, only twenty-eight had voted in a recent contest. Widely dispersed throughout the nation, the policyholders were rendered powerless by their sheer numbers: they could not be easily organized, and any one vote against management was inconsequential. Nor could policyholders depend on the corporations' directors to safeguard their interests. In the 1890s, insurance company boards had adopted a policy of deference to the firms' chief executives—one that would become commonplace in public corporations in the following decades. Even though the boards of the major insurance companies were a "Who's Who" of New York financial, business, and political elites, the directors acted powerless. "In fine," the Nation observed, "directors do not direct."[27]

Had the policyholders somehow overcome their collective action problem, they faced a series of other hurdles created by the recent corporate law reforms. The "race to the bottom" that began when New Jersey loosened its laws to lure reincorporation by large corporations, like Standard Oil and American Tobacco, translated into increasingly lax rules of corporate governance. Older rules that held managers liable for negligent decision-making were replaced by the "business judgment rule," which effectively immunized management from liability for bad decisions so long as those decisions were made in good faith to serve the business. Shareholders saw their legal right to inspect the books and records diminished. Laws requiring unanimous shareholder consent for fundamental changes in the business were watered down to allow rule by the majority. Even this became a mere formality due to the introduction of preferred shares that lacked voting power and the widespread use of proxy voting in shareholder elections—an innovation traceable to John Winthrop and the Massachusetts Bay Company back in the 1600s. With power concentrated in executives' hands, each company, Hughes concluded, had been turned into "an autocracy, maintained almost without challenge."[28]

Given the separation of ownership and control in the insurance companies, the hurdles facing policyholders were "simply overwhelming," according to Harvard economist Charles J. Bullock, writing in the midst of the scandal. Insurers, Bullock warned, had become typical of "'high finance,' which, whatever its form, always means irresponsible control of other persons' money."[29]

* * *

AMID CHARLES EVANS HUGHES'S discoveries of exorbitant salaries and cronyism in the insurance business in the Great Wall Street
Scandal, the corporate wrongdoing that "most shocked the public"
was George Perkins's revelation that executives were taking from the
till to contribute to political campaigns. This, too, was widely seen as a
form of self-dealing. The contributions were thought to serve the selfish interests of executives rather than the true interests of the companies or their policyholders.[30]

In the public eye, the money given to candidates belonged to the
policyholders. Yet executives had used the policyholders' money to
support political candidates many of the policyholders would not
themselves support. As the *New York Herald* put it, "An insurance
company has a vast number of policy holders of all shades of political
belief. To take money in which a rabid Democrat has a beneficial interest and devote it to the election of a Republican is unfair on its face."
Campaign contributions forced policyholders to associate with partisan politics against their will, and thus were different in kind from
other types of business decisions about how to spend the company's
money, such as whether to open a branch office or launch a marketing
campaign. Political donations also served to undermine the value of
the individual policyholder's own vote. Humorist Finley Peter Dunne
captured it well with "Mr. Dooley," his inimitable Irish working man,
in a piece published shortly after Perkins's testimony: "Th' joke iv it
was that half th' money belonged to dimmycrats. . . Haw, haw! There
they were out West losin' their jobs an' havin' their morgedges fore-
closed all f'r love iv Bryan, an' here was their money down east fightin'
again thim. They beat thimsilves. An' they didn't know it."[31]

The corporate executives involved insisted that the political contributions were just smart business. Echoing Mark Hanna, Perkins said a
company "ought to contribute . . . 25 cents, 50 cents, a dollar or 10 cents
from each policyholder to protect his interests" when threats arose, "as
in the McKinley campaign" to defeat Bryan. Yet if the contributions were
made to protect the policyholders' interests, why were they kept secret,

hidden in the accounting books such that policyholders might never discover them? New York Life had even filed a sworn affidavit to Texas lawmakers denying having made any political contributions. According to Hughes's Final Report, "The devious methods taken to conceal the payments of this sort are confessions of their illicit character."[32]

The facts uncovered by Hughes's committee also undermined the executives' defense that they had given to defeat Bryan. In fact, the companies gave more in the 1904 campaign, in which Bryan was not a candidate, than in the 1896 or 1900 campaigns, in which he was. The Democrats in 1904 had run instead Alton Parker, a bland New York judge, chosen largely because he was the antithesis of the radical, antibusiness, and twice-defeated Bryan. With no shortage of sarcasm, Hughes wondered, "The size of contribution I suppose indicates the remoteness of the danger?"[33]

Questions turned to what benefits the insurance executives were really receiving for their generosity. The suspicion was that the contributions were not to help the company or the policyholders but to help management. Company executives used the money to gain access to elected officials—and to secure favorable legislation that protected them in their jobs. Newspapers seized upon a prominent illustration, the recently enacted reform of New York's insurance law known as "Section 56." The new law required policyholders who wanted to sue insurance executives for breach of their fiduciary duties to first obtain the permission of the state attorney general. This "reform," like the larger changes occurring in corporate law, only made it harder for policyholders to hold management accountable. Parker, whose earlier charge that Roosevelt had received corporate money was vindicated by the Perkins revelations, said the contributions from business were designed to guarantee the "triumph of that party which will better serve [the executives'] personal financial interest and will—for contributions, past, present, and future—continue to protect their interests by lenient legislation." The result was "unfettered management." Old protections that had once guarded the interests of policyholders had been "removed by the legislature at the instigation of the Wall Street insurance corporations and gamblers," noted muckraking journalist B. O. Flowers. Executives had perfect freedom "to use the trust funds of policy holders recklessly and wastefully."[34]

The contributions to Roosevelt were seen in a similar light. In 1905, Republican senator John Dryden of New Jersey had introduced a bill with Roosevelt's backing to give regulatory authority over insurance to the federal government. Insurance had been traditionally regulated by the states, but company executives were growing weary of having to comply with (then) forty-six different state insurance regimes. They backed Dryden's plan, hoping for a set of uniform, national laws through a federal Bureau of Insurance. As Dryden himself admitted, this would "make it so much easier to shape policy." Lest there be any doubt, the companies handpicked the bureau's first would-be superintendent even before the bureau was voted on in Congress. The bill was never passed, in part because life insurance contributions confirmed the suspicion that a federal takeover of insurance law could, in the words of the usually business-friendly *Independent*, "render impregnable the position and power of a comparatively small number of men in the insurance business."[35]

Few people thought that the problems of accountability and political misuse of company money were truly unique to the insurance business. According to the *New York Times*, the money "contributed by the life insurance companies" was "but a drop in the bucket as compared with the total contributions by railroads and other great corporations." The "indications" were that "many insurance secrets are also Wall Street secrets."[36]

* * *

THE EMBODIMENT OF THE populist opposition to Wall Street and big business was Louis D. Brandeis, who was first inspired to focus on the organizational dynamics and dangers of the modern corporation by the Great Wall Street Scandal. Building upon Hughes's discoveries about the nature of political and corporate corruption, Brandeis would become the nation's most astute and nuanced thinker about corporations.

By all accounts brilliant, Brandeis began Harvard Law School at the age of 18, where he received the highest grades in the school's history— a record held until the school changed its grading system nearly eighty years later. Neither his youth nor his Jewish identity affected him in the classroom, although the former did pose a problem when it came time for graduation. Harvard's rules required students to be at least 21 to receive a low degree, and Brandeis was only 20. On the morning of commencement, Brandeis was surprised to learn the faculty had voted to waive the rule and allow him to be graduated with his class. The Harvard professors were only the first to be so impressed by Brandeis to rewrite the rules for him. It would happen again shortly after graduation when, with the backing of the chief justice of the Massachusetts Supreme Court, he was allowed to join the bar without taking an examination. Most notably, it would occur in 1916 when Woodrow Wilson broke from long-standing tradition and nominated Brandeis to become the first Jew on the Supreme Court.[37]

The insurance investigation was a turning point for Brandeis, much as it was for Hughes. After Harvard, Brandeis had opened up a law office in Boston, where he represented local businessmen, such as Edward Filene of the eponymous department store, and worked sporadically on public interest matters. In his free time, he wrote scholarly articles with his law partner, Samuel Warren, on esoteric legal subjects; one was on "the law of ponds." Another article argued for courts to recognize a novel legal right: the "right to privacy." Published in the *Harvard Law Review* in 1890, Brandeis and Warren's right to privacy article has been called "certainly the most influential law review article ever written." After becoming involved with the Great Wall Street Scandal as counsel to the New England Policy-Holders Committee, Brandeis would focus ever more of his time on political activism. The controversy also exposed him to the dynamics of the corporation that would influence his most important intellectual contributions to the understanding of corporate capitalism.[38]

In October of 1905, as Hughes's hearings continued, Brandeis gave a speech at the Commercial Club in Boston, a half-century-old group

INSPIRED BY THE LIFE INSURANCE INVESTIGATION,
LOUIS BRANDEIS ARGUED THAT MODERN
CORPORATIONS WERE TOO BIG AND ALLOWED
EXECUTIVES TO MISUSE OTHER PEOPLE'S MONEY.

formed to promote "the commercial prosperity and growth of the City of Boston." In that speech, Brandeis articulated for the first time the two insights into the modern corporation for which he would become famous: "the curse of bigness" and "other people's money" corruption.[39]

The life insurance companies were becoming dangerously large, Brandeis warned. Like the "Bosses of the Senate" in Keppler's political cartoon, these companies had achieved a size and level of influence dangerous to democracy. Insurance policies were valued at nearly $13 billion, greater than the value of all the nation's railroads combined, and the companies held more than $2.5 billion in assets, three times the combined capital of all of the nation's banks. Annual return on investment for the insurers was more than $600 million, greater than the annual budget of the federal government. Unlike industrial or manufacturing corporations whose assets were "permanently invested in lands, buildings or machinery," the "capital of the life insurance companies, on the other hand, is mainly free capital." This liquidity made insurance companies, more so than even banks, "the creditors of our great industries," with the power to control not only insurance but nearly every other industry. Those "who control these great insurance companies" exert "a predominating influence upon the business of the country."[40]

Eventually, Brandeis would expand his criticism beyond insurance companies and apply it more generally to large corporations and the trusts, like Standard Oil and American Tobacco. He became nothing less than the "most influential critic of trusts during his generation." Brandeis was convinced that huge, industry-dominant corporations were less efficient than smaller firms. In an era of unprecedented consolidation, nearly all segments of the marketplace were being controlled by one company or a few companies acting in concert. Brandeis, like Roosevelt, feared these firms became dominant not through natural growth but through market manipulation and the stifling of competition. Small-scale entrepreneurs, who in Brandeis's view gave the American economy its traditional vitality and innovative edge, were being squeezed out. Moreover, companies were becoming so large and their businesses so diverse that no one could gain the necessary expertise to manage them well. Indeed, the same group of investment bankers was effectively directing the major companies in nearly all industries through interlocking directorates, leading to poor service at excessive cost.[41]

Yet for the populist Brandeis, intellectual heir to Jefferson, the evils of enormity were not primarily economic; they were moral. Great size was noxious to democracy and individual liberty. "Half a century ago, nearly every American boy could look forward to becoming independent as a farmer or mechanic, in business or professional life," Brandeis explained in a congressional hearing a few years after the Great Wall Street Scandal. "Today, most American boys" were destined to "work in some capacity as employees of others." As a result, they will not build up strong and independent characters, forsaking freedom to make a living. "There cannot be liberty without industrial independence," he believed, "and the greatest danger to the people of the United States is in becoming, as they are gradually more and more, a class of employees."[42]

Focusing on the curse of bigness also helped Brandeis to differentiate between "good" corporations and "bad." Hardly the socialist critic of capitalism some of his opponents assumed, he was instead a Jeffersonian convinced of the virtues of economic and political decentralization. He saw his reform agenda as necessary to prevent the United States from falling victim to the socialistic and revolutionary zeal cascading through Europe at the turn of the century. American workers and consumers were accustomed to liberty and self-direction, two victims of the industrial workplace, where authority was concentrated in the hands of supervisors. In the absence of reform, the disempowered would eventually demand more and more benefits from the government. By refusing to change, Brandeis told the crowd at the Commercial Club, the "great captains of industry and finance" were "the chief makers of socialism."[43]

Brandeis's most famous explanation of the curse of bigness came decades later, when he was a justice on the Supreme Court. In *Louis K. Liggett Company v. Lee*, decided in 1933 near the end of his tenure, he dissented from the court's decision to invalidate a Florida law designed to limit the spread of chain stores. Brandeis argued that the law should be upheld because the rise of national chains, "by furthering the concentration of wealth and power" and reducing competition, was "thwarting American ideals; that it is making impossible equality of opportunity; that it is converting independent tradesmen into clerks; and that it is sapping the resources, the vigor, and the hope of the small cities and towns." Due to these "giant corporations," he wrote, "individual initiative and effort are being paralyzed." Invoking a metaphor that would capture how many in his day viewed the large corporation, Brandeis warned of a "Frankenstein monster" over which the people, the corporation's creators, were losing control.[44]

Besides the size of the new modern corporations, Brandeis was also concerned about their internal organization—and how it enabled management to misuse other people's money. In 1914, Brandeis would publish a collection of essays on these issues under the title *Other People's Money: And How the Bankers Use It*, which became an instant classic and remains an iconic analysis of why and how American corporate finance and management should be reformed. Yet it was nine years earlier, in his reflections at the Commercial Club, that he initially identified the problem. The Great Wall Street Scandal had exposed that executives of the great insurance companies were using the policyholders' money against the policyholders' interests. The "American people have entrusted to the managers of these large companies" their savings, which have since been used "selfishly" and "dishonestly," through "exorbitant salaries," "persistent perversion of sacred trust funds to political purposes," and an "elaborate system of fraud" in bookkeeping.[45]

While Brandeis became the most famous critic of "other people's money" corruption, the notion was not new. The same concern was raised about the very first English stock corporation, the Muscovy Company of 1555. The company's innovative approach to raising money through the sale of stock was the brainchild of Sebastian Cabot, who was not a financier but, rather, an explorer. He sought to raise funds to finance an expedition to establish a trade route from England to Russia through the icy northern seas. Unlike Christopher Columbus, who relied upon an "elaborate array of sponsors and patrons" to finance his voyages, Cabot adapted a practice he had witnessed in Italy, where groups of people bought little pieces, or shares, of a business and would divide the profits. When Cabot proposed to do the same for his venture, business traditionalists scoffed, predicting he would squander away the investors' money. Nonetheless, with few other investment options, English merchants and notables bought up the full issue of shares. Cabot still faced hardships, such as when one of his first ships was shipwrecked in Lapland, only to be found a year later with the crewmen's bodies frozen in place. Yet he established the trade route, and the Muscovy Company gained a monopoly on Russian furs, tallow, and other commodities. The investors who took a

chance on Cabot were richly rewarded; the first English stock corporation remained in operation for nearly four hundred years, felled finally
by the Russian Revolution of 1917.[46]

Concern about corporate leaders misusing other people's money
reached a new level of urgency in the years surrounding the Great Wall
Street Scandal. Insurance companies held in trust the money of millions of people, giving executives more money to play with than ever
before and increasing exponentially the number of victims. Insurance companies, however, were not the only corporations financed
with other people's money. The decade before Brandeis's speech to the
Commercial Club saw an unprecedented rise in stock ownership by
the public. The aggregate value of stocks and bonds of corporations
listed on the country's major exchanges went from under $1 billion in
1898 to over $7 billion only four years later. The number of companies
listed on the exchanges increased just as dramatically. Nearly everyone
with money to invest wanted to share in the gains. Taking advantage
of this growing demand for stock were two reporters, Charles Dow
and Edward Jones, who in 1889 launched a daily newsletter of stock
prices and information about public companies they called the *Wall
Street Journal*.[47]

By focusing on the misuse of other people's money, Brandeis added
important nuance to the Progressive era's uprising against the large
corporation. The trusts and other big businesses of the era were not
just the overwhelmingly powerful titans of industry portrayed in Keppler's "Bosses of the Senate." They also posed a threat to the people
within them—the members, like policyholders and stockholders—
from managerial misconduct. Because of the way these organizations
raised money, ordinary Americans had become an integral part of
them. The people provided the financing that made corporate corruption possible. Their savings and investments were the electric charge
that pulsed the Frankenstein monster to life. Brandeis's realization
was essentially that, if one looked closely, Keppler's titans were actually made up of millions of tiny, ordinary people. We the people had
become we the corporations.

* * *

IN FEBRUARY OF 1906, four months after Brandeis's speech, Hughes's committee issued its Final Report on the insurance investigation, charging the companies with both political and financial corruption. It was not merely that campaign spending enhanced the power of the corporations. The corruption was a modern sort that emerged from changes in the corporate form itself. Echoing Brandeis, the report warned that the separation of ownership from control in modern corporations allowed executive officers to use other people's money "virtually as their own." Political expenditures by corporations were wrong, and Hughes offered a populist solution: corporate political spending should "be expressly prohibited and treated as a waste of corporate moneys."[48]

President Roosevelt, eager to salvage his public image, agreed. The day after Perkins's testimony about corporate campaign contributions, Roosevelt met with his top advisors to begin plotting a response. At first the administration insisted that even if the campaign had received corporate money, Roosevelt had never been influenced by the gifts. When that did not dampen the public outrage, Roosevelt endorsed Hughes's recommendation. "All contributions by corporations to any political committee or for any political purpose should be forbidden by law," Roosevelt announced in his State of the Union address of December 1905. Roosevelt rested his justification on the concerns about other people's money revealed by the Great Wall Street Scandal and described by Brandeis in his speech at the Commercial Club: "Directors should not be permitted to use stockholders' money for such purposes."[49]

In Congress, the corporate contribution ban proposed by Hughes and endorsed by Roosevelt was sponsored by an unlikely ally to either man, South Carolina senator "Pitchfork" Ben Tillman. A natural showman who earned his nickname after a speech threatening to poke President Grover Cleveland, a fellow Democrat, with a farm tool, Tillman despised Roosevelt. Part of the reason was partisan politics,

AFTER USING CORPORATE MONEY TO WIN REELECTION,
PRESIDENT THEODORE ROOSEVELT PROPOSED A BAN ON
CORPORATE MONEY IN ELECTIONS TO SALVAGE HIS
TRUST-BUSTING PUBLIC IMAGE.

but Tillman's racism also had something to do with it; he bristled at Roosevelt's daring to dine at the White House in 1901 with Booker T. Washington, the leading African American intellectual of his day. Like many southern Democrats, Tillman hated federal legislation almost as much as he hated racial minorities, arguing often for states' rights and limited federal power. Yet, like many states' rights advocates before and since, Tillman could be a fair-weather federalist. A federal law banning corporations from making any monetary contributions to federal campaigns was an opportunity to rub salt in Roosevelt's wound and make it harder for the Republican Party, and the Yankees who ran the nation's largest business corporations, to control Congress.[50]

Enacted in 1907, the Tillman Act was landmark legislation on money in politics. Outside of civil service reform, the Tillman Act was the first significant effort by Congress to regulate how money was raised or spent in election campaigns. The ban set a precedent for federal regulation of campaign finance that would be followed repeatedly in the years to come: the Publicity Act of 1910, which required disclosure of certain contributions; the Taft-Hartley Act of 1947, which prohibited contributions from labor unions; the Federal Election Campaigns Acts of 1971 and 1974, which imposed contribution and spending limits; and the Bipartisan Campaign Reform Act of 2002, whose restrictions on independent expenditures by corporations would be challenged in *Citizens United*. The Tillman Act also demarcated a clear limit to the political rights of corporations: they had no right to influence electoral politics. The public outcry from Perkins's revelations would also propel a wave of similar legislation at the state level banning corporate spending in state elections.

The Great Wall Street Scandal would also launch Hughes's distinguished career. Although Hughes might have worried about being blacklisted by an angry Republican establishment, his service on the committee had the opposite effect. Seeking to take back the initiative after the embarrassing discoveries, the Republican Party, like Roosevelt himself, embraced the cause of reform. The same year the Tillman Act was signed into law, Hughes, just two years from being a little-known corporate lawyer, was elected governor of New York as a Republican. Soon after, there were rumors that Hughes would be a viable candidate for president of the United States in 1908. He did not run, although he was asked by William Howard Taft to be his vice president. In 1910, he accepted another offer from Taft instead, this one to join the Supreme Court of the United States. Like campaign finance law, Hughes's historic career was just beginning.

* * *

AT THE SAME TIME Congress and the states were enacting campaign finance laws to limit the political spending of corporations, the Supreme Court was once again confronting questions about the constitutional rights of corporations. The issue before the high court in 1907, the year of the Tillman Act, was not whether corporations could be prohibited from making political contributions. The question instead was whether corporations had the freedom of association. The court's opinion in that case and a series of other freedom of association cases would nonetheless influence how the courts would rule on the constitutionality of the campaign finance restrictions on corporations a decade later.

Although the Supreme Court had held that corporations had only property rights but not liberty rights, corporations still pushed the justices to extend to businesses liberty rights, such as the freedom of association. The 1907 case involved the Western Turf Association, a company that operated horse tracks, which sought a declaration that corporations have a fundamental right to associate only with those with whom they wished to do business. The specific person Western Turf did not want to associate with was Hyman Greenberg, a racing form publisher the company forcibly ejected from its state-of-the-art racetrack at Tanforan in San Mateo County, California. Western Turf already had an exclusive contract with another racing form provider, but California law prohibited places of public amusement from denying admission to any person of age with a valid ticket. The company challenged the law, claiming it interfered with the corporation's right to control whom it does business with. Forcing the company to admit Greenberg was the equivalent of allowing a "newspaper reporter to force his way into a private reception."[51]

The Supreme Court, however, ruled in favor of Greenberg. The justices in *Western Turf Association v. Greenberg* held that equal access laws do not infringe corporations' rights. This was not a property right, the court explained, and even if it were, California was within its traditional power to regulate property "not only for the public health, the public morals, and the public safety, but for the general or common good, for the wellbeing, comfort, and good order of the people." The right here was a liberty right, one associated with personal freedom and autonomy. And the Constitution refers, the court said, only to "the liberty of natural, not artificial persons." The Court's decision not only affirmed the distinction between property and liberty rights, but also provided an important precedent for later civil rights laws mandating equal access to public accommodations and places of public amusement.[52]

The next year, 1908, the freedom of association returned to the court in *Berea College v. Kentucky*. While the Western Turf Association had business reasons motivating its constitutional claims, Berea College in Kentucky had moral ones. At the time, the college, which was organized as a corporation like one of the earliest corporate rights litigants, Dartmouth College, was the only racially integrated school in the South. After Roosevelt's fateful dinner with Booker T. Washington at the White House, Kentucky lawmakers hardened their segregationist resolve and passed a law prohibiting any school from having a racially integrated student body. The college challenged the law on various grounds, including interference with its right to choose its own students. It was unconstitutional, the college argued, to prohibit "the voluntary association of persons of different races" absent compelling reasons.[53]

Kentucky's defense rested on the Supreme Court's embrace of racial segregation a dozen years earlier in *Plessy v. Ferguson* (1896). Just as the court then had upheld a law requiring racially segregated railway cars, now the justices should affirm Kentucky's authority to require racially segregated schools. Although the relatively enlightened leaders of the college would probably have liked to see *Plessy* overturned, their lawyers had to accept the decision for purposes of Berea's case. They told the justices that Kentucky's law should be struck down despite *Plessy*. The difference in the two cases, the lawyers argued, was that unlike Kentucky's law, the law in *Plessy* was designed to protect white people from being forced to associate involuntarily with people of other races. In other words, the law in *Plessy* might be seen to further associational freedom rather than restrict it. Kentucky's law, by contrast, prevented Berea's students, all of whom attended voluntarily, from associating with people of their choice.[54]

The court upheld Kentucky's law and rejected Berea College's assertion of the freedom of association. The opinion was written by

Justice David Brewer, Stephen Field's nephew and one of the foremost advocates of the liberty of contract jurisprudence. Although the educational corporation's claims might be valid if raised by an individual, the state was "under no obligation to treat both alike," Brewer wrote. "In creating a corporation a State may withhold powers which may be exercised by and cannot be denied to an individual." The unique nature of the corporate form justified distinct treatment. Corporations, for one, had charters granted by the state that were subject to revision by the legislature. (Although corporate charters were deemed inviolate contracts by the Supreme Court in the *Dartmouth College* case in 1819, Kentucky had followed the advice of Justice Joseph Story's concurring opinion in that case and explicitly reserved the power to amend charters.) Here, Brewer held, all Kentucky had done was to amend Berea College's charter. The argument was a stretch, as the law never even mentioned the college's charter much less purported to revise it. Yet the decision was consistent with the broader framework articulated by the court in previous corporate rights cases of the *Lochner* era: corporations had property rights, not liberty rights.[55]

* * *

NO LIBERTY RIGHT IS more important to a nation committed to democratic self-governance than the right to speak freely about electoral politics. In *Citizens United*, the Supreme Court held that corporations enjoyed this constitutional right, but the issue first arose nearly a century earlier, in the 1910s, when corporations first challenged the bans on corporate contributions to political campaigns enacted in the wake of the Great Wall Street Scandal. The trigger for those earlier challenges was the temperance movement. As advocates pushed for local referendums to ban alcohol, brewing companies fought back against the measures by making illegal expenditures. When they were prosecuted, the corporations became constitutional first movers, asserting for the first time that laws restricting money in politics violated the freedom of speech. Although the issue did not reach the Supreme Court, the state and lower federal courts did confront the question of free speech rights for corporations long before *Citizens United*.

Within the liquor industry, the beer companies had been the most politically active, even before temperance began to take hold. During the Civil War, when President Abraham Lincoln proposed a tax on malt liquors to help defray the costs of the fight, beer makers mobilized to form the nation's first trade group to lobby against the proposal. The United States Brewers Association was not able to defeat the tax, but its political engagement from then on paid dividends. Although Congress repeatedly raised taxes on distilled spirits in the years that followed, the tax on malt liquors remained low.[56]

One impact of the relatively low taxes on beer as compared to other forms of alcohol was a vast increase in beer sales. Between 1860 and 1900, the annual consumption of beer per adult rose dramatically from five gallons to twenty-three gallons. The beer companies were also helped by technological inventions of the Gilded Age, such as pasteurization and artificial refrigeration, both of which extended the shelf life of beer and enabled national distribution. Business boomed—but so did the backlash against alcohol in the form of temperance advocacy. With Carrie Nation quite literally using her hatchet to wreck saloons in the Midwest, the movement to restrict alcohol won headlines and gained political momentum. Nation's home state of Kansas was the first to outlaw alcohol in 1881. By 1912, eight other states had followed suit, along with individual counties in more than half the other states.[57]

Nonetheless, the Brewers Association remained focused on keeping beer taxes low, more or less ignoring the growing push for alcohol restrictions—at least until 1913. That year Congress passed the Webb-Kenyon Act, making it illegal to ship alcohol into dry states and counties. The law spurred efforts for national prohibition and woke the brewers to the seriousness of the threat. The beer companies, operating on their own or through the auspices of the Brewers Association, committed to becoming more politically active in trying to defeat prohibition. They began to spend corporate money on campaigns, even though such expenditures were illegal under the Tillman Act and similar state laws.[58]

The Lansing Brewing Company was one of the beer makers that

made illegal corporate contributions. When Ingham County, Michigan, held a local option election in 1914, Jacob Gansley, an officer and director of the company, secretly gave $500 of the corporation's money to the Personal Liberty League, the organization leading the opposition. Gansley was convicted of violating Michigan's campaign finance laws and, in his appeal, asserted that the ban on corporate campaign spending was unconstitutional. Corporations, he argued, had the same free speech right as individuals "to make such lawful expenditures as may be necessary to protect their interests" in elections.[59]

The Michigan Supreme Court in *People v. Gansley* ruled against the company. The court's opinion in the 1916 case was authored by Chief Justice John W. Stone, a populist when it came to corporations and someone who happened to know quite a bit about political campaigns, having run for elective office no fewer than seven times. Although he understood the value of campaign spending to promote a political agenda, Stone emphasized the differences between natural persons and corporations when it came to elections. If "the stockholders and officers of the Lansing Brewing Company desire, as individuals, to contribute to the campaign fund, it was their privilege so to do." They were entitled to "freely speak, write, and publish their views." The company itself, however, had "no right to participate in the elective franchise." Borrowing the distinction previously made by the Supreme Court, Stone explained that the law here did not interfere with property rights and that the constitutional guarantee in question, a liberty right, "relates to natural and not artificial persons." "The Lansing Brewing Company was created under our statute," Stone concluded succinctly, not for political purposes but "for the purpose of manufacturing beer."[60]

Beer makers also challenged the federal Tillman Act in another case arising out of the 1914 elections, *United States v. United States Brewers Association*. To support "wet" candidates, the Brewers Association and more than seventy beer companies made contributions to candidates for federal office—in clear violation of the Tillman Act. The brewers argued that the ban on corporate contributions "violated the first amendment of the constitution, in that it attempts to prohibit,

Beer is Food

Beer is Food

Lansing Brewing Co.

Manufacture it from Purest
of Hops and Malt.

PURE, HEALTHFUL *and* INVIGORATING

Try our AMBER CREAM
Bottled Beer

IT SUITS THE MOST FASTIDIOUS

Brewery: *Cor. Turner and Clinton Sts.*
BOTH PHONES

LANSING, MICH.

ADVERTISEMENT FOR THE LANSING BREWING COMPANY, WHICH
CHALLENGED A BAN ON CORPORATE MONEY IN ELECTIONS
ALMOST A CENTURY BEFORE *CITIZENS UNITED*.

make criminal, and punish, the freedom of speech and of the press
in the discussion of candidates and of political questions involved in
such elections." The federal court disagreed. Although the court was
not convinced that campaign finance laws burdened speech rights
at all—modern free speech doctrine would only arise in the years to
follow—it also emphasized the differences between corporations and
individuals when it came to participating in elections. Echoing Roger
Taney, the federal court said that corporations "are not citizens of the
United States, and, so far as the franchise is concerned, must at all
times be held subservient to the government and the citizenship of
which it is composed." Spending money to influence elections was,

like the right to vote, one of the central "means of participation in the government," and as such was limited to natural people. Individuals had a right to vote but the "time has not come," the court noted wryly, "when the right of suffrage will be extended to the artificial beings known as corporations."[61]

Even though these early cases on political rights for corporations were brought during the *Lochner* era, the courts nonetheless ruled consistently against the corporations. The Great Wall Street Scandal of 1905 had prompted Congress and state legislatures to prohibit corporate money in elections to combat corruption, and the courts agreed that such laws were justifiable restrictions. In both the legislatures and the courts, corporations were viewed as fundamentally different from ordinary individuals when it came to questions of democratic participation. That understanding would remain the law of the land for almost a hundred years, until *Citizens United*.

* * *

TODAY, THE SCANDAL TOUCHED off by Charles Evans Hughes's interrogation of George Perkins has been largely lost to popular memory. Although the discovery of corporate campaign contributions to Theodore Roosevelt threatened to undermine the trustbuster's legacy, the controversy is mentioned only in passing, if at all, in many of his biographies. Roosevelt saved his image, in part by proposing groundbreaking legislation to ban corporate money in federal elections. His success in that effort was highlighted by the very fact that, despite his reelection campaign's reliance on sizeable corporate gifts, he is still remembered today as a crusader against big business and the trusts.[62]

Like Roosevelt, Perkins too was only set back temporarily by the scandal—although it seemed much more calamitous for him at first. Held up as the embodiment of political corruption, Perkins, who was forced to quit his job at New York Life, was attacked from the pulpit in Sunday sermons and from columns in the daily papers. He was also brought up on criminal charges by New York District Attorney William Travers Jerome, who had previously prosecuted Edwin Hale for stealing money from MacAndrews & Forbes. Perkins was also charged with stealing company money, and using it to further the personal interests of New York Life's executives rather than the business interests of the company.[63]

Perkins escaped jail, however, when the New York Court of Appeals threw out Jerome's charges. The court said Perkins had not had the requisite criminal intent, given that the expenditures had been authorized by the company's board. Moreover, the contributions took place before such donations were explicitly banned by laws like the Tillman Act, so Perkins could not be prosecuted for violating campaign finance rules. Instead, the court said that policyholders would have to find recourse in corporate law for what the judges readily termed a "misappropriation" of company funds. What the judges left unstated, however, was that late nineteenth-century reforms in corporate law had only further separated ownership from control, making it harder than ever to hold management accountable for such wrongdoing.[64]

Perkins's friends, including Roosevelt, stuck by him through the difficult years. He remained a Morgan partner until 1910, when he decided to focus his energies away from business and toward electoral politics. He went from being Morgan's right-hand man to Roosevelt's, and became the strategist behind the former president's bolt from the Republican Party to form the Bull Moose Party in 1912. Even though their quixotic effort divided the Republican vote and helped lead to Woodrow Wilson's victory—only the second Democrat elected president in half a century—Perkins was nonetheless welcomed back into the GOP. Few others could match his shrewdness and connections. In the election of 1916, Perkins even mustered the courage to endorse and campaign for the GOP presidential nominee of that year, the man who had disregarded Perkins's warning and brought him years of public humiliation, Charles Evans Hughes.[65]

Hughes had to resign from the Supreme Court to run. For all his intellectual and prosecutorial gifts, however, Hughes was a poor campaigner and, in an upset, lost by only a few thousand votes to the incumbent Wilson. The lesson of his failed candidacy—that the judicial temperament is ill-suited to the rigors of the type of modern, commercial-style campaign first envisioned by Mark Hanna—

would discourage future Supreme Court justices from running for national executive office. (William O. Douglas came closest in 1940 and 1944 when he was considered for vice president by Franklin Roosevelt.) Losing the presidency and a lifetime seat on the Supreme Court within months of each other, however, did not seem to faze the gifted Hughes. Like a cat with nine lives, he would go on to serve as secretary of state to two presidents and, in 1930, would be appointed again to the Supreme Court of the United States, this time as chief justice.

When Hughes was confirmed the second time, the leading voice of anticorporate populism on the high court was Louis Brandeis. Nominated by Wilson in 1916, Brandeis owed his nomination to Perkins and Roosevelt's foolhardy third-party campaign in 1912. Brandeis and Hughes, the two men who together had helped inspire the restrictions on corporate power of the early twentieth century, served together for nine years. Like so many of their predecessors, they too would confront the perennial question of constitutional rights for corporations. Given their backgrounds, the two might have been expected to vote without hesitation to limit corporate rights. Yet the same progressive impulses that led them to push for new limits on corporations around the time of the Great Wall Street Scandal would lead them to do precisely the opposite in the 1930s. As we will see, they would ultimately vote to expand corporate rights, including the right to free speech. Paradoxically, Brandeis and Hughes would help break down the *Lochner* court's distinction between property rights and liberty rights, and further set the course of the Constitution toward *Citizens United*.

PART FOUR

THE RISE OF LIBERTY RIGHTS FOR CORPORATIONS

—

IN THE TWENTIETH CENTURY, CORPORATIONS WON
LIBERTY RIGHTS, SUCH AS FREEDOM OF SPEECH AND
RELIGION, WITH THE HELP OF ORGANIZATIONS LIKE
THE CHAMBER OF COMMERCE.

—

CHAPTER 7

Discrete and Insular Corporations

THE SUPREME COURT HAS DECIDED OVER 32,500 CASES AND published more than 25,500 majority opinions, filling up nearly 600 hefty volumes of the *United States Reports*. Yet arguably the most important words ever written by the court can be found in a single footnote. That footnote, which came in a 1938 case little known outside of law schools, led to *Brown v. Board of Education*, invalidating racial segregation; *Reynolds v. Sims*, establishing one person, one vote; and *Obergefell v. Hodges*, guaranteeing same-sex couples the right to marry. Lawyers and judges know footnote number four in *United States v. Carolene Products Company* to be the germinal seed of modern constitutional law. The footnote marks the end of the *Lochner* era, when the court devoted itself mainly to protecting economic and property rights, and the beginning of the *Brown* era, when the court's primary role became protecting civil rights and civil liberties.[1]

The footnote in question was written by Justice Harlan Fiske Stone, a former corporate lawyer and dean of Columbia Law School, who was nominated to the court in 1925 by his college roommate, President Calvin Coolidge. Their long friendship was not the sole reason Coolidge chose Stone; the president fully expected his old friend to share his pro-business leanings. Indeed, one senator opposed Stone's confirmation precisely because the nominee had "spent all his life in an atmosphere of big business, of corporations, of monopolies, and of trusts." Yet, once confirmed, Stone disagreed with most of his *Lochner* court colleagues about the need to strike down regulations on business. "Courts are not the only agency of government that must be assumed to have the capacity to govern," Stone argued. Elected officials too should be allowed room to experiment with economic policy. Endorsing "self-restraint," Stone insisted that for "unwise laws . . . appeal lies, not to the courts, but to the ballot and to the processes of democratic government."[2]

Stone's view was reflected in footnote four, which suggested that when it came to economic matters, the "political processes . . . can ordinarily be expected to bring about repeal of undesirable legislation." If lawmakers enact bad laws, the people and interest groups adversely affected by them will have incentive to lobby, advocate, and vote for change. Because we can usually rely on the democratic process in those circumstances, there is little need for the courts to second-guess lawmakers. In another set of cases, however, Stone's footnote proposed a more active role for the court. Where, for example, a law restricts the normal operation of the political processes, such as by restricting the free discussion of ideas, the court should exercise very careful scrutiny and strike down the law if necessary to reopen the pathways of democracy. The court ought to play a similarly aggressive role, the footnote offered, when reviewing laws targeting "discrete and insular minorities," who are too often and too easily subject to persecution by the majority.[3]

When Stone wrote about political persecution, he was not just referring to racial minorities; he also meant political minorities, like those Stone had witnessed being silenced in the 1910s. After the Russian Revolution of 1917, a red scare swept the nation; socialists, labor activists, anarchists, and immigrants were targeted for prosecution and deportation, usually for little more than speaking out against World War I. At Columbia, Stone fought attempts by Nicholas M. Butler, the university's domineering president, to purge the faculty of socialists; Stone later said that Butler believed "true academic free-

JUSTICE HARLAN FISKE STONE WROTE THE LANDMARK
FOOTNOTE THAT RESHAPED AMERICAN LAW AND HELPED
JUSTIFY THE GRADUAL EXTENSION OF LIBERTY RIGHTS TO
CORPORATIONS.

dom is identical with that of a citizen in the German Reich—the freedom to do what he is told by his Fuehrer and entourage." In 1920,
Stone drafted a resolution on behalf of the New York City Bar Association criticizing the New York Assembly for suspending five duly
elected members because of their socialist views. He also served on
the War Department's Board of Inquiry, which adjudicated claims
of conscientious objectors, and came to appreciate the war dissenters' sincerity even if he disagreed with their tactics. The lesson Stone
learned was that while lawmakers could reliably make economic policy, they could not be trusted to preserve the rights of political outcasts and minorities.[4]

Although Stone may have had racial minorities and socialist radicals in mind, corporations too would claim to be the victims of politi-

cal persecution. The most important early illustration of this came in the 1930s, and the corporations involved were political dissenters—newspaper companies that Huey Long, the infamous "Kingfish" of Louisiana, tried to silence for opposing him. The newspapers challenged Long's efforts by asserting a constitutional right to freedom of speech and of the press. Although this right had been held to be a "liberty" right, the newspapers' case arrived at the Supreme Court at an advantageous time. For the first time, the justices were reading the First Amendment vibrantly and calling into question laws designed to silence political radicals. The newspapers' case became wrapped up in the court's larger commitment to fighting government censorship, and the court abandoned the distinction made in the *Lochner* years between property rights and liberty rights. Nearly seventy-five years before *Citizens United*, the Supreme Court held that newspaper corporations had First Amendment rights.

* * *

IT TOOK AN IRREPRESSIBLE DEMAGOGUE like Huey Long to make Louisiana's major newspaper companies look like victims of political repression. Like Jefferson, Jackson, and Bryan before him, Long, the fiery, outspoken, 34-year-old governor of Louisiana, was a populist who denounced big corporations and a political system skewed against the common man. Elected in 1928 by the largest margin of victory in the state's history, Long pursued an impressive array of reforms to serve a population mired in abject poverty: new schools, free textbooks, paved roads, bridges, university expansion, and old-age pensions. Yet Long was also an autocrat who exercised near complete control over all aspects of state government and harbored no tolerance for dissent. He was the Kingfish, and when Louisiana's big city newspapers refused to support his policies, Long determined to silence them.[5]

When Long was elected, Louisiana had a large number of newspapers, 163 in all. Most were weeklies with small circulations in the state's predominantly rural parishes; these papers supported Long throughout his tenure. Yet a rift opened up almost immediately

LOUISIANA GOVERNOR HUEY LONG SOUGHT TO PERSECUTE
HIS OPPONENTS, INCLUDING MEDIA CORPORATIONS.

between Long and the major urban dailies, such as the *New Orleans Times-Picayune*, the *Baton Rouge Morning Advocate*, and the *Shreveport Times*, largely over how to tax the state's biggest corporation and largest employer, Standard Oil. The once legendary monopoly was no longer the national political powerhouse it had been before being broken up, but it remained Louisiana's largest employer and one of the few businesses not devastated by the economic crisis of 1929. To finance his expensive education reforms, Long proposed to raise taxes on oil. The urban papers, especially those in Baton Rouge, where Standard Oil had its biggest refinery, came out against Long's proposal, warning it would lead to a spike in unemployment at a time of serious economic instability. Long was outraged.[6]

Long fought dirty, and after Capital City Press, the publisher of the *Baton Rouge Morning Advocate*, came out against the tax, Long tried to blackmail the company's owner and editor, Charles Manship. "Cut out those spite editorials," Long warned Manship, whose brother was in a state-run psychiatric asylum, "or I'll get out a statement that will hurt you." Manship refused to back down and Long—if nothing else, true to his word—leaked to friendly reporters that syphilis had driven the newspaper man's brother mad.[7]

Long's outrageous attempt to blackmail Capital City was said to have "aroused the indignation of every newspaper man in the state." The major dailies turned against the governor and began portraying him as a tyrant. The *Morning Advocate* called Long a "conscience-less" and "dangerous" official who relied on "graft, corruption and debauchery"; the *Times-Picayune* wrote that he was an "unbalanced dictator" eager "to set up a personal despotism as irresponsible and oppressive" as those emerging in post–World War I Europe. The *New Orleans States* went so far as to label Long a "liar, crook, petty larceny thief and scoundrel." Only a year into Long's governorship, the urban papers began calling for his impeachment.[8]

Long beat the impeachment effort and immediately declared war on the state's biggest newspaper companies. "These daily newspapers have been against every progressive step in the state," he said, "and the only way for the people of Louisiana to get ahead is to stomp them flat." Stomping on opponents is what Long did best. When public officials in Shreveport sought state approval to acquire land for an airbase, Long refused, complaining that the city's papers treated him poorly. His machine established a state board of censors to review movies and newsreels. He set up another state board to select which papers would carry official government notices, and let it be known that papers that opposed him would be excluded. Several papers dependent upon that revenue abruptly stopped discussing political issues altogether. In an incident that gained national attention, Long threatened to shut down the Louisiana State University newspaper after it published an unflattering article about him: "I'm not going to stand for any students criticizing Huey Long."[9]

The centerpiece of Long's attack on the press was an advertising tax on large-circulation newspapers enacted in 1934. By then, Long had left the governor's mansion to become a senator, but as contemporaries recognized, "his grasp upon the destinies of the state [was] stronger than it ever was." Long returned from Washington to oversee passage of the advertising tax law, moving the sitting governor out of his office to manage the vote. Louisiana Act No. 23 imposed a 2 percent tax on advertising receipts for periodicals with a weekly circulation of 20,000 or more. The circulation threshold meant that the small, rural weekly newspapers that tended to support Long—about 150 of the 163 total papers in the state—were exempt. The tax burden was shouldered solely by the 13 largest urban dailies, like Manship's *Morning Advocate*, all but one of which had opposed Long.[10]

On the floor of the state legislature, the advertising tax was justified as a measure to raise revenue for the state to finance educational reforms, like free textbooks for schools. The Louisiana strongman, however, offered his own, more censorial justification, saying the "lying newspapers should have to pay for their lying." "I'm going to help these newspapers by hitting them in their pocketbooks," he explained. "Maybe then they'll try to clean up." In a widely distributed political circular, Long said that the "big Louisiana newspapers tell a lie every time they make a dollar. This tax should be called a tax on lying, two cents per lie."[11]

Manship's *Morning Advocate* complained that Long's advertising tax was a threat to free speech and the free press. Long intended the tax to intimidate the newspapers into supporting the government orthodoxy, with the implicit threat of even higher taxes for any future dissent. If Long could impose special taxes on newspapers for opposing him, the *Morning Advocate* editorialized, "the guarantee of a free press, written in the Constitution of the United States, is at an end."

In fact, however, the Supreme Court was only first breathing life into the Constitution's guarantees of freedom of speech and freedom of the press in the 1930s. And corporations would play an influential role in the rise of judicial protection of these fundamental rights.

* * *

ALTHOUGH THE FIRST AMENDMENT is central to America's legal identity, the Supreme Court did not vibrantly protect the freedom of speech or the freedom of the press until the twentieth century. While there had long been considerable debate about freedom of expression—including the brewing companies' challenges to the Tillman Act and similar state bans on corporate campaign contributions—World War I was a turning point. In response to the silencing and persecution of political dissenters, the court began to invigorate the First Amendment. Among the dissidents who inspired the court were the Louisiana newspaper corporations.[12]

One reason for the long delay between the adoption of the First Amendment in 1791 and the court's embrace of the freedom of expression in the early twentieth century was the text of the Constitution. It says, *"Congress* shall pass no law," suggesting that it applies only to federal laws, not to laws passed by the state or local governments. For much of American history, the federal government did not regulate speech very often, and when it did the courts usually refused to interfere. First in 1798 and then again during World War I, with the Espionage Act of 1917 and the Sedition Act of 1918, Congress did enact laws making "disloyal" speech a crime.[13]

President Woodrow Wilson aggressively enforced the law, rounding up socialists, radicals, and pacifists, especially in immigrant communities. More than 1,500 people were prosecuted, including labor leader and four-time presidential candidate Eugene Debs; he ran his fifth campaign from a prison cell after the Supreme Court upheld his ten-year sentence for making a speech against the draft. A movie producer was even sentenced to ten years for a film about the American Revolution because it portrayed Britain, now an ally, in a negative light. The federal prosecution of political dissenters also justified similar repression by state and local governments, by industry, and even by universities—as Harlan Fiske Stone discovered as dean of Columbia law school. Historians remember the World War I crackdown on dissent as "one of the greatest restrictions on civil liberties in American history."[14]

The experience with political persecution during the World War I era opened the eyes of many Americans to the dangers of censorship. Among them was Supreme Court justice Oliver Wendell Holmes Jr.

Appointed by Teddy Roosevelt, Holmes voted to uphold restrictions on speech and the press early in his tenure. In 1907, for example, Holmes wrote the majority opinion for the Supreme Court in *Patterson v. Colorado* upholding a conviction of a newspaper publisher for publishing critical articles and cartoons about state judges. The purpose of the freedom of the press, Holmes said then, was to prohibit only prior restraints on publication and did "not prevent subsequent punishment" of publishers for publishing articles "deemed contrary to the public welfare." With the World War I prosecutions of political minorities, however, Holmes's views began to evolve, and American attitudes toward freedom of expression would soon follow.[15]

Holmes began to articulate a new, more vibrant vision for the First

JUSTICE OLIVER WENDELL HOLMES BREATHED LIFE
INTO THE FIRST AMENDMENT'S GUARANTEES OF
FREEDOM OF SPEECH AND OF THE PRESS.

Amendment in the case of Jacob Abrams, a Jewish immigrant from Russia who was sentenced to twenty years in prison for distributing leaflets critical of President Wilson. Although the Supreme Court upheld the conviction in *Abrams v. United States*, decided in 1919, Holmes filed a dissenting opinion. He wrote that while government could restrict speech that presented a clear and present danger to public safety, Abrams's "silly leaflet" threatened no harm. Joined by Justice Louis Brandeis, Holmes warned that "persecution for the expression of opinions" was always tempting, but experience showed that once-unshakable truths have often been disproved by advancing knowledge. Introducing a libertarian metaphor from the world of commerce that would come to define the freedom of expression in both law and popular culture, Holmes wrote that "the ultimate good desired is better reached by free trade in ideas—that the best test of truth is the power of the thought to get itself accepted in the competition of the market." The marketplace of ideas, not the government, should decide which views prevail.[16]

Another case involving political persecution led the Supreme Court to say, for the first time, that freedom of speech was a "liberty" right under the Fourteenth Amendment. The question arose not in the context of corporate rights but rather in the context of a doctrine with a similar name, "incorporation." That is the constitutional doctrine that determines which provisions of the Bill of Rights apply to the states. Although the Supreme Court traditionally read the Bill of Rights to apply only to the federal government, the court began to require states to adhere to those rights too around the turn of the twentieth century. The court held that certain fundamental rights among the first eight amendments were "incorporated" through the due process clause of the Fourteenth Amendment to apply to the states. In the case of Benjamin Gitlow, an anarchist convicted for publishing books said to advocate the overthrow of the government, the Supreme Court held the freedom of speech was also a limit on state and local laws. *Gitlow v. New York* was a groundbreaking ruling that greatly expanded the scope of free speech protections—although Gitlow himself did not benefit. Finding the prosecution justified, the Supreme Court upheld his conviction, over another dissent by Holmes and Brandeis.[17]

While pushing out the boundaries of the First Amendment, the court had still never invalidated a law for violating the freedom of expression. The very first Supreme Court cases striking down laws on speech or press grounds were handed down in the spring of 1931— and one of those early cases involved a corporation. *Near v. Minnesota* involved a Minnesota law that allowed the shuttering of newspapers that created a "public nuisance" by distributing "malicious, scandalous and defamatory" material. The law was designed to silence one man in particular, Jay M. Near, and his sleazy scandal rag, *The Saturday Press*. Described as "anti-Catholic, anti-Semitic, anti-black, and anti-labor," Near was a constant thorn in the side of Minneapolis politicians. His vulgar brand of yellow journalism accused them of incompetence, graft, conspiracy, and just about every other crime, rarely backed by a scintilla of evidence. The politicians repaid the favor and attempted to use the public nuisance law to permanently stop the publication of his paper. Near claimed the law infringed his First Amendment press rights as an unconstitutional prior restraint on speech.[18]

Near was not styled a corporate rights case. Formally, at least, it was a case about Jay Near's own constitutional rights as an individual. The lawsuit was nonetheless spearheaded and bankrolled by the Tribune Company, the corporation that owned the powerful and influential *Chicago Tribune*. One of the most respected papers in the country, the *Chicago Tribune* was the polar opposite of Near's tabloid. Robert McCormick, the *Tribune*'s strong-willed and visionary publisher, nevertheless saw Near's case as an opportunity to set a First Amendment precedent that would extend to his corporation's newspapers too. McCormick was prescient, as the court ruled in Near's favor and struck down the Minnesota law for infringing the freedom of the press. Unlike Benjamin Gitlow, Near won his case, but he did not benefit either; Near's paper shuttered soon after and he died in obscurity five years later. Meanwhile, McCormick commemorated the victory by etching a quote from the Supreme Court's opinion about the special role of the press into the marble walls of the lobby of Tribune Tower in Chicago. Large media corporations like McCormick's would be the primary beneficiaries of the lawsuit brought in the name of Near's scurrilous little outfit.

Even after *Near v. Minnesota* established more vibrant protections for freedom of the press, the law nonetheless appeared to be on the side of Huey Long when it came to the advertising tax. *Near* was a prior restraint case and the court had never held that free speech applied to any other kinds of burdens. The Louisiana advertising tax was not a prior restraint because it did not prevent the thirteen newspapers from publishing anything. It only taxed their advertising revenue. Nonetheless, the newspapers had one thing in common with the radicals and outcasts, like Jacob Abrams, Benjamin Gitlow, and Jay Near. The newspapers, too, were political dissenters facing persecution by powerful government officials eager to quiet them. The advertising tax, like the Sedition Act and the Minnesota public nuisance law, was used to punish and silence those who challenged government orthodoxy.

The American Newspaper Publishers Association, with a push from the *Tribune*'s McCormick, urged the Louisiana newspaper corporations to sue. "The press and the nation must stand solidly with the Louisiana newspapers in this fight, for other brazen demagogues will follow any Long success." Repeating a common refrain in the corporate rights movements, the ANPA said the papers' lawsuit should be "if necessary carried to the U.S. Supreme Court!"[19]

* * *

CHARLES MANSHIP AND HIS Capital City Press took the lead in organizing the newspaper corporations' challenge to Long's advertising tax in the fall of 1934. Two New Orleans lawyers, Eberhard P. Deutsch and Esmond Phelps, were hired to handle the case. Deutsch was the founding partner of one of the city's leading law firms. Phelps, the scion of a local aristocratic family, usually represented corporations like Western Union and the Texas and Pacific Railroad and was also a bitter enemy of Long. When the Kingfish was impeached, Phelps volunteered to lead the effort to remove him.[20]

The hurdles the two men faced were significant. In addition to the fact that the advertising tax was not a prior restraint, the newspapers were corporations. The federal and state courts had two decades earlier held that corporations did not have free speech rights in cases involving the bans on corporate political spending. More recently, *Gitlow* had held that free speech was a "liberty" right under the Fourteenth Amendment, and the court had consistently held over the previous thirty years that corporations have only property rights. Despite the obstacles, the newspaper companies filed suit, portraying Long's law as an act of political persecution—"an attempted reprisal or punishment by the dominant political faction of the state . . . against the daily press of the state for its past opposition, and a threat of further reprisals in the event of further or future opposition."[21]

The named defendant in the lawsuit was Alice Grosjean, the supervisor of public accounts. From one perspective, Grosjean was something of a political pioneer. At the tender age of 24, she was appointed Louisiana's secretary of state, the only woman in the country of any age to hold such a high government post. Her rise to power, however, was not due to education; the high-school dropout was Long's mistress. The Kingfish was so smitten with her that he once moved her into the Governor's Mansion over the predictably vociferous objections of his wife, who promptly moved out. Long relied on Grosjean for more than companionship, however. He appointed her, along with other allies, to important positions in state government to solidify his iron-fisted control.[22]

Grosjean, however, was not a lawyer. The job of defending the tax fell to the state attorney general, Gaston L. Porterie, another of Long's cronies. The year before the newspaper companies' lawsuit, Porterie had been expelled from the state bar for ethics violations. The bar determined that he had improperly used his position as attorney general to quash an investigation into election fraud by the Long machine. Long appreciated Porterie's loyalty more than the bar did and ordered the legislature to "make me a new bar." Porterie was promptly named president of the new bar association and retained his position as the state's leading law enforcement official.[23]

Even though the law was on Long's side, cronyism had its costs.

The state might have been better served if the unschooled Grosjean herself had appeared in court. Porterie and his lead counsel in the case, Charles Rivet, made an embarrassing series of mistakes defending the advertising tax. Most glaringly, they were not up to date on current Supreme Court case law. They argued, for instance, that freedom of speech and freedom of the press were only restrictions on Congress, not the states, even though *Gitlow* and *Near* had held precisely the opposite. In almost a comedy of errors, Porterie and Rivet also devoted the lion's share of their constitutional argument to the wrong clause of the Constitution. Although Charles Manship and the newspapers challenged the advertising tax as a violation of the "liberty" guaranteed by the Fourteenth Amendment's due process clause, Porterie and Rivet focused on the privileges or immunities clause—an entirely irrelevant provision of the Constitution that had been effectively gutted a half-century earlier in the *Slaughter-House Cases*.[24]

Because they focused on the wrong constitutional provision, Porterie and Rivet all but ignored the most persuasive argument on their side: a consistent line of precedent holding that corporations had property rights but not liberty rights. Instead of emphasizing this point, Porterie and Rivet mentioned it only in passing, as if it were an afterthought. Perhaps the Louisiana state bar was onto something when it tried to stop Porterie from practicing law. In any event, once the case was in the Supreme Court, with significant cutting-edge constitutional issues on the line, it became clear that Porterie and Rivet were in over their heads.

* * *

IN THEIR DEFENSE OF LONG'S advertising tax, Porterie and Rivet argued that newspaper corporations were no different from any other type of business corporation. Just as the state had the authority to impose a tax on oil companies for refining oil, it could tax newspaper companies for selling advertising. The news trade was just another business properly subject to state regulation and taxation. Although the newspapers portrayed themselves as victims, Porterie and Rivet argued instead that they were successful corporations unhappy that Louisiana was preventing them from maximizing profits.

The notion that corporations should devote themselves to maximizing profits is often taken to be one of the bedrock principles of corporate law and governance. In the early history of corporations, however, business corporations were much different; as Blackstone wrote in his *Commentaries*, corporations could only be formed if they served public purposes. Today, in part because of the *Dartmouth College* case, that rule no longer applies, and modern business corporations are considered private entities that need not serve any explicitly public objective. Indeed, corporate officers who failed to focus on the profitability of the business, at least in the long term, would be in breach of their fiduciary duties. If the transformation of the corporation from public to private was begun in 1819 with *Dartmouth College*, involving storied lawyer Daniel Webster, it was completed exactly a century later with a case involving another American legend, Henry Ford.

Ford, the visionary carmaker behind the Model T and the assembly line production process, was sued in 1916 by two business partners, James and Horace Dodge. The Dodge brothers, who built Ford's engines and owned 10 percent of Ford Motor Company stock, had been made immensely wealthy from their relationship with the company; their $10,000 investment netted them more than $32 million. Yet the brothers were unhappy that Ford refused to maximize profits even more, running the company in ways designed to benefit employees and the larger community instead of stockholders. In 1914, for example, Ford announced that he would begin paying workers $5 a day, double their previous wages, even though job applicants were plentiful. Every year the company lowered the price of cars even as significant improvements were introduced and inventory sold out. Ford had decided the stockholders were earning enough, explaining that he did "not believe that we should make such an awful profit on our cars."[25]

In 1916, Ford announced that his company would not distribute a special dividend to stockholders despite having on hand an extraordinary cash surplus of $60 million. With Europe at war, Ford justified the decision as necessary to prevent the "discharge of a large number of employees in case there should be a sudden depression of business." Ford also detailed a plan to use some of the surplus to build the largest manufacturing plant in the world at River Rouge outside of Detroit, which would allow him to lower prices for consumers even more.[26]

The Dodge brothers, who would go on to build quite a successful car company of their own, condemned Ford for running his corporation "as a semi-eleemosynary institution and not as a business institution." Helping employees and the larger public were goals "worthy in themselves but not within the scope of an ordinary business corporation." Ford was obligated to run the company in the interests of stockholders, which meant distributing to them the cash surplus. The brothers' lawsuit raised an important question: Can corporations be run in the interest of stakeholders like employees, customers, and the larger community—or must they be managed to maximize profits?

During the trial, the outspoken Ford insisted that his company had the right to make business decisions in the interests of the public

HENRY FORD WITH JAMES AND HORACE DODGE.

even if stockholders had to sacrifice. The Ford Motor Company was organized "to do as much good as we can, everywhere, for everybody concerned," Ford testified, and only "incidentally to make money." He could have claimed that his corporation would benefit in the long run from these policies, as executives often do today when pressed to defend socially responsible policies, but Ford stubbornly refused on principle. "My ambition," Ford said, is "to spread the benefits of this industrial system to the greatest possible number, to help them build up their lives and their homes."[27]

Citing Ford's testimony, the Michigan Supreme Court ruled against Ford and his public-spirited view of the corporation. While corporations might lawfully make "an incidental humanitarian expenditure of corporate funds," the court held, they could not commit to "a general purpose and plan to benefit mankind at the expense" of stockholders. Although judges typically defer to corporate executives under the "business judgment rule," which says that courts will not second-guess business decisions made in good faith, here Ford had offered no valid business reason to refuse to distribute a special dividend. Even if the company kept enough money to build the River Rouge plant—which was a legitimate business move—there would still be $30 million in cash reserves on hand and a steady flow of additional revenue from ever-increasing car sales. "A business corporation is organized and carried on primarily for the profit of the stockholders," the court explained. "The powers of the directors are to be employed for that end. The discretion of directors is to be exercised in the choice of means to attain that end, and does not extend to a change in the end itself."[28]

Dodge Brothers v. Ford Motor Company has become "an iconic statement that corporations have no obligations beyond the bottom line," according to corporate law scholar Kent Greenfield. The economist Milton Friedman captured this view of the corporation in the title of a well-known article he wrote for the *New York Times Magazine* in 1970: "The Social Responsibility of Business Is to Increase Its Profits." Of course corporations can take measures that *also* benefit other stakeholders, yet the majority view is that such activity must ultimately be in the long-term interests of the company and its stock-holders. Genuine corporate social responsibility—done *purely* to serve employees, customers, or society, at the long-term expense of stockholders—would be a breach of management's fiduciary duties.[29]

This principle of "shareholder wealth maximization" has become deeply engrained in America's corporate culture. Critics, however, blame this one-dimensional—some say "pathological"—view of the corporation for any number of corporate misdeeds, from the Deepwater Horizon oil spill of 2010, which was linked to safety shortcuts taken to prop up share prices, to Enron's accounting fraud, done to hide debt from investors. Nonetheless, today nearly every law student reads the Ford case and learns that, by law, a corporation exists to further the interests of stockholders, not the interests of employees, customers, or the larger community. For those who believe that corporations should be more than profit-maximizing automatons, *Dodge v. Ford Motor Company*, writes Greenfield, is "corporate law's original sin."[30]

* * *

IN THE LOUISIANA ADVERTISING tax case, Eberhard P. Deutsch and Esmond Phelps, the lawyers for the newspaper companies, sought to portray their clients as being fundamentally different from ordinary profit-maximizing corporations. These companies played a special role in a democratic society. They were an essential part of "the press" protected by the Constitution, and their unique mission was "to gather and disseminate information" in order to educate voters and keep the government in check. Press corporations would not fulfill those important social functions if the government could punish them for publishing things contrary to government dogma.[31]

When Deutsch and Phelps's case reached the Supreme Court in January 1936, the justices were in yet another new home—and on the verge of a new mission. The justices, who were hearing cases for the first time in their Cass Gilbert–designed neoclassical marble palace, would soon abandon the *Lochner*-era commitment to the liberty of contract and make a new one to preserve civil rights and civil liberties. Huey Long was dead, the victim of an assassin's bullet at the age of 42. Despite his youth, the Kingfish had gained national notoriety as a demagogue and a tyrant who abused government power to muffle political rivals. One of Long's final embarrassments came when, drunk, he got into a fistfight in the bathroom of a swank Long Island country club. As the national media hounded him, Long lashed out, bragging about how he had silenced Manship's Capital City Press and the other urban dailies in his state: "The newspapers in Louisiana have learned their lesson. They don't try anything like this down there. They don't dare!"[32]

It was this image of Long, the dough-faced persecutor of political opponents, that animated the arguments in the Supreme Court. The newspaper companies portrayed themselves as political dissenters being silenced for countering the powerful Long. The advertising tax was not just an ordinary tax on a business; it was an effort by Long's forces to manipulate the political process and stifle the voice of Long's opponents.

In a sign of how newspapers across the country appreciated the implications of the case, Deutsch and Phelps were joined on the briefs and in the Supreme Court hearing by Elisha Hanson, the general counsel of the American Newspaper Publishers Association. Largely due to the efforts of the *Chicago Tribune*'s McCormick, the association was now fully committed to establishing broader freedom of the press protections. The association's newsletter, *Editor & Publisher*, likened Long's attacks on the newspapers to the subjugation of dissidents in Germany. It was doubtful, the newsletter wrote, "if Hitler, Goering, and Goebbels have a lower estimate of a free and democratic process than this brazen, loud mouthed, smirking arriviste from Louisiana."[33]

Before the justices in January of 1936, the Louisiana papers hammered the same theme. They quoted Long's widely distributed circular admitting his motives: "The lying newspapers are continuing a vicious campaign" against Long's policy programs, the pamphlet said. "We managed to take care of that element here last week. A tax of 2% on what newspapers take in was placed upon them. That will help their lying some." If Long had wanted just to raise revenue by taxing advertising, the law should have applied to all newspapers. Instead, it applied only to thirteen of them, twelve of which were outspoken opponents of Long.

The thirteenth paper was *The Lake Charles American-Press*, published by the American Press Company, which had supported Long. Yet the inclusion of that paper did not mean the tax was a neutral revenue measure. The Louisiana papers again quoted Long, who had admitted that the American Press Company's paper was only included by necessity. "There was only one [large] newspaper in the State that had not joined up with the gang opposing me," Long had said. Lawmakers "tried to find a way to exempt *The Lake Charles American-Press* from the advertising tax, but did not think we could do it," Long explained, "but we would have done it if we could."[34]

The lawyers also told the justices that the very purpose of the First Amendment was to prevent the government from silencing political dissenters. "That amendment was written to protect the people in their right to have a press free from restraint from whatsoever hostile source the threat of restraint might spring, and from any method sought to be applied—whether that method be censorship, licensing, taxation, seditious libel, injunction, writ of attachment or anything else." Although the court had only previously held that prior restraints on publication were prohibited by the First Amendment, the lawyers argued that the Founders had broader concerns and sought to protect against any law that stifled or censored speech because it opposed government orthodoxy.

* * *

THE JUSTICES THAT DECIDED the constitutionality of the Louisiana advertising tax were deeply divided over many constitutional issues, especially pertaining to the regulation of business. Those divisions would manifest themselves in the justices' deliberations over *Grosjean v. American Press Company*, even as the case presented a rare instance of consensus on the ideologically riven court: all the justices thought Huey Long's law was unconstitutional. The disagreement was over why. In their debates over that key question, the justices largely overlooked the newspapers' identity as corporations. The justices saw this case through the lens of emerging First Amendment principles and concern for the persecuted, all but ignoring the corporate rights aspect of the controversy.

On one side of the court was a group of relatively strong pro-business justices, all appointed long before the Great Depression: George Sutherland, James McReynolds, Pierce Butler, and Willis Van Devanter. Nicknamed the "Four Horsemen of Reaction," they were proponents of the *Lochner* jurisprudence and saw their role as enforcing limits on government's authority to regulate property rights and the free market. They voted consistently against Roosevelt's New Deal programs. The Four Horsemen clashed with the "Three Musketeers": Louis Brandeis, Harlan Stone, and Benjamin Cardozo, the court's liberals, who thought the Constitution permitted government considerably more leeway over economic matters. The two swing votes on the court were Owen Roberts, who tended to side with the Horsemen, and the formidable Chief Justice Charles Evans Hughes, who had seen firsthand how business corrupted politics during the Great Wall Street Scandal of 1905 and now often joined the Musketeers.[35]

In this case, the Musketeers were led by Cardozo, the rare instance of a judge so renowned that he was appointed to the Supreme Court by a president of the opposite political party—a situation impossible to imagine today. A Democrat who had profoundly shaped the law as chief justice of New York's highest court, Cardozo was widely thought to be the only man worthy of filling Oliver Wendell Holmes's seat when the legendary jurist retired in 1932. Nominated by Republican Herbert Hoover, Cardozo became a leader of the progressive wing of the court. In the newspaper case, Cardozo argued that Long's advertising tax was unconstitutional because it infringed a civil liberty, the freedom of the press. Although the law was not a prior restraint, Cardozo agreed with the newspapers that the First Amendment should be read more broadly to protect against other forms of regulation, such as taxes, that could similarly stifle democratic debate. In a modern society, the free exchange of ideas required expansive free speech protections.[36]

THE JUSTICES OF THE SUPREME COURT WHO DECIDED THE
LOUISIANA NEWSPAPERS CASE. STANDING, LEFT TO RIGHT:
OWEN ROBERTS, PIERCE BUTLER, HARLAN STONE, BENJAMIN
CARDOZO. SITTING, LEFT TO RIGHT: LOUIS BRANDEIS,
WILLIS VAN DEVANTER, CHARLES EVANS HUGHES, JAMES
McREYNOLDS, GEORGE SUTHERLAND.

The Horsemen, led by Sutherland, a native Englishman who grew up in the wilds of Utah Territory in the 1870s, agreed the law was unconstitutional but argued instead that the problem was one of business taxation. Louisiana could tax all newspapers or no newspapers but could not only tax those newspapers with circulation in excess of 20,000. Regardless of whether Long and lawmakers sought to stifle opponents, a tax law could not arbitrarily apply only to a subset of businesses. Such discriminatory taxes, in the view of the Horsemen, were a way for the government to choose winners and losers in the marketplace. As Sutherland had written in a previous case, differential rates of taxation were "a mere subterfuge by which the members of one group of taxpayers are unequally burdened for the benefit of the members of other groups similarly circumstanced." For the Musketeers, who believed government was within its powers to set different tax rates, the Louisiana law burdened liberty and interfered with democracy. For the Horsemen, the law burdened business and interfered with the free market.[37]

Sutherland was assigned to write the majority opinion, which prompted Cardozo to draft a concurrence emphasizing the civil liberties aspect of the case. Cardozo's concurring opinion was so powerful, Sutherland found the justices gravitating away from his own argument. Instead of allowing Cardozo to steal away his majority opinion, Sutherland agreed to revise his own opinion to give more weight to the freedom of the press.

In February of 1936, as Americans were being reminded of the dangers of political persecution in newspaper stories about athletes marching past Adolf Hitler at the winter Olympics, the Supreme Court issued its opinion in *Grosjean v. American Press Company.* Sutherland's opinion integrated concerns about taxation and political persecution: "The form in which the tax is imposed is in itself suspicious," Sutherland wrote. The "plain purpose" of the tax was "penalizing the publishers and curtailing the circulation of a select group of newspapers." Once again, the government was picking winners and losers. Yet, due to Cardozo's influence, Sutherland also portrayed the case as one about persecution and democracy.[38]

"For more than a century prior to the adoption of the [First] amendment—and, indeed, for many years thereafter," Sutherland's opinion explained, "history discloses a persistent effort on the part of the British government to prevent or abridge the free expression of any opinion which seemed to criticize or exhibit in an unfavorable light, however truly, the agencies and operations of the government." The advertising tax was "a deliberate and calculated device in the guise of a tax to limit the circulation of information to which the public is entitled in virtue of the constitutional guaranties." Echoing the argument of Manship and the Louisiana dailies, Sutherland recognized the special role the press plays in a democracy: "A free press stands as one of the great interpreters between the government and the people."

The court's decision in *Grosjean* was a landmark in the history of free expression in America. Yet in the justices' internal debate over how to view the tax, one of the central issues in the case was obscured: the newspapers were corporations claiming to have liberty rights under the Constitution. Even if Long's law went too far, how did Capital City Press and the other newspaper corporations involved have any constitutional right to challenge it?

Justice Sutherland's opinion for the court breezed right over the issue on a corporationalist wind. Louisiana "contends that the Fourteenth Amendment does not apply to corporations; but this is only partly true," Sutherland wrote. "A corporation, we have held, is not a 'citizen' within the meaning of the privileges and immunities clause. But a corporation is a 'person' within the meaning of the equal protection and due process clauses, which are the clauses involved here." That was the entirety of the court's discussion of corporate rights— and it was fundamentally misleading. While the court had said that corporations were people, it had also repeatedly held that corporations did not have liberty rights. The rights protected by the First Amendment, the court had clearly held in *Gitlow*, were liberty rights.

The court was able to gloss over the corporate rights issue in part because Louisiana's attorneys, Gaston Porterie and Charles Rivet, had done such an incompetent job briefing and arguing the case. They had focused on the wrong clause of the Constitution, the privileges or immunities clause, so the justices were able to dispense with their arguments easily. Ordinarily, the justices might feel compelled to correct such an error rather than seizing on it. Yet neither of the court's two factions had strong reason to intervene. Cardozo and the Musketeers were eager to expand the freedom of the press against Long's repressive tactics and strengthen the First Amendment's protections more generally. Their commitment to expansive free speech principles meant inevitably that media corporations, which were becoming the public's main source of information, would have to be protected. Sutherland and the Horsemen, meanwhile, were willing to blur the distinction between property rights and liberty rights in order to overturn the discriminatory taxes. If newspaper companies could also assert First Amendment claims to strike down such laws, the case amounted to an important victory for the free market. The end result of the justices' agreement on the outcome was a Supreme Court case that afforded an unambiguous liberty right to corporations. Moreover, the court had portrayed the corporate speech involved as appropriate, legitimate, and even necessary in the democratic process.

In the decades that followed, the freedom of the press would become one of the hallmarks of American law and politics. Yet rarely acknowledged is that it was corporations that were behind many of the earliest and most important cases; newspaper companies like the Louisiana media corporations were constitutional first movers whose cases invigorated constitutional protections that would also be enjoyed by individuals. When the Supreme Court issued its ruling in 1964 establishing the right to criticize public figures without fear of libel, the First Amendment claim was asserted by the New York Times Company. In 1971, when the justices held that President Richard Nixon could not stop publication of the classified *Pentagon Papers*, the constitutional claimant was not leaker of the documents Daniel Ellsberg but the New York Times Company and the Washington Post Company. The right to a free press was certainly not limited to media corporations but, unlike most individuals, newspaper companies and broadcasters had the resources to litigate whenever new restrictions were imposed. As A. J. Liebling of *The New Yorker* quipped, "Freedom of the press is guaranteed only to those who own one."[39]

Though well known for its impact on First Amendment law, *Grosjean* also marked a turning point in the history of corporate rights. For the first time in American history, the Supreme Court held that corporations have the right to freedom of speech and freedom of the press under the Constitution. Corporations no longer only had property rights; they also had a right associated with liberty. Indeed, they were treated as valuable participants in America's democratic debates—a vision of the corporation that would appear again in the Supreme Court's opinion in *Citizens United*.

CHAPTER 8

Corporations, Race,
and Civil Rights

I N THE EARLY TWENTIETH CENTURY, THE SUPREME COURT began to focus on civil liberties in response to the persecution of socialists like Jacob Abrams and the silencing of newspapers like Charles Manship's Capital City Press. By mid-century, the court, under the leadership of Earl Warren—often named alongside John Marshall as the greatest chief justices in American history—had finally begun to embrace a commitment to racial equality to match its commitment to free speech. Racial minorities, as much as if not more than political dissenters, needed the judiciary to protect them from the tyranny of the majority. The civil rights movement provided the court with the opportunity to more fully realize Harlan Fiske Stone's proposal from *Carolene Products* to recast the court as a bulwark against the persecution of minorities. At the same time, the civil rights movement also led the Warren court to expand the constitutional protections for corporations, affording at least some of them another liberty right they had previously been denied—the freedom of association.

Corporate rights became entangled with the civil rights movement in 1956, when elected officials across the South determined to aggressively persecute civil rights activists, especially the National Association for the Advancement of Colored People. Founded in 1909 by famed African American scholar W. E. B. DuBois and others, the NAACP had already made considerable headway by the time of the crackdown. *Brown v. Board of Education*, decided two years earlier, promised to end segregated public schools. The Montgomery bus boycott of 1955, triggered by longtime NAACP member Rosa Parks's refusal to move to the back of a city bus, brought widespread condemnation of Jim Crow. Integrationists had gained the political and legal momentum, and reactionaries decided it was time to put the nation's leading advocate of civil rights out of business.[1]

Of course, the NAACP was not a business. Yet it was organized as a corporation, a nonprofit membership corporation under New York law. It was the NAACP's status as a corporate entity that Alabama and its young, ambitious attorney general, John Patterson, tried to use to destroy the organization. Patterson was elected to that post in 1954 after his father, Albert Patterson, the original Democratic nominee, was gunned down for promising a crackdown on organized crime. The son ran in his father's place, and turned his attention to the equally popular (and much less dangerous to himself) issue of fighting racial integration. His strategy paid off, and within four years he was elected governor of Alabama on an anti–civil rights platform.[2]

Alabama was a central battlefield in the war over racial equality. The bus boycott triggered by Parks propelled a 26-year-old local pastor at the Dexter Avenue Baptist Church in Montgomery into the national limelight and a leadership position in the movement; Martin Luther King Jr. would also write his momentous *Letter from Birmingham Jail* (1963) behind Alabama bars. Civil rights protestors would bravely cross the Edmund Pettus Bridge in Selma, where their bold activism was met with brutality. White terrorists in Alabama bombed the homes of activists Ralph Abernathy, E. D. Nixon, and King, along with the Sixteenth Street Baptist Church, killing four girls attending Sunday school. Freedom Riders were attacked with pipes and bats in the state, their bus set on fire. Often the violence was at the hands of government officials, like Eugene "Bull" Connor, the Birmingham public safety commissioner who sicced German Shepherds and trained fire hoses on marchers.

The Alabama attorney general's war against the NAACP began in 1956, Patterson's first year in office. He filed a lawsuit charging the organization with failing to register as a "foreign" corporation. Under Alabama law, out-of-state corporations doing business within the state were required to file with the government a copy of their articles of incorporation and designate a local agent to receive legal documents. The NAACP had never filed these documents in the belief that the rules did not apply to a nonprofit, and officials had never before requested them. Although the organization offered to register and fulfill the requirements, which were really no burden at all, Patterson asked a state court to order the NAACP to also turn over a list of its members. The ostensible reason was to enable the attorney general's

JOHN PATTERSON ARGUED THAT THE NAACP
DID NOT HAVE THE FREEDOM OF ASSOCIATION
BECAUSE IT WAS A CORPORATION.

office to more fully investigate the NAACP's activities in Alabama but many speculated the real motive was to intimidate the organization's members, who faced potential violence if identified.[3]

In places like Alabama, the local courts could not be counted on to protect discrete and insular minorities from persecution, and the NAACP was ordered to turn over its membership list. When the organization refused, it was held in contempt and fined a crippling $100,000. The NAACP, led by legendary attorneys Thurgood Marshall and Robert Carter, turned to the Supreme Court for relief, arguing that the organization had a constitutional right to freedom of association. In the *Lochner* era, the Supreme Court had refused to extend this right to corporations, be they businesses like Western Turf Association, which tried to exclude competitors from its horse tracks, or schools like Berea College, which fought to maintain an integrated student body in the face of Jim Crow. The NAACP would succeed where those other types of corporations had failed. Its victory would safeguard the nation's most vital civil rights organization from persecution, and also win for corporations—at least nonprofit corporations—the protections of another liberty right under the Constitution.

* * *

CAN A CORPORATION BE BLACK? If corporations like the Louisiana newspapers persecuted by Huey Long could be political outcasts, could corporations also be ascribed a racial identity? At first, the question sounds absurd. Corporations are legal fictions, devices created by people to achieve certain goals such as making money. Even if corporations might usefully be thought to be "persons" for some legal purposes, viewing them as having a race or an ethnicity seems to take the metaphor too far. Supreme Court justice Hugo Black, whose views on corporations and the Constitution would shape the corporate rights jurisprudence of the mid-twentieth century, likely gave voice to a commonplace sentiment when he wrote, "Corporations have neither race nor color."[4]

In a nation whose history is so intimately tied up with race and color, however, it was inevitable that questions about the racial iden-

tity of corporations would arise. The first known cases came in the
Jim Crow era. The South's obsession with separating the races led to
any number of inanimate objects being deemed to have a race; courts
"recognized and gave countenance to black blood, black churches,
black cemeteries, black books (even Bibles), and much more," according to legal scholar Richard Brooks. When African Americans in the
South began to earn enough money to start their own incorporated
businesses around the end of the nineteenth century, the courts were
forced to decide whether those corporations were black too.[5]

The People's Pleasure Park Company was one such corporation.
Owned by Joseph P. Johnson, a former slave who rose to the upper
echelon of Virginia's African American society through service in the
state's black militia, the company opened a popular amusement park
for people of color outside of Richmond in 1906. Whites who lived
nearby were upset that Johnson's amusement park brought so many
African Americans into their community and sought to shut it down.
They sued, pointing to the racially restrictive covenant in the deed for
the park's land, which prohibited sale to "a person or persons of African descent" or any other "colored person." Such covenants became
commonplace in the early twentieth century as one of the primary
ways to enforce residential segregation. Although the Supreme Court
of the United States would rule in 1948 that such deed restrictions were
unconstitutional, the People's Pleasure Park case arose in the Virginia
Supreme Court forty years earlier, when the neighbors sought to use
the racially restrictive covenant to annul the sale of the land to Johnson's company.[6]

One might expect the justices of the Virginia Supreme Court to
have viewed this case through the lens of Jim Crow. It came before
them in 1908, when racial lines were hardening in the South and the
gains from Reconstruction were being stripped away. The Supreme
Court had given constitutional imprimatur to racial segregation a
decade earlier in *Plessy v. Ferguson*. Laws banning interracial marriage were being enacted, as were laws requiring separate schools and
literacy tests to vote. White racial resentment was feeding a surge in
lynching and other forms of antiblack violence. Within a few years of

the People's Pleasure Park case, the growing oppression would lead to the Great Migration, as southern blacks moved in large numbers to northern cities.

At the turn of the century, hostility toward minorities was not only aimed at African Americans, of course; white minorities, whether ethnic or religious, often confronted a government insensitive to their rights. Indeed, not too long before the People's Pleasure Park case, the Supreme Court of the United States had decided another corporate rights case with undertones of discrimination. The law at issue in *The Late Corporation of the Church of Jesus Christ of Latter-Day Saints v. United States*, decided in 1890, was a federal law dissolving the Mormon Church, which had been organized as a religious corporation. Citing the unlawful practice of polygamy, Congress revoked the church's charter of incorporation and authorized the seizure of all the church's property, save for houses of worship. The church and several of its members, including George Romney—a distant relative of future presidential candidate Mitt Romney—challenged the law. At the time, Utah was not yet a state, and the court upheld the law on the basis of Congress's broad powers to regulate the territories. If that was the formal reason for the decision, the informal one was the justices' anti-Mormon biases. Describing polygamy as a "repugnant" and "nefarious . . . blot on our civilization," the court opined that any "organization of a community for the spread and practice of polygamy is, in a measure, a return to barbarism."[7]

The justices of the Virginia Supreme Court could easily have manifested a similar enmity to Johnson's "colored" amusement park. Yet the court, even though it upheld racial segregation in numerous other cases, unexpectedly ruled in favor of the People's Pleasure Park. The Virginia jurists were not struck by a bolt of racial egalitarianism. Rather, they ignored the deed restriction because of corporate law, coupled with concerns about disrupting creditor contracts. Relying on "general principles relating to the legal nature of corporations," the court explained that the People's Pleasure Park Company was "a legal entity distinct from the persons composing it." The "one important fact" in the case, the court explained in a way that evoked the

Taney court precedents, was that "in the eye of the law" the corporation had an "existence separate and distinct from the individual or individuals composing it." Johnson's company, in other words, was clearly a legal person: its own, separate, legally identifiable entity that was not reducible to its members. Simply because the corporation's owner and customers were black did not make the corporation a "colored person."[8]

The Virginia court did something the Supreme Court of the United States has only occasionally done in constitutional law cases involving corporations by embracing the principle of corporate personhood. The court said that the identity and rights of the Park's owner do not determine the scope and nature of the corporation's rights. Corporations were entities with their own rights and their own legal identities. And although Jim Crow courts declined to ascribe a race to corporations, by the end of the twentieth century the law would indeed allow corporations to be black.

* * *

WHEN THE NAACP FACED OFF against Alabama's John Patterson a half-century after the People's Pleasure Park case, the issue was not the race of corporations but their rights. Even the famed Supreme Court advocate Thurgood Marshall, like Horace Binney, Daniel Webster, and Delancey Nicoll before him, would argue for recognizing new rights for corporate entities.

Few, if any, lawyers in American history enjoyed more success than Marshall and his chief deputy, Robert Carter. In 1944, four years after founding the NAACP's Legal Defense Fund, Marshall hired Carter fresh out of military service and Howard Law School, where Carter had been mentored by Marshall's mentor, Charles Hamilton Houston. Together, Marshall and Carter developed and implemented the litigation strategy that brought down the doctrine of separate but equal. Although Marshall, who went on to become the first African American solicitor general and first African American Supreme Court justice, may be better remembered today, Carter's contributions to the NAACP's civil rights work were immeasurable. Carter was only thirty-three when he made his first Supreme Court argument; he briefed and argued parts of *Brown*; and he won a series of landmark race cases after succeeding Marshall as general counsel of the NAACP. Carter, like Marshall, would also be appointed to the federal bench, serving with distinction on the United States District Court in New York for forty years.[9]

In the Alabama case, *NAACP v. Alabama ex rel. Patterson*, Marshall and Carter argued that forcing the NAACP to reveal its membership list would violate the constitutional rights of both the corporation and its members. The organization claimed that the NAACP had "its own right of freedom of association" that would be infringed by the mandated disclosure. Like the Louisiana newspaper companies that distinguished themselves from ordinary business corporations by citing the special role of the press in a democracy, Carter and Marshall

THURGOOD MARSHALL (FOURTH FROM LEFT) AND
ROBERT CARTER'S (SECOND FROM LEFT) FIGHT
AGAINST RACIAL SEGREGATION LED THEM TO DEFEND
THE RIGHTS OF NONPROFIT CORPORATIONS.

argued that the NAACP was unique too. Unlike a profit-maximizing business, the NAACP was a "political organization" that "seeks to influence public opinion and affect the political structure to achieve its objectives." Although a corporation, the NAACP was truly a voluntary membership organization operating in the public interest.[10]

While the NAACP's lawyers highlighted how the entity was different from an ordinary corporation, Patterson emphasized the ordinariness of the NAACP's corporate status. Referring to the NAACP over and over again as "the corporation," Patterson emphasized that it was subject to state supervision like all other corporations. Because the NAACP was a corporation, it did not have any right of freedom of association that might allow it to keep its membership list secret. "A corporation, being an artificial entity, is subject to the restraints of the police power more than a natural person and has fewer rights," Patterson argued. With a nod to *Grosjean*, Patterson insisted that while the "rights of a corporation" might include the "freedom of the press," they "do not include freedom of association" or "a right of privacy." Indeed, in the *Western Turf Association* case, the Supreme Court had held that corporations did not have associational freedoms.[11]

Marshall and Carter highlighted how the NAACP was a victim of political persecution, not unlike the newspaper companies targeted by Huey Long. The NAACP, too, was being harassed for challenging government orthodoxy. "This case cannot be properly considered without being viewed against the background and setting in which it arose," Marshall and Carter's brief argued. The NAACP's victory in *Brown* required racial integration of schools and, in response, "Alabama officials have committed themselves to a course of persecution and intimidation of all who seek to implement desegregation." "The truth is that Alabama seeks, in these proceedings, to silence petitioner and its members" and "eradicate opposition" to Jim Crow. Rather than viewing the NAACP as a corporation, Marshall and Carter saw the NAACP as one of the political dissenters Justice Harlan Fiske Stone had worried about in his *Carolene Products* footnote.

* * *

ONE JUSTICE WHOSE VOTE the NAACP could usually count on was Hugo Black, whose diminutive size and southern manners could easily obscure his forceful personality and dogged determination. Given his background, Black's frequent votes in favor of the NAACP were surprising to many. Prior to his nomination to the Supreme Court in 1937 by fellow New Dealer Franklin Roosevelt, Black had been a member of the Ku Klux Klan. Although the revelation of his Klan membership almost derailed his chances, once on the bench Black became, as his obituary in the *New York Times* observed, "a champion of civil rights and liberties."[12]

Black's solid support for the NAACP and his membership in the Klan were, paradoxically, driven by the same realization: he understood how deeply entrenched racism was in places like Alabama. Like John Patterson, Black was a native Alabaman, and like the reactionary state attorney general, Black recognized early on that success in Alabama electoral politics meant support for racial segregation. Seeking to expand his base in one of his early election campaigns, he joined the Klan. Later in life, he recognized that, because of that same deep-seated racism in the South, racial justice would never come without an unrelenting push by the Supreme Court.

As much as Black championed civil rights, he was an equally vigorous opponent of corporate rights. Even more so than Chief Justice Roger Taney a century earlier, Black argued forcefully against constitutional protections for corporations. As a young trial lawyer, Black steadfastly refused to represent corporate clients, bragging that he was not "a railroad, power company, or a corporation lawyer." When Black was in the Senate, he often railed against moneyed corporations in the southern populist vein of Jefferson and Jackson. Once he became a justice, he quickly staked out his populist position against corporate constitutional rights.[13]

In 1938, just four months after Black was sworn in, the Supreme Court decided a case called *Connecticut General Life Insurance Company v. Johnson*, which, like the NAACP case, involved state restrictions on foreign corporations. California had required out-of-state insurance companies that did business in California to pay taxes even

A CHAMPION OF CIVIL RIGHTS, JUSTICE HUGO BLACK WAS
OUTSPOKEN IN HIS OPPOSITION TO CORPORATE RIGHTS.

on insurance contracts formed outside the state. A life insurance company from Connecticut challenged the law—another in the seemingly
endless corporate lawsuits against such restrictions that stretched back
a century to the Taney court. By the 1930s, the Supreme Court had
largely sided with the foreign corporations. Following this later trend,
the Supreme Court in *Connecticut General Life Insurance* struck down
the California law. Black, however, dissented. Even though none of the
parties had raised the issue, Black argued that Justice Stephen Field
had been wrong about the scope of corporate rights under the Fourteenth Amendment. In Black's view, the amendment afforded corporations no rights whatsoever.[14]

Challenging a half-century of precedent recognizing corporations to have at least property rights under the Fourteenth Amendment, Black rested his case on the original meaning of the Fourteenth Amendment. No one who voted to ratify the Fourteenth Amendment knew they were "granting new and revolutionary rights to corporations," Black insisted. Mocking Roscoe Conkling's "secret history" of the drafting of the Fourteenth Amendment, Black criticized the court's 1886 ruling in *Santa Clara County v. Southern Pacific*, which, Black said, "decided for the first time that the word 'person' in the amendment did, in some instances, include corporations." Black's reliance on *Santa Clara* was not only incorrect, but stunningly so given that he was arguing for that very case to be overturned. Regardless, in Black's view, the Fourteenth Amendment was designed "to protect weak and helpless human beings," not "to remove corporations in any fashion from the control of state governments." People had constitutional rights; corporations did not.

It was a bold stance to take for someone only four months on the job. Not only had Black breached the court's protocol by reaching out to decide an issue neither briefed nor argued by the parties, but he dared propose a novel and sweeping reinterpretation of the Fourteenth Amendment. His views, however, never gained the support of a majority of the court.

In one 1946 case, however, the Supreme Court momentarily embraced another of Black's idiosyncratic views about corporations—and nearly brought about a constitutional revolution. Ever since the Founding, the Constitution has been understood to be mainly a limitation on government, not a limitation on private actors. The Fourteenth Amendment, for example, says "No *State* shall" deny equal protection and due process. Someone can only claim to have his or her individual rights violated when the government has burdened those rights. This is known as the "state action" requirement. By comparison, if a private person prevents someone from speaking or practicing her religion, the Constitution offers no protection or remedy. (There is one exception: the Thirteenth Amendment, which directly prohibits private individuals from holding another person in servitude.) The fact that the state action requirement is as old as the Constitution itself was no reason, in Black's mind, to keep it. He thought corporations should be required to respect and enforce individual rights too.

The 1946 case, fittingly, came out of Alabama. Grace Marsh, a Jehovah's Witness, had been arrested for distributing religious literature in the tiny town of Chickasaw, located on Mobile Bay, just off the Gulf of Mexico. Chickasaw looked like any of a hundred other small towns that dotted the South. Houses crowded around a short business block, which had a barbershop, drugstore, post office, and a grocery—a southern variant of a *Saturday Evening Post* tableau. The businesses were easily accessible from a four-lane public highway, which brought in supplies for Chickasaw's primary employer, the Gulf Shipbuilding Corporation. During World War II, the company and the town had prospered due to contracts with the Navy. Chickasaw's most distinguishing feature was one a visitor like Marsh might not even notice: it was a company town, wholly owned and operated by the Gulf Shipbuilding Corporation.[15]

On Christmas Eve in 1943, Grace Marsh visited Chickasaw's business block to hand out copies of *Watchtower*, the official magazine of the Jehovah's Witnesses. A sheriff's deputy, who was paid by Gulf

THE MAIN BUSINESS STREET OF CHICKASAW, ALABAMA, 1953.

Shipbuilding to police the devoutly Christian town, demanded she stop, citing company policy prohibiting the distribution of literature on the streets. Marsh refused and was convicted for criminal trespass onto the company's private property. Marsh challenged her conviction as a violation of her rights of free speech and freedom of religion.

When Marsh's case made it to the Supreme Court in the winter of 1945–1946, only a decade had passed since *Grosjean*, but the court had been busy expanding the scope of First Amendment protections. Many of the cases involved Jehovah's Witnesses, another group of persecuted outsiders. A common tenet of faith among Jehovah's Witnesses was the obligation to proselytize in person, but that often ran afoul of laws prohibiting such activity, some of which were enacted precisely to stop the Jehovah's Witnesses. In a series of important decisions, the court, in the early days of its historic embrace of vibrant free speech protection, struck down laws prohibiting the distribution of literature on the streets; laws banning people from going door-to-door; and restrictions on the solicitation of charitable contributions. By guaranteeing the right of Jehovah's Witnesses to engage in political and religious advocacy in public places, the court was living up to the promise of Justice Harlan Fiske Stone's footnote in *Carolene Products* by protecting minorities from government persecution.[16]

Grace Marsh's case, however, was different. Although she too was being punished for proselytizing, the government was not the one silencing her. Gulf Shipbuilding, a private company, was. Because of the state action doctrine, she had no case; private companies were not obligated to respect individual rights. So when Justice Black wrote a majority opinion for the Supreme Court ruling in her favor in January of 1946, the outcome was unexpected, to say the very least. Although Black recognized that private property owners usually have the right to exclude whomever they want from their property, the "more an owner, for his advantage, opens up his property for use by the public in general," the more the owner has to respect the constitutional rights of the public. Here, Chickasaw's business block was "accessible to and freely used by the public in general." Because Chickasaw was a town—even if it was really a *company* town—it could not silence religious minorities.[17]

Marsh v. Alabama fundamentally flipped the constitutional status of corporations. Ever since Daniel Webster's *Dartmouth College* case, corporations were deemed to be private entities, which like ordinary people could assert individual rights *against* the government. In *Marsh*, Black reimagined Gulf Shipbuilding to be *akin* to the government instead and bound to respect the constitutional rights of others. In a dissenting opinion, Black's friend and fellow New Dealer Justice Stanley Reed gently chided him for his "novel Constitutional doctrine." While the doctrine was new, Black's view harkened back in some ways to early America. In the colonial era, corporations like the Massachusetts Bay Company also served as governments.

Black's belief that some corporations should be treated like governments under the Constitution was not solely a product of his eccentricities. Other mid-century thinkers came to similar conclusions in light of the pervasive influence of large corporations on people's lives. The same year as *Marsh v. Alabama*, a management consultant named Peter Drucker wrote *Concept of the Corporation*, a pioneering study of the management structure of General Motors, the world's largest corporation. Drucker likened GM to the US government, but noted that corporations do more than governments to set "the standard for the way of life and the mode of living of our citizens." Drucker was not a critic of the corporation; he admired the efficiency of the large corporation and the contribution business made to social welfare. Still, he admitted that the modern corporation was, quite unlike government officials, "responsible to no one."[18]

The trend to view the corporation as a de facto government continued to gain high-profile adherents in the 1950s. Adolph Berle Jr., the economist who coined the terminology of the "separation of ownership and control," built on Black and Drucker in 1952: "Some of these corporations are units which can be thought of only in somewhat the way we have heretofore thought of nations." With "sufficient economic power" to burden "the constitutional rights of an individual to a material degree," corporations ought to be "subject to constitutional limitations . . . as is the state itself." Berle fearlessly predicted that, in light of *Marsh v. Alabama*, the day would soon come when corporations would be bound to respect individual rights as a matter of course. Their private property would become public space.[19]

An astute observer of the modern corporation, Berle was not, however, a particularly talented prognosticator of constitutional law. Despite growing awareness of the power and influence of the large corporation, Black's decision in *Marsh* never caught on. Never again would the court rule that the Constitution required large corporations as such to respect individual rights. Instead, the court returned to saying that corporations were, like individuals, themselves protected by the Constitution. *Marsh* was never overturned, but neither did it become an important precedent. Instead, it continues to live to this day in a state of constitutional purgatory, essentially a dead letter but still on the books. Now the case, when remembered at all, is dismissed as a sui generis response "to the special history and circumstances of the Southern company town"; as those towns faded from the economic scene in the decades that followed, so did Black's unusual approach to corporations and the Constitution.[20]

The fate of *Marsh* was strikingly different from that of *Santa Clara County v. Southern Pacific Railroad*. Even though the court explicitly refused to decide whether corporations were protected by the Fourteenth Amendment in *Santa Clara*, that decision would be frequently cited for establishing that rule.

One reason the seed planted by Black in *Marsh* never again bore fruit was pragmatic. Not all corporations had power comparable to that of the government. The large corporation gained most of the media and scholarly attention, but the vast majority of corporations were small businesses. From the corner drugstore to the local Chinese restaurant, the twentieth century saw small business owners increasingly organize their businesses as corporations, lured by the promise of limited liability. Yet these corporations did not have power and influence similar to the government's. As even Berle admitted, "In the absence of very considerable concentration of economic power in a given area, the problem does not arise." The court faced the difficult if not impossible question of separating out those corporations with government-like power from those without it.

Another reason Black's view of corporations as governments withered can be gleaned from the controversy over the NAACP's membership list in *NAACP v. Alabama ex rel. Patterson*. As the NAACP's experience made clear, sometimes corporations were indeed the victims of political repression by the government and needing of constitutional protection. The NAACP in Alabama, at least, was much less less like Gulf Shipbuilding, a massive corporation that controlled a whole town, and more like Grace Marsh, a dissenter being silenced. The NAACP case thus presented Black with a dilemma. To support the NAACP meant accepting that at least some types of corporations had at least some constitutional rights.

* * *

ALABAMA'S JOHN PATTERSON HAD many allies in his effort to stop racial integration after *Brown*. In 1956, over one hundred representatives and senators signed the Southern Manifesto, which encouraged states to resist the Supreme Court's decision. The next year, as the controversy over the NAACP's membership list was making its way to the Supreme Court, Arkansas governor Oral Faubus deployed the state's National Guard to prevent the "Little Rock Nine," a group of fearless African American students, from integrating Central High School. In 1958, the same year the court would decide the NAACP's membership list case, the justices felt obligated to issue the unprecedented decision in *Cooper v. Aaron*, which forcefully declared that state officials were indeed obligated to obey federal court orders mandating integration. In this environment, the NAACP's case was a major civil rights case, not just a minor dispute about the scope of corporate rights.

No one understood better than Black the depths of southern intransigence. And although Black recognized in the justices' conference that the "fact that the petitioner is a corporation raises a background problem similar to the *Berea College* case"—referring to the *Lochner* era decision that refused to extend the freedom of association to an educational corporation—he was adamant that a unified front of justices was essential to enforcing the court's rulings. As a result, Black explained to Justice John Marshall Harlan II, who would ultimately author the court's opinion in the membership list case, that he was "willing to go a long way to obtain such unanimity" in civil rights cases.[21]

Harlan, the grandson of the nineteenth-century justice with the same name, was a moderate on the liberal Warren court. He sided with the majority in the Warren court's major race cases, but often expressed reservations about the judiciary becoming "a general haven for reform movements." He proposed a compromise to decide the NAACP membership list case—one that echoed the first corporate rights case, *Bank of the United States v. Deveaux*. Like Horace Binney, the lawyer for the Bank, Harlan suggested piercing the corporate veil. The court need not say anything about whether the NAACP had rights of its own. Instead, the NAACP should be allowed to assert and defend the constitutional rights of its members. The NAACP's members were

JUSTICE JOHN M. HARLAN II AUTHORED THE SUPREME COURT'S OPINION IN *NAACP V. ALABAMA EX REL. PATTERSON*.

unquestionably people, and they had the full panoply of constitutional rights, including liberty rights like the freedom of association. While recognizing that the court "has generally insisted that the parties rely only on constitutional rights which are personal to themselves," Harlan's opinion held that the court would look past the corporate form and base the decision instead on the associational rights of members. The decision was, as Black thought necessary, unanimous.[22]

Harlan's opinion departed from *Bank of the United States* in one important way. Although the court pierced the corporate veil, Harlan suggested that such an approach was justified in this case precisely because the NAACP was *not* a business. It was, instead, a voluntary, nonprofit membership corporation and the people who joined did so specifically "to make more effective the expression of their own views" about racial justice. Unlike a business corporation, there was a unique "nexus" between the NAACP and its members that made the two "in every practical sense identical." Given the NAACP's status as a voluntary, nonprofit membership organization, it could act as the members' representative. For all intents and purposes, the corporation bore the rights of its members—in this case, the freedom of association, a right of personal liberty.

NAACP v. Alabama ex rel. Patterson would be celebrated as an important landmark in both the civil rights movement and the development of First Amendment principles. "Effective advocacy of both public and private points of view, particularly controversial ones, is undeniably enhanced by group association," Justice Harlan's opinion explained. "It is beyond debate that freedom to engage in association for the advancement of beliefs and ideas is an inseparable aspect of the 'liberty' assured by" the Constitution. For the NAACP, however, the fight was hardly over. Southern resistance would bring the question of corporate rights back to the Supreme Court in *NAACP v. Button* (1963), where the justices held that "though a corporation," the NAACP could assert freedom of association "on its own behalf" while it could also "assert the corresponding rights of its members."[23]

The freedom of association established in the NAACP cases would be used primarily by advocacy groups, not business corporations, to fight against repressive laws. Yet the court's language was broad. "Of course, it is immaterial whether the beliefs sought to be advanced by association pertain to political, economic, religious or cultural matters," Justice Harlan explained. In time, the notion that business corporations were a form of association dedicated to constitutionally protected advocacy on economic matters would fuel the expansion of political speech rights for business.

* * *

TODAY, ONE MIGHT ASSUME that the seemingly bizarre question that confronted the Virginia Supreme Court in the People's Pleasure Park case of the Jim Crow era—whether corporations can have a racial identity—would have long ceased to be relevant. Unlike during the early twentieth century, when states were aggressively using race to segregate people in all areas of social life, race is no longer the focus of many laws. Nonetheless, the law today does allow corporations to claim a race or ethnicity.

Although Justice Black wrote that corporations could not have a race, the law once again refused to embrace his views. Consider the case of Flying B, a trucking company owned by Sikhs, with Sikh drivers, that contracted with oil giant ARCO to haul fuel through Washington State. ARCO's Seattle supervisor peppered Flying B's drivers with racial epithets and made their lives miserable. He refused to sign delivery papers. He made them wait in the rain when other drivers were allowed inside. He forced them to clean up other drivers' spills, one time directing a Sikh trucker to take the "rag from your head and clean it." He also degraded Flying B's non-Sikh drivers for working for Sikhs. When Flying B complained, ARCO terminated the contract.[24]

Flying B sued, claiming ARCO discriminated against the company on the basis of race. Following Justice Black, ARCO argued that because Flying B was a corporation it had "no racial identity." ARCO was willing to concede that Flying B could bring a lawsuit for breach of contract; corporations have always had the right to make and enforce contracts. But Flying B could not bring a lawsuit for racial discrimination under federal civil rights laws. The federal court disagreed. The ARCO supervisor treated the company and its employees in a discriminatory manner. And he did it because the company was owned and operated by Sikhs. As a result, the court said, "Flying B undoubtedly acquired an imputed racial identity." Here, ascribing a racial identity to a corporation was necessary to give teeth to antidiscrimination law.

Corporations today can also have a legally recognized racial identity under affirmative action policies. Federal law provides that companies with 51 percent minority control and ownership can be certified as "Minority Business Enterprises," which qualifies them for a variety of contracting, banking, and training programs for economically and socially disadvantaged groups. States have similar programs, the result of which is effectively to classify particular companies as African American, Hispanic American, or Native American. In contrast to the People's Pleasure Park case of a century ago, which treated the corporation as a person—its own independent legal entity, distinct from the people who owned it—the minority business enterprises policies represent a form of veil piercing. The courts look to the racial identity of the owners and graft that race onto the corporation.[25]

The Flying B case and the affirmative action programs arise under statutes passed by Congress or the state legislatures, not the Constitution. If Congress or the states wanted to exclude corporations from these programs, they could pass new laws through the ordinary legislative process. Constitutional protections are more durable because they cannot be legislated away. While the Supreme Court has never explicitly held that the Constitution recognizes corporations to have racial identities, the justices have nevertheless come very close—effectively reaching the same result indirectly. Only the beneficiaries were not corporations run by socially disadvantaged minorities like Flying B; they were instead corporations run by whites.

Since the late 1970s, the Supreme Court has often been criticized for reading the Constitution's protections against racial discrimination more to the benefit of whites than to the benefit of historically subjugated minorities. Previously, during the Warren court of the 1950s and 1960s, the Supreme Court had read the Constitution to upend Jim Crow, fulfilling the promise of Justice Harlan Fiske Stone's footnote in *Carolene Products*. Yet those decisions helped feed a backlash, and after the election of Richard Nixon in 1968, Republican presidents who ran against liberal judicial activism would appoint ten consecutive Supreme Court justices. The remade court curtailed busing to integrate schools and made it harder to sue for racial discrimination.²⁶

In one way, however, the justices made it easier to prove discrimination—against whites. Beginning with a 1978 case, *University of California v. Bakke*, the court began to insist that affirmative action policies, such as minority set-aside programs, satisfy constitutional law's hardest test, "strict scrutiny." *Bakke* suggested strict scrutiny was necessary because race-based affirmative action was another form of racial discrimination, raising the same concerns as Jim Crow laws. The effect of *Bakke* was to make it easier to challenge affirmative action polices as unconstitutional.²⁷

Although strict scrutiny for affirmative action grew out of *Bakke*, that case split the justices and, as a result, there was no controlling majority opinion. The first two Supreme Court cases to have a clear majority in favor of strict scrutiny for affirmative action involved business firms who claimed to be victims of racial discrimination: Adarand Constructors, Inc. and the J. A. Croson Company, the former a corporation and the latter a limited liability company. Both companies were owned by whites, and both sued to overturn minority set-asides, claiming that such race-conscious programs violated the Constitution's guarantee of equal protection. The companies were, in a way, constitutional first movers whose fight to establish their own rights would later be exploited by individuals.

The Supreme Court sided with the companies generally, although without explicitly addressing whether corporations, as such, could have a racial identity. Yet the court's reasoning unquestionably assumed that those companies did indeed have racial characteristics. To have standing to challenge an affirmative action policy, someone must show that the policy caused her an injury. Only if Adarand Constructors, Inc. and J. A. Croson Company were discriminated against on account of race could they claim to have suffered a unique harm from the racial preferences. As one federal court admitted, the Supreme Court in these cases "implicitly recognized that corporations can have racial characteristics by allowing white owned corporations to challenge contractor set asides."[28]

The business victories marked a retreat of sorts from Justice Harlan Fiske Stone's footnote in *Carolene Products*. For a half-century after the 1937 decision in which Stone insisted that special judicial protection was necessary for "discrete and insular minorities," the court had largely followed that advice. The court struck down speech restrictions targeting political dissenters, dismantled Jim Crow, and generally committed itself to preserving civil rights and civil liberties. Stone's justification for stricter judicial review of laws burdening minorities was grounded in political power: minority groups were easily victimized by the majority. Yet in the affirmative action cases, the justices abandoned that rationale, giving special judicial protection to the white majority. It was another example of reform adopted to help the powerless that was exploited and transformed by corporations to benefit the powerful.

The Supreme Court justice who first suggested that race-based affirmative action be subject to strict scrutiny was Lewis F. Powell Jr., a Nixon appointee who authored the *Bakke* opinion. Another area of constitutional law in which Powell would have a tremendous influence was corporate rights. For just as Daniel Webster was the Corporation's Lawyer, Lewis Powell was the Corporation's Justice.

∨

CHAPTER 9

—

The Corporation's Justice

A T PHILIP MORRIS'S ANNUAL CHRISTMAS LUNCHEON IN December of 1971, Joe Cullman, the tobacco giant's chief executive, gave a warm sendoff to a longtime member of the board of directors who was leaving to take a new job. Although the two men had been close friends since childhood, Cullman's elaborate tribute proved he was not disappointed by the departure of Lewis F. Powell Jr., who after all was severing formal ties with the company to become a justice on the Supreme Court. Cullman had prepared a state-of-the-art multimedia production, complete with special effects, music, and film clips, to honor Powell. The tribute was a spoof on the popular 1950s television history show, *You Are There*, and featured the program's actual host, legendary news anchor Walter Cronkite, who recounted the highlights of Powell's life interspersed with humorous and touching reenactments. As Powell and his wife Jo looked on joyously, the tribute reimagined when a younger Powell was first pursuing Jo and asked her father for his blessing. "Yes," the father replies, "she says you are a supreme courter!"[1]

The festive mood belied the fact that Philip Morris and the tobacco industry—indeed, much of corporate America—had been the targets of withering attacks over the better part of the previous decade. Few people felt this as acutely as Cullman, Philip Morris's CEO since 1957. During that time, he had seen his company's products demonized as a health risk after waves of studies exposed the dangers of smoking. Strict new federal laws restricted cigarette advertising and required warning labels on cigarette packages. Those regulations were not far from Cullman's mind during his tribute to Powell. About halfway through, Cullman paused to announce "this important message from our sponsor" and played an ad for Philip Morris cigarettes—one that the company was prohibited by recent reforms from airing on broadcast television.

Tobacco regulation was just one small swell in a tidal wave of populist reforms enacted in the 1960s and early 1970s that curtailed traditional business practices in the interests of consumers, workers, and the environment. In a remarkably productive six-year stretch, Congress passed the Clean Air Act, the Clean Water Act, the National Environmental Policy Act, and the Consumer Product Safety Act, along with new regulations establishing safety standards for automobiles, prohibiting dangerous chemicals in children's products, and strengthening food safety. The laws reflected Americans' loss of faith in industry. In 1966–1967, over half of Americans reported having "a great deal of confidence" in corporate leaders, but by 1974–1976, that number had dropped precipitously to 20 percent.[2]

The unquestioned leader of the reform movement was Ralph Nader, a tireless populist advocate for curbing corporate power whom *Newsweek* magazine featured on its cover dressed as a knight in shining armor. *Time* magazine called Nader the "nation's No. 1 consumer guardian," who had prompted "much U.S. industry to reappraise its responsibilities and, against considerable odds, created a new climate of concern for the consumer among politicians and businessmen." Nader carried on the spirit of the Muckrakers and, like Upton Sinclair exposing the slaughterhouses or Henry Demarest Lloyd warning of Standard Oil's monopoly, he unmasked how corporations harmed consumers in the unyielding pursuit of profit. Nader, *Time* wrote, was "almost solely responsible" for the wave of "major federal laws" regulating business.[3]

The year 1971, when Philip Morris had its luncheon send-off for Lewis Powell, was a critical one in the battle between populist reformers and big business. Earlier that year, Nader had founded Public Citizen to advocate for consumers with the motto, "Corporations have their lobbyists in Washington, D.C. The people need advocates too." Using sophisticated methods to mobilize grassroots pressure on lawmakers, Public Citizen quickly became a leading voice for curbing corporate power. Yet 1971 was also the year the seeds of a comeback for corporate America were planted—by none other than Powell. In August, two months before he was nominated to the Supreme Court, Powell wrote a lengthy memorandum for the Chamber of Commerce outlining the threats posed by the likes of Nader to the free enterprise system and detailing how business should fight back. Although the memorandum was not discovered until a year after Powell's confirmation, once revealed it became a rallying cry for business leaders across the country. Indeed, the Powell Memorandum became an influential strategic planning document of the emerging New Right—a coalition of free market advocates and religious conservatives that swept Ronald Reagan into the White House in 1980, pushed for deregulation of industry, and reasserted the influence of business in American politics.[4]

At the luncheon, Joe Cullman teased Lewis F. Powell for his strong ties to one corporation in particular. An early skit featured Powell's elementary school teacher asking him, "What does the 'F' stand for in your name?" to which Powell replied, "Philip Morris, ma'am." Powell's ties to tobacco went back a remarkably long way; his ancestor Nathaniel Powell arrived with the Virginia Company's first ships in 1607 and survived to see the development of tobacco as the colony's first profitable crop. Indeed, the future Supreme Court justice was born less than sixty miles from Nathaniel Powell's plantation, located off a tiny tributary of the James River still known after four hundred years as Powell's Creek.[5]

Cullman's tribute surveyed Powell's impressive resume: a decorated army intelligence officer during World War II, a leading lawyer in Richmond, and president of the American Bar Association. "However," Cullman continued, "his career reached a new high, when Mr. Joseph F. Cullman said to him, 'Congratulations, Lewis, you have just been elected to the board of directors of Philip Morris Incorporated!' "[6]

Yet only after Lewis Powell left the Philip Morris board and joined the Supreme Court would he come to be called "the most powerful man in America." He was one of four justices named by President Richard Nixon, who set out to dismantle the liberal Warren court of the 1950s and 1960s. Under the chief justiceship of Earl Warren, the court had issued a reliable stream of liberal rulings desegregating schools, expanding the rights of criminal defendants, guaranteeing sexual privacy, and giving private citizens wide leeway to bring antitrust suits against business. Nixon's court, by contrast, would end busing, limit the scope of civil rights laws, and curtail securities fraud and antitrust suits. Powell became the Supreme Court's swing vote, and while he occasionally sided with the liberal Warren court holdouts on social issues, the author of the Powell Memorandum was a corporationalist who voted more consistently to expand the rights of corporations and protect industry from burdensome regulation and lawsuits.[7]

While the Supreme Court's conservative turn in the 1970s has been well documented, one aspect of that transformation warrants closer examination: how the remade court dealt with the constitutional rights of corporations. Both Ralph Nader and Lewis Powell would play starring roles in that drama. Nader and his advocacy group Public Citizen spearheaded a landmark case on behalf of consumers that relied on an innovative "listeners' rights" theory of the First Amendment—one that, ironically, would result in broader speech rights for businesses. Then, in another case soon after, Powell would use Nader's listeners' rights theory to justify extending to corporations the First Amendment right to engage in political speech about elections. Together, these two cases would speed along the political revitalization of corporate America. And they would set in place the final foundation stones in constitutional doctrine for *Citizens United*.

As Joe Cullman finished up his lavish tribute to Powell, the voice of Walter Cronkite once again filled the room. "The elevation of Lewis Powell to the highest court in the land . . . adds to the lustre, the stature and the nobility of our Supreme Court," the news anchor declared. "And *you were there*!" Cullman then called Jo Powell up to receive a farewell gift before presenting one to her husband. "It is customary for friends and associates to present a newly appointed Supreme Court justice with his robes of office," Cullman announced. "It is therefore a great honor and privilege for me to present you with this robe on behalf of your friends as you enter the exalted chambers of the court, and leave the crass world of commercialism." Powell being robed by the chief executive of one of America's most powerful corporations was a sign of the future direction of corporate rights.

* * *

TALL, AFFABLE, AND A BIT GAUNT, the bespectacled Lewis Powell was said to resemble a "kindly country pharmacist." His genteel southern manners—he never swore and was unfailingly polite—enhanced the perception. While known for his "qualities of temperament" and willingness to compromise as a justice, Powell could also be strident and immoderate on certain issues. It was his harsh views of criminal justice that first attracted Nixon's attention. When Powell was the president of the American Bar Association in the mid-1960s, he gave a series of speeches on criminal justice in which he bashed liberals who blamed rising crime on structural racism or the lack of economic opportunity in minority communities. Instead, Powell said, the "root cause of the crime crisis which grips our country" was "excessive tolerance" of "substandard, marginal, and even immoral and unlawful conduct." As he told the Senate during his confirmation hearings, "The need is for greater protection—not of criminals but of law-abiding citizens."[8]

Another issue about which Powell had very rigid views was Ralph Nader's progressive reform movement. Like Sinclair Lewis's Babbitt, Powell still believed in the promise and potential of business, even as it faced new regulations of unprecedented number and scope. His position was laid out in the memorandum he wrote for the Chamber of Commerce in the summer of 1971.

The memorandum was the product of a series of conversations

JUSTICE LEWIS POWELL ADVOCATED FOR BUSINESS TO BECOME
MORE POLITICALLY ACTIVE AND WROTE A SUPREME COURT
OPINION PROTECTING CORPORATE POLITICAL SPEECH.

between Powell and his friend Eugene Sydnor Jr., a prominent Richmond businessman who ran the Southern Department Stores chain
and served on the board of the national Chamber of Commerce.
Sydnor was a proponent of the view that businessmen needed to be
more active politically. He first learned that lesson as a state senator
in Virginia in the mid-1950s, when the state was roiled by debates over
school integration. Sydnor opposed the policy of "massive resistance"
because he feared the pitched battles over racial segregation were bad
for Virginia's economy. His pro-business voice was nonetheless easily
drowned out by the sirens of racism, and Virginia became a leader in
the southern revolt against *Brown*.[9]

The need for business interests to become better organized politically became the subject of Sydnor and Powell's colloquy in 1971. The topic fascinated Powell, who clipped and saved articles from popular magazines like *Fortune* and *Barron's* about the faltering political position of business, the growing opposition to concentrated wealth, and the rise of socialism on college campuses. Sydnor encouraged Powell to write up his memorandum and sent him helpful editorials about the political position of business from the *Wall Street Journal*. One editorial Sydnor sent focused on perhaps the most publicized conflict of the era between a reformer and big business—the battle between Ralph Nader and General Motors.

Nader became America's most famous anticorporate crusader thanks to the bumbling way that General Motors, America's biggest car company, tried to silence him. Nader had first written about automobile safety in a student paper at Harvard Law School, which he expanded into a book after graduation. Published by a startup publisher in 1965, *Unsafe at Any Speed* was a wonky policy book filled with data about what Nader called the "designed-in dangers" of American cars. The book was an exhaustive muckraking critique of one of the nation's iconic commercial products. It showed that carmakers spent millions of dollars on comfort and styling but did little to improve car safety, despite nearly 40,000 fatalities and 1.5 million injuries per year. Most damning was Nader's accusation that executives and engineers of the car companies knew of their cars' design flaws and yet, driven by profit, failed to correct them.[10]

One of Nader's featured examples was the Corvair, a popular sports car manufactured in the 1960s by Chevrolet, a division of GM. After Nader's book was published, the carmaker hired a private detective agency headed by Vincent Gillen, a former FBI agent, to find dirt on Nader, who was preparing to testify before a Senate subcommittee on automobile safety. In 1966, Gillen sent out agents to look into Nader's personal life, to see if the crusader was into "women, boys, etc.," and to determine if he liked "drinking, dope" or anything else scandalous.[11] When Morton Mintz of the *Washington Post* reported that Nader was being tailed, Senator Abraham Ribicoff, the chairman of the Senate subcommittee, was outraged at the apparent harassment of a congressional witness. He demanded GM president James Roche appear before the Senate, where the humiliated car executive was forced to apologize repeatedly.[12]

The incident made Nader famous overnight, much as Charles Evans Hughes was catapulted into the public limelight by George Perkins's revelations of corporate campaign contributions in the Great Wall Street Scandal of 1905. Sales of Nader's book skyrocketed, and Congress soon after passed two major auto safety laws. The *Washington Post* called Nader the "one-man lobby for the public" who had "prevailed over the nation's most powerful industry." Nader, however, would soon have help; this being the apex of political activism in the 1960s, young adults from around the country volunteered to work for him. Called "Nader's Raiders," they were charged with exposing the harm and corruption of other industries as Nader had done for automobiles: collect reams of data, write detailed investigative reports, and advocate for reform. In the ensuing years, Nader's acolytes published devastating indictments of the corporations that polluted the air, dirtied the water, and exposed people to deadly chemicals. Not surprisingly, then, Powell's Memorandum identified Nader as "the single most effective antagonist of American business."[13]

Under the title "Attack on American Free Enterprise System," the Powell Memorandum insisted that "no thoughtful person can question" whether capitalism was under siege from within. The "extremists of the left," including "Communists, New Leftists and other revolutionaries" in the universities and the media were "waging ideological warfare against the enterprise system." To counter Nader and his powerful reform movement, the Powell Memorandum advised that "it is essential that spokesmen for the enterprise system—at all levels and at every opportunity—be far more aggressive than in the past." Like the Southern Pacific Railroad back in the 1880s, corporate America had to assert itself aggressively and creatively against populist reform. In Orwellian tones, Powell wrote that the battle should be waged on all fronts: liberal professors teaching the youth to "despise the American political and economic system" must be challenged; textbooks "should be kept under constant surveillance"; the "national

RALPH NADER CAME TO REPRESENT THE
MOVEMENT TO REFORM AMERICAN BUSINESS
IN THE 1960S AND 1970S.

television networks should be monitored" and "equal time" for pro-
business views demanded; and "scholarly articles" on the benefits
of capitalism should be produced and disseminated widely to shape
Americans' attitudes.

To win this war of ideas required business to greatly enhance its
political organization and advocacy. Corporations "must learn the lesson learned by labor and other self-interested groups. This is the lesson
that political power is necessary; that such power must be assiduously
cultivated." Too often, businessmen were reluctant to speak out on
policy, fearing their companies would be tainted by the perception of
partisanship. When they did engage the public, they tended to misplay
their hands—as Powell's friend Joe Cullman knew all too well.

LEWIS POWELL'S CHILDHOOD FRIEND AND PHILIP MORRIS
CEO, JOSEPH CULLMAN, BECAME A LEADING, IF INEFFECTIVE,
SPOKESPERSON FOR TOBACCO COMPANIES.

As a spokesperson for the tobacco industry, Cullman was one of the rare businessmen of his era who had long been willing to participate in public debates over policy. He testified on Capitol Hill against health warning labels on cigarette packages and took to the airwaves to defend tobacco. He had the passion but not the judgment to be an effective messenger. In January 1971, only months before Powell wrote his memorandum, Cullman had appeared on the national television news program *Face the Nation* and insisted, contrary to all evidence, that cigarettes were neither addictive nor a health hazard. When one of the show's panelists asked him about a study finding that smoking during pregnancy led to reduced birth weight, a tone-deaf Cullman replied, "Some women would prefer having smaller babies."[14]

Powell was certain corporate America could do much better. Businessmen had to recognize their shared interest in defending the free enterprise system, rather than just fighting for their own company or industry. "Strength lies in organization, in careful long-range planning and implementation, in consistency of action over an indefinite period of years, in the scale of financing available only through joint effort, and in the political power available only through united action and national organizations." Joe Cullman should not be the only one on television arguing against tobacco regulation; every businessman had an interest in curtailing burdensome government mandates, no matter which industry was targeted this time around.

One battlefront Powell believed to be especially important was the courts. With the Warren court still fresh in memory, Powell reminded readers of his memorandum, "Under our constitutional system, especially with an activist-minded Supreme Court, the judiciary may be the most important instrument for social, economic and political change." Nader and the organizations on the left understood this. "Labor unions, civil rights groups and now the public interest law firms are extremely active in the judicial arena," the memorandum explained, "often at business' expense." The courts were a "neglected opportunity" for business corporations to assert their own rights.

Sydnor was thrilled with Powell's memo. In a thank-you note, Sydnor complimented Powell for his "excellent presentation of the vitally important case for American Business to go on the offensive after such a long period of inaction and indecision." In a sign of how seriously Powell and Sydnor took the memo and its goals, the men soon after drove two hours from Richmond to Washington, DC, to present the plan in person to a vice president of the US Chamber of Commerce. They hoped the memorandum might make a difference, and they likely expected the Chamber to take up at least some of Powell's recommendations. What they could not have imagined, however, was how influential the Powell Memorandum would turn out to be for both the Chamber and the country.[15]

* * *

IN 1969, AT THE HEIGHT of Ralph Nader's popularity, his father Nathra, a Lebanese immigrant, was asked about the activist's exceptional record of defeating America's most powerful corporations. "We're very proud of Ralph," Nathra answered. Yet not even a populist icon featured on the cover of *Time* and *Newsweek* could skirt the universal lament of parents: "But we wish he would get married soon."[16]

The consumer crusader's only marriages would be professional—and none was more successful than the one to Alan Morrison, the intense, steely-eyed New York lawyer with whom Nader cofounded Public Citizen's litigation arm, the Public Citizen Litigation Group, in 1972. Morrison was an unabashed liberal who had become a lawyer so he could work to improve society. The "big guys didn't need representation," Morrison explained. "The little guys did." When Morrison was working as a government attorney, one of his interns, who had been a Nader's Raider the summer before, introduced the two Harvard Law graduates.[17]

Nader brought Morrison into Public Citizen to set up a litigation shop. Reform through legislation was valuable, but Nader wanted Public Citizen to pursue lawsuits to protect the interests of consumers too. Often the law was already on the side of consumers but simply was not being properly enforced. Government agencies had the power but, due to industry capture or influence, not the will. Nader sought out what he called "a corps of . . . public-interest lawyers" who could pursue a case "year after dreary year as it proceeds through the regulatory agencies, the Congress, the courts, the executive branch bureaucracy." The Public Citizen Litigation Group would serve in that role and find considerable success—even though one of Nader and Morrison's greatest triumphs would redound largely to the benefit of big business.[18]

At the top of Morrison's agenda when he joined Public Citizen was to free up competition in the professions. Lawyers, doctors, opticians, accountants, and other professionals operated under long-standing rules that restricted their ability to advertise, limited how they could solicit clients, or required them to charge minimum fees. Although the rules were justified as measures to protect consumers, Morrison believed they did the opposite. Adopted by state licensing authorities and professional associations, such rules resulted in artificially high prices and made it harder for the poor to find adequate services. Instead of helping consumers, the rules, according to Morrison, served the interests of "lawyers who already had clients and who were probably the ones who wrote the rules."[19]

Lynn Jordan was one of the consumers hurt by the rules. A middle-class woman in suburban Virginia, Jordan suffered long-term health problems that eventually resulted in a hysterectomy. Her diet of pre-

ALAN MORRISON (LEFT), WHO LED RALPH NADER'S CONSUMER ADVOCACY LITIGATION GROUP, DEVELOPED AN INNOVATIVE AND INFLUENTIAL THEORY OF FREE SPEECH THAT ULTIMATELY HELPED COMMERCIAL SPEAKERS.

scription medicines was expensive, so she set out to find the best prices from the local pharmacies. The information was difficult to come by. Pharmacists in Virginia, like those of thirty-three other states, were prohibited from advertising the prices of prescription drugs. Many refused even to give customers prices over the telephone for fear of having their licenses revoked by the Virginia State Board of Pharmacy for "unprofessional conduct." Jordan was not deterred. It was the age of Nader and everywhere around her the law was bending toward the protection of consumers and away from corporate interests. Together with a group of like-minded amateur consumer activists, Jordan organized a survey of prescription drug prices in northern Virginia and Richmond. They found that prices for the same dosage of medicine varied wildly. For forty tetracycline tablets, a patient could pay $1.20 in one pharmacy and $9.00 in another—a difference of almost 650 percent. Without going from pharmacy to pharmacy, patients would never know there was a cheaper alternative.[20]

Morrison learned of Jordan's survey of drug prices from a Naderite working across the hall from his office. Although Morrison's focus had been on challenging restrictions on advertising by lawyers, he quickly saw that Virginia's ban on advertising drug prices had several advantages as a test case. Drug prices were objective and verifiable, unlike subjective claims about the quality of a lawyer. "We knew that attacking lawyer advertising rules would be difficult, not just because they existed in every state, but also because they were so universally accepted," Morrison remembered. And the judges who would be asked to rule on their lawfulness were chosen from among the "elite lawyers" who benefited the most from the advertising bans. Those judges, however, would not have the same stake in preserving restrictions on pharmacists.[21]

Morrison still had to discover a viable legal theory to support his challenge to the restrictions on drug prices. Advertising was considered "commercial speech," which the Supreme Court had said was not protected by the First Amendment in a 1942 case, *Valentine v. Chrestensen*. A natural showman, Francis Chrestensen owned a decommissioned US Navy submarine that he would dock in ports along the Atlantic coast, charging visitors 25¢ a tour. When war broke out in Europe, he sought to capitalize on the news by docking his submarine, dubbed the *Fighting Monster*, at a city-owned pier in lower Manhattan within sight of the Statue of Liberty. The city refused to grant him permission to use its pier, forcing Chrestensen to dock at an out-of-the-way spot up the East River. Without views of Lady Liberty, Chrestensen needed to stir up business, so he printed out handbills touting his *Fighting Monster* and offering visitors the chance to see "the only submarine used for exhibition purposes in the world." The handbills, however, were illegal. New York police informed Chrestensen that distributing commercial handbills was prohibited by the city's antilitter laws.[22]

Chrestensen was not one to be easily deterred, as his ex-wife discovered a few years before the dispute with New York police. Along with a local constable in Montreal, she had tried to serve Chrestensen with legal papers relating to their divorce, only to see the crafty captain retreat to his submarine, raise the Stars and Stripes, and warn the constable that any trespass would amount to a hostile invasion of American territory. As the flustered constable tried to figure out what to do, Chrestensen set back out to sea on the *Fighting Monster*, leaving his wife ashore to complain to reporters, "Never let your husband buy a submarine." In New York, that same creative streak led Chrestensen to seize upon an exception in the city's antilitter laws that permitted handbills containing political protests. On the flip side of his advertisements, he printed up a diatribe accusing local officials of acting "in a dictatorial manner" by refusing to allow him to moor at the city-owned pier. The city's police commissioner, Lewis J. Valentine, known to be a "stern" and "fearless police man, who hated dishonesty," was not amused and warned Chrestensen to stop distributing the handbills or face arrest. Chrestensen sued, claiming infringement of his right to freedom of speech.[23]

Like the police commissioner, the justices of the Supreme Court had little patience for Chrestensen's antics. In a terse opinion only a few paragraphs long, the court dismissed the entrepreneur's novel claim. "This court has unequivocally held that the streets are proper places for the exercise of the freedom of communicating information and disseminating opinion," the court wrote. "We are equally clear that the Constitution imposes no such restraint on government as respects purely commercial advertising." Unlike Huey Long's tax on the Louisiana newspapers, the antilitter law was not designed to persecute political dissenters. Although the court offered little explanation of why commercial speech was categorically excluded from the First Amendment, Chrestensen and his *Fighting Monster* had nonetheless met their match.[24]

Commercial speech—the advertising of drug prices—was precisely what Alan Morrison wanted the court to protect. And even if the court back in 1942 had not offered a thorough justification for excluding commercial speech from the First Amendment, *Valentine* remained good law and sound arguments could be made to support it. One of the traditional justifications for free speech, for example, was that it served democracy by enabling people to become informed citizens through the open discussion of ideas; advertising for commercial products, however, did not promote political self-governance in any obvious way. Another justification for free speech rested on self-realization, positing that individual expression helped people to develop their faculties and their identities. Most commercial speakers, however, were corporations or businesses for which advertising was simply about maximizing profit. Nevertheless, Nader had told Morrison "to test the outer limits of the law," so in July of 1973 the Public Citizen Litigation Group filed suit in federal court against the Virginia Board of Pharmacy on behalf of Lynn Jordan and others.[25]

There was one aspect of Morrison's case that would prove especially fateful: his plaintiffs were pharmacy customers, not pharmacists. Public Citizen's mission was to help consumers, not the businesses that sold to them. Yet this posed a dilemma for Morrison. Consumers like Lynn Jordan were not being denied the right to speak in any way. The law did nothing to stop Jordan from paying to take out an ad in the newspaper listing the price of drugs. It was a professional regulation that applied only to licensed pharmacists, and none of Morrison's plaintiffs were licensed pharmacists.

Like the crafty Captain Chrestensen, Morrison came up with an innovative solution. He would frame the case around the rights of listeners. Instead of focusing on how censorship harmed the speaker who was silenced, he would focus on the harms to the audience deprived of the information. The ad ban, he would argue, restricted the right of the *listeners* to hear what a pharmacist might say. The recipients of speech had their own, independent constitutional "right to know" that was equally entitled to First Amendment protection, regardless of any rights of the pharmacists. The drug ban was a perfect vehicle for such an argument because the primary injury from Virginia's law was not felt by pharmacists, who wrote the law and benefited from it. The people hurt the most were consumers, the would-be recipients of the censored speech.[26]

Around the same time Morrison was strategizing his consumer rights lawsuit, Martin Redish, a recent law school graduate aiming to become a law professor, published a law review article offering a similar, listeners' rights theory of the First Amendment. In the first half of his article, Redish argued that *Valentine* was wrongly decided and that commercial advertising, like political and artistic expression, was socially valuable. As Morrison would do in the pharmacy case, Redish argued that commercial speech provided consumers with essential information in the easiest, most accessible way. "Since advertising performs a significant function for its recipients, its values are better viewed with the consumer, rather than the seller, as the frame of reference." The identity of the speaker was irrelevant; it was the listeners' rights that mattered. If Morrison had discovered Redish's article, he would have found helpful reasoning and perhaps even a few citations he could have used in his briefs in Lynn Jordan's case.[27]

He would also have found a bright, bold red flag warning of the dangers inherent in a listeners' rights theory of free speech. The second half of Redish's article illustrated how this way of thinking about the First Amendment would apply to a number of current controversies, including the recently enacted federal law prohibiting tobacco advertising on television. Redish admitted that, under his approach to the First Amendment, the question was close. While recognizing the public health justifications behind the law, Redish also argued that consumers had a right to hear any truthful information the tobacco companies had to share. If so, then perhaps the ban on tobacco advertising was unconstitutional. Redish's article provided an ominous sign of how the law might develop—and who exactly would benefit—if the Supreme Court accepted the listeners' rights theory.

* * *

BY THE TIME MORRISON'S case arrived at the Supreme Court in 1975, everyone involved understood that much more than prescription drug ads was at stake. For Morrison, who planned to challenge bans on lawyer ads later, the pharmacy case was about establishing the consumer's right to know. Virginia, meanwhile, defended the ban as part of the long-standing tradition of state regulation of the professions designed to protect consumers; were this ban to fall, Virginia's lawyers argued, it would cast doubt on any number of laws governing how lawyers, doctors, dentists, and others solicit clients. Both sides claimed to be helping consumers—even as the case would, in the end, mostly help corporations.[28]

While Morrison hoped the justices would articulate broad principles that could be deployed in his next case, he also wanted to win this one. That meant keeping the justices focused on drug ads rather than the more controversial issue of lawyer ads. Morrison repeatedly emphasized the narrowness of the issue before the court. "There is only one question," he told the justices, "and that is the constitutionality of the Virginia statute which prohibits the advertising of the price of prescription drugs." Justice Byron "Whizzer" White knew better. White, who earned his memorable nickname as a professional football player—he led the National Football League in rushing in 1938 as a running back for the Pittsburgh Steelers franchise—was a force on and off the bench. Off the bench, he was known for his rough play on the basketball court located surprisingly on the top floor of the Supreme Court Building. (Clerks dutifully called White "the best player on the highest court in the land.") On the bench, he asked tough questions and, although appointed by liberal president John F. Kennedy, was impossible to pigeonhole ideologically. He opposed abortion rights, gay rights, and, as we will see, corporate rights. "I suppose your next case is going to involve advertising for lawyers," White suggested to Morrison. Just as Morrison was about to answer, however, White uncharacteristically let Morrison off the hook. "That's all right," White said knowingly, "you don't have to answer that one."[29]

When the court issued its opinion in *Virginia Pharmacy Board v. Virginia Citizens Consumer Council* in May of 1976, the vote was 7–1 in favor of Morrison. (As it has more recently, the Supreme Court then was operating with only eight justices; William O. Douglas, a liberal icon appointed by Franklin D. Roosevelt, had retired from the court the day after oral argument in Morrison's case.) The majority decision was written by Justice Harry Blackmun, one of the four Nixon appointees. Blackmun was in his fifth term on the court and was already well on his way to becoming somewhat of a liberal icon himself as the author of the 1973 majority opinion in *Roe v. Wade*. That decision, however, which is today often criticized as liberal judicial activism, was not reflective of the general tilt of Blackmun's jurisprudence in his early years on the court. He and the conservative chief justice Warren Burger were known as the "Minnesota Twins," in part because they were lifelong friends from St. Paul, but also because they voted together in lockstep. In those first five terms on the court, Blackmun voted with Burger in 87 percent of the closely divided cases and with the liberal William Brennan in only 13 percent.[30]

Blackmun's opinion in *Virginia Pharmacy* appeared, like *Roe*, to be a liberal decision, one that would help consumer rights activists like Nader. Blackmun heartily embraced Morrison's novel listeners' rights theory of the First Amendment. Even without a pharmacist whose own speech was restricted, the First Amendment "protection afforded is to the communication, to its source and to its recipients both." A consumer like Lynn Jordan had an "interest in the free flow of commercial information" that "may be as keen, if not keener by far, than [her] interest in the day's most urgent political debate." This was especially so for "the poor, the sick and particularly the aged," who spent a disproportionate amount of their income on prescription drugs. The First Amendment's guarantee of free speech is "enjoyed by the appellees as recipients of the information, and not solely, if at all, by the advertisers themselves." The court held that commercial advertising was constitutionally protected—and, in doing so, insisted that the identity of the speaker was irrelevant.[31]

Following Morrison's lead, Blackmun characterized the ruling as narrow. Although the court was overturning *Valentine* and adopting a potentially expansive new theory of the First Amendment, Blackmun took pains to point out that some "forms of commercial speech regulation are surely permissible." False and deceptive commercial speech could be limited, and Blackmun also said that commercial speech deserved less protection than political speech. In answer to White's question at oral argument, Blackmun included a footnote saying the decision should not be read to call into doubt advertising bans by other professionals, like physicians and lawyers.

Lewis Powell was not one to lean instinctively in favor of Ralph Nader and Public Citizen, and he explicitly disagreed with the listeners' rights theory of the First Amendment. During deliberations in the pharmacy case, Powell jotted down in his case file that "there is no Const[itutional] right to know." The First Amendment was about protecting the rights of speakers, not the rights of listeners. Yet Powell also thought the advertising restrictions on pharmacists were foolish, and many other conservatives were starting to agree. The Nixon administration was pursuing a broad agenda of deregulating the nation's airlines, banking, and telecommunications industries, and saw the advertising ban in that same light. Two weeks after oral argument in Morrison's case, the administration filed its own suit to strike down a drug price advertising ban as an unlawful restraint of trade under federal antitrust law—similar to the claims brought against the American Tobacco Company and the Tobacco Trust back in the early 1900s. Meanwhile, newspapers reported that Nixon's Federal Trade Commission was considering new rules to *require* pharmacists to publicize their prices. Despite Powell's clear trepidation about the listeners' rights theory, he cast his vote with the majority to invalidate the drug price advertising ban.[32]

The lone dissenter in the case was Justice William Rehnquist, another Nixon appointee, and he saw the case as anything but narrow. With longish hair and thick, mutton chop sideburns, Rehnquist looked like one of the counterculture radicals Nixon railed against rather than the strict, states' rights conservative he was. Rehnquist, in fact, had spent most of his career involved with the Supreme Court, clerking for Justice Robert Jackson in the 1950s, vetting judicial nominees for the Nixon administration, and serving on the court himself for thirty-three years, the last nineteen as chief justice. His approach to cases involving corporate rights was evocative of another chief justice, Roger Taney. On this issue at least, both were populists who thought states should have broad leeway to regulate business and who opposed expansive constitutional rights for corporations.[33]

"The logical consequences of the court's decision in this case are far-reaching indeed," warned Rehnquist. Not only would the court's ruling inevitably "extend to lawyers, doctors, and all other professions," it would also lead to "active promotion of prescription drugs, liquor, cigarettes, and other products." In a prescient passage, Rehnquist predicted that pharmaceutical companies would soon be hawking their drugs directly to consumers: "Don't spend another sleepless night," he predicted the ads might say. "Ask your doctor to prescribe Seconal without delay." Rehnquist also saw the red flags that Martin Redish, the aspiring law professor, had highlighted in his article on commercial speech. Although consumers might be helped in this one case, the court's ruling would nonetheless call into question a wide variety of laws regulating "existing commercial and industrial practices" beyond advertising. Rehnquist's dissent in *Virginia Pharmacy* would turn out to be one of the most farsighted opinions in the history of the Supreme Court.

Never one to agree with Rehnquist, the *New York Times* hailed Nader and Morrison's case as "a significant victory for consumers." The two progressive activists agreed, with Morrison expressing satisfaction with the majority's sweeping listeners' rights theory of the First Amendment, which he said would likely lead to other advertising bans, such as those on lawyers, being struck down. Indeed, the very next term, the justices adhered to the logic of *Virginia Pharmacy* and invalidated a ban on lawyer advertising. Although Morrison was not the lawyer behind the lawyer ad case, he was nonetheless thrilled with the result; Nader and Morrison had always hoped the pharmacy case would have a broad impact.[34]

And it did. The case was arguably the last great victory for consumer rights in the 1970s, a legal swan song, as Nader and the progressive Left were quickly being overtaken by a mounting conservative backlash. Over the next two decades, the doctrine created by *Virginia Pharmacy* would rarely be used by consumers like Lynn Jordan but would be invoked instead by tobacco companies challenging restrictions on tobacco advertising; gaming interests seeking to overturn restrictions on television and radio ads for casinos; the liquor industry in an effort to invalidate laws limiting alcohol advertising; and dairy producers hoping to defeat requirements to disclose the use of synthetic growth hormones. And, as we will see, the decision was also used to justify the extension of political speech rights to corporations even before *Citizens United*. By 2011, the impact of Public Citizen's drug advertising lawsuit was recognized to be so contrary to consumer interests that Robert Weisman, the president of Public Citizen, called for the entire line of commercial speech cases to be overturned. It was a poignant, First Amendment version of buyer's remorse.[35]

* * *

IN 1976, THE YEAR *Virginia Pharmacy* was decided, the Ad Council, an organization that produced and distributed public service announcements, launched a major initiative to "create greater understanding of the American economic system." The Ad Council had been the creative force behind some of the most iconic advertising campaigns of the twentieth century: the "Loose Lips Sink Ships" ads to support World War II bonds; the "Smokey the Bear" ads on wildfire prevention; and "The Mind Is a Terrible Thing to Waste" ads for the United Negro College Fund. With financial support from what the Ad Council described as a "who's who in American business," the new multimillion-dollar campaign to defend free enterprise, which included television ads, newsletters, and educational materials for schools, was a direct outgrowth of Lewis Powell's memorandum to the Chamber of Commerce.[36]

When it was first written, the Powell Memorandum was marked "confidential," intended only for the leaders of the Chamber of Commerce and perhaps a small group of Powell and Sydnor's friends. The memo did not become public until many months after Powell's confirmation when, in September of 1972, Jack Anderson, the legendary columnist for the *Washington Post*, received a leaked copy and wrote an explosive piece about it. Calling the memo "so militant that it raises a question about [Powell's] fitness to decide any case involving business interests," Anderson hoped the American public would rise up against the court's newest justice. Anderson's column, however, had a very dif-

ECONOMIC EDUCATION ON TV
THE COMPETITIVE ENTERPRISE SYSTEM

This clever new 60-second public service announcement
sells THE COMPETITIVE ENTERPRISE SYSTEM.

DETAIL OF THE AD COUNCIL'S MARKETING CAMPAIGN TO
PROMOTE FREE ENTERPRISE TO AMERICA'S YOUTH.

ferent result: it led the Chamber to publicize the letter widely, which
in turn inspired corporate America to rise up against Nader and the
reform movement.[37]

The impact of the memorandum was felt quickly. Within a year of Anderson's column, a Chamber of Commerce task force could plausibly claim, "Millions of Americans—including many prominent business executives—have read it" and "hundreds of thousands of copies have been circulated." The Chamber enthusiastically endorsed Powell's call to arms, as did business tycoons like Joseph Coors, John M. Olin, and Richard Mellon Scaife, in addition to major American corporations like U.S. Steel, General Electric, Dow Chemical, and Kraft. One sign of the new political orientation of industry was the growth in the number of corporations with "government affairs" lobbyists in Washington, which surged over 500 percent between 1968 and 1978.[38]

The Powell Memorandum touched off what one historian called "an explosion of efforts to recast Americans' understanding of business and economics and to rehabilitate the public image of corporations." In this war of ideas, a central role was played not only by the Ad Council but also think tanks devoted to free-market principles and reduced government regulation, such as the Heritage Foundation (1973), the Cato Institute (1974), and the Manhattan Institute (1978). Although founded earlier, the American Enterprise Institute grew from a staff of 19 and a budget of $879,000 in 1970 to a staff of 135 and a budget of over $10 million in 1980. With financing from business interests, the think tanks did for corporations what Nader's Raiders did for consumers. They gathered information, analyzed it, and publicized it to the public and to lawmakers to influence legislation. The main difference was that when Nader's Raiders went their separate ways as the reform movement slowed in the mid-1970s, the conservative and libertarian think tanks were growing stronger and soon flourished.[39]

Spurred by the memorandum, the Chamber of Commerce revamped itself to become one of the most influential lobbying organizations in Washington. That the Chamber would play such an overtly political role would have outraged its first president, a Chicago lawyer named Henry A. Wheeler. Originally founded as a government agency to facilitate information sharing between lawmakers and industry, the Chamber was privatized in 1912 with the blessing of President

CONFIDENTIAL MEMORANDUM

ATTACK ON AMERICAN FREE ENTERPRISE SYSTEM

TO: Mr. Eugene B. Sydnor, Jr.   DATE: August 23, 1971
           Chairman
           Education Committee
           U.S. Chamber of Commerce

FROM: Lewis F. Powell, Jr.

      This memorandum is submitted at your request as a
basis for the discussion on August 24 with Mr. Booth and others
at the U.S. Chamber of Commerce. The purpose is to identify the
problem, and suggest possible avenues of action for further
consideration.

Dimensions of the Attack

William Howard Taft, the brother of Tobacco Trust prosecutor Henry Taft. Wheeler doggedly kept the Chamber out of partisan politics. When President Taft asked the Chamber to support his reelection bid, Wheeler refused, insisting on the need to preserve the organization's neutrality. The Chamber, Wheeler said, "will not, I trust, ever in its history become a lobbying organization." When Powell was writing his memo in the summer of 1971, the Chamber had a large membership but remained politically moribund. As one vice president put it, the Chamber had "no muscle either in the executive branch or on Capitol Hill."[40]

Powell's memo triggered a complete overhaul of the Chamber's approach to politics—and, more broadly, ushered in a new era in which business lobbyists would come to dominate lawmaking in Washington. The Chamber established its own think tank, the National Chamber Foundation, to publish pro-business research. It began a series of public education campaigns to defend free enterprise, even hiring Hanna-Barbera Studios, the makers of the popular primetime cartoons *The*

Flintstones and *The Jetsons*, to create animated public service announcements promoting capitalism to children. The Chamber also mimicked Nader's style of grassroots lobbying to mobilize business. With a network of 2,800 state and local chambers and over 200,000 business firm members to generate telephone calls, letters, and editorials, the Chamber developed into "one of the best grassroots lobbying organizations in America." The Chamber's politics became increasingly hostile to regulation, opposing proposals for healthcare reform, campaign finance law, consumer protection laws, and environmental legislation. Its politics were also more partisan, with the overwhelming majority of the Chamber's activity going to help Republicans. In 2012, the Chamber devoted $58 million to election campaigns and—in stark contrast to Wheeler's prediction—more than $135 million to lobbying; no organization in the country besides the political parties themselves spent more on politics.[41]

Washington politics would also be reshaped by the Business Roundtable, founded in 1972 on the basis of the Powell Memorandum and "in the belief that business executives should take an increased role in the continuing debates about public policy." Bryce Harlow, a Procter & Gamble representative who came to be known as "unofficial dean" of Washington lobbyists, recalled that, due to the social welfare regulation of the Nader era, "the danger had suddenly escalated. . . . We had to prevent business from being rolled up and put in the trash can" by Congress. Harlow, along with the chief executives of Campbell Soup, U.S. Steel, General Electric, and Alcoa, recruited an exclusive membership of Fortune 500 CEOs to launch what an early consultants' report called a "total attack program." In addition to funding pro-business publicity campaigns in *Reader's Digest*, the most popular magazine in the country, the Roundtable launched an innovative government relations strategy that made it, according to one source, "the most powerful lobby in Washington." Instead of sending paid representatives like Harlow to meet with members of Congress, the Roundtable would send CEOs from the nation's largest companies. As one staffer acknowledged, lobbyists could be "shunted over to a legislative assistant. But the chairman of the board is going to get to see the senator."[42]

From his seat on the Supreme Court, Powell thought it would be inappropriate of him to promote the memorandum even as it gained fame and influence. Yet when people wrote to Powell asking for a copy, he unfailingly directed them to the Chamber. And although a Supreme Court justice could not engage in the sort of advocacy proposed in the memorandum, Powell's position gave him other unique opportunities to shape the law and to promote the memorandum's goals. One case in particular, a dispute over the referendum process in Massachusetts, enabled him to write his vision of politically active business corporations into the First Amendment of the Constitution. And Ralph Nader and Alan Morrison's victory in the *Virginia Pharmacy* case would help him do it.

* * *

THE CONTROVERSY OVER MASSACHUSETTS'S referendum process had begun years earlier, in 1962, when reformers sought a state-wide vote on an amendment to the commonwealth's constitution to allow for a progressive income tax. At the time, Massachusetts's constitution required a flat income tax, but liberal reform groups argued that a graduated tax that imposed higher rates on those who earned the most was more equitable. Richard Hill, the chairman of the First National Bank of Boston and "New England's most influential banker," was among the top earners in the region, and he was committed to stopping the graduated tax amendment.[43]

Hill sat on the boards of the region's largest companies, including United Fruit Corporation, Boston Edison, NYNEX (later Verizon), Polaroid, Raytheon, and John Hancock Mutual Life. Politically active, Hill had earned top honors in *Who Rules Boston?*, a book that ranked the city's power brokers. He was a graduate of Dartmouth College, like Daniel Webster, and he chaired the college's Board of Trustees a century and a half after that board hired the Corporation's Lawyer to bring one of the earliest lawsuits to establish constitutional rights for corporations in *Dartmouth College v. Woodward*. Following Webster's footsteps, Hill, a member of the brand new Business Roundtable who shared Powell's view of the necessity of

RICHARD HILL (RIGHT), WHO FOUGHT TO ALLOW
CORPORATIONS TO SPEND ON POLITICS,
AT A GROUNDBREAKING FOR FIRST NATIONAL
BANK OF BOSTON, 1968.

corporate activism, would also lead a series of lawsuits to expand
corporate rights.

Under Massachusetts's law, corporations like First National Bank
were prohibited from making political expenditures. In 1907, Massachusetts was one of the many states that, like Congress, barred corporate spending on campaigns in the wake of Charles Evans Hughes's
discoveries in the Great Wall Street Scandal. Nonetheless, the Massachusetts law contained a loophole. It did not apply to companies that
wished to spend on ballot measures "materially affecting any of the
property, business or assets of the corporation." Taking advantage of

this exception, Hill and executives from several other Massachusetts corporations, including Digital Equipment Corporation and Gillette, forged a successful campaign to defeat the graduated tax amendment. Six years later, in 1968, the graduated tax proposal went before the voters a second time, only to lose once more in the face of significant corporate spending by Hill's company and others.[44]

In 1972, lawmakers in Massachusetts decided to try a third time to pass the graduated tax amendment, even if it meant changing the rules of the political game. They revised the corporate political spending law to narrow the loophole Hill's corporation had used to defeat the earlier referendums. Under the new law, corporations could still finance expenditures on ballot propositions that materially affected their businesses, with one exception: any measure "concerning the taxation of the income, property or transactions of individuals" was to be deemed automatically immaterial to business interests. In legalese, taxes on individuals were "conclusively presumed" to be irrelevant to any business.

At Hill's direction, First National Bank filed suit to protect its rights, and Massachusetts's highest court ruled in the bank's favor. The court held that the graduated tax measure on the 1972 ballot would authorize lawmakers to impose graduated taxes on both individuals *and* corporations, and thus the measure was not immaterial to First National. The court did not say that First National had a First Amendment right to participate in ballot measure elections. It only held that the law, as written, permitted political expenditures in these circumstances. With financing from First National, opponents of the graduated tax outspent supporters 6–1 and the proposal was defeated once again.[45]

In 1975, Massachusetts lawmakers sought a fourth vote on a graduated tax and changed the rules again. Now corporations were prohibited from spending on any measure related "solely" to individual taxation—and, this time, the measure placed on the ballot was explicitly limited to individuals.

Hill remained undaunted. Like an increasing number of businesspeople in the years after publication of the Powell Memorandum,

Hill was convinced of the need to defend the interests of business, and his resolve had only been fortified by the stagnating economy of the mid-1970s. Beginning in 1973, a deep two-year recession brought on by the international oil crisis was eating into corporate profits. Many business executives, who were already questioning the dominant philosophy of active government intervention to manage the economy, blamed the recent wave of Nader-inspired regulation. Their companies faced billions of dollars in new compliance costs and "the government," a 1975 issue of *Fortune* complained, "is now present—either in person, or somewhat like Banquo's ghost, in disturbing spirit—at every major business meeting." The marketplace, in many businessmen's view, needed an exorcism to get rid of burdenson regulation.[46]

Certain that a progressive income tax on individuals would further inhibit economic growth and make it harder to recruit top-notch talent to Massachusetts, Hill and other businessmen had first lobbied to stop the legislature from putting the measure on the ballot. When that failed, they outspent opponents and defeated the measure on Election Day— several times. When lawmakers threw up new hurdles, the businessmen went to court to protect their interests. It was precisely the type of relentless, assertive mobilization of business envisioned by the Powell Memorandum. And the final word on whether Massachusetts could prohibit corporations from spending money to influence ballot campaigns would rest with the court on which sat the memorandum's author.

* * *

WHEN POWELL WAS A STUDENT at Harvard Law School in the 1930s, one of his professors was Felix Frankfurter, the brilliant, Austrian-born cofounder of the American Civil Liberties Union who also served as one of President Franklin Roosevelt's closest advisors during the New Deal. After Roosevelt appointed Frankfurter to the Supreme Court in 1939, the liberal academic became a conservative judge, consistently arguing for judicial restraint at a time when the court's liberal majority was growing increasingly bold. In a 1946 case, Frankfurter warned the court to stay out of election cases in particular. Things like the drawing of congressional districts were inherently partisan, and judges lacked the requisite expertise and understanding of how elections work to make sound decisions. Election cases were, Frankfurter said, a "political thicket" that would ensnare unsuspecting judges.[47]

In the mid-1970s, as the battle in Massachusetts between lawmakers and Richard Hill raged, the Supreme Court disregarded Frankfurter's advice and issued some of the most important, controversial, and, in the eyes of some, wrongheaded decisions in recent memory. One case stood out above the others, *Buckley v. Valeo*, decided in 1976. In *Buckley*, the court held that campaign finance laws could restrict the size of contributions *to* candidates but not the amount of spending *by* candidates and others. *Buckley*'s split-the-baby compromise, which had the unfortunate effect of forcing candidates to engage in an endless cycle of fund-raising, has been roundly criticized by Democrats, Republicans, federal and state regulators, politicians, contributors, and political fund-raisers—in short, nearly everyone involved in the financing of elections.[48]

One reason *Buckley* was so problematic was the court's rejection of equality as a guiding principle in campaign finance law. The court said that lawmakers could seek to prevent bribery or the appearance of corruption, but they could not try to enhance the equality of voices in the political community. The court applied this principle to strike down limits on "independent expenditures"—money spent to support candidates but without prior coordination with the campaigns. As a result, individuals could spend unlimited sums on advertisements promoting their favored candidates, so long as they did so "independently." *Citizens United* would extend to corporations the same right to make unlimited independent expenditures, and cite *Buckley* for support.

Although the court in *Buckley* insisted that equality was "wholly foreign to the First Amendment," in fact that principle ran throughout the institutional design of American politics. Every citizen had one vote, political debates gave each candidate equal time, and legislative districts were required to be drawn evenly to ensure equal representation. After *Buckley*, however, equality was something campaign finance law was uniquely prohibited from promoting. And that was good news for Richard Hill and First National Bank, whose strategy was to outspend their opponents.

When the Supreme Court heard arguments in First National's case in November of 1977, the lawyers were afforded the benefit of the equality principle the justices had rejected in *Buckley*: each side was given exactly thirty minutes to argue at the lectern. Francis H. Fox, the attorney for First National, who would go on to become one of the antiabortion movement's leading lawyers, admitted there were no previous Supreme Court cases clearly holding that corporations had the same First Amendment rights as individuals. Nonetheless, he argued, *Virginia Pharmacy* implicitly recognized the free speech rights of businesses to advertise drug prices. Moreover, Massachusetts's corporate spending law was designed to reduce the "undue influence of wealth," which was just another way of equalizing voices.[49]

Massachusetts, whose legal team was led by Francis X. Bellotti, the commonwealth's popular attorney general, argued that the law was not designed to promote political equality but was about "preserving the integrity of the referendum." Besides, "business corporations are simply quite different from natural persons." Massachusetts emphasized the line drawn by the Supreme Court at the turn of the twentieth century between property rights and liberty rights. Business corporations "do not have First Amendment rights per se" nor do they "exercise other purely personal rights such as the privilege against self-incrimination." The only exception was for a media corporation, such as the Louisiana newspaper companies or the *New York Times*, for whom it was "in its charter or it is part of its business" to engage in speech.

Although Massachusetts harkened back to the corporate rights jurisprudence of the early twentieth century, it was now a new era—one in which business interests were more determined than ever to have their voices heard, both in politics and in court. One sign of that new activism was the half-dozen friend-of-the-court (or "amicus") briefs filed in First National Bank's case, including ones by pro-business groups like the Associated Industries of Massachusetts, the New England Council, the Pacific Legal Foundation, and the Chamber of Commerce. Amicus briefs, which provide the justices with additional information and arguments besides those presented by the parties to a case, were once rare. In the 1950s, for example, only about fifty such briefs were filed per year, often by liberal groups like the American Civil Liberties Union. Today, the justices receive about eight hundred amicus briefs a year, despite taking about half as many cases as they did in the 1950s. The most frequent friends of the court are now commercial interests and business trade groups that followed Powell's advice, like the Chamber.[50]

Powell was a predictable vote in favor of Hill and First National Bank. The question remained whether the arguments made at hearing and in the amicus briefs filed by business interests would be enough to secure a majority in favor of corporate political speech rights.

* * *

AFTER THE HEARING IN *First National Bank of Boston v. Bellotti*, the justices met in their private conference to discuss and vote on the case. The conference is a closed-door meeting of the justices and no one else, not even law clerks or secretaries, is allowed in the room. The chief justice is the first to speak about a given case and then each justice, in order of seniority, states his or her own view. No justice is allowed to talk a second time until every justice has had the opportunity to speak once. The conference, in other words, just like oral argument in the Supreme Court, nods to a principle of equality when it comes to speech similar to the one rejected in *Buckley v. Valeo*.

In the typical case, the justices meet, vote, and assign someone to write the majority opinion. Although the justices are permitted to change their minds up until the day the final, written opinion is released to the public months after the private conference, the votes usually do not change. One justice will write the opinion for the court and the justices who supported that position in the conference will sign on, perhaps making a few suggestions about wording or emphasis. Every once in a while, however, the tidy decision-making process turns tumultuous, and a case is completely transformed once the writing begins. That is precisely what happened in the *First National Bank* case, making what would be a minor decision written by the court's most liberal justice, William Brennan, into a groundbreaking one written by Lewis Powell.

Although the conference and the justices' deliberations are all conducted in secret, the story of the *First National Bank* case can be pieced together by examining the papers of the justices who have since retired or passed. Powell's notes from the conference reveal initially that most of the justices, whether liberal or conservative, agreed that Massachusetts had gone too far. Brennan argued that the court did not need to rule broadly that corporations had free speech rights. Instead, the court could rule narrowly, striking down only the "conclusive presumption" that individual tax measures were immaterial to any corporation's business. Massachusetts had already decided to allow corporations to spend on ballot measures that were material to their businesses. There was no valid reason for denying them the opportunity to show that individual taxes were material too. The problem with Massachusetts's law, in Brennan's view, was not that it restricted corporate spending on politics but that it was a bald-faced effort to manipulate the outcome of a particular election.[51]

As the justices went around the table discussing the Massachusetts law, nearly all of them concurred with Brennan that a narrow ruling would suffice to decide this case. Two justices disagreed, White and Powell. White was the only justice who believed that Massachusetts's law should be upheld in its entirety. He argued that this case was simply about whether corporations had political speech rights, and in White's view, corporations had no such rights whatsoever. They were, he argued, artificial entities that enjoyed special privileges like limited liability, and Massachusetts was free to impose whatever limits it wanted, broad or narrow, on their political advocacy.[52]

The corporationalist Powell also disagreed with Brennan, but in the other direction: he thought the court should rule broadly that corporations had the same freedom of speech as individuals. The problem in Powell's view was not just the "conclusive presumption" that individual taxes were immaterial to any business; Massachusetts had no authority to restrict corporate spending at all, whether the issue was material to a company's business or not. Like individuals, corpora-

THE JUSTICES OF THE SUPREME COURT WHO DECIDED *FIRST
NATIONAL BANK OF BOSTON*. STANDING, LEFT TO RIGHT:
WILLIAM REHNQUIST, HARRY BLACKMUN, LEWIS POWELL,
JOHN PAUL STEVENS. SITTING, LEFT TO RIGHT: BYRON WHITE,
WILLIAM BRENNAN, WARREN BURGER, POTTER STEWART,
THURGOOD MARSHALL.

tions should be free to determine for themselves when to speak about
politics. As he wrote on the margins of a document in his case file, the
Massachusetts law had to be struck down "unless the court is willing
to say that corporations have inferior 1st A[mendment] rights."[53]

None of the other justices, however, thought it necessary to make
such a broad declaration of equal speech rights for corporations. This
case could be decided on the narrower grounds suggested by Brennan, and each side could claim a small victory. First National would
be the nominal victor, and Massachusetts's legal decree that individual
tax measures were immaterial would be invalidated. Yet Massachusetts could still require the bank to prove in court that a graduated tax
on individuals was material to its business. If First National failed to
make such a showing, it could still be prohibited from making political expenditures to defeat the referendum.

The chief justice assigned the opinion to Brennan. It appeared as if Powell had lost the opportunity to issue an expansive ruling giving business the political speech rights he thought necessary to fight back against reformers. Yet the case was about to take an unexpected turn.

* * *

WILLIAM BRENNAN WAS ONE of the most influential justices ever to sit on the Supreme Court. Appointed in 1956 by President Dwight Eisenhower, a Republican, Brennan became the intellectual leader of the Warren court—so much so that some people thought it should be called the Brennan court. By the time the Massachusetts law on corporate political spending came before Brennan and the other justices, however, the brash liberalism of the 1960s was being overtaken by a rising conservative tide that followed the channel suggested by the Powell Memorandum. Brennan still achieved some notable liberal victories after President Nixon transformed the court—including *Furman v. Georgia*, temporarily outlawing the death penalty; *Roe v. Wade* (1973), guaranteeing women the right to abortion; and *Craig v. Boren* (1976), prohibiting sex discrimination. Nonetheless, by the time he retired in 1990, Brennan had gone from being the potent instigator of the Warren court to the great dissenter of the Rehnquist court. The Massachusetts case involving First National Bank was one of the key turning points.[54]

As Brennan began drafting the opinion, he found himself in a quandary. He had originally proposed a narrow ruling, focused only on the "conclusive presumption"—the part of Massachusetts's law that decreed individual tax measures off limits for corporations. Yet as he thought through the issue, Brennan became increasingly convinced that such a limited ruling would be an abdication of the court's duty to provide a clear and final resolution to the controversy. First National would win this case but still remain uncertain if it could spend money to defeat the graduated tax measure. The two sides would soon be right back in court arguing over whether the measure was, in fact, material to First National's business. In all likelihood, the case was going to return to the Supreme Court, where the justices would eventually have to decide whether and how states could restrict corporate spending on ballot measures.

A few weeks after the conference, Brennan sent around a note to the other justices expressing his view that the "constitutionality of the general ban" on corporate political expenditures "must also be decided." Powell had been right at the conference to suggest the court reach that broader question. Yet unlike Powell, Brennan said he would go along with Justice White and vote to uphold Massachusetts's ban in its entirety. Pointing to the Tillman Act prompted by Charles Evans Hughes's investigation into the Great Wall Street Scandal of 1905, Brennan wrote, "Corporate spending as a corrupting influence in the political process has long been a national concern and has produced numerous corrupt practices acts, federal and state, ever since Theodore Roosevelt some 75 years ago urged their passage as necessary to curb the abuse to enhance representative democratic government." As the justices in conference had agreed to decide the case on the narrower issue of the "conclusive presumption," Brennan suggested that he was no longer the best person to write the opinion.[55]

Powell was incredulous, writing "Wow!" in the margins of his copy of Brennan's memo. Yet Brennan had also provided Powell with an opportunity. Several days later, Powell circulated a note of his own. He agreed with Brennan that the justices should address the larger question of corporate speech rights but argued again for striking down the entire law. Powell's note set out his view of the merits in detail and served as a none-too-subtle invitation to Chief Justice Burger to reassign the opinion to him.[56]

Burger complied and offered Powell the chance to write the court's opinion. Powell, however, faced immediate challenges. Now that they were focused on the broad question of the political speech rights of corporations, justices began to peel off and side with Brennan and White. Thurgood Marshall, who argued for the rights of nonprofit membership corporations when he was with the NAACP, now agreed with the dissenters who thought business corporations could be restricted in their political spending. Burger, too, soon began to waver, as he was often known to do, and circulated a memo expressing reluctance about "taking any step which would undermine state and federal Corrupt Practices Acts," like the Tillman Act. Moreover, Burger wrote, "It seems to me that there are differences between the First Amendment rights of an individual as compared with a corporate-collective body." Corporate politics raised the problem that Brandeis had long ago identified as "other people's money" corruption; stockholders, Burger complained, are "rarely, if ever" consulted before corporate money is spent on politics. Burger declined to say exactly how he would vote on the case, but it was looking increasingly as though there were four votes against Powell's position. His majority was teetering.[57]

Then Powell received the alarming news that Rehnquist was going to vote with Brennan, White, Marshall, and potentially Burger. As Rehnquist's opinion in the *Virginia Pharmacy* case had suggested, he was a states' rights justice rather than a pro-business justice like Powell. Rehnquist had thought the case could be decided on narrower grounds, but now that the justices were focused on the broader question of whether states could ever prohibit corporate political speech, Rehnquist would side with Massachusetts. If Burger carried through on his threat to do the same, the vote would be 5–4 against Richard Hill, First National Bank, and Lewis Powell.

Desperate to save his majority, Powell attempted to turn Rehnquist. There was an unspoken camaraderie between the two Nixon appointees. They had gone through the confirmation process together, both having been nominated on the same day and sworn in on the same day. Powell thought he might be able to persuade Rehnquist of the importance of this issue to the future of free enterprise, and he sent a note requesting some time to talk. "As you are a man of reason (especially when you agree with me)," Powell offered with a touch of ingratiating humor, "I would like to have about a ten-minute 'shot' at you to amplify my arguments." The outreach, however, proved unsuccessful, and two weeks later Rehnquist distributed a dissent arguing that corporations had no political speech rights under the First Amendment.[58]

Powell had to find a way to preserve his majority. There were now four solid votes against him—Brennan, White, Marshall, and

Rehnquist—and the unreliable chief justice was on the fence. Powell also had reason to believe Blackmun was wavering now too. He had to come up with a way to frame his opinion to keep Burger and Blackmun on board.

Powell allayed the chief justice's fears about undermining the Tillman Act and similar laws by adding language to his draft opinion that distinguished ballot measures from candidate elections. In an election for candidates, outside spending might be corrupting because the candidate who benefited might feel indebted to the spenders. A ballot measure campaign, Powell said, "presents no comparable problem" because there is no candidate involved. Although Powell's distinction was questionable—ballot measure campaigns are often closely associated with particular candidates and elected officials, raising similar threats of indebtedness to funders—Burger was satisfied.

The indecisive and vacillating Blackmun required another approach. Especially during his early years on the Supreme Court, Blackmun was known for agonizing endlessly over his votes. It was not false modesty but a lack of confidence that led Blackmun to describe his own draft opinions as "feeble." In the conference, Blackmun had expressed support for corporations having at least some free speech rights of a commercial nature, which was the logical implication of his own opinion in *Virginia Pharmacy*. Yet, as Powell noted in his file, Blackmun was "not fully persuaded" that the First Amendment prohibited states from restricting corporate *political* speech. Moreover, Blackmun's clerk, who had written an early memorandum summarizing the case that was distributed to all the justices, suggested that states could legitimately restrict corporate political spending as a way to protect shareholders.[59]

Powell found a way to secure Blackmun's vote by constitutional leveraging: he would exploit Blackmun's earlier opinion in *Virginia Pharmacy* to keep him in the majority. From the beginning, Powell had seen this case as one about whether corporations had the same free speech rights as individuals. Yet it had become clear that such an argument would not likely command a majority. *Virginia Pharmacy* offered an alternative pathway to victory. Powell could make this case about the rights of listeners, not about the rights of corporations. Just as Virginia's ban on advertising prescription drug prices interfered with the flow of commercial information to consumers, Massachusetts's ban on corporate spending interfered with the flow of political information to voters. Although corporations had long been limited in making political expenditures, under *Virginia Pharmacy* the identity of the speaker was irrelevant. Despite the fact that Powell had indicated in the deliberations over *Virginia Pharmacy* that he did not believe that listeners had a "right to know," he could nonetheless use Alan Morrison and Ralph Nader's theory, developed in the context of individuals, to keep Blackmun's vote and win broader rights for corporations.[60]

The idea to focus on the rights of listeners rather than the rights of corporations was apparently first suggested to Powell by Nancy Bregstein, one of his law clerks. Like many young women in the mid-1970s, Bregstein was wont to shatter glass ceilings. She had integrated Yale University as part of its first female undergraduate class and was graduated in 1973 *magna cum laude*. At the University of Pennsylvania Law School, she was the first female editor-in-chief of the law review. After her clerkship with Powell, she would go on to become one of only a handful of women partners in the major Washington, DC, law firms. Never one to shy away from a fight, she later founded CeaseFirePA, a group seeking to prevent gun violence, even as the gun rights movement was becoming one of the most powerful forces in modern American politics. Back in 1978, when she was clerking for Powell, Bregstein was one of only seven women among the court's thirty-two clerks.[61]

In a memorandum to Powell in the First National Bank case, Bregstein wrote, "This case is very easy or very difficult, depending on one's choice of a major premise. If one begins, as did the Massachusetts court, by placing predominant emphasis on the view that corporations are unique because of their artificial existence and their status as creatures of state law, it is not difficult to conclude that their rights are not infringed" by the law. That had been White's view at the conference. "If, on the other hand, one conceives of the problem in terms of *what* is prohibited rather than *who* is guaranteed a certain right," Bregstein continued, "then the fact that appellants are corporations takes on a different significance." Under the latter view, the First Amendment protects speech about important matters of public policy "regardless of the identity of the speaker." Bregstein's argument was grounded in *Virginia Pharmacy*: ignore the identity of the speaker and focus on the substance of the speech and its potential benefits to the people who hear it.[62]

Powell wrote the court's opinion in *First National Bank of Boston v. Bellotti* precisely along those lines. He left out any mention of corporations having the same free speech rights as individuals. In contrast to his personal notes, which identified the issue in the case as the "1st Amend. rts of corps.," his opinion said the opposite: "The proper question therefore is not whether corporations 'have' First Amendment rights and, if so, whether they are coextensive with those of natural persons. Instead, the question must be whether [Massachusetts's law] abridges expression that the First Amendment was meant to protect." Because the law here restricted political speech valuable to the public at large, it was unconstitutional regardless of the identity of the speaker. "It is the type of speech indispensable to decisionmaking in a democracy, and this is no less true because the speech comes from a corporation rather than an individual." The speech itself was protected: absent compelling reasons, the government could not deprive "this proposed speech of what would be *its* clear entitlement to protection." Blackmun's vote held—and Powell maintained his majority in the closely divided 5–4 decision.[63]

Powell's opinion admitted that the right involved in the case, the freedom of speech, was a liberty right—exactly the sort of right the court in the *Lochner* era had said was inapplicable to corporations. Back then, the justices recognized corporations to have property rights but not liberty rights, and turned away the brewing companies who claimed they had a free speech right to spend their money to influence referendum elections. In the years since, however, corporations had won a growing share of liberty rights. Indeed, as Powell observed in his opinion, the justices had affirmatively rejected the idea that corporations were limited to property rights forty years earlier when they extended free speech protections to the Louisiana newspaper corporations in the Huey Long case, *Grosjean v. American Press Company.*

* * *

THE SUPREME COURT'S DECISION in *First National Bank of Boston v. Bellotti* would have surprised J. W. Sullivan, the crusading late nineteenth-century journalist who introduced Americans to the initiative and referendum process. Borrowing from Switzerland, Sullivan, a populist, thought that having citizens vote directly on proposed laws would diminish the power of the "great trusts and railroad corporations" that often dominated state legislatures. His 1892 book, *Direct Legislation by the Citizenship*, proposed ballot measures as the way "the American plutocracy might be destroyed," and captured the attention of progressive activists—especially after the election of 1896, when Republican William McKinley used corporate money raised by Mark Hanna to hand a crushing defeat to William Jennings Bryan and the reform movement. Animated by the same desire to shield democratic politics from the influence of corporations that inspired the wave of laws banning corporate contributions to candidates in the wake of Charles Evans Hughes's insurance investigation, direct democracy was adopted in twenty states before World War I. Ballot measures became popular as a way of skirting corrupted officials in order to further reforms like women's suffrage, the eight-hour workday, and the breakup of monopolies.[64]

In the years after Lewis Powell led the Supreme Court to rule that corporations had a First Amendment right to speak and spend freely on ballot measures, this type of lawmaking became even more popular, with an average of forty referendums per year nationwide. Corporations, empowered with the same legal right to finance ads on ballot measure campaigns as individuals—yet benefiting from the special privileges that enabled them to raise unusually large amounts of capital—have become the loudest voices. In 2014, the top dozen contributors to ballot measure campaigns nationwide were corporations and business trade groups. Outspending opponents by margins as high as 16–1, as Monsanto Company did to defeat a Colorado measure requiring labeling of products with genetically modified organisms, business won 96 percent of its campaigns that year. The device that J. W. Sullivan imagined as the cure for corporate political influence had been transformed by Powell and the Supreme Court into another arena for corporations to dominate.[65]

The same year the Supreme Court decided *Bellotti,* Joseph Cullman, the tobacco executive who organized the extravagant multimedia tribute to Lewis Powell, stepped down after twenty years at the helm of Philip Morris. When Cullman took over back in 1957, Philip Morris had ranked dead last in sales among major American tobacco producers. By the time he retired in 1978, however, the company was second only to R. J. Reynolds, which Philip Morris would soon overtake. The company's turnaround was almost entirely due to Cullman's imaginative rebranding of a single cigarette that Philip Morris had long marketed to women without much commercial success. Cullman directed future campaigns to aim for male consumers by featuring rugged, virile men like cowboys. Before long, Marlboro cigarettes were among the best-selling products in the world and Cullman was being called "the most successful tobacco merchant since Buck Duke."[66]

Powell similarly enjoyed great success, profoundly shaping the law both before and after his appointment to the Supreme Court. When he wrote the Powell Memorandum in 1971, the law was moving in the progressive direction of Ralph Nader, and business interests were on the defensive. Yet Powell's passionate cri de coeur gave voice to the prevailing fear within the business community—and offered detailed, comprehensive solutions. Powell, who was born in 1907 just as Teddy Roosevelt was signing into law the Tillman Act banning corporate contributions to candidates, would transform America's political and corporate landscape by the time he passed away in 1998 at the age of 91. The Reagan Revolution of 1980, which was built around the vision articulated in the Powell Memorandum, ushered in a conservative era committed to free markets, small government, pro-business tax policies, and deregulation of industry. The shift was so profound that it shaped the agendas of both major political parties. In the early 1990s, Democrats, fearful after losing five of the previous six presidential elections, also adopted more centrist, business-friendly rhetoric in an effort to regain their Election Day competitiveness.

One of Powell's most lasting influences was on the role of business advocates before the Supreme Court. Following the Powell Memorandum's suggestion, the Chamber of Commerce established its own law firm, the National Chamber Litigation Center (NCLC) in 1977, just as the *Bellotti* case was wending its way up through the courts. With the motto, "In the Case of The Government v. Business, NCLC Is Your Strongest Ally," the Chamber's litigation arm fought for free enterprise the way Ralph Nader and Alan Morrison's Public Citizen Litigation Group fought for consumers. The NCLC filed cases and amicus briefs seeking to restrict class actions, limit punitive damages, curtail environmental regulation, and make it harder for employees to sue for discrimination—and became the nation's most influential business-oriented legal advocacy group. Today, the organization wins nearly 70 percent of its Supreme Court cases. Carter Phillips, a Washington lawyer who has argued scores of cases in the nation's highest court, says that no private entity "has more influence on what cases the Supreme Court decides and how it decides them than the National Chamber Litigation Center." [67]

Indeed, the battle between Powell and Nader is still carried on in the Supreme Court, in cases pitting the NCLC against Public Citizen. In 2007, the two litigation outfits faced off in a lawsuit brought by a man who suffered serious complications when a catheter manufactured by Medtronic burst during an angioplasty procedure. The injured patient sued Medtronic for marketing a defective product and the company, backed by the NCLC, argued that the suit should be thrown out of court because federal regulators had approved the catheter for sale. Although Nader and Morrison had long since left Public Citizen, the organization was still representing consumer interests and handled the patient's appeal, arguing that lawsuits such as his were the "sole means of obtaining compensation for injuries caused by medical devices." [68]

The court that heard the Medtronic case had, like the larger political environment, been reshaped since the 1960s, when Warren and

Brennan had led the Supreme Court to embrace progressive reform. The court now included six justices, selected by presidents of both parties, whose nominations had been endorsed by the Chamber of Commerce as good for business interests. The Medtronic decision, which came down in February of 2008, was 8–1 in favor of the NCLC and the medical device company. On that same day, the Supreme Court also ruled in favor of the NCLC in two other cases, both of which limited state efforts to hold business accountable for wrongdoing. Amidst reports that lawyers at Public Citizen were "demoralized and discouraged," Robin Conrad, the charismatic leader of the NCLC, gloated about her three victories in a single morning, a high court hat trick: "I don't think I've ever experienced a day at the Supreme Court like that."[69]

The buoyant Conrad nonetheless had little time to celebrate. From her office in the Chamber of Commerce's majestic, Corinthian-columned building in Washington—designed by Cass Gilbert, the same man who designed the Supreme Court's majestic, Corinthian-columned building in Washington—Conrad had to begin strategizing for the next term's slate of cases. One of those cases was a seemingly insignificant dispute about the niggling details of campaign finance law, involving a little-known nonprofit named Citizens United that had used some corporate money to finance a political documentary. That case, like *Bellotti*, would also be converted from a minor one of little importance into a landmark corporate rights decision with a profound impact on American law and politics.

CHAPTER 10

—

The Triumph of Corporate Rights

*C*ITIZENS UNITED BEGAN AS A LAWSUIT NO ONE THOUGHT could be won. None of the heavyweight Washington, DC, lawyers were interested in taking on the case when Citizens United, a conservative political advocacy group, sought out counsel in 2007. Lawyers like Ted Olson, who represented George W. Bush in *Bush v. Gore* and had since become the dean of an emerging group of elite Supreme Court specialists in Washington, preferred cases they could win. And Citizens United's proposed lawsuit to challenge the federal law restricting corporate spending on election ads was a long shot. Since the early twentieth century, when courts turned away the brewing companies that challenged the Tillman Act and similar state bans, courts had consistently ruled that corporations could be subject to special restrictions in funding campaigns for public office. Although Justice Lewis Powell's decision in *Bellotti* had carved out an exception for ballot measure campaigns, the Supreme Court had subsequently affirmed the constitutionality of bans in campaigns for candidates—most recently in 2003, when the justices upheld the very same provisions Citizens United would ultimately challenge. Olson and the several other lawyers who turned Citizens United's case down knew that the court rarely reconsidered its own decisions after only four short years.

Citizens United, in other words, was exactly the type of case that Jim Bopp Jr., the tall, white-haired lawyer from Terre Haute, Indiana, loved to take. "Jim has always been in the position of making arguments that other people thought were wild-eyed, went too far," said Trevor Potter, a former chairman of the Federal Election Commission, the main federal agency charged with enforcing the nation's campaign finance laws. For over twenty years, Bopp, an outspoken Tea Party conservative, had spearheaded a relentless crusade of lawsuits seeking to overturn restrictions on money in politics. "We need *more* spending on elections," Bopp insisted, arguing whenever he could for a libertarian approach to campaign finance laws—one that saw nearly all government regulation of money in politics as a violation of the First Amendment. No case was too small; he once represented a student who challenged a college's $100 spending limit in student council races. He had won big cases, too, including several at the Supreme Court. Even before Bopp signed on to represent Citizens United, he had been accused of turning campaign fund-raising into an ungoverned, anything-goes, Election Day version of the Wild West. "The Wild West?" Bopp laughed, "That's freedom."[1]

Like Ted Olson, Bopp was an accomplished lawyer with ties to the Republican Party and a track record of success at the Supreme Court. The similarities, however, ended there. Bopp worked out of a tiny law office in Indiana, where he primarily represented individuals and ideological groups suing to limit abortion and campaign finance law; big business, he said, would not hire him. Olson was a fantastically successful partner at the powerhouse law firm of Gibson, Dunn & Crutcher, where he represented the nation's biggest corporations out of the firm's Washington office. Bopp was gleefully contemptuous of liberals—he liked to call President Barack Obama a "socialist"—while Olson was married to a Democrat and hosted parties for a bipartisan coterie of Washington insiders. Olson's shirts had French cuffs, Bopp's had plastic buttons. Both were Republicans but each represented a different branch of the conservative movement of the early twenty-first century. Bopp was the Supreme Court equivalent of the Tea Party insurgent from the heartland who was tired of compromise and wanted to radically reshape the law to promote conservative values. Olson was more the genteel face of a Republican elite in Washington that was content to push the law more gingerly.[2]

There was some professional animosity between Bopp and Olson, too, and Bopp often complained that he should have received credit for Olson's greatest victory, *Bush v. Gore*, the case that decided the contested 2000 presidential election. Although Olson had been Bush's lawyer in the Supreme Court, Bopp insisted that he had developed the winning legal theory adopted by the Supreme Court and that Bush won the case and the presidency in spite of Olson. Nevertheless, Olson was the one Bush rewarded by naming him to the prestigious post of solicitor general, while Bopp went back to Terre Haute. The friction between Bopp and Olson that grew out of *Bush v. Gore* would also color *Citizens United*—which, like that earlier case, quickly became one of the most controversial decisions in the history of the Supreme Court. Once again, Bopp would claim to do much of the legwork and Olson would receive most of the credit for winning a groundbreaking decision that fundamentally reshaped American politics.[3]

Citizens United, which held that corporations (and unions) have a First Amendment right to spend their money to influence elections for public office, sparked a backlash, including a nascent movement to amend the Constitution to eliminate all constitutional protections for corporations. Critics accused the Supreme Court of judicial activism; the justices, it was said, had read new rights into the Constitution. While the charge was not completely without foundation, the *Citizens United* decision also followed well-established patterns drawn over the course of the previous two centuries of corporate rights cases. *Citizens United*, in other words, is best understood as the most recent manifestation of a long, and long overlooked, corporate rights movement.

* * *

AMERICAN POLITICS IN THE first decades of the twenty-first century suffered from increasing polarization, with the widening gap between Republicans and Democrats making compromise nearly impossible. Polarization had many contributing factors, including a changing media environment that rewarded bluster and stridency. Perhaps the most important cause was what political scientists call "partisan realignment"—a reshuffling of the coalitions that form the two main political parties. For most of the twentieth century, both parties had distinctively liberal and conservative wings. In 1964, President Lyndon Johnson famously (and, perhaps, apocryphally) said the Civil Rights Act he signed that year would cost Democrats the South for a generation; whether or not Johnson was right about the cause, the one-party South did switch to the Republican Party over the following three decades. Meanwhile, northeastern liberals defected from an increasingly southern-dominated Republican Party to join the Democrats. Partisan realignment meant that liberals were nearly uniformly concentrated in the Democratic Party and conservatives in the GOP. Americans' political attitudes had not necessarily changed that much, but the political parties had been radically transformed.[4]

In this age of hyper-partisanship, the Washington, DC–based advocacy group Citizens United thrived. Originally started in 1988 by the political consultant behind the notorious Willie Horton ad that derailed Michael Dukakis's presidential campaign, the organization set out in 2007 to bring down another Democratic presidential candidate, Hillary Clinton. By then, it was under the leadership of David Bossie, an audacious political operative who had long been a thorn in the sides of the Clintons. During Bill Clinton's presidency, Bossie had been an investigator for the House and the Senate, working on probes into several Clinton scandals, including ones involving the White House Travel Office and the suicide of Vince Foster. Bossie, however, was forced to resign in disgrace after being caught doctoring tapes to make it appear that Hillary Clinton was guilty of defrauding clients of her Arkansas law firm. Nonetheless, he would stage a political comeback with the Citizens United organization, and he would eventually taste the fruit of victory over the Clintons in 2016 when he served as deputy campaign manager to Donald Trump.[5]

Back in 2007, Bossie and his organization decided to make a hard-hitting, feature-length documentary about Hillary Clinton, the presumptive front-runner in the 2008 election. Bossie had first been

DAVID BOSSIE, THE PRESIDENT
OF THE ADVOCACY GROUP CITIZENS UNITED.

inspired to turn his partisan attentions to filmmaking by Michael
Moore and his successful 2004 documentary, *Fahrenheit 9/11*, a
harshly critical exposé of President George W. Bush and his family's
connections to Saudi-funded terrorist networks. Moore's film was a
box-office success—and the advertisements for it served, in Bossie's
view, as effective campaign ads for John Kerry, Bush's opponent in the
presidential campaign that year. Citizens United's movie about Hillary Clinton was unimaginatively titled *Hillary: The Movie*, and the
substance was no more nuanced. It featured a litany of pundits derid-
ing Clinton as corrupt, deceitful, and driven by a desire for power.[6]

It was perfectly lawful for Bossie to make his documentary, regardless of how one-sided it might have been. The problem was that Citizens
United, which intended to broadcast the documentary on television
through video-on-demand, had used corporate money to finance the
project. Under the terms of the Bipartisan Campaign Reform Act
of 2002, corporate money could not be used to finance what the law
called "electioneering communications"—basically, ads about candidates broadcast on television or radio in the weeks prior to an election.
The most significant regulation of money in politics since Watergate, the Bipartisan Campaign Reform Act effectively expanded the
Roosevelt-era prohibition on corporate contributions to candidates to

apply also to ads featuring candidates. While the law allowed corporations to finance ads through their political action committees (PACs), which raised money from employees and shareholders through voluntary donations, companies were prohibited from using general treasury funds, their main pot of money.[7]

Citizens United had accepted some contributions from businesses and used that money to finance a small portion of the costs of *Hillary: The Movie*. Because of that corporate financing, however, Citizens United was likely to run into trouble at the Federal Election Commission. The commissioners had previously indicated that a documentary about a candidate produced by a political advocacy group like Citizens United might well be deemed an "electioneering communication" under the Bipartisan Campaign Reform Act. Michael Moore was able to air his film because it had been made by a reputable and experienced production company that was regularly in the business of making commercial films. An election-year biopic of one of the major candidates by an explicitly political group like Citizens United, by contrast, would be seen as motivated by partisanship, not profit. If so, then Bossie would not be able to air *Hillary: The Movie* or advertisements for it in the weeks just before the election—precisely when it might have the most impact. Rather than abandon his movie, Bossie decided to hire a lawyer and fight.

* * *

THE LAWSUIT IN *CITIZENS UNITED* threatened to open up a loophole to allow corporate money in candidate elections much as *Bellotti* had allowed corporate money in ballot measure campaigns. Yet despite the long-standing prohibitions on corporate contributions passed in the wake of Charles Evans Hughes's investigation of corruption in the life insurance companies, corporations had already gained a toehold in candidate races—through PACs. Labor unions had invented the PAC as a way to skirt laws prohibiting unions from contributing to candidates. Corporations, however, were astute legal leveragers and once again were able to exploit progressive reforms to enhance the power of business.

Corporations might never have gained the right to form PACs were it not for legendary film director Cecil B. DeMille. Often called the "founding father of Hollywood," DeMille made seventy films between 1913 and 1956. With hugely popular titles like *The Ten Commandments*, *Cleopatra*, and *The Greatest Show on Earth*, which won the Academy Award for Best Picture in 1952, DeMille was one of the most successful directors of all time. In the 1940s, he was as much a celebrity as the stars who appeared in his films. Unlike with David Bossie, however, it was not a movie that put DeMille at the center of controversy. It was instead his immensely popular radio program, *Lux Radio Theatre*, which enjoyed a weekly audience of over 20 million people—nearly 20 percent of the US population.[8]

DeMille, like all radio performers of his day, was a member of a union, the American Federation of Radio Artists. In 1944, the Los Angeles chapter of AFRA decided to impose a special assessment of $1 on every local member to be used to defeat Proposition 12, a right-to-work measure on the California ballot that would prohibit closed union shops. DeMille, a fervent anti-Communist, supported Proposition 12 and refused to pay the assessment. The union, he said, was "demanding, in a word, that I cancel my vote with my dollar." What was cancelled instead was DeMille's radio program, once AFRA suspended DeMille from the union.[9]

DeMille's protest garnered considerable publicity, both because of his celebrity and because the political activity of unions was a hot-button issue in the 1940s. Although unions historically had not been active in funding elections, the 1936 election had marked a shift. One year earlier, in 1935, President Franklin Roosevelt secured passage of the National Labor Relations Act, a law that was called "the Magna Carta of Labor" because it formally recognized the legal right of workers to bargain collectively as a union. Roosevelt's opponent in the 1936 race was Republican Alf M. Landon, who promised to repeal the NLRA. The two largest unions in the country, the Congress of Industrial Organizations (CIO) and the American Federation of Labor (AFL), decided they had to get involved to save the law and made large contributions to pro-union Democrats and Roosevelt's reelection fund.[10]

FAMED MOVIE DIRECTOR AND RADIO PERSONALITY
CECIL B. DeMILLE PROTESTED AGAINST MANDATORY UNION
DUES USED FOR POLITICAL PURPOSES.

The unions' political activity triggered a congressional investigation that resulted in a recommendation that unions, like corporations, be barred from making political contributions to candidates. That recommendation was not acted on immediately—in part because union spending in the 1936 race was so successful in electing allies to Congress—but a series of unpopular labor stoppages during World War II created the political will to limit the unions. In 1943, Congress prohibited unions from striking and making political contributions to candidates for federal office for the duration of the war.[11]

The war was still on when AFRA imposed its special assessment on

DeMille. The union's spending, however, was in support of a state election, not a federal one, so it was not covered by the federal ban. While AFRA's political activity was lawful, many people were outraged. Even union members supportive of union politics saw DeMille's story as a cautionary tale. They too could be forced to pay for political advocacy they did not support, or else risk losing their jobs. After the war ended, Congress made the union money ban permanent, adding it to the existing ban on corporate contributions in the Taft-Hartley Act of 1947. In a nod to DeMille, the law also barred unions from punishing members who refused to pay special assessments designed for political purposes even in state elections. Lawmakers thought that unions, like corporations, should not be able to use a member's money on politics the member did not support.[12]

Money in politics is often likened to water: it seeps inevitably into any cracks in the barriers that campaign finance law erects to restrain it, eventually making the openings bigger and bigger to allow ever more money to flow through. That is how union money found its way into candidate elections, the result of a determined effort by union leaders to exploit the fissures in the law. In the 1940s, the CIO decided to experiment by setting up a committee distinct from the CIO itself to do political advocacy work. Even though the CIO funded and managed the Congress of Industrial Organizations Political Action Committee, or CIO-PAC, the latter was technically a separate entity from the union. As a result of that separation, CIO-PAC was not a labor union covered by the ban, even though the union exercised complete control over the PAC. Using the union's funds, CIO-PAC paid for publicity, pamphlets, and radio ads to help elect pro-labor candidates. CIO-PAC also instituted a "dollar drive" to raise funds from union members to contribute directly to candidates. Other unions soon followed suit and formed their own political action committees.[13]

Over the next thirty years, union PACs flourished, despite operating in a legal gray area. Nothing in the law explicitly allowed them, and the wink-and-a-nod separation between a union and its PAC led to accusations that unions were simply flouting the law. There were occasional prosecutions, a few of which made it to the Supreme Court.

Although the justices danced around the legal questions surrounding PACs, without ever clarifying entirely their legal basis, a few guiding principles were established. One was the distinction between a union's general treasury funds, which Congress was entitled to prohibit from being used for electioneering, and funds from members "fairly said to have been obtained on a voluntary basis." In 1972, for instance, the court in *Pipefitters Local v. United States* held that the ban on union contributions did not apply to "political funds financed in some sense by . . . voluntary contributions." The "dominant concern" behind the law, the court explained, was "to protect the dissenting shareholder or union member," which was not implicated if the money was given willingly for political purposes.[14] A union's PAC was like the NAACP in *NAACP v. Alabama ex rel. Patterson*: a voluntary membership organization that people join specifically to exercise First Amendment rights.

Pipefitters included a curious phrasing of the dominant concern behind the ban: "to protect the dissenting shareholder or union member." There were, however, no shareholders or corporations involved in the case, which dealt with a labor union. Nevertheless, the court suggested that corporations could form PACs too. Even without any effort whatsoever, corporations had gained new legal rights to influence democratic elections.

Unlike unions, however, corporations showed little interest in forming PACs prior to the Powell Memorandum of 1971. A handful of companies, mostly California-based aerospace firms looking for government contracts, formed "good government" or "civic action" committees, but the funds contributed remained small. Corporations tended to avoid partisan politics, fearing the taint of partisanship. Moreover, the uncertain legal basis for PACs dissuaded risk-averse corporate executives who feared being prosecuted.

In 1972, executives at Goodyear Tire & Rubber, Phillips Petroleum, and a dozen other corporations were not as risk-averse as most of their peers and simply broke the law banning corporate contributions in order to help President Richard Nixon's reelection campaign. Revealed in the Watergate investigation, this illicit corporate giving was one of the inspirations for Congress to overhaul the campaign finance system in 1974 and 1976. The Federal Election Campaign Act amendments of those years imposed strict new limits on money in politics. At the heart of the reforms were limits on contributions *to* candidates and limits on expenditures *by* candidates. Although supporters expected the law to minimize the pressure to raise money, it was never very effective. Part of the blame, as we have seen, can be ascribed to the Supreme Court, which in *Buckley v. Valeo* (1976) upheld the limits on contributions but struck down those on expenditures. The result, ironically, was that candidates had to spend even more time raising ever more money, as the contributions they could accept were capped but expenditures were unlimited. Labor unions also shared the blame for the law's ultimate ineffectiveness in limiting money in politics. Due to a strong push by organized labor, Congress inserted into the amendments clear rules explicitly allowing PACs.[15]

Unions wanted the PAC rules but corporations exploited the legal reforms with remarkable effectiveness. Once PACs were given the imprimatur of Congress and the clarity of federal legislation, the number of corporate PACs surged. By 2002, when Congress enacted the Bipartisan Campaign Reform Act and adopted new limits on corporate and union money in elections, there were over 1,670 PACs affiliated with corporations, compared to just over 325 affiliated with labor unions. The union effort to avoid the contribution ban served ultimately to legitimate, for the first time, corporate spending to influence the election of candidates.[16]

* * *

ALTHOUGH THE BIPARTISAN CAMPAIGN Reform Act allowed a corporation to fund election ads if the money were raised through a PAC, *Hillary: The Movie* had been partially financed with ordinary, general treasury funds from business. David Bossie, certain that the FEC would crack down on his documentary, began interviewing lawyers. He met with some of the leading attorneys in Washington, but Bossie recalled that "nobody showed a passion." "When you're dealing with a cause-oriented outcome, you want whoever you hire to be passionate about it," Bossie explained. You want a lawyer who will "go hammer and tong for us, who is going to fight every step, every half step."

Ted Olson did not appear to be that lawyer.[17] "I don't think he took me seriously," recalled Bossie after their meeting. One reason Olson might have been skeptical is that the Supreme Court had consistently upheld laws prohibiting corporations from using general treasury funds to influence candidate races. Although the court had accorded corporations free speech rights to spend in ballot measure campaigns in *First National Bank of Boston v. Bellotti* and had permitted corporations to form PACs like unions, the justices had drawn the line at attempts to influence candidate elections with general treasury funds. The two most important rulings were *Austin v. Michigan Chamber of Commerce*, decided in 1990, and *McConnell v. Federal Election Commission*, decided in 2003.

The *Austin* case involved the same law first challenged by the Lansing Brewing Company during the debates over Prohibition, Michigan's ban on corporate money in political campaigns. Although the beer maker had lost that early challenge, the Michigan branch of the Chamber of Commerce decided to try again seventy years later, following the advice of the Powell Memorandum to become more assertive in defending its rights. The Supreme Court, however, upheld Michigan's law, pointing to the "unique legal and economic characteristics" of the corporate entity: "special advantages—such as limited liability, perpetual life, and favorable treatment of the accumulation and distribution of assets." These benefits were designed to enable corporations to raise capital, yet they also enabled corporations to use "resources amassed in the economic marketplace to obtain an unfair advantage in the political marketplace." Because of their special advantages in raising capital and their diverse group of stockholders, corporations had more limited rights to spend money on electoral politics than ordinary people.[18]

Austin was difficult, if not impossible, to square with Justice Powell's opinion in *Bellotti*. Although the two decisions could be distinguished superficially—with *Bellotti* applying to ballot measure campaigns and *Austin* to candidate races—the two decisions were otherwise at loggerheads. Powell had insisted the identity of the speaker was irrelevant; the court in *Austin* relied explicitly on the distinctive characteristics of the corporate speaker. Powell had suggested that dissenting share-holders were irrelevant; *Austin* declared that fact essential. Powell had written that corporations contribute meaningfully to public debate; *Austin* said they distort democratic deliberation. Yet *Austin* did not purport to overturn *Bellotti*, so both precedents remained on the books, their seeming tension papered over by the flimsy distinction between ballot measure campaigns and candidate races.

The second case, *McConnell*, took its name from Kentucky senator Mitch McConnell, who led a sweeping legal challenge to the Bipartisan Campaign Reform Act in 2003, just after the law was signed. A divided Supreme Court upheld most of the law, including the restrictions on corporate financing of electioneering communications. The court's opinion was jointly authored by Justice John Paul Stevens, a Gerald Ford appointee who had voted with Powell in *Bellotti* but had become steadily more liberal over his tenure, and Justice Sandra Day O'Connor, who was chosen by Ronald Reagan to be the first woman on the Supreme Court. Stevens and O'Connor pointed to the long history of special restrictions on corporations in campaign finance, dating back to the Great Wall Street Scandal of 1905 and "President Theodore Roosevelt's call for legislation forbidding all contributions by corporations." Relying heavily on *Austin*, the *McConnell* majority explained, "We have repeatedly sustained legislation aimed at 'the corrosive and distorting effects of immense aggregations of wealth that are accumulated with the help of the corporate form and that have little or no correlation to the public's support for the corporation's political ideas.'"[19]

Even though *McConnell* had been decided only four years prior to Citizens United's movie, Jim Bopp was more than willing to take the case. Bopp subscribed to a libertarian theory of campaign finance law that was growing increasingly popular in conservative circles at the turn of the twenty-first century. The libertarian theory held that government regulation of money in politics distorted the free operation of the marketplace of ideas and therefore violated the First Amendment. This view of campaign finance law was first deployed in campaign finance cases in the 1970s by liberals, namely the American Civil Liberties Union, which led the challenge to the Watergate era reforms in *Buckley v. Valeo*. The libertarian theory of campaign finance law was nonetheless attractive to conservatives who opposed government regulation generally—and to those who thought the Republican Party would be the primary beneficiary of fewer restrictions. Bopp, who had become one of the leading proponents of the libertarian theory in the Supreme Court, rarely passed on an opportunity to challenge a campaign finance law.

Moreover, Bopp thought that the relevant circumstances had changed drastically since 2003—that is, the personnel on the court had changed drastically. In 2005, O'Connor retired and Chief Justice William Rehnquist, the longtime critic of corporate rights who dissented in *Bellotti*, passed away. President Bush replaced them with Sam Alito and John Roberts, respectively. Although the two new justices' views on restrictions on corporate money in politics were unclear, Bopp was sure that both would share his libertarian view that campaign finance law had gone too far and needed to be reined in.

Even before the *Citizens United* case, Bopp had already won a telling victory in the Roberts court in another campaign finance case dealing with the Bipartisan Campaign Reform Act's restrictions on corporate spending. In June of 2007, as the Citizens United organization was

CITIZENS UNITED'S ORIGINAL ATTORNEY, JIM BOPP, FOUGHT TO SCALE BACK CAMPAIGN FINANCE LAW, INCLUDING RESTRICTIONS ON CORPORATE POLITICAL SPENDING.

completing its documentary about Clinton, Bopp represented an anti-abortion group in *Federal Election Commission v. Wisconsin Right to Life*. In that case, Bopp argued that, under the First Amendment, the FEC could only enforce the law against corporate-financed ads that unambiguously endorsed or opposed a candidate; merely mentioning a candidate by name was not enough. The Supreme Court, in a 5–4 opinion written by Chief Justice Roberts and joined by Justice Alito, agreed. Without calling into question the constitutionality of the basic provisions of the Bipartisan Campaign Reform Act restricting corporate money, the justices nonetheless opened up a significant loophole in the law. Now corporations could finance ads that featured candidates if the ads could be plausibly said to be about issues. So long as the ad did not expressly advocate for or against particular candidates, it would not be deemed an "electioneering communication" subject to the legal limits on corporate cash.[20]

The advocacy group Citizens United, however, did not benefit immediately from the court's new approach to the Bipartisan Campaign Reform Act. A few months after the court's decision in *Wisconsin Right to Life*, the FEC determined that *Hillary: The Movie* was an "electioneering communication." The film, the FEC said, "is susceptible of no other interpretation than to inform the electorate that Senator Clinton is unfit for office, that the United States would be a dangerous place in a President Hillary Clinton world, and that viewers should vote against her." The movie, the FEC ruled, was not about issues. As the film's title suggested, it was about a candidate.[21]

* * *

JIM BOPP HAD HIS own ideas about how the law should work and was not one to back down easily. It was that character trait that had led to the rivalry with Ted Olson over who deserved credit for *Bush v. Gore*. The disputed presidential election of 2000, which pitted George W. Bush against Al Gore, turned on the vote count in Florida. Although Florida election officials declared Bush the winner by a narrow margin of less than 2,000 votes—giving the Republican a majority in the Electoral College—Gore challenged the results. The Florida Supreme

Court ruled largely in Gore's favor, and ordered a statewide recount. The Florida court, however, did not set out clear standards for how to determine whether a questionable vote, such as one with a hanging chad, should count. Each county was to make its own determinations.

Bopp, like many politically active lawyers, sought to lend his services to the cause of his preferred candidate—in this case, Bush. After discussing with his small team of lawyers in Indiana potential ways to challenge the Florida court's ruling, Bopp hit upon an innovative legal theory: the Florida recount violated the Fourteenth Amendment's guarantee of equal protection of the laws. This was the same provision Roscoe Conkling and the Southern Pacific Railroad had invoked back in the Gilded Age in seeking to immunize corporations from discriminatory taxation. Bopp's argument was that the recount violated equal protection because of the lack of uniform, statewide standards. A voter whose ballot had two hanging chads might have her vote counted in one county, but another voter with the same ballot might have her vote rejected in a different county. When Bopp first suggested this argument to Bush's lawyers, however, they dismissed it out of hand. Bush's team was skeptical of the equal protection argument, perhaps because the courts had never before required strict equality for how different counties tabulate votes. Some counties might use one type of voting machine that has a higher error rate than the machines used in another county, and yet no court had ever called into question such disparities, which were commonplace. Bopp was told that "under no circumstances" would his equal protection theory be the basis of Bush's lawsuit.[22]

Instead of equal protection, Ted Olson focused on another provision of the Constitution, Article II, which required that presidential electors be appointed "in such Manner as the *Legislature*" of a state directed. This provision was violated, Olson claimed, because the Florida Supreme Court, not the state's legislature, had ordered and managed the recount. Bopp was rebuffed but not deterred. Certain that the Bush legal team was making "tactical and strategic errors," Bopp pursued his own independent challenge to the Florida recount on behalf of a group of Florida voters. Days before Olson's argument in the Supreme Court, a federal court of appeals endorsed Bopp's equal protection argument and issued the first injunction against the recount. That last-minute victory for Bopp was hard for Olson, who favored the Article II theory, to ignore, and Olson included a short discussion of Bopp's equal protection theory in the final pages of his brief to the Supreme Court, almost as a throwaway. During the hearing at the Supreme Court, Olson emphasized the Article II theory and did not even mention equal protection at all in his main argument, addressing it only on rebuttal.[23]

The Supreme Court, of course, ruled in Bush's favor, putting a halt to the Florida recount. A majority of justices, seven of the nine, held the recount violated the Constitution's equal protection clause because each county used its own, potentially divergent, standards to count votes. Only three justices adopted Olson's Article II theory. If Bopp had not stubbornly pursued his own lawsuit to stop the Florida recount, the Supreme Court might not have had the winning equal protection argument even presented to it. Nonetheless, Olson was the one praised in the press as Bush's savior and appointed by the new president to be solicitor general.[24]

It was in Olson's role as solicitor general that he first became involved with the Bipartisan Campaign Reform Act's corporate spending restrictions. As the federal government's main advocate before the Supreme Court, Olson was responsible for defending laws passed by Congress. So when Senator McConnell challenged the Bipartisan Campaign Reform Act in 2003, Olson successfully argued that the law was constitutional. Although Olson could not have known it then, he would eventually find himself back in the Supreme Court arguing to overturn the very same provisions of the law—arguing, in essence, against himself—in the *Citizens United* case.

* * *

JIM BOPP SAID THAT THE *Citizens United* lawsuit was inspired by another landmark Supreme Court case that changed America, *Brown v. Board of Education*. "The strategy that was used to overturn 'separate but equal' was not to challenge [it] directly," Bopp explained, "but to demonstrate that it was not workable by raising extreme applications of it." Thurgood Marshall and the NAACP exposed the fallacy of segregation by bringing cases challenging egregiously unequal facilities. In *Sweatt v. Painter*, for example, a 1950 case decided four years prior to *Brown*, the NAACP challenged the separate law school established by the University of Texas, which was little more than a roped-off area of the state capitol building. Only after showing the absurdity of separate but equal in practice did the NAACP ask the court to declare an end to all state-sponsored racial segregation.[25]

Bopp employed a similar strategy in his libertarian quest to tear down campaign finance law. He had not challenged the constitutionality of bans on corporate money in *Wisconsin Right to Life* but instead sought to undermine such bans incrementally. In the *Citizens United* case, he would use *Hillary: The Movie* to highlight the outrageousness and impracticality of the Bipartisan Campaign Reform Act's restrictions, and make the loophole created in *Wisconsin Right to Life* even bigger.

There were two unusual features of the Citizens United organization's documentary that made application of the Bipartisan Campaign Reform Act seem extreme. First, it was a feature-length movie, not the kind of commonplace campaign advertisement that members of Congress had in mind when they voted for the law. Although the statute's language could plausibly be read to cover *Hillary: The Movie*, as the Federal Election Commission had done, the documentary, which was slated to air by video-on-demand, was by all accounts an unusual, borderline case.

Second, Citizens United was a nonprofit political advocacy group, not a business corporation. Typically, such organizations are recognized to have political speech rights and are allowed to engage in explicit political advocacy; that is, after all, their essential purpose. As the Supreme Court explained in the *Austin* case, nonprofit advocacy groups, in contrast to business corporations, do not have huge aggregations of capital raised in the economic marketplace. They are also unlikely to have any dissenting shareholders, as anyone who contributes to an explicitly political group presumably supports that group's politics. Nonetheless, David Bossie's organization had received some

A SMALL AMOUNT OF CORPORATE MONEY WAS USED
TO FINANCE *HILLARY: THE MOVIE*, LEADING TO THE
CITIZENS UNITED CASE.

small contributions from business corporations and used that money
to help finance the movie. Had Citizens United not used any corporate
money, or used only corporate PAC money, the organization would
have had no legal problem airing the documentary. Nevertheless, the
FEC ruled that because Bossie had used some corporate money, *Hillary: The Movie* could not be shown in the weeks before an election
under the Bipartisan Campaign Reform Act.

Despite these two unusual features of Citizens United's case, Bopp and Bossie still faced seemingly insurmountable hurdles, as became clear in the first federal court hearing in the case, held in January of 2008. When Bopp first learned the identity of the three judges selected at random to hear the case, he must have been pleased, as two were well-known conservatives: A. Raymond Randolph, an appointee of George W. Bush, and Royce Lamberth, an appointee of Ronald Reagan. Lamberth in particular had a history of rulings against the Clintons. According to the liberal *Mother Jones* magazine, Lamberth had "a reputation as a Clinton basher." Yet, like the lawyers who could not summon the passion to take on Bossie's case, the judges were not very sympathetic to Bopp's argument that *Hillary: The Movie* was "issue-oriented" speech rather than an appeal to voters to cast their ballots against Clinton the candidate.[26]

"What is the issue?" asked Randolph.

"That Hillary Clinton is a European Socialist," Bopp replied. "That is an issue."

"Which has nothing to do with her campaign?" Lamberth asked incredulously. "Once you say, 'Hillary Clinton is a European Socialist,' aren't you saying vote against her?"

No, said Bopp, because the movie did not say explicitly that anyone should vote one way or another. "Oh, that's ridiculous," replied Lamberth. When Bopp insisted that *Hillary: The Movie* was investigative journalism and likened it to the celebrated television news program *60 Minutes*, Lamberth laughed out loud. By the time the hearing ended, it was clear to Bopp that victory would have to come, if at all, from the Supreme Court.

* * *

IN OCTOBER OF 2008, nine months after Judge Lamberth mocked Jim Bopp's argument in the *Citizens United* case, the leading conservative lawyers in Washington assembled at the Capitol Hill Club, located just blocks from the Supreme Court. The club was said to be "one of the most popular gathering spots in Washington for lawmakers, government officials and other members of the political establishment." That night the club was hosting a celebration for Ted Olson, who was being honored as the "Lawyer of the Year" by the Republican National Lawyers Association.[27]

Many arrived at the club early to watch the final presidential debate of the year and root for Republican John McCain, whose campaign was reeling. The economy was in dire crisis, and both McCain and the incumbent Republican president George W. Bush appeared overwhelmed by what came to be known as the Great Recession, the worst economic downturn since the Great Depression of the 1930s. Unemployment doubled, housing prices dropped 30 percent, and the stock market plunged. Meanwhile, the candidacy of Democrat Barack Obama, vying to be the first African American elected president, was surging into the final month of the campaign on the promise of bringing hope and change to Washington.

Once the fete of conservative lawyers began, John Ashcroft, Bush's former attorney general, rose to give a tribute to Olson. So did William Kilberg, "the labor lawyer of choice for corporate America" and Olson's law partner at Gibson Dunn. Trevor Potter, the former chairman of the FEC and general counsel to McCain's presidential campaign, also praised the superstar lawyer—and for good reason. Unlike Jim Bopp, Potter was not a proponent of the libertarian theory of campaign finance law; in fact, he had been responsible for drafting the Bipartisan Campaign Reform Act's restrictions on corporate money, which Olson had successfully defended in the *McConnell* case when serving as solicitor general.[28]

Olson had left the solicitor general's office in 2004 to return to his lucrative private practice at Gibson Dunn. In part due to his numerous appearances before the Supreme Court as solicitor general, Olson was part of an emerging school of elite Washington lawyers who specialized in arguing at the nation's highest court. Early America was known to have an illustrious Supreme Court bar made up of luminary advocates, such as Horace Binney, Daniel Webster, William Wirt, and Philip Barton Key—each of whom argued early corporate rights cases. By 1986, however, William Rehnquist, who became the chief justice that year, remarked, "There is no such Supreme Court bar at the present time." The lawyers who appeared before the justices had typically

CITIZENS UNITED'S SECOND ATTORNEY, TED OLSON, WAS THE
DEAN OF AN ELITE GROUP OF SUPREME COURT SPECIALISTS
WHO TYPICALLY REPRESENTED CORPORATIONS.

worked on a case from the beginning, and most had never previously argued at the Supreme Court.[29]

Yet while Rehnquist was stating his view, a new Supreme Court bar was being born. The renaissance began in 1985, when Rex Lee, Reagan's solicitor general, left government to join the law firm of Sidley Austin, where he started an innovative practice focused specifically on the Supreme Court. Within the first two years, Lee had argued eight cases before the justices—at the time, an unheard of number for a lawyer in private practice. Soon all the major law firms in DC were creating specialized Supreme Court practices to compete with Sidley. They hired lawyers who had gone to the top schools, clerked on the Supreme Court, or worked in the solicitor general's office—and, whenever possible, all three. Olson headed up Gibson Dunn's practice. Wilmer Hale hired Clinton's solicitor general, Seth Waxman. Kirland & Ellis brought on Ken Starr, of future Whitewater fame. Among the most successful of these advocates was John Roberts, who, after serving as deputy solicitor general, led the group at Hogan & Hartson and argued thirty-nine cases in the Supreme Court before being tapped to be chief justice.

These lawyers quickly earned a reputation for winning high-stakes cases in the rarefied milieu of the Supreme Court. A Reuters study in 2014 found that the elite Supreme Court lawyers were far more likely than other lawyers to have their cases accepted for review by the Roberts court. Because of their expertise, the members of the Supreme Court bar knew what kinds of arguments appealed to the justices—and they quickly gained the name recognition to impress the justices' law clerks, who did most of the vetting of potential new cases. Reuters also found that a mere eight lawyers accounted for 20 percent of oral arguments in the Supreme Court. Olson was one of them.[30]

The elite Supreme Court bar was criticized for being overwhelmingly white and male, but what really united its members were the clients: corporations seeking to vindicate business interests. When Rex Lee founded Sidley Austin's Supreme Court practice, he sought out paying business clients, such as those companies that were heeding the Powell Memorandum's advice and litigating to defend corporate interests. Lee brought in "a virtual Who's Who of the nation's major industries" from "banking, mining, railroads, electric utility, and telecommunications." Today, most members of the elite Supreme Court bar work for national law firms that primarily represent corporations. "Working for corporate clients is the bread and butter of our practice," explained Ashley Parish, a Supreme Court lawyer at King & Spalding. "It's the nature of the business." Individuals and minorities rarely benefited from this unique high court expertise. "Business can pay for the best counsel money can buy," explained Justice Ruth Bader Ginsburg, unlike many ordinary citizens. The rise of the elite Supreme Court bar became another way in which corporations enhanced their sway in court.[31]

The specialized Supreme Court lawyers do represent individuals on occasion, usually in criminal cases or those dealing with social issues that are not likely to create conflicts of interest with the firms' corporate clients. Olson, for example, signed on to lead a highly publicized challenge to California's ban on same-sex marriage just a month after being honored at the Capitol Hill Club. Yet Olson's typical clients at the Supreme Court were major corporations. He had argued cases on behalf of Philip Morris, DaimlerChrysler Corporation, Medtronic, Inc., Aetna Life Insurance Company, and ARC America Corporation.[32]

Most members of the elite Supreme Court bar are not driven by ideology but by the practice. The greatest challenge for any lawyer who wants to argue before the Supreme Court is obtaining cases. The court decides only about seventy cases a term, creating heated competition among the top lawyers for clients. Whether liberal or conservative, Democrat or Republican, the lawyers of the Supreme Court bar thus tended to represent businesses because those were the most frequent litigants willing to pay for their services. The renowned Laurence Tribe, a liberal professor at Harvard Law School who worked opposite Olson in *Bush v. Gore*, for example, has represented clients like Peabody Energy, General Electric, and the Petroleum Marketers Association of America in the Supreme Court seeking to curtail environmental regulation. Critics say lawyers like these are "hired guns"—a label that, no matter how often unfair, is applied to lawyers because of the nature of their work as temporary fiduciaries. Certainly for most of the elite, specialized Supreme Court lawyers, the proverbial game *is* the thing.[33]

Having argued a number of cases in the Supreme Court, Jim Bopp was a member of the elite Supreme Court bar. Yet, as usual, he did not quite fit in with the inside-the-beltway crowd. No other member of this cadre of Supreme Court specialists worked out of Indiana, and Bopp's clients were not typically corporations. Almost invariably, he represented conservative-leaning advocacy groups, like Citizens United and Wisconsin Right to Life, or individuals on a political mission. Bopp was a true believer—and he preferred to represent clients who furthered his vision of the Constitution. Bopp would not take a case just to have another argument in the Supreme Court. He was seeking to move the law. It was that commitment to the cause that had led David Bossie to hire Bopp rather than someone like Olson to represent Citizens United.[34]

Yet Bossie, who was present at the Capitol Hill Club reception to honor Olson, began to have second thoughts as he watched Olson receive his Republican Lawyer of the Year award. "I'm sitting there, thinking about my case," Bossie recalled. "Every Republican lawyer in town is there. Bill Kilberg of Gibson Dunn gets up to introduce Ted and says Ted Olson has won x number of cases and he's the winningest Supreme Court lawyer. I've known Ted forever and I said to myself, 'How is it I am not in Ted Olson's hands?'"[35]

A month later, in November of 2008, the Supreme Court agreed to hear Bossie and Bopp's case—or, rather, Bossie and Olson's case. Although Bopp had written and filed the paperwork requesting the justices to hear the dispute, Bossie decided he wanted Olson to argue the case instead. Bossie did not feel any special obligation to Bopp, even though Bopp had overseen the case from the beginning and ushered the case to the Supreme Court. "Look, if you get to the Super Bowl with your second-string quarterback and your first stringer comes off the injured reserve list, you put him back in," Bossie explained, before backtracking. "Not that Jim is second string." Yet Bossie's metaphor was revealing. Olson was *not* the first-string quarterback sitting out because of an injury; he had not even been on the team. Despite Bopp's expertise in campaign finance, his track record of success at the Supreme Court, and his commitment to Bossie's cause, the lawyer from Terre Haute was seemingly destined to be thought of as second best when compared to a quintessential Washington player like Olson.[36]

* * *

SAMUEL ALITO WAS TO the Supreme Court bench what Jim Bopp was to the Supreme Court bar. Both were brilliant lawyers whose work, at the highest levels of the law, brought them to Washington, where neither quite fit in. Both were strong social conservatives whose political philosophies were formed in reaction to the 1960s counterculture. And they would both play central though easily overlooked roles in the *Citizens United* case. Bopp's contributions would be obscured because he withdrew from the case after David Bossie hired Ted Olson, unwilling to be second string to Olson. Alito's influence could be missed because he would not write any opinion in the case. Nonetheless, Alito was the justice most responsible for transforming *Citizens United* from a relatively minor case chipping away at the Bipartisan Campaign Reform Act to a landmark ruling on the free speech rights of corporations.

Alito's conservatism was fermented as a young man at Princeton in the late 1960s, which the justice recalled as a "time of turmoil." "I saw some very smart people and very privileged people behaving irresponsibly," Alito explained. "And I couldn't help making a contrast between some of the worst of what I saw on the campus and the good sense and the decency of the people back in my own community," a middle-class neighborhood in Trenton, New Jersey. While the radical Students for a Democratic Society were blockading buildings to protest the university's involvement with the Vietnam War, Alito joined the ROTC. The next year, the university decided to end ROTC training on campus in response to student pressure. "I was more than disappointed that they threw ROTC off campus," Alito remembered. "It was an unprincipled thing to do."[37]

Alito witnessed firsthand how the tumult of the era took a heavy toll on the once prosperous Trenton. More than two hundred businesses were ransacked during a week of riots in April 1968, touched off by the assassination of Martin Luther King Jr. The department stores, furniture shops, and markets that had populated the downtown business district never returned. Without those businesses, Trenton descended into poverty and blight. By 2016, the per capita income of residents was less than $18,000, well below the national average. "The riots killed Trenton," said historian Charles Webster. Alito agreed, "The city never really recovered."

Perhaps with the memory of how vital thriving businesses had been to Trenton's fortunes, Alito leaned decidedly in favor of business interests as a judge. When the Bush administration was looking to replace Justice Sandra Day O'Connor on the Supreme Court, the US Chamber of Commerce was asked to vet potential nominees, a sign of how much political influence the Chamber had gained since Powell's Memorandum. The Chamber gave Alito high marks. During his fifteen years on the federal court of appeals, Alito had ruled consistently to limit corporate exposure to lawsuits, cabin federal regulation, and narrow employee rights. "He would be a liability restrainer," concluded Stan Anderson, the legal-affairs lobbyist for the Chamber. Once confirmed to the high court, one of Alito's first majority opinions was *Ledbetter v. Goodyear Tire & Rubber Company*, decided in 2007, which limited the ability of employees to recover for discrimination in the workplace. (Congress shortly after revised the law to reverse the court's decision.) A study by political scientist Lee Epstein, law professor William Landes, and Judge Richard Posner found that Alito voted in favor of business more often than any other justice to sit on the Supreme Court since 1946.[38]

Alito was the most pro-business justice on what arguably was the most pro-business Supreme Court in decades. Epstein, Landes, and Posner's study also found that Chief Justice John Roberts was the second most business-friendly justice of the last seventy-five years, and Justices Clarence Thomas, Anthony Kennedy, and Antonin Scalia were all in the top ten. The Roberts court's tilt in favor of business manifested itself in high-profile cases like *Citizens United* but also in others that garnered far less attention. "The Supreme Court has altered federal procedure in dramatic ways, one step at a time, to favor the business community," noted Arthur Miller, a well-known law professor and legal commentator. Indeed, Epstein, Landes, and Posner concluded that the Roberts court was "much friendlier to business than either the Burger or Rehnquist Courts" that preceded it.[39]

At the first Supreme Court hearing in Citizens United's case, held in March of 2009, Ted Olson sought only to move campaign finance law one small step in favor of the business community. Unlike Bopp, Olson was not ideologically committed to tearing down the nation's campaign finance regime. After all, he had previously defended the Bipartisan Campaign Reform Act in the Supreme Court. Olson was a lawyer's lawyer, and his strategy was to win the case for the Citizens United organization without unsettling the law any more than necessary. That meant Olson would make narrow, fact-specific arguments about *Hillary: The Movie* that did not threaten to undermine the broader set of rules on corporate money in elections.[40]

Olson told the justices that the Bipartisan Campaign Reform Act was intended to apply to advertisements, not feature-length documentaries broadcast over video-on-demand. Moreover, Citizens United's documentary was financed with only a trivial amount of corporate money. The court, Olson argued, should simply interpret the Bipartisan Campaign Reform Act to not apply to *Hillary: The Movie*.

Bopp thought these were the wrong arguments to make. The heart of the case, in Bopp's view, was the FEC's determination that Citizens United's film was about a candidate, not issues. As in *Wisconsin Right to Life*, Bopp thought it was more important to broaden the law's exception for speech about issues. Open up that loophole more, and the corporate spending restrictions would be effectively irrelevant; corporations would be able to fund ads about candidates under the guise of issue advertising. By making more narrow, fact-based arguments, however, Olson risked winning the case in a way that Bopp thought "would have made no impact on the law." A Supreme Court determination that *Hillary: The Movie* was not covered because it was broadcast over video-on-demand or because it had only a trivial amount of corporate funding would not "safeguard free expression in a meaningful way." Olson's arguments would carve out a this-day, this-movie-only exception to the Bipartisan Campaign Reform Act, but the corporate money ban would remain strong and in effect, with the *Wisconsin Right to Life* loophole made no larger. Such a result would not have satisfied Bopp, a committed soldier in the libertarian war on campaign finance law.[41]

"I do recognize that people like Ted Olson, who make their reputation on winning Supreme Court cases, they have different ways of looking at things," said Bopp. Such lawyers "within the beltway . . . they recognize that they have to win and so they come up with these really narrow grounds for winning just so they can get a 'W.'" Nonetheless, David Bossie did not mind Olson's narrow reframing of the case. "All I wanted to do was win something," he admitted. But Bopp, the activist, criticized Olson's arguments for that same reason. They were, in Bopp's view, "simply designed to win the case, no matter what." Olson was a fixer while Bopp was a fighter.[42]

At oral argument, Justice Antonin Scalia was similarly disappointed with Olson's narrow arguments. "Wait, are you making a statutory argument now or a constitutional argument?" If the only question was whether the Bipartisan Campaign Reform Act should be read to apply to video-on-demand documentaries with minimal corporate funding, then the case was indeed pretty minor. It was not a case of constitutional significance but one of statutory interpretation—and, because it would likely only impact this one movie, a relatively insubstantial statutory interpretation case at that.[43]

Scalia was one of the most influential justices in American history, in large part because of his tireless advocacy, both in public and in his opinions, on behalf of originalism—the philosophy that says judges should interpret the Constitution to preserve the original understanding of those who drafted and ratified it. Although there is little evidence the Framers meant to protect the rights of corporations, Scalia nonetheless believed that campaign finance laws like the Bipartisan Campaign Reform Act that burdened corporate speech were unconstitutional. Indeed, Scalia's votes in corporate political speech cases owed less to founding-era history than to intellectual currents swirling around the University of Chicago in the 1970s, when Scalia was a law professor there before joining the bench. The University of Chicago was the hub of the law and economics movement, which employed neoclassical economic theory to understand legal rules. Law and economics assumed that people were rational actors who usually maximized their own self-interest and that government regulation typically led to inefficient allocation of resources. Like the libertarians opposed to campaign finance law, law and economics adherents thought that if the government stayed its hand, people in a free market would gravitate toward the best, most productive outcomes. In the late 1970s and early 1980s, an era of deregulation and business backlash against big-government progressive reform, law and economics had tremendous appeal.[44]

When it came to corporations, law and economics promoted markets, not government regulation, as the proper way to prevent corporate wrongdoing. Adherents of this philosophy rejected the notion that corporations were entities created by the state that ought to be subject to significant regulation. Instead, they viewed the corporation as a "nexus or hub of privately structured contractual arrangements" among stockholders, creditors, employees, and managers, all of whom participate voluntarily in the enterprise. Government generally should not interfere with these voluntary contractual relationships by, say, enacting laws designed to protect stockholders. Instead, such matters should be left to the contracting parties to negotiate among themselves. If stockholders cared enough about some form of protection—such as preventing executives from contributing corporate money to candidates—they would bargain to obtain it. If that was too costly, stockholders unhappy with management's political contributions could simply sell their shares.[45]

Although Scalia never claimed to be a proponent of law and economics, distinct traces of this free market approach to corporations can be found in his opinions on corporate money in politics. In *Austin v. Michigan Chamber of Commerce*, for example, Scalia dissented, arguing that the Michigan corporate spending restriction was an unconstitutional, "paternalistic measure to protect the corporate shareholders of America." Such fatherly oversight by the government was unwarranted, in Scalia's view, because people voluntarily buy stock in corporations knowing that management can do whatever it wants to pursue profit. "That," he wrote, "is the deal." Corporations, Scalia said, were "voluntary associations," and a shareholder dissatisfied with management decisions, such as whether to spend corporate money on political ads, always had the "ability to sell his stock." For Scalia, as for proponents of law and economics, the answer was not government regulation but the capital markets.[46]

In Citizens United's case, Scalia seemed dissatisfied that these larger questions about the constitutionality of campaign finance restrictions on corporations were not on the table. Olson was asking the court instead to rule more narrowly that the Bipartisan Campaign

Reform Act simply did not apply to Citizens United's movie at all. *Hillary: The Movie* was not the type of "electioneering communication" Congress had intended to cover. "You're saying that this isn't covered by [the law]," asked an exasperated Scalia. "Yes," replied Olson.[47]

Alito, seated three seats to Scalia's left, saw the case in broader terms. After Olson sat down, Deputy Solicitor General Malcolm Stewart, a veteran lawyer in the solicitor general's office, rose to defend the FEC's determination that *Hillary: The Movie* was the equivalent of an election ad. Alito, whose shrewdness often led him to ask the most difficult questions that cut right to the heart of an advocate's case, had one prepared for Stewart. If Congress could prohibit an ad mentioning the name of a candidate because it was financed with corporate money, Alito asked, could Congress also prohibit the publication of a book mentioning a candidate if it were financed with corporate money?

Stewart had argued more than forty cases before in the Supreme Court and yet, at that moment, the lessons of his experience temporarily abandoned him. Yes, Stewart replied. Restrictions on corporate spending, such as those in the Bipartisan Campaign Reform Act, "could have been applied to other media as well." There was an audible gasp in the courtroom. "That's pretty incredible," replied Alito. "The government's position is that the First Amendment allows the banning of a book if it's published by a corporation?" Suffice to say, it is never the right answer in the Supreme Court to say the government can ban books.

Stewart realized that he had been caught in Alito's trap and immediately tried to clarify that all he meant was that the government could regulate how campaign material was *financed*. "I'm not saying it could be banned. I'm saying that Congress could prohibit the use of corporate treasury funds and could require a corporation to publish it using" PAC funds. That is, after all, what the Bipartisan Campaign Reform Act did. The law did not ban election ads by corporations so much as dictate such ads be financed through a PAC. And, Stewart noted, the Bipartisan Campaign Reform Act explicitly exempted book publishers and other media outlets, applying only to a narrow class of "electioneering communications" broadcast over television or radio in the weeks before an election. Alito's hypothetical, no matter how dramatic, was far removed from the case at hand.

The damage, however, had been done. One justice after another pushed Stewart to explain how the First Amendment could allow the government to ban books simply because those books were published by a corporation. "If we accept your constitutional argument," Chief Justice Roberts said, "we're establishing a precedent that you yourself say would extend to banning the book, assuming a particular person pays for it." Suddenly, *Citizens United* was no longer a case about the applicability of the Bipartisan Campaign Reform Act to *Hillary: The Movie*. Now the issue was whether the government could ban books. Olson had tried to narrow the issues as much as possible, willing to eke out a victory. Alito opened the case back up, making it instead about broad, foundational questions of free speech and censorship.

As Alito transformed the case, Jim Bopp watched silently from the back of the courtroom. Although the hard wooden benches were not nearly as inviting as the velvet cushions that comforted the society women who frequented the court in the Gilded Age, Bopp had been too committed to the cause to stay away. "I'm sitting there, answering the questions in my mind," he recalled. Even though Olson, not Bopp, stood at the podium on behalf of Citizens United, Bopp's voice still resonated in the courtroom. It was in fact Bopp who had first called the justices' attention to banning books. In his original filing asking the justices to hear the case, Bopp had colorfully warned that the government's argument would allow "high-tech 'book burnings' without restriction."[48]

* * *

WHEN THE JUSTICES MET in conference later that week to decide the case, the four liberal justices were prepared to rule against Citizens United and the five conservative justices, including Roberts and Alito, voted in Citizens United's favor. As chief justice, Roberts had the authority to determine who would write the court's opinion, and he kept it for himself. The draft he circulated weeks later followed Olson's narrow arguments, holding that a feature-length documentary financed with only a trivial amount of corporate money and aired over video-on-demand was not covered by the Bipartisan Campaign Reform Act. Roberts, a former member of the elite Supreme Court bar, saw this case as one to move the law incrementally.

Roberts's draft opinion was consistent with the view he expressed around the time of his confirmation about the proper role of the court in a democracy. Then Roberts had extolled the virtues of narrow rulings that respected as much as possible the judgments of Congress and the court's own precedent. The court's legitimacy, he said, was threatened by sweeping 5-4 decisions on high-profile, controversial issues that took on a partisan tint. Instead, Roberts expressed the desire for his legacy to be that of a chief justice who, like a baseball umpire, simply called "balls and strikes." Such an approach, he said, would promote consensus and keep the court out of the political thicket. Roberts was ideologically conservative but, like Olson, he preferred a long game with incremental movement. "If it is not necessary to decide more to a case," he said, "then in my view it is necessary not to decide more to a case."[49]

Soon after Roberts was confirmed, Scalia was asked what he thought about Roberts's goal of unifying the court around narrow rulings that avoided controversy, prompting the outspoken jurist to laugh, "Good luck!" His skepticism was borne out in the *Citizens United* case. The other justices in the majority—Alito, Scalia, Thomas, and Kennedy— pushed back against Roberts's halting approach. They circulated an opinion of their own, written by Kennedy, that went much further than Roberts's. Although many liberals hailed Kennedy for his progressive rulings in favor of gay rights, the same libertarian impulse that led him to oppose bans on gay sex and same-sex marriage also translated into a strong skepticism about campaign finance reform. Over the course of his more than two decades on the court, Kennedy had voted consistently to strike down limits on money in politics. He had dissented in both *Austin* and *McConnell*.[50]

Kennedy, Alito, and the others wanted to go broad and declare that the Bipartisan Campaign Reform Act's corporate money provisions violated the First Amendment. The court, they believed, should not focus on the narrow question of whether the Bipartisan Campaign Reform Act applied to this one movie but on the bigger question of whether corporate political expenditures could be limited at all. They shared Jim Bopp's libertarian theory of campaign finance and wanted Roberts to join them in overturning *Austin* and *McConnell*. Their draft opinion was a bold corporationalist statement on the expansive rights of corporations that blew well past anything Olson had requested. After some deliberation, Roberts, whose narrow opinion had not built the type of consensus he might have hoped, decided to go along with his less compromising colleagues. He withdrew his narrow opinion and signed on to their precedent-shattering one, which promised to fundamentally revamp the laws regulating money in politics.[51]

Roberts's switch infuriated the court's liberal justices, especially David Souter. A taciturn, mild-mannered New Englander who habitually ate the same lunch nearly every day—a cup of yogurt and an apple—Souter abandoned his usual congeniality and wrote a scathing dissent. He was not upset that the side he favored was going to lose; Souter, who for eighteen years was on the losing side of many Rehnquist and Roberts court decisions, was already used to that. The majority, in his view, was violating the court's well-established traditions governing how cases are to be decided. One long-standing norm on the court was that the justices would not reach questions that had not been briefed and argued by the parties. This ensured the justices had a full record and the benefit of adversarial argument before making decisions. Olson had not asked the court to decide whether the Bipartisan Campaign Reform Act provisions were unconstitutional in their entirety. Nor had he asked the court to overturn *Austin* and *McConnell*. Neither had the lower court developed an evidentiary record on issues relating to those broad constitutional questions. Souter accused the majority of simply deciding, without following the proper procedures, sweeping and controversial questions of law— contrary to the minimalist, consensus-building approach Roberts had promised during his confirmation. Souter, who was planning to retire that summer, would leave the court with a parting shot that let everyone know Roberts had betrayed his own legacy.

After spirited debate among the justices, Roberts and the conservative justices withdrew their far-reaching opinion. At the same time, they refused to back down completely. The justices agreed instead to hold another hearing in the case, only this time the lawyers would be instructed specifically to focus on whether the restrictions on corporate expenditures were constitutional. If the liberal justices thought the larger constitutional questions should not be decided absent briefing and argument, then the answer was to brief and argue them. A second hearing in the *Citizens United* case was slated for September of 2009.

The outcome, however, was a fait accompli. All the justices knew that there were now five votes to overturn *Austin* and *McConnell* and invalidate the Bipartisan Campaign Reform Act's restrictions on corporate funding of campaign ads. Justice Stevens would later write woefully, "Essentially, five justices were unhappy with the limited nature of the case before us, so they changed the case to give themselves an opportunity to change the law."[52]

* * *

WHEN THE *CITIZENS UNITED* case returned to the Supreme Court in September of 2009, signs of progress in America's historic civil rights movements were everywhere. Pathbreaking women's rights lawyer Ruth Bader Ginsburg, who had won some of the earliest successful sex discrimination cases in the Supreme Court, was on the bench. She was joined by Clarence Thomas, only the second African American justice, and the first Latina justice, Sonia Sotomayor, who filled the seat vacated over the summer by Justice Souter. *Citizens United* was Sotomayor's first case as a justice. It was also the first Supreme Court case for Elena Kagan, who had been the first woman dean at Harvard Law School and was now serving as the first woman solicitor general. Although she had no prior experience as an appellate advocate, she would have to hold her own in the highest court in the land against formidable adversaries: Olson, the dean of the Supreme Court bar, and Floyd Abrams, a renowned First Amendment lawyer who had argued for a libertarian approach to free speech in a number of landmark First Amendment cases and was now appearing on behalf of Senator McConnell. Unfortunately for Kagan, the *Citizens United* case presented its own form of glass ceiling. No matter how well she performed her job, she was bound to lose.

The return of *Citizens United* was also a sign of how much progress had been made by another, lesser-known civil rights movement—the one for corporations. It was exactly two hundred years after Horace Binney and the Bank of the United States brought the first corporate rights case to the Supreme Court in 1809. In those years, corporations had gained the protections of nearly all of the most significant individual rights provisions in the Constitution: rights of property, contract, and access to court; the right to be free from unreasonable searches and seizures; equal protection and due process; the right against double jeopardy and the right to counsel; the right to trial by jury; freedom of the press and freedom of association; commercial speech rights and even a limited right to speak on electoral politics under *Bellotti* and the union PAC cases. Although corporations had not won the right to vote, with the *Citizens United* case they were on the precipice of winning the right to use their amassed resources to influence candidate elections.

On paper, it did not appear to be an auspicious time for Ted Olson and the Citizens United organization to argue for expansive constitutional rights for corporations. The country was still reeling from the Great Recession, and public anger was directed at the nation's banks and other financial institutions that had received massive bailouts after speculative investments in subprime mortgage derivatives, popular but opaque securities with hidden risks, went bust. The firms, like the East India Company in the colonial era, were deemed "too big to fail." The crisis helped propel Barack Obama into the White House, and the new president proposed a number of monetary policies and reforms to stimulate the economy. These measures, coupled with the bailouts, led to a backlash among grassroots conservatives, who staged protests around the country in early 2009 calling for smaller government and lower taxes. The protestors called themselves the "Tea Party," borrowing the name from the famous Boston rabble rousers who threw overboard the tea of the East India Company, which had also been the recipient of a massive government bailout. The modern-day Tea Party quickly became the political engine driving the Republican Party, railing against not only Obama and the bailouts but also "RINOs"— Republicans In Name Only—such as the Washington party elites who claimed allegiance to conservative principles but sacrificed them to win the admiration of the mainstream media.[53]

Even if the cultural zeitgeist was marked by renewed hostility to big business, inside the Supreme Court the justices had not changed much at all—save for Sotomayor's replacement of Souter—and the votes in the *Citizens United* case had effectively been cast. Nevertheless, the representatives of the women's and minority rights movements' progress took aim at constitutional protections for corporations. Ginsburg asked Olson if there was any difference between the First Amendment rights of individuals and corporations. Referencing the Declaration of Independence, she noted that a "corporation, after all, is not endowed by its creator with inalienable rights." True, replied Olson, but the court had previously held that corporations had First Amendment rights in cases like *Bellotti* and *Grosjean v. American Press Company*, the Louisiana newspaper tax case that first held media corporations had freedom of the press.[54]

Sotomayor, following the example of Justice Hugo Black, the most vocal opponent of corporate rights in the history of the Surpeme Court, asked Floyd Abrams if the problem was the very idea of corporate rights. The Framers of the Constitution did not set out to give rights to corporations; the courts were the ones who expanded corporate freedoms. "There could be an argument made that *that* was the court's error to start with," she suggested, "not *Austin* or *McConnell*, but the fact that the court imbued a creature of state law with human characteristics." No, said Abrams, the court was correct to extend free speech to corporate entities. Political speech of the sort Citizens United wanted to engage in was "at the core of the First Amendment." The court in cases like *Virginia Pharmacy* had held that speech should be protected if its content is valuable to listeners, regardless of the identity of the speaker.

That Abrams, who was ideologically committed to a laissez-faire approach to speech, would attack the corporate money provisions of the Bipartisan Campaign Reform Act was no surprise. On behalf of the ACLU and others, he had consistently fought campaign finance laws as unduly restrictive of free speech. The ACLU, for instance, had been one of the primary challengers to the federal campaign finance laws in *Buckley v. Valeo*. Olson, however, was in the awkward position now of challenging provisions of a statute that he had previously defended before this very court in the *McConnell* case. As a result, he made claims to the justices that were directly contradicted by his own previous statements before the court.

In the *Citizens United* case, Olson told the court that the Bipartisan Campaign Reform Act was a "ban on speech by corporations." "What the government has done here is prohibit speech," he insisted. In *McConnell*, however, Olson said precisely the opposite, insisting then that the Bipartisan Campaign Reform Act "does not 'ban' any speech, but instead merely limits the manner in which a corporation or labor union may finance certain speech" by requiring PAC funding. In the *Citizens United* case, Olson said "there is no evidence that corporate and union independent expenditures" are corrupting, and criticized the government for being "unable to point to any congressional finding that corporate expenditures result in the corruption of legislators." In *McConnell*, by contrast, Olson had described the "massive record" compiled by Congress that "establishes that federal office-holders and candidates are aware of and feel indebted to corporations and unions that finance electioneering advertisements on their behalf." In the *Citizens United* case, Olson argued that the Bipartisan Campaign Reform Act provisions were "a dramatically underinclusive means" of combatting corruption. In *McConnell*, Olson had said the same provisions were a "carefully 'targeted'" and "narrowly tailored" means to "directly advance compelling government interests in eliminating real and apparent corruption." Olson's performance in the *Citizens United* case gave ample ammunition to those who called the elite members of the Supreme Court bar hired guns.[55]

When it was time for Kagan to address the court, she began by saying she had "three very quick points to make about the government position. The first is that this issue has a long history," she said, pointing to the Roosevelt-era Tillman Act. "For over a hundred years Congress has made a judgment that corporations must be subject to special rules when they participate in elections, and this Court has never questioned that judgment. Number 2...." "Wait, wait, wait, wait," Justice Scalia interrupted, welcoming her to the lightning fast pace of oral arguments at the Supreme Court. As lawyers quickly learn, you rarely have time to make three points, even very quick ones, before a justice will stop you with a question.

Kagan's success in making all three of her points did not really matter. She was going to lose anyway, and she knew it. She tried to persuade the court to take a narrow route similar to the one originally proposed by Olson and merely carve out an exception for the *Hillary* movie instead of overturning the corporate money provisions in their entirety. In response to a question by Roberts, Kagan was left to reply, "If you are asking me, Mr. Chief Justice, as to whether the government has a preference as to the way in which it loses, if it has to lose, the answer is yes." Even here, however, the outcome was a foregone conclusion. The justices had already decided the government was going to lose—and corporations were going to win—big.

* * *

THE AIR WAS FREEZING and the sky overcast on the morning of January 21, 2010, when David Bossie arrived at the Supreme Court to hear how the court had ruled in the *Citizens United* case. He came without Ted Olson, who was in California litigating the gay marriage case. Bossie could be reasonably certain of victory, although the exact shape of the court's ruling remained to be seen. From his perspective, the oral argument had certainly gone well. Yet even though Bossie was not a lawyer, he knew that oral argument could be misleading and the behind-the-scenes deliberations among the justices could result in surprising and unexpected rulings.

Precisely such deliberations after the first hearing in the *Citizens United* case had led the justices to order another round of oral argument. After the second hearing, though, there was little left for the

THE JUSTICES OF THE SUPREME COURT WHO DECIDED *CITIZENS UNITED*. STANDING, LEFT TO RIGHT: SAMUEL ALITO, RUTH BADER GINSBURG, STEPHEN BREYER, SONIA SOTOMAYOR. SITTING, LEFT TO RIGHT: ANTHONY KENNEDY, JOHN PAUL STEVENS, JOHN ROBERTS, ANTONIN SCALIA, CLARENCE THOMAS.

justices to negotiate. Justice Kennedy reworked the concurring opinion that he and Justices Alito, Scalia, and Thomas had written months earlier, turning it into a majority opinion with Chief Justice Roberts's support. Justice Stevens adapted Justice Souter's scathing draft dissent into one on behalf of himself and the three other dissenters, Justices Ginsburg, Breyer, and Sotomayor. Stevens borrowed so much from his retired colleague's unpublished opinion that he originally included a footnote acknowledging the debt, although it was removed before the dissent was published.

When Bossie took his seat in the courtroom, however, all that backstage maneuvering remained a secret. After the marshal called the court to order and the justices filed in through the break in the tall red velvet curtains behind the bench, Justice Kennedy began to summarize the court's ruling. The breadth of Kennedy's corporationalist decision quickly became clear. Corporations and unions, Kennedy explained, had a First Amendment right to make expenditures in elections for candidates for political office. The corporate spending restrictions of the Bipartisan Campaign Reform Act, by burdening this right, were unconstitutional in their entirety. Kennedy also revealed that the court had overturned *Austin* and *McConnell*, the two most important precedents for restricting political speech by corporations.[56]

Given the public uproar that *Citizens United* would eventually provoke, perhaps the most surprising thing about the decision was what it omitted. For as Kennedy read out loud from his opinion, not once did he mention corporate personhood. He never said that corporations are people, and nothing in his opinion turned on the notion. Corporate personhood—the idea that a corporation is an entity with rights and obligations separate and distinct from the rights and obligations of its members—is entirely missing from the court's opinion. The court afforded broad free speech rights to corporations, but not because they were people. Instead, like many of the earlier corporate rights cases, the *Citizens United* decision obscured the corporate entity and emphasized the rights of others, like shareholders and listeners.

Citizens United repeatedly described the corporation as "an association that has taken on the corporate form." "If the First Amendment has any force," Kennedy read out loud from the opinion, "it prohibits Congress from fining or jailing citizens or associations of citizens for simply engaging in political speech." By treating corporations as associations, *Citizens United* echoed the two-centuries-old argument of Horace Binney, the young, creative lawyer who argued the earliest corporate rights case, *Bank of the United States v. Deveaux*. Calling a corporation "a mere collection of men," Binney had persuaded the Supreme Court back then to look past the corporate entity, to pierce the corporate veil and focus on the rights of the corporation's members. Rather than treating the corporation as a legal person with rights of its own, both *Deveaux* and *Citizens United*—and many cases decided in the interim—allowed corporations to assume the rights of other people, namely the corporations' members.

Not only were corporations associations of citizens rather than independent legal persons, the Supreme Court in *Citizens United* suggested these associations were being persecuted. The court described corporations as "disfavored speakers" and criticized the Bipartisan Campaign Reform Act for threatening to penalize "disfavored associations of citizens—those that have taken on the corporate form" for making political expenditures. This portrayal of corporations as a sort of discrete and insular minority subjected to discriminatory and hostile legislation had its roots in the corporate rights cases of the mid-twentieth century. The Supreme Court had recognized the right of Louisiana's newspaper corporations to freedom of the press after the companies had been singled out for punitive, censorial taxes by Huey Long. The court subsequently responded to southern efforts to shut down the NAACP because of its ideology by recognizing the organization's right to freedom of association. Justice Kennedy's opinion in *Citizens United* similarly imagined corporations, even big business, to be victims. Although corporations are usually thought to be among the most powerful and influential players in American politics, *Citizens United*'s view that corporations should not be subject to political persecution by a hostile government was not entirely new.[57]

Citizens United also reflected the listeners' rights theory of free speech Justice Lewis Powell had used to justify extending political speech rights to corporations in *Bellotti*. As the *Citizens United* decision explained, "The First Amendment protects speech and speaker, and the ideas that flow from each." The Bipartisan Campaign Reform Act restricted political speech, the most valuable form of expression under the First Amendment, and thus was unconstitutional. "Political speech is indispensable to decision-making in a democracy and this is no less true because the speech comes from a corporation rather than an individual." Here the Supreme Court was following the listeners' rights theory of the First Amendment first proposed by Ralph Nader's Public Citizen Litigation Group in the *Virginia Pharmacy* case and then applied to corporate speech in ballot measure campaigns by Powell. If the speech was valuable, then it was protected regardless of the identity of the speaker. The Constitution, according to *Citizens United*, forbade the government from "distinguishing among different speakers, allowing speech by some but not others."[58]

Finally, *Citizens United* was consistent with the law-and-economics perspective on the superfluousness of laws designed to protect shareholders articulated by Justice Scalia's dissent in *Austin v. Michigan Chamber of Commerce*. With regard to corporate political activity, *Citizens United* said, there is "little evidence of abuse that cannot be corrected by shareholders through the procedures of corporate democracy." Although the court did not elaborate, the reference was clearly to shareholders' ability to vote for directors and shareholder proposals. Because shareholders could control the political activity of their corporations through board elections or via shareholder proposals to prohibit management from making political expenditures, there was no need for government regulation to protect them. Besides, as Scalia had previously argued, dissatisfied shareholders could simply sell their shares.

After reading from his opinion summary for about nine minutes, Justice Kennedy concluded and turned the floor over to Justice Stevens to read from the dissent.* Other justices had written opinions too; Chief Justice Roberts and Justice Scalia, for example, wrote separate concurrences to defend their votes against the inevitable charges against them: that Roberts, the consensus-builder, had abandoned minimalism, and that Scalia, the originalist, had extended rights to corporations the Framers never imagined. Yet justices can choose whether to read from their opinions in open court, and only Stevens responded to the majority's decision.

The 90-year-old jurist, with his flash of white hair and baritone voice, spoke haltingly, pausing often and fumbling his words. (He would later say that his trouble reading aloud his *Citizens United* dissent that day was a factor in his decision to retire from the court the following summer.) Yet there was no mistaking Stevens's passion. He

---

* The opinion of Justices Stevens, Ginsburg, Breyer, and Sotomayor was a partial dissent and partial concurrence. Those justices agreed with the majority with regard to another part of Citizens United's case beyond our focus here, the organization's challenge to the Bipartisan Campaign Reform Act's disclosure provisions. By a vote of 8–1, the disclosure provisions were upheld. On the issue of corporate spending, however, Stevens et al. were dissenters and are referred to this way in the text for clarity.

read for over twenty minutes, and although his tone was measured his words carried over the anger and frustration of the now-retired Justice Souter. "I must emphatically disagree with today's all-changing decision," Stevens declared.[59]

One of the majority's most significant mistakes was to suggest "the First Amendment absolutely and categorically prohibits any regulation of speech that distinguishes on the basis of the speaker's identity, including its identity as a corporation." In fact, Stevens, who had served on the court for thirty-five years, observed that over the course of his long tenure the court had often considered the speaker's identity in free speech cases. Just a few years earlier, in 2007, the same five justices in the *Citizens United* majority upheld special restrictions on the speech of public school students. Back then, Chief Justice Roberts had endorsed the principle that "the constitutional rights of students in public school are not automatically coextensive with the rights of adults" and admitted that "the same speech" in another setting "would have been protected." In a 2006 case, the Roberts court had similarly held that government employees had more limited speech rights than ordinary people. "The Government routinely places special restrictions on the speech rights of students, prisoners, members of the Armed Forces, foreigners and its own employees," Stevens noted. If the identity of the speaker were irrelevant, then foreign governments and foreign corporations had the exact same right to influence American elections as citizens of the United States. Stevens, who had served as a naval intelligence officer during World War II, warned, "The Court's new rule would have accorded propaganda broadcast to our troops by Tokyo Rose . . . the same threshold protection as a speech by General MacArthur."[60]

When it came to political speech about elections, Stevens noted that the law had always made identity-based distinctions. The Internal Revenue Code, for example, completely prohibits organizations formed under section 501(c)(3), such as charities and churches, from engaging in any electoral advocacy. Yet a social welfare organization formed under 501(c)(4) is entitled to engage in a moderate amount of political campaigning so long it is not the organization's "primary" function. The First Amendment has never been thought to prohibit these long-standing differences in how the law treats these distinct types of organizations, even when it comes to restrictions on core political speech.[61]

The Supreme Court itself would affirmatively endorse a clear identity-based distinction in federal campaign finance law less than two years after the *Citizens United* decision insisted the identity of the speaker was irrelevant. In 2012, the court in *Bluman v. Federal Election Commission* summarily affirmed a lower court ruling that had upheld a ban on political contributions and spending by foreign nationals residing in the United States. Because it was a summary affirmance, the justices did not publish an opinion explaining their reasoning. Indeed, the decision might have been hard to explain. The lower court held that, although foreign nationals within the country have many of the same rights as citizens, the "government may exclude foreign citizens from activities intimately related to the process of democratic self-government." Just as foreign nationals, on the basis of their identity alone, could be barred "from voting and serving as elected officers . . . [i]t follows that the government may bar foreign citizens . . . from participating in the campaign process that seeks to influence how voters will cast their ballots in the elections." Had *Citizens United* applied that same logic to corporations, which cannot vote in federal elections or serve in elected office, the case might well have come out differently.[62]

In *Citizens United*, Justice Stevens accused the majority of unbridled judicial activism. Echoing Souter's earlier criticism of the majority for reaching out to decide questions none of the advocates had even raised, Stevens proclaimed, "While the court tells us that we are asked to reconsider *Austin* and *McConnell*, it would be far more accurate for them to say, 'We have asked ourselves to reconsider those cases and to do so without the benefit of any evidentiary record that might shed light on the issues that the court addresses.'" The *Citizens United* decision, according to Stevens, was "a radical change in the law," breaking from long-standing tradition that dated back to Charles Evans Hughes, the Great Wall Street Scandal, and the Tillman Act. In Stevens's written dissent, the justice expanded on the accusation, even deploying the chief justice's words against him: "The majority has transgressed yet another 'cardinal' principle of the judicial process: 'If it is not necessary to decide more, it is necessary not to decide more.'"

Judicial activism is often just a label given to court rulings someone opposes. In *Citizens United*, however, the charge was not without justification. The court's majority had finessed the case so the justices could decide a major constitutional issue that had not originally been briefed and argued by the parties. The court had also struck down key provisions of a law passed by Congress, and in doing so overturned *McConnell*, a precedent that was less than seven years old. What had changed in the intervening years? Not much more than the personnel on the court.

Yet it would be a mistake to view *Citizens United* as a novelty, as an ungrounded invention of the Roberts court with little basis in law or history. *Citizens United* was in fact the culmination of a two-hundred-year struggle for constitutional rights for corporations. The decision was built upon foundations first laid in the early 1800s. Ever since, corporations have fought to win a greater share of the individual rights guaranteed by the Constitution. First they won constitutional protection for the core rights of corporations identified by Blackstone in his *Commentaries*: rights of property, contract, and access to court. Then they won the rights of due process and equal protection under the Fourteenth Amendment and the protections of the criminal procedure provisions of the Constitution. In the early twentieth century, the court said that there were nonetheless limits to the constitutional rights of corporations: they had property rights but not liberty rights. Eventually, however, the court broke down that distinction and began to recognize corporations to have liberty rights such as freedom of the press and freedom of association. While corporate rights reached new heights with *Citizens United*, the scaffolding had been built up over two centuries of Supreme Court decisions.

Once Stevens finished reading from his dissent, the chief justice adjourned the court and the justices disappeared back behind the

red velvet curtains. David Bossie excitedly went out to meet reporters waiting for a statement in the plaza in front of the Supreme Court
Building. "I am grateful and humbled by today's ruling," Bossie said.
Corporations could now "participate fully and freely in the election
process." Bossie then stopped to "take an opportunity to thank a few
people." He first named Ted Olson and his team from Gibson Dunn,
who "poured their hearts and souls into this case. . . . Ted Olson has
been a dear friend." After naming more than half a dozen others,
including the wife of the coexecutive producer of *Hillary: The Movie*,
Bossie finally came around to Jim Bopp. Referring to him only as "Jim,
our first lawyer," Bossie said he was "one of the foremost First Amendment lawyers in the country."[63]

Bopp had earned that reputation by winning important free speech
challenges to campaign finance laws in the Supreme Court, yet it had
not been enough to persuade Bossie to stick with him when Citizens
United's case reached the justices. And not long after the Supreme
Court's ruling in January of 2010, Bossie, as the broad scope of his
victory became more clear, seemed to forget Bopp's contributions altogether. Olson, Bossie told one interviewer, was "singularly responsible
for our winning this case."[64]

* * *

THE PUBLIC BACKLASH TO *Citizens United* was swift, and to the
justices almost certainly unexpected. Rarely does a Supreme Court
decision on a subject as dry as campaign finance law stir the public's
outrage. Less than a week after the court's ruling, President Obama
denounced the decision in his State of the Union address. Standing
before members of Congress, illustrious visitors, and even several of
the justices, Obama said, "With all due deference to separation of
powers, last week the Supreme Court reversed a century of law that
I believe will open the floodgates for special interests—including foreign corporations—to spend without limit in our elections. I don't
think American elections should be bankrolled by America's most
powerful interests or, worse, by foreign entities." Democratic lawmakers rose to their feet in applause, contrasting sharply with the stillness

PROTEST AGAINST CONSTITUTIONAL RIGHTS FOR CORPORATIONS
AT THE SUPREME COURT ON THE SECOND ANNIVERSARY OF
CITIZENS UNITED, JANUARY 20, 2012.

of the justices, who by custom remained seated and unmoved by the cheering. Only Justice Alito acknowledged the president's comment, shaking his head in disagreement and mouthing, "Not true."[65]

Although partisans on both sides were quick to condemn the exchange—with Republicans accusing Obama of exaggerating the court's decision and Democrats criticizing Alito for denying the decision's impact—Obama and Alito were both partially correct. Alito was right to object to the president's statement that the court had "reversed a century of law." To the extent Obama was referring to the Tillman Act of 1907, which banned corporate contributions to candidates, his statement was inaccurate. Technically, at least, that law was not at issue in *Citizens United*, which ruled only on the constitutionality of the Bipartisan Campaign Reform Act provisions that were enacted in 2002. And while the court had reversed two precedents, *Austin* and *McConnell*, those cases were nothing near a century old. Yet Obama was right that the logic and reasoning of *Citizens United* fundamentally undermined the legal basis for *any* special restrictions on corporate money in elections. The court had held that the corporate identity of the speaker was not grounds for limiting political speech, even though that had been the justification for over a century of campaign finance limits on corporate money.

Obama predicted that the *Citizens United* decision would open the floodgates for America's wealthiest interests to exert even more influence over elections, and spending in the next presidential election cycle of 2012 rose dramatically. Corporations were now allowed to spend general treasury funds to finance independent expenditures in favor of, or against, candidates for office. They also gained the right to contribute to "Super PACs"—a special type of political action committee that, unlike ordinary PACs, was able to accept unlimited contributions from corporations and individuals so long as their independent expenditures were not coordinated with any federal candidate. In 2012, businesses publicly gave over $70 million to Super PACs, lead by the Chevron Corporation, which contributed $2.5 million to House Speaker John Boehner's Congressional Leadership Fund. Some analysts speculated that corporations would have given more if Super PAC contributions did not have to be disclosed. As one corporate lobbyist noted, given the possibility of political donations offending customers and clients with different views, "nondisclosure is always preferred."[66]

Corporations eager to assert themselves in politics but fearful of exposure directed their money instead to other types of political advocacy groups that were not required to disclose their contributors. Trade associations, nonprofit 501(c) organizations, and so-called "527 committees" were responsible for most of $300 million in "dark," or undisclosed, money flowing into the 2012 races. It was revealed that Prudential, Merck & Company, and Dow Chemical each gave over $1 million to the US Chamber of Commerce to fund political expenditures. Computer chip maker Qualcomm, which was forced to admit its political spending as part of a settlement of a lawsuit, gave $2.8 million to dark money groups in 2012—far more than the company gave in otherwise disclosed contributions. In Montana, a political group named Western Tradition Partnership solicited money from companies by highlighting the lack of sunshine: "Corporate contributions are completely legal under this program. There's no limit on how much you can give. It's confidential. . . . No politician, no bureaucrat, no radical environmentalist will ever know."[67]

Corporations have not been the only ones to increase their political spending in the wake of the *Citizens United* decision; wealthy individuals and unions have also embraced the new ability to spend unlimited sums on independent advertisements. The Center for Public Integrity, a campaign finance watchdog group, estimated that in 2012 there was nearly $1 billion in new political spending traceable to *Citizens United*. And that number only reflects spending on *federal* races, where there is already an overwhelming amount of money. Although the data are hard to come by, there is evidence of significant spending increases at the state and local level too. In races for judges, mayors, district attorneys, and county commissioners, campaign expenses are historically quite small. As a result, corporations and others can have a much greater impact on the outcome with far less money than would be possible in federal races.[68]

Corporations gained new means of influencing American elections from the *Citizens United* decision, despite the fact that the case was not brought by a business like so many other of the most important corporate rights cases of the past. *Citizens United* was the handiwork of a small nonprofit group—and thus follows the handful of cases that involved corporations that were not themselves business firms, including *Dartmouth College v. Woodward* and *NAACP v. Alabama ex rel. Patterson*. The victories of these nonbusiness corporations nonetheless often redounded to the benefit of business firms, which were able to leverage them in the pursuit of their own profit.

The *Citizens United* decision also triggered a public backlash. Polls showed that eight in ten Americans were opposed to the Supreme Court's decision. The opposition crossed party lines, with 85 percent of Democrats, 76 percent of Republicans, and 81 percent of independents saying *Citizens United* was wrongly decided. Even five years after the ruling, an overwhelming majority of Americans polled, 78 percent, said the ruling should be overturned. Hillary Clinton and Bernie Sanders, the two main Democratic candidates in the 2016 presidential race, both said that overturning *Citizens United* would be a litmus test for their Supreme Court nominees—a level of opposition known to only a handful of notorious cases in American history, such as *Roe v. Wade*, the abortion decision.[69]

Perhaps the most visible manifestation of the public reaction to the *Citizens United* decision came in 2011 with Occupy Wall Street, a series of populist political protests against income inequality and the role of money in politics that began in New York and, according to the *Washington Post*, quickly "spread like wildfire around the country." The original Occupy protestors, who camped out in Zuccotti Park in lower Manhattan for two months, displayed signs testifying to the role they believed cases like *Citizens United* played in distorting democracy: "Corporations Are Not People," "Democracy Not Corporatization," "Revoke Corporate Personhood." They claimed to speak for the "99 percent," the broad mass of Americans who lacked the money and influence to fight against big business and the moneyed elite.[70]

One of the ironies of the Occupy Wall Street protests was that their success in raising public awareness about corporate power might not have been possible were it not for the political influence of a corporation. The protestors had expected to use either Bowling Green Park, the site of the famous "Charging Bull" sculpture that serves as the unofficial mascot of Wall Street, or the street in front of another downtown skyscraper nearby. When the New York City Police Department discovered the protestors' intended destinations, however, they roped those public areas off and the protestors were forced to look elsewhere. They found their way to Zuccotti Park, a privately owned green space and plaza about a block away from their original site. The park had been created in 1968 by U.S. Steel as part of a deal with New York City to permit the company to build a neighboring skyscraper that exceeded the city's height limits. One of the conditions of that agreement was that the park had to be kept open to the public at all times. As a result, when the Occupy protestors arrived, the current owner of the land, a commercial real estate company, believed it was powerless to close down the protest. The Occupy protestors were able to set up their tents and capture the attention of the American public thanks in part to the political deal making of a powerful corporation.[71]

The Occupy protestors adopted a resolution endorsing a constitutional amendment to overturn *Citizens United*:

Convinced that one critical threat to authentic democratic self-governance comes from the fact that corporations have been defined as legal persons, . . . Be it resolved that the New York General Assembly of Occupy Wall Street joins the millions of citizens, grassroots organizations and local governments across the country in calling for an Amendment to the Constitution to firmly establish that money is not speech, that human beings, not corporations, are persons entitled to constitutional rights, and that the rights of human beings will never again be granted to fictitious entities or property.

Support for such a constitutional amendment to eliminate constitutional rights for corporations was widespread, and stretched across the usual partisan lines. One of the leading proposals in Congress was sponsored by Representative Walter Jones Jr., a conservative Republican from North Carolina. "The status quo is dominated by deep-pocketed special interests," Jones explained, "and that's simply unacceptable to the American people." A constitutional amendment was endorsed by liberal public interest organizations such as Common Cause, Move to Amend, Free Speech for People, and even Public Citizen, whose lawsuit on behalf of consumers in the 1970s unwittingly set in place one of the doctrinal foundations for *Citizens United*. By 2016, sixteen states, including California, Colorado, Montana, New Mexico, Oregon, Vermont, and West Virginia, and hundreds of municipalities, had passed resolutions of support for a Twenty-Eighth Amendment to clarify that constitutional rights belong to human beings, not corporations.[72]

"I just hope they spend every waking minute and even stay up late at night working on that amendment," said Jim Bopp. The original lawyer behind the *Citizens United* case had experience with unsuccessful constitutional amendments. For years, he had promoted a different sort of "personhood" amendment, one that would declare the unborn to be "persons" protected by the Constitution. Yet after years of trying unsuccessfully to mobilize popular support, Bopp had come to realize that changing the Constitution on controversial issues through the amendment process was nearly impossible. Given the remote chances, a constitutional amendment to overturn *Citizens United* was exactly what a vigorous opponent of campaign finance law like Bopp wanted reformers to spend their time on. "I hope that is all they do for the next several centuries. Because it will be that long."[73]

Better to fight in court, where Bopp had discovered it was far easier to change how the Constitution was interpreted. That was, at least, the approach taken by corporations since the earliest days of the nation. The Framers did not explicitly provide corporations with any rights in the text of the Constitution, and the document was never formally amended to extend rights to corporations, the way it was for women and racial minorities. Yet corporations had nonetheless secured nearly all the same rights as individuals through a two-centuries-long effort concentrated on the Supreme Court.

Corporate Rights and Wrongs

I N THE SUMMER OF 2011, A YEAR AND A HALF AFTER THE SUPREME
Court announced its decision in the *Citizens United* case, Mitt Romney, an aspiring candidate for the Republican presidential nomination,
climbed up onto the famous Soapbox at the Iowa State Fair. Ringed by
bales of straw, Romney, a private equity investor who had been governor of Massachusetts, was given twenty minutes to make his pitch
to the fairgoers who gathered closely around. The crowd that greeted
him was combative. They continually interrupted with shouted questions and jeers as the presidential hopeful tried to explain his policy
on funding Social Security. Romney said he opposed policies that
would "raise taxes on people." A heckler who thought taxes should
be raised on business instead shouted in response, "Corporations!" In
what would become one of the notable gaffes of his campaign, Romney
replied, "Corporations are people, my friend."[1]

Romney's comment, caught on video, touched off a storm of criticism. Corporate personhood had become a controversial catchphrase
since *Citizens United*, and Romney was accused of repeating the same
mistake as the Supreme Court by suggesting that corporations had
equal standing to individuals under the law. Romney, however, was
trying to make a different point. "Everything that corporations earn

ultimately goes to people," he said next. "Where do you think it goes?" Romney was not saying that corporations, as such, were people with the same rights as individuals. He was saying that corporations were simply associations of people. His view was that when it came to policymaking one should ignore the corporate entity and focus instead on the people behind it. Dating back to Blackstone, however, corporate personhood in the law has traditionally meant that corporations are independent entities whose rights and obligations are separate and distinct from the rights and obligations of their members. Romney was mimicking the Supreme Court, but not in the way critics imagined. Rather, Romney and the justices used the language of personhood but employed the logic of piercing. They called corporations "people," yet pierced the corporate veil, looking right through the corporate form to base the decision on the rights of the corporations' members.

The centerpiece of Romney's presidential campaign was a promise to repeal and replace President Obama's signature legislation: the Patient Protection and Affordable Care Act. Popularly known as "Obamacare," the healthcare law triggered a wave of legal challenges,

AT THE IOWA STATE FAIR SOAPBOX, PRESIDENTIAL CANDIDATE MITT ROMNEY SAID, "CORPORATIONS ARE PEOPLE, MY FRIEND."

including a historic, high-profile Supreme Court case on the law's mandate that nearly all individuals have or buy health insurance. In a 2012 decision that surprised many court watchers, the court upheld the health insurance mandate in a narrow 5–4 decision in which Chief Justice John Roberts sided with the court's four liberal justices. It was only the second time Roberts sided with the liberals in a 5–4 decision since joining the high court—and one possible explanation was *Citizens United.* As in that case, the four conservative justices argued for a broad ruling that went much further than necessary to resolve the dispute; they were prepared to strike down not only the individual mandate but the entire 2,700-page law, which included hundreds of provisions completely unrelated to the mandate. Perhaps Roberts was not willing to go along again with such an aggressive approach in another highly politically charged case that threatened to undermine his stated desire for a legacy as a minimalist who kept the court out of politics.[2]

There was, however, one legal challenge to a smaller piece of Obamacare that succeeded, and it involved the rights of corporations. Hobby Lobby Stores, Incorporated, a national chain of craft stores with over 23,000 employees, filed suit against an Obamacare regulation that required large employers to include birth control in their employees' health insurance plans. The owners of Hobby Lobby, David and Barbara Green and their three children, were Evangelical Christians who believed some of the mandated forms of birth control caused abortion, which the Greens opposed on religious grounds. Although technically the Greens themselves were not required by the law to provide birth control coverage—the mandate fell on the corporate entity, not the owners personally—the Greens felt the law interfered with their religious freedom and directed the company to challenge the requirement.[3]

Hobby Lobby, joined by another for-profit company with religious owners, Conestoga Wood Specialties, sued the federal government, claiming the mandatory birth control coverage violated the Religious Freedom Restoration Act, or RFRA. Enacted by a nearly unanimous vote in 1993 after a Supreme Court ruling narrowing the scope of the First Amendment's free exercise clause, RFRA entitled people to an exemption from federal laws that imposed a substantial burden on their sincerely held religious beliefs. Hobby Lobby's claim, in other words, was not based on the Constitution, like the other corporate rights cases that have arisen in the Supreme Court over the past two centuries. Nonetheless, RFRA was designed to enhance rights of religious liberty associated with the First Amendment. And although the law was enacted with the religious rights of individuals in mind, Hobby Lobby and Conestoga Wood Specialties were constitutional leveragers that sought to use the statute to protect their businesses.[4]

In June of 2014, the Supreme Court, in another 5–4 ruling, sided with the company in *Burwell v. Hobby Lobby Stores, Inc.* Justice Sam Alito wrote the majority opinion for the same five justices who voted to strike down limits on corporate political spending in *Citizens United*, including the chief justice. Alito's opinion held that Hobby Lobby and Conestoga Wood Specialties, even though they were for-profit companies, had religious liberty rights under RFRA and were entitled to an exemption from the birth control coverage requirement. Over the dissent of the four liberal justices, including Elena Kagan, who had replaced Justice John Paul Stevens, the Supreme Court for the first time explicitly recognized that business corporations had religious freedom.[5]

The Supreme Court's decision in *Hobby Lobby* was a near perfect embodiment of the more than two-hundred-year history of corporate rights jurisprudence. Although the case was formally about a federal statute, not the Constitution, the decision hewed closely to the reasoning and logic of so many previous cases extending constitutional rights to corporations. Like the late nineteenth-century rulings that extended due process and equal protection rights to corporations, *Hobby Lobby* said that corporations were people. Under RFRA, the federal government was prohibited from substantially burdening "a *person's* exercise of religion." The court held that business corporations were included, largely because of the Dictionary Act, another federal law that officially defined the terms used in federal statutes. The Dictionary Act provided that "unless the context indicates otherwise," the word *person* should be read to apply to "corporations, companies, associations, firms, partnerships, societies, and joint stock companies, as well as individuals." As a result, the court expansively read the law to protect the rights of corporations, which deployed those rights to overturn a regulation of their business practices.

Yet, as with many previous Supreme Court cases invoking corporate personhood, the underlying logic of *Hobby Lobby* reflected instead piercing the corporate veil. "A corporation is simply a form of organization used by human beings to achieve desired ends," Justice Alito explained. "When rights, whether constitutional or statutory, are extended to corporations, the purpose is to protect the rights of these people." Protecting the "free-exercise rights of corporations like Hobby Lobby, Conestoga, and [others] protects the religious liberty of the humans who own and control those companies." Hobby Lobby was entitled to assert religious rights, Alito wrote, to protect "the religious liberty of the Greens." Alito, in other words, looked right through the corporate form and focused instead on the people who made up the corporation. Properly understood, Alito's decision, like *Citizens United*, represented a rejection of corporate personhood. Instead of treating the corporation as an independent legal entity, with rights separate from those of its members—as the Taney court did in the mid-1800s—the Supreme Court once again collapsed the distinction. Hobby Lobby was the Greens, and the Greens were Hobby Lobby.[6]

In dissent, Justice Ruth Bader Ginsburg called the majority's opinion one of "startling breadth." Any corporation, public or private, closely held or public, could claim those same rights in order to gain an exemption from other forms of business regulation to which the owners of a company objected. Indeed, in the months after the *Hobby Lobby* decision came down, a number of businesses asserted a religious right to discriminate against same-sex couples—although, at least at first, with little success. Alito insisted that Ginsburg was wrong and that "our holding is very specific." The court had only held this one regulation invalid, and there were other ways for the government to provide birth control to women. Moreover, Alito also emphasized that Hobby Lobby was a closely held corporation and "it seems unlikely" that publicly held corporations "will often assert" religious rights. In the *Citizens United* case, Alito had helped transform Ted Olson's narrow claim into a broad, groundbreaking decision that significantly changed the law; in the *Hobby Lobby* case, Alito sought to portray his broad, groundbreaking decision as a narrow one that barely moved the law at all.

* * *

WITH INTRICATELY ETCHED WOOD paneling on the walls and ornate stained glass in the windows, the faculty lounge at the Yale Law School exuded the formality and tradition of the Ivy League, and that did not suit Leo Strine at all. The brilliant and outspoken chief justice of the Delaware Supreme Court, Strine had been invited to deliver the Ralph K. Winter Lecture, a prestigious speaking engagement named after a federal judge and Yale alumnus known for his rulings on business and corporate law issues. After a laudatory introduction by the law school's dean, Strine stood up in front of the faculty, students, and distinguished visitors gathered in the solemn room and immediately began to undress. "I'm a judge, so I'm going to do this," he announced, and with the ardor of an escaped convict shedding his prison jumpsuit Strine pulled off his suit jacket, revealing colorful suspenders busy with vivid cartoons of jazz musicians.[7]

Strine's lecture at Yale—a school, you may recall, named after Elihu Yale, one of the stockholders made rich by the East India Company— took place in October of 2015, a year after the *Hobby Lobby* decision. By then, the 51-year-old jurist had already proven himself to be the most influential and charismatic figure in the world of corporate law. Prior to becoming the chief justice of Delaware, Strine served for sixteen years on Delaware's Court of Chancery, the nation's leading court for corporate law. Delaware, with over 60 percent of Fortune 500 companies and more than 900,000 businesses incorporated in the state, had won the so-called "race to the bottom" begun at the end of the nineteenth century when New Jersey loosened its laws to attract Rockefeller's Standard Oil and other trusts. Although New Jersey eventually strengthened its corporate code, Delaware followed the Garden State's earlier example and continually made its corporate law rules more permissive and friendly to management, becoming the leading state of choice for America's corporations. To handle the legal disputes arising from all these corporations, the judges on the Court of Chancery developed special expertise in corporate law, unique in the nation.[8]

When Strine was first appointed to the Chancery court, he was only 34, a precocious age for a judge. Nonetheless, he quickly dispelled any skepticism stemming from his inexperience by working around the clock and writing clear, learned opinions that proved his mastery of the nuances of corporate law. Strine's rulings were "extremely well crafted legally," said Charles Elson, director of the Weinberg Center for Corporate Governance at the University of Delaware. Indeed, within a few years, Strine was being called the Chancery court's "leading voice." Certainly he was the court's most entertaining one, sprinkling into his opinions and proceedings references to music and pop culture, from reality television star Snooki to the novelist John Cheever. Unlike many judges, Strine did not shy away from public speaking—or from speaking his mind. The *Wall Street Journal* called him "about the closest thing to a celebrity in the buttoned-up world of corporate law."[9]

"It's a little bit daunting to be here," Strine began his Winter Lecture, acknowledging with a touch of false modesty the presence of some of the nation's leading legal scholars. In fact, no one was more qualified to speak about the topic of Strine's address: how the Supreme Court decisions in the *Citizens United* and *Hobby Lobby* cases were profoundly mistaken from the perspective of corporate law. In Strine's view, the court's rulings reflected serious confusion about the nature of corporations and how they operated. Strine, a modern-day Louis Brandeis who favored legal rules built around the empirical reality of human behavior, suggested that the justices who wrote those opinions, simply put, "don't know much corporate law."

Strine was a strong proponent of free markets and often opposed heavy-handed regulation of business. Unlike many critics of the *Citizens United* decision, for example, Strine was a vocal critic of the Sarbanes-Oxley Act, calling the federal law imposing strict new rules on corporate executives to increase transparency "misguided." Yet he

DELAWARE CHIEF JUSTICE LEO STRINE DELIVERS THE 2015
RALPH K. WINTER LECTURE AT YALE LAW SCHOOL.

was not a corporationalist committed to expansive rights for corporations, and he believed that judges should base their decisions in corporate rights cases on an accurate understanding of how corporations
and corporate law actually work. By that metric, at least, the *Citizens
United* and *Hobby Lobby* decisions went awry.

Stine took issue with the view expressed in *Citizens United* that
stockholders unhappy with corporate political spending could use
"the procedures of corporate democracy" to stop it, or simply sell
their shares. "Now, that's not really true," Strine said. The Supreme
Court had misunderstood "how ordinary humans now invest in corporations. It's just not the same as it was back in the day—back in
the 70s, before Disco and New Wave," he added with a smirk. Today,
most "stockholders own stock through intermediaries," such as pen-

sion and mutual funds, "not directly." Individual investors in pension and mutual funds are not entitled to vote in corporate elections, so they have no access to the procedures of corporate democracy. Even if they could vote, the widespread use of proxy voting gives management nearly unfettered control over corporate election outcomes—as revealed by the Great Wall Street Scandal more than a century earlier. Echoing Charles Evans Hughes, Strine insisted that the "reality is so-called stockholder democracy provides little restraint on management's political spending."

Nor was it realistic, in Strine's view, to believe that dissatisfied stockholders could sell their shares. Pension and mutual fund investors "don't choose which stocks the intermediaries invest in or even which intermediary manages their funds in some circumstances." Funds do not typically allow individual investors to pick which corporations they will own. And while mutual fund investors may be able to move in and out of fund portfolios, people who invest through pension funds are typically, according to Strine, "stuck in."

Strine's understanding of how ordinary people invest in corporations stemmed not just from his expertise in corporate law but also from his experience growing up in a working-class family. His parents were row house kids in Baltimore who married as teenagers and skipped college to work and raise a family. While his father worked for a department store, his mother worked her way up the ladder of a bank in Wilmington. If people like Strine's parents had retirement savings, it would most likely be in a pension. Yet they could not control which companies their retirement money was invested in—at least not without significant legal penalties. "If you take your money out of your 401(k), there is expropriatory levels of taxation," even if you sell because of political dissent, Strine noted. "So once you entrust that money to the market, it stays there." The law, in other words, strongly discourages people from selling their shares. Contrary to the assumptions behind *Citizens United*, Strine said, "investors have little control over the day-to-day business decisions of corporations and little choice but to invest."

One of the Supreme Court's most glaring errors, in Strine's view, was piercing the corporate veil. As he wrote in a law review article published the same year as his lecture at Yale, such an approach was "at odds with historical understandings of the corporation and the reality of diverse stockholder ownership." From the perspective of corporate law, "it was not credible to equate the view of the corporation to those of its diverse and changing stockholders." Perhaps it might have made sense for the court to treat a corporation as an association back in the day of Horace Binney and Daniel Webster, when corporations typically were made up of small groups of local investors and had only a handful of employees. Today, however, a corporation seeking to spend on politics could be a multinational enterprise with tens of thousands of employees and an equally large number of stockholders. Many of those stockholders might hold their shares only for minutes—or less— as a play on the stock market; others, such as the majority of Americans who own stock in companies through pension and mutual funds, likely do not even know the names of the companies in which they are invested. Corporations were not political associations like the NAACP or a PAC. Given the reality of modern-day stockholding, Strine said it was hard to believe that "General Electric, Wal-Mart, McDonald's, etc., exist because their stockholders wish to come together and have those corporations, through their managers, 'speak' on behalf of the stockholders" on matters of electoral politics.[10]

Corporations were not associations under the long-standing law of corporations, they were people. A corporation is "a distinct entity that is legally separate from its stockholders, managers, and creditors. This is the whole point of corporate law after all." Pick up any textbook on the law of corporations and the first lesson is always the same: the corporation is a legal person—an independent legal entity separate from the people who own and work for it. Because of that personhood, stockholders in the modern corporation were not personally responsible for the company's debts; if a corporation broke a contract or harmed someone, the victim had to sue the corporate entity, not the members of the corporation. As the Supreme Court itself has said in ordinary business law cases, a "corporation and its stockholders are generally to be treated as separate entities."[11]

The *Hobby Lobby* decision, in Strine's view, similarly failed to recognize the separate personhood of the corporation. "There's a whole, deep corporate law problem with figuring out whether a corporation has a religion," Strine argued. "And what [the justices] did was conflate the family which controlled Hobby Lobby with the corporation." The court looked right past the distinct legal status of the corporation and based the decision on the religious beliefs of the Green family. By allowing the company to claim the religious rights of its shareholders, the *Hobby Lobby* decision abandoned the principles of corporate personhood.

Strine's remarks raised an important question: What if the Supreme Court had taken corporate personhood seriously in a case like *Hobby Lobby*? If so, the justices would not have asked whether the Green family had religious beliefs that were offended by the birth control coverage requirement. They would have asked instead whether Hobby Lobby, the corporation itself, as an independent entity in the eyes of the law, should be recognized to have religious beliefs. The members of the Green family were wholly distinct legal persons, whose rights were not at issue. The Green family depended on that separation to protect their personal assets; they would have insisted on a strict boundary between them and the corporate entity if a customer had fallen in a Hobby Lobby store and sued the Greens personally for damages. Like the liability for the customer's injury, the birth control mandate was imposed on the corporate entity alone. Whatever reasons there might be for recognizing for-profit corporations to have religious beliefs—and there were good arguments to be made on both sides—at least the court would be focused on the corporation, not the Greens.[12]

Over the course of American history, corporate personhood has *not* led to expansive constitutional protections. In fact, when the Supreme Court has broken from its usual pattern and treated a corporation as a truly separate legal person with distinct rights of its own, the result has usually been more limited rights for business. Under Chief Justice Roger Taney, the court viewed the corporation as a legal person separate from its members but nonetheless scaled back corporate constitutional protections, much to the displeasure of Daniel Webster. In

the *Lochner* era, the courts vacillated but often did treat the corporation as a person—and cabined the ability of corporations to claim
the protections of the right against self-incrimination, the freedom of
association, and the freedom of speech. The court held that corporations have a Fourth Amendment right against unreasonable searches
and seizures, yet the scope of that protection was less than it was for
individuals. Because those judges did not confound the rights of the
corporation with the rights of the corporation's members, they properly asked which rights corporations, as such, should have and then
tailored those rights to the particular circumstances of the corporate
form. Corporations were legal persons but they were not necessarily
the same as human beings and, as a result of those distinctions, were
afforded fewer and more circumscribed constitutional rights.

At Yale, Strine pointed to the "obvious differences between flesh
and blood citizens and corporate citizens." Corporations lack "the
capacity or inclination to think and act like a human being with the
full range of human concerns." For Strine, this was not a matter of
metaphysics; it was a basic principle of corporate law. "Corporations
must put profit first under the predominant corporate law in the
United States, that of my own state, Delaware." Indeed, ever since
the Dodge brothers sued to stop Henry Ford from pursuing policies to benefit employees and the broader public without regard to
stockholders, the law required that all corporate activity be designed
in the long run to enhance profits. Officers had to obey that legal
mandate or risk being held in violation of their fiduciary duties to
the corporation. As a result, corporations are not truly "free" in the
way that individuals can be. A person can choose her own values,
preferring to prioritize personal wealth, social welfare, the environment, or law and order. A corporation, however, is legally obligated
to prioritize profit, at least in the long term. Corporate law purports
to prohibit corporations from exercising the very autonomy often
thought to be essential to rights of political participation and religious liberty.[13]

As Strine neared the end of his talk, he said that he was "going
to finish—and you'll be glad to hear the word 'finish,'" he said with

a wry smile, by asking whether the recent decisions of the Roberts court were just examples of "this is the balls and strikes, as a certain judge said? Or does it evidence judges willing to depart from principles of restraint and move the law in a direction they think is better for society?" Given the Constitution's silence on the issue of corporations, Strine's question was one that could have been asked of all the corporate rights cases dating back to the early 1800s.

* * *

THE MORA COUNTY COMMISSION meets in a small, drab, prefabricated office off Highway 518 in a remote part of northern New Mexico. Although the temporary structure serves as the seat of government for this small community (population 4,881), the parking lot is unpaved and it sits next door to a dilapidated house with boarded-up windows. The entrance to the prefab is marked with a hand-painted wooden sign that says "Mora County Court House" in bright, slightly uneven letters. In May of 2013, John Olivas, the chairman of the commission, stood out in front of the sign talking to a reporter from an international news agency. Although the foreign press rarely took an interest in the doings of tiny Mora County, Olivas and the other commissioners had made headlines earlier that spring when they enacted the nation's first countywide ban on fracking, the controversial drilling technique believed to cause earthquakes and water pollution. "Approximately ninety-five percent of the people in our community don't want oil and gas," Olivas explained to the journalist. "They want to protect the water. They want to protect the air. They want to protect the environment."[14]

Olivas, the main sponsor of the ordinance to ban fracking, was tall and lean, with a boyish face that masked his stubborn resolve. He came from hardy stock; his family was among the earliest settlers of this high-mountain outpost back in 1835 when it was still part of Mexico, and they fought against the US takeover in 1848. An outfitter by trade, Olivas often went into the Pecos Wilderness alone to hunt 700-pound elk with only a bow and arrow. With the fracking ban, however, Olivas and the Mora County Commission had taken aim at more

THE MORA COUNTY COURTHOUSE IN NEW MEXICO.

formidable quarry. Not only were they targeting the wealthy oil and gas companies that owned mineral leases to more than 30,000 acres of land in the county, they were also seeking to overturn *Citizens United* and indeed the entire two-hundred-year line of Supreme Court cases establishing constitutional rights for corporations.

"For well over a century now, corporations have used those 'rights' to stop efforts, like ours, which seek to use local lawmaking to protect our communities from harmful corporate activities," said Olivas. Citing recent lawsuits brought by businesses to challenge laws requiring the labeling of dairy products and regulating the siting of cell phone towers, Olivas insisted that "our lawmaking authority as 'we the people' has been largely eliminated." With a populist tone that harkened all the way back to Thomas Jefferson and Roger Taney, Olivas warned that "private corporations have been granted increasing power to dictate the future of our communities."

Olivas's ordinance, titled the "Mora Community Water Rights and Self-Governance Act," declared that the oil and gas companies who wanted to frack in the county had no constitutional rights. "Corporations in violation of the prohibitions enacted by this ordinance, or seeking to engage in activities prohibited by this ordinance [such as fracking], shall not have the rights of 'persons' afforded by the United States and New Mexico Constitutions, nor shall those corporations be afforded rights under the 1st or 5th amendments to the United States Constitution or corresponding sections of the New Mexico Constitution, nor shall those corporations be afforded the protections of the commerce or contracts clauses within the United States Constitution or corresponding sections of the New Mexico Constitution." Instead, the ordinance endorsed a different set of rights: the local residents' "right to water," "right to a sustainable energy future," and "right to self-government."

When the Mora County Commission first met in the prefab to deliberate over Olivas's bold, populist measure, they were carrying on a tradition that traced directly back to the Virginia Company and the first legislative assembly in Jamestown. Although separated by four centuries and nearly two thousand miles, both the colonists and the Mora County commissioners were small, desperate communities seeking to assert some control over their environment. Yet the world had changed so much in the intervening years. Jamestown was a fragile corporate outpost in the vast expanse of America, the Virginia Company quite literally the only corporation on these shores. By 2013, however, corporations had become the dominant form of business enterprise and were pervasive in every corner of America—even little Mora County, a tiny outpost whose people were attempting to assert what they saw as their last vestiges of popular sovereignty.

Like the colonists of Jamestown, the people of Mora County faced daunting odds. While flush with a fighting spirit, Mora County lacked the resources to be able to compete with the oil and gas giants, such as the subsidiary of Royal Dutch Shell that filed suit in January of 2014 to challenge Olivas's ordinance. The annual budget of Mora County was reported to be less than $1 million, while Shell was the sixth largest company in the world and had annual revenues of over $270 billion.

By filing suit to protect its rights in federal court, the Shell subsidiary corporation, like the Mora County Commission, was also carrying on a tradition—one that went back to Horace Binney, the Bank of the United States, and the first corporate rights case. The Bank was the first corporation to use the federal courts to challenge a local law; its victory established the precedent that, even though the text of the Constitution guarantees the right to sue in federal court only to "Citizens," corporations enjoyed that right too. Chief Justice John Marshall's decision in *Bank of the United States v. Deveaux* would be the germinal seed of more than two centuries of corporate rights cases—up to and including the Shell subsidiary's lawsuit against Mora County.

The Shell subsidiary claimed Olivas's ordinance denied the company a number of corporate constitutional rights. The law denied the corporation the right of access to federal court by prohibiting corporations seeking to engage in fracking from having any legal right to challenge the law in any tribunal, state or federal. The ordinance was said to violate the company's property rights—an argument that would have been appreciated by Daniel Webster. The company further argued that the ordinance violated the company's rights to equal protection and due process under the Fourteenth Amendment, 130 years after Roscoe Conkling deceived the Supreme Court in pursuit of those same rights for the Southern Pacific Railroad. Mora County's ordinance, the company said, was "motivated by animus" and was "directed at a politically unpopular group," similar to Huey Long's advertising tax, Alabama's persecution of the NAACP, and, according to *Citizens United*, campaign finance laws restricting corporate spending.

The oil company's constitutional arguments were anything but innovative; this corporation was not a constitutional first mover. The Supreme Court had extended all of these constitutional protections to corporations. Those decisions came from an institution that for much of its history has leaned decidedly in favor of business—often under the leadership of influential justices, like Stephen Field and Lewis Powell, who were committed to expansive rights for corporations. At the same time, corporations have also won constitutional rights when their cases became caught up in larger political controversies or jurisprudential shifts, such as the civil rights movement or the rise of modern free speech doctrine. It was, ironically, the New Deal and Warren courts that extended to corporations rights of "liberty" that the famously business-friendly *Lochner* court had rejected.

Judge James Browning, the federal judge who presided over the challenge to Mora County's fracking ban, was no stranger to the oil business. During his summers in college he worked in the oilfields, and his father had been an employee of Texaco. Yet Browning was passionate about the law. He traced his inspiration to a book about John Marshall that he found in the fourth grade, when as a young, voracious reader Browning set out to read every book in the local public library. The book recounted in depth the *Dartmouth College* case, celebrating Marshall's opinion that established the constitutional status of corporations as private entities. Browning went to law school at the University of Virginia, located about 125 miles from Jamestown, and then clerked on the Supreme Court for Justice Lewis Powell four years after the landmark *Bellotti* decision. The Shell subsidiary, however, did not need Browning to take after his corporationalist mentor and expand the rights of corporations in order to win. The law was already on the company's side.[15]

In January of 2015, Judge Browning struck down the Mora County ordinance. His decision rested largely on the most controversial of corporate constitutional rights: freedom of speech. Mora County's ordinance unconstitutionally purported to strip away the First Amendment rights of any corporation "seeking to engage" in fracking, Browning ruled. A century ago, when the federal courts were turning away free speech cases brought by brewing companies seeking to stem the rising tide of Prohibition, the ordinance might have been upheld. Back then, the federal courts insisted that corporations had rights of property but not rights of liberty. In the years since, however, the Supreme Court had gradually recognized corporations to have ever-greater protections under the First Amendment, beginning with the Louisiana newspapers in the 1930s. By the time of the Mora County case, the justices had afforded corporations broad rights of political and commercial speech too. In light of this clear line of precedent, Browning had little choice but to invalidate the ordinance.

"It is well established, however, that corporations have constitutional rights," Browning explained. "To find support for the long history of corporate constitutional rights, the court needs to look no further than" Mora County's own briefs, which listed "numerous cases in which the Supreme Court recognized" such protections. "The Defendants' argument that corporations should not be granted constitutional rights, or that corporate rights should be subservient to people's rights, are arguments that are best made before the Supreme Court—the only court that can overrule Supreme Court precedent—rather than a district court." Corporate constitutional rights were a product of Supreme Court decisions and so, absent a constitutional amendment like the one proposed by Occupy Wall Street, only the justices could declare an end to them.[16]

The justices would not have the opportunity to reconsider the long, complicated history of corporate rights in the Mora County case. The lawsuit by the Shell subsidiary worried many local residents, who feared that defending the law and paying damages and legal fees to the company could bankrupt the already impoverished county. Six months after the lawsuit was filed, John Olivas lost his bid for reelection to the county commission, which subsequently decided not to appeal Browning's ruling. The effort to turn back the remarkably successful corporate rights movement would have to wait for another day—and another, more deep-pocketed challenger who, like the wealthy and powerful corporations that fought to gain constitutional rights over the course of American history, could afford the costs of litigation.

Nearly two hundred years ago, in one of the very first corporate rights cases, Chief Justice Marshall wrote, "A corporation is an artificial being, invisible, intangible, and existing only in contemplation of law." In so many ways, the corporation has remained invisible in constitutional law ever since. Although corporations have won the lion's share of constitutional protections, the corporate rights movement has remained largely unnoticed by the public at large—despite many of the cases being high-profile controversies that drew considerable public attention contemporaneously. The Supreme Court has contributed to the cloaking of the corporation by looking right through the corporate form and basing the rights of the corporation on the rights of the people associated together within it. While calling corporations "people," the justices have usually rejected the core principle of corporate personhood: the independent legal standing of the corporation, with rights and duties separate and distinct from those of its members.

Lawyers and historians have extensively studied the civil rights movements for racial minorities, women, and others, making those stories central to our understanding of the Constitution and of America itself. Corporations, too, have had a civil rights movement of sorts. Although *Citizens United* and *Hobby Lobby* brought new public attention and scrutiny to corporate rights, long before those controversial cases were decided corporations had already taken their place among *We the People*.

ACKNOWLEDGMENTS

—

ONE BENEFIT OF A BOOK THAT TAKES TOO MANY YEARS to write is that the deliberate pace offers the chance to discuss the ideas and stories with a large number of people. I am indebted to the insights offered and inspired by Steve Bainbridge, Tamara Belinfanti, Joan Biskupic, Josh Blackman, Margaret Blair, Sam Bray, Rick Brooks, Judge James Browning, Devon Carbado, Wah Chen, David Ciepley, Jeff Clements, Mitchell Duneier, Garrett Epps, Jason Epstein, Andreas Flexner, David Gans, Nancy Gordon, Malcolm Harkins III, Dan Klerman, Russell Korobkin, Naomi Lamoreaux, Jessica Levinson (for the title), Ajay Mehrotra, Judith Miller, Hiroshi Motomura, Doug Nejaime, William Novak, Karen Orren, Tamara Piety, Kal Raustiala, Sergio Alberto Gramitto Ricci, Larry Rosenthal, David Savage, Lynn Stout, Eugene Volokh, the participants in the *Corporations and American Democracy* convening of the Tobin Project, the participants in the *Corporations as Legal Persons: Taking Entity Status Seriously* workshop, and the students in my 2013 and 2015 Constitutional Theory seminars at UCLA School of Law. I will forever be indebted to the friends who read the manuscript and pushed me to make it better, including Ryan Azad, Stuart Banner, Stephen Breyer, Kent Greenfield, Rick Hasen, David Leyva, Louis Marshall, Darrell Miller, Alan Morrison, Frank Partnoy, Elizabeth Pollman, Richard Re, Ed Renwick, Ganesh Sitaraman, Irwin Winkler, Margo Winkler, and James Zagel.

A veritable army of librarians and research assistants helped me uncover the wealth of detail necessary to tell the story of corporate rights, and this book would not have been possible without Amy

Atchison, Thomas Cochrane, Stephanie Der, Robert Double, Meredith Gallen, Daniel Gibbons, Lucy Jackson, Katherine Kamlowsky, Sarah Levesque, Sam Moniz, Nicole Nour, Jaqi Schock, Terry Stedman, Vicki Steiner, Zachary Taylor, Stephanie Thomas-Hodge, Amy Takeuchi Wanlass, and Brooke Zarouri. A special thanks to Linda O'Connor, who keeps me well stocked in extremely well-trained research assistants. Elsa Duong, Cheryl Kelly Fischer, and Rebecca Fordon were tireless in finding and securing the rights to images. My two assistants, Rusty Klibaner and Sherry Yuan, were unfailingly helpful with organizational details. Deans Jennifer Mnookin and Rachel Moran of the UCLA School of Law provided the funds necessary to finance my research.

The final chapters benefited immensely from interviews with Jim Bopp, Michael Dukakis, Trevor Potter, John Paul Stevens, Leo Strine, and others; each graciously gave their time and memories. Lynn Nesbit, my superb agent, guided me through the process of writing this book from beginning to end. At W. W. Norton & Company, Marie Pantojan provided needed assistance at every turn, and Ed Klaris gave his thoughtful legal advice. No one did more than my fantastic editor Bob Weil to improve the manuscript and sharpen the history.

One final note of gratitude to two special people who shape everything I do, Melissa Bomes and Dani Winkler. My love for you is boundless.

CHRONOLOGY
OF CORPORATE RIGHTS

—

separate legal identity and certain rights, including property, contract, and access to court.

1773:   Boston Tea Party – The colonists demonstrate their anger toward the English government and the East India Company, the recipient of a huge bailout, by dumping the corporation's tea into Boston Harbor.

FIRST CORPORATE RIGHTS CASES, 1787–1860

1787:   Constitutional Convention – The Framers design the Constitution of the United States, influenced by their experience with colonial corporations.

1809:   *Bank of the United States v. Deveaux* – In the first corporate rights case, Horace Binney persuades the Supreme Court to recognize corporations' right of access to federal court under Article III of the Constitution and the Judiciary Act.

1819:   *Dartmouth College v. Woodward* – The Supreme Court under Chief Justice John Marshall adopts Daniel Webster's argument that corporations are private entities, akin to individuals, under the contract clause of the Constitution.

1837:   *Charles River Bridge Company v. Warren Bridge Company* – In a defeat for Daniel Webster, the Supreme Court under Chief Justice Roger Taney refuses to read monopoly privileges into a corporate charter.

1839:   *Bank of Augusta v. Earle* – The Taney court holds that corporations do not have the privileges and immunities of citizens under the comity clause of Article IV of the Constitution.

1853:   *Marshall v. Baltimore & Ohio Railroad Company* – The Taney court uses corporate personhood to make corporations more easily amenable to suit in federal court.

PROPERTY BUT NOT LIBERTY RIGHTS, 1861–1935

1882:   *San Mateo County v. Southern Pacific Railroad Company* – Roscoe Conkling misleads the justices about the history and meaning of the Fourteenth Amendment in a test case designed to win rights of equal protection and due process for corporations.

1886: *Santa Clara County v. Southern Pacific Railroad Company* – Reporter of Decisions J. C. Bancroft Davis includes an inaccurate headnote saying the Supreme Court held that corporations were persons under the Fourteenth Amendment.

1888: *Pembina Consolidated Silver Mining Company v. Pennsylvania* – Justice Stephen Field's majority opinion announces that corporations are persons entitled to equal protection and due process under the Fourteenth Amendment.

1896: Marc Hanna – As William McKinley's campaign manager, he revolutionizes election campaigns and, for the first time, actively solicits corporate money for a presidential race.

1897–1936: *Lochner* Era – Although often friendly to business, the court establishes a new boundary on the rights of corporations, entitling them to property rights but not liberty rights.

1906: *Hale v. Henkel* – The Supreme Court holds corporations do not have the Fifth Amendment right against self-incrimination but do have a limited Fourth Amendment right against unreasonable searches and seizures.

1907: Tillman Act – After the revelations of the Great Wall Street Scandal, Congress enacts the first modern campaign finance law, a ban on corporate contributions to federal candidates.

1907: *Western Turf Association v. Greenberg* – The Supreme Court rules that corporations do not have the freedom of association, a liberty right.

1908: *Berea College v. Kentucky* – The court affirms that corporations, even educational corporations not organized for profit, have no right of association.

1916: Brewers Cases – The Michigan Supreme Court and a federal court hold that corporations have no right to influence elections and uphold bans on corporate money in campaigns.

1919: *Dodge Brothers v. Ford Motor Company* – An influential case that stands for the principle that business corporations must be run in the interests of stockholders.

LIBERTY RIGHTS, 1936–CURRENT

1936: *Grosjean v. American Press Company* – The Supreme Court rules that the First Amendment right of freedom of the press extends to newspaper corporations.

1942: *Valentine v. Chrestensen* – The Supreme Court holds that commercial speech is not protected by the First Amendment.

1946: *Marsh v. Alabama* – In an unusual case, the Supreme Court determines that a company town run by a corporation must respect individual rights.

1958: *NAACP v. Alabama ex rel. Patterson* – The Supreme Court holds that a voluntary membership corporation can assert its members' rights of association.

1971: Lewis Powell – Months before being nominated to the Supreme Court, he authors an influential memorandum to the Chamber of Commerce outlining how business could better defend its interests.

1976: *Virginia Pharmacy Board v. Virginia Citizens Consumer Council* – Siding with Ralph Nader's consumer rights group, the Supreme Court adopts the listeners' rights theory of free speech to protect commercial speech.

1978: *First National Bank of Boston v. Bellotti* – Justice Lewis Powell authors the Supreme Court's opinion recognizing corporations have a free speech right to influence ballot measure campaigns.

1990: *Austin v. Michigan Chamber of Commerce* – The Supreme Court declares restrictions on corporate money in candidate election campaigns constitutionally permissible, distinguishing *Bellotti*.

2003: *McConnell v. Federal Election Commission* – Reaffirming *Austin*, the Supreme Court upholds the federal law barring corporations and unions from financing "electioneering communications."

2010: *Citizens United v. Federal Election Commission* – The Supreme Court holds that corporations have a First Amendment right to spend money to influence candidate elections, overturning *Austin* and *McConnell*.

2014: *Burwell v. Hobby Lobby Stores, Inc.* – The Supreme Court declares corporations have religious freedom under a federal statute.

NOTES

—

INTRODUCTION: ARE CORPORATIONS PEOPLE?

1. Conkling and his deceptive account of the drafting of the Fourteenth Amendment are discussed in more detail in chapter 4, infra.
2. See Citizens United v. Federal Election Commission, 558 U.S. 310 (2010); Richard McGregor, "Obama Launches Re-Election Campaign," *Financial Times*, May 6, 2012; Greg Stohr, "Bloomberg Poll: Americans Want Supreme Court to Turn Off Political Spending Spigot," *Bloomberg News*, September 28, 2015, available at https://www.bloomberg.com/politics/articles/2015-09-28/bloom berg-poll-americans-want-supreme-court-to-turn-off-political-spending-spigot; Allegra Pocinki, "16 States Call to Overturn 'Citizens United,'" July 8, 2013, available at http://www.publicampaign.org/blog/2013/07/08/16-states-call -overturn-%E2%80%98citizens-united%E2%80%99.
3. See Burwell v. Hobby Lobby Stores, Inc., 134 S.Ct. 2751 (2014).
4. Cass R. Sunstein, "The Supreme Court Follows Public Opinion," in *Legal Change: Lessons From America's Social Movements*, ed. Jennifer Weiss-Wolf and Jeanine Plant-Chirlin (2015), 21. On social movements and the Constitution, see Jack M. Balkin and Reva B. Siegel, "Principles, Practices, and Social Movements," 154 *University of Pennsylvania Law Review* 927 (2006); William N. Eskridge Jr., "Channeling: Identity-Based Social Movements and Public Law," 150 *University of Pennsylvania Law Review* 419 (2001). David Cole, *Engines of Liberty: The Power of Citizen Activists to Make Constitutional Law* (2016).
5. See Adolf A. Berle and Gardiner C. Means, *The Modern Corporation and Private Property* (1948), liii. Among those who noticed and wrote about the constitutional rights of corporations before *Citizens United* were Carl J. Mayer, "Personalizing the Impersonal: Corporations and the Bill of Rights," 41 *Hastings Law Journal* 577 (1990); Susanna K. Ripken, "Corporations Are People Too," 15 *Fordham Journal of Corporate & Finance Law* 97, 118 (2009); Henry N. Butler and Larry E. Ribstein, *The Corporation and the Constitution* (1995); Peter J. Henning, "The Conundrum of Corporate Criminal Liability: Seeking a Consistent Approach to the Constitutional Rights of Corporations in Criminal Prosecutions," 63 *Tennessee Law Review* 793 (1996); Gregory A. Mark, "The Personification of the Business Corporation in American Law," 54 *University of*

Chicago Law Review 1441 (1987); Ted Nace, *Gangs of America: The Rise of Corporate Power and the Disabling of Democracy* (2003); Thom Hartmann, *Unequal Protection: The Rise of Corporate Dominance and the Theft of Human Rights* (2002); Scott R. Bowman, *The Modern Corporation and American Political Thought: Law, Power, and Ideology* (1995).

Only the freedom of speech for corporations had been subject to extensive study before *Citizens United*, mostly in the area of campaign finance law. See, e.g., Daniel J. H. Greenwood, "Essential Speech: Why Corporate Speech Is Not Free," 83 *Iowa Law Review* 995 (1998); Richard L. Hasen, "Campaign Finance Laws and the Rupert Murdoch Problem," 77 *Texas Law Review* 1627 (1999); Thomas W. Joo, "The Modern Corporation and Campaign Finance: Incorporating Corporate Governance Analysis into First Amendment Jurisprudence," 79 *Washington University Law Quarterly* 1 (2001); Martin H. Redish and Howard M. Wasserman, "What's Good for General Motors: Corporate Speech and the Theory of Free Expression," 66 *George Washington Law Review* 235 (1998); Jill E. Fisch, "Frankenstein's Monster Hits the Campaign Trail: An Approach to Regulation of Corporate Political Expenditures," 32 *William & Mary Law Review* 587 (1991); Victor Brudney, "Business Corporations and Stockholders' Rights Under the First Amendment," 91 *Yale Law Journal* 235 (1981); Mark Tushnet, "Corporations and Free Speech," in *The Politics of Law*, ed. David Kairys (1982), 253.

Since *Citizens United*, scholarly attention to corporate constitutional rights has increased dramatically. See, e.g., Margaret M. Blair and Elizabeth Pollman, "The Derivative Nature of Corporate Constitutional Rights," 56 *William & Mary Law Review* 1673 (2015); Elizabeth Pollman, "Reconceiving Corporate Personhood," 2011 *Utah Law Review* 1629; Reuven S. Avi-Yonah, "*Citizens United* and the Corporate Form," 2010 *Wisconsin Law Review* 999; Darrell A. H. Miller, "Guns, Inc.: *Citizens United, McDonald*, and the Future of Corporate Constitutional Rights," 86 *New York University Law Review* 887 (2011); Lucian A. Bebchuk and Robert J. Jackson Jr., "Corporate Political Speech: Who Decides?," 124 *Harvard Law Review* 83 (2010); Ryan Azad, "Can a Tailor Mend the Analytical Hole? A Framework for Understanding Corporate Constitutional Rights," 64 *UCLA Law Review* 452 (2017); Anne Tucker, "Flawed Assumptions: A Corporate Law Analysis of Free Speech and Corporate Personhood in *Citizens United*," 61 *Case Western Reserve Law Review* 497 (2010); Monica Youn, "First Amendment Fault Lines and the *Citizens United* Decision," 5 *Harvard Law & Policy Review* 135 (2011); Robert Post, *Citizens Divided: Campaign Finance Reform and the Constitution* (2014); Lucian A. Bebchuk and Robert J. Jackson Jr., "Shining Light on Corporate Political Spending," 101 *Georgetown Law Journal* 923 (2013); Ilya Shapiro and Caitlyn W. McCarthy, "So What if Corporations Aren't People?," 44 *John Marshall Law Review* 701 (2011); Sonja R. West, "The Media Exemption Puzzle of Campaign Finance Laws," 164 *University of Pennsylvania Law Review Online* 253 (2016); Richard L. Hasen, *Plutocrats United: Campaign Money, The Supreme Court, and the Distortion of American Elections* (2016); Michael W. McConnell, "Reconsidering *Citizens United* as a Press Clause Case," 123 *Yale Law Journal* 412 (2013); Kent Greenfield, "In Defense of Corporate Persons," 30 *Constitutional Commentary* 309 (2015); Ciara Torres-Spelliscy, *Corporate Citizen? An Argument for the Separation of Corporation and State* (2016); Jessica A. Levinson, "We the Corporations?: The Constitutionality of Limitations on Corporate Speech after *Citizens United*," 46 *University of San Francisco Law Review*

307 (2011); Burt Neuborne, "Of 'Singles' Without Baseball: Corporations as Frozen Relational Moments," 64 *Rutgers Law Review* 769 (2012); Thomas Wuil Joo, "Corporate Speech and the Rights of Others," 30 *Constitutional Commentary* 335 (2015); David H. Gans and Douglas T. Kendall, "A Capitalist Joker: The Strange Origins, Disturbing Past, and Uncertain Future of Corporate Personhood in American Law," 44 *John Marshall Law Review* 643 (2010); Jeff Clements, *Corporations Are Not People: Reclaiming Democracy From Big Money and Global Corporations* (2d ed., 2014). On the longer history of corporate constitutional rights cases in the Supreme Court, see Blair and Pollman, "The Derivative Nature of Corporate Constitutional Rights," and Ruth H. Bloch and Naomi Lamoreaux, "Corporations and the Fourteenth Amendment," in *Corporations and American Democracy*, ed. Naomi R. Lamoreaux and William J. Novak (2017), 286.

6. On the Supreme Court's repeated failure to rule on the side of women, racial minorities, and the common people more generally, see Ian Millhiser, *Injustices: The Supreme Court's History of Comforting the Comfortable and Afflicting the Afflicted* (2016).

7. See Lee Epstein et al., "How Business Fares in the Supreme Court," 97 *Minnesota Law Review* 1431 (2013); Jeffrey Rosen, "Supreme Court Inc.," *New York Times*, March 16, 2008. See also Adam Liptak, "Corporations Find a Friend in the Supreme Court," *New York Times*, May 4, 2013. For a fuller analysis of, and some skepticism about, the business leanings of the recent Supreme Court, see Jonathan H. Adler, ed., *Business in the Roberts Court* (2016).

8. On the political activity of large firms, see David Vogel, *Fluctuating Fortunes: The Political Power of Business in America* (1989); Wendy L. Hansen and Neil J. Mitchell, "Disaggregating and Explaining Corporate Political Activity: Domestic and Foreign Corporations in National Politics," 94 *American Political Science Review* 891 (2000); Amy J. Hillman, "Determinants of Political Strategies in US Multinationals," 42 *Business & Society* 455 (2003); Martin B. Meznar and Douglas Nigh, "Buffer or Bridge? Environmental and Organizational Determinants of Public Affairs Activities in American Firms," 38 *Academy of Management Journal* 975 (1995).

9. See Ganesh Sitaraman, "The Puzzling Absence of Economic Power in Constitutional Theory," 101 *Cornell Law Review* 1445 (2016); Benjamin I. Page et al., "Democracy and the Policy Preferences of Wealthy Americans," 11 *Perspectives on Politics* 51 (2013); Kay Lehman Schlozman et al., *The Unheavenly Chorus* (2012); Martin Gilens, *Affluence and Influence: Economic Inequality and Political Power in America* (2012). On the ties between regulated industry and business political activity, see Kevin Grier et al., "The Determinants of Industrial Political Activity, 1978–1986," 88 *American Political Science Review* 911 (1994); Amy J. Hillman and Michael A. Hitt, "Corporate Political Strategy Formation: A Model of Approach, Participation, and Strategy Decisions," 24 *Academy of Management Review* 825 (1999). On the profit motive in motivating corporate political activity, see Neil J. Mitchell et al., "The Determinants of Domestic and Foreign Corporate Political Activity," 59 *Journal of Politics* 1096 (1997). See also Amy J. Hillman et al., "Corporate Political Activity: A Review and Research Agenda," 30 *Journal of Management* 837 (2004).

10. On the shareholder wealth maximization norm, see Stephen M. Bainbridge, "In Defense of the Shareholder Wealth Maximization Norm," 50 *Washington & Lee Law Review* 1423 (1993).

CHAPTER 1: IN THE BEGINNING, AMERICA WAS A CORPORATION

1. On the original understanding of corporate rights, see Jonathan A. Marcantel, "The Corporation as a 'Real' Constitutional Person," 11 *University of California Davis Business Law Journal* 221 (2011).

2. See James Stancliffe Davis, *Essays in the Earlier History of American Corporations* (1917), 332 and especially Appendix B: "American Charters to Business Corporations, 1781–1800." Some of these corporations received multiple charters from different states but are counted here as a single business enterprise. The two corporations that would assert constitutional rights would be Dartmouth College and the Charles River Bridge Company.

3. See Jonas V. Anderson, "Regulating Corporations the American Way: Why Exhaustive Rules and Just Deserts Are the Mainstay of U.S. Corporate Governance," 57 *Duke Law Journal* 1081, 1100–1101 (2008); Thom Hartmann, *Unequal Protection: The Rise of Corporate Dominance and the Theft of Human Rights* (2004), 63. See also Thomas Jefferson, Letter to George Logan (November 12, 1816), in *The Works of Thomas Jefferson* (Federal ed.), ed. Paul Leicester Ford (1904–1905); Robert S. Alley, ed., *James Madison on Religious Liberty* (1985), 91; James Wilson, "Of Corporations," in *The Collected Works of James Wilson*, ed. Kermit L. Hall and Mark David Hall (2007).

4. See Charles A. Beard, *An Economic Interpretation of the Constitution* (1941), 133–151; Forrest McDonald, *We the People: The Economic Origins of the Constitution* (1958), 38–92; Robert A. McGuire, *To Form A More Perfect Union: A New Economic Interpretation of the United States Constitution* (2003), 54; Eric Hilt and Jacqueline Valentine, "Democratic Dividends: Stockholding, Wealth, and Politics in New York, 1791–1826," 72 *Journal of Economic History* 332, 340–341 (2012).

5. On the Jamestown colony, see Bernard Bailyn, *The Barbarous Years: The Peopling of British North America: The Conflict of Civilizations, 1600–1675* (2012); John Darwin, *Unfinished Empire: The Global Expansion of Britain* (2013); Virginia Bernhard, *A Tale of Two Colonies: What Really Happened in Virginia and Bermuda?* (2011); John C. Miller, *The First Frontier: Life in Colonial America* (1966); Karen Ordahl Kupperman, *The Jamestown Project* (2009).

6. See Kupperman, *The Jamestown Project*, 20–34; Bernhard, *A Tale of Two Colonies*, 8.

7. On the Virginia Company's corporate form, see Miller, *The First Frontier*, 15–26; Bernhard, *A Tale of Two Colonies*, 7, 16. On the investors, see Kupperman, *The Jamestown Project*, 214, 242–243. The available data reflect the price of shares and the number of investors after the Virginia Company was reorganized and a second "public offering" was made in 1609.

8. On Thomas West, see Samuel Willard Crompton, "De La Warr, Baron," in *American National Biography Online*, available at http://www.anb.org/articles/01/01-00206.html; Henry Browning, *The Magna Charta Barons and Their American Descendants* (1898), 159; Robert Alonzo Brock and Virgil Anson Lewis, *Virginia and Virginians: Eminent Virginians, Executives of the Colony of Virginia* (1888), 15–16; Alexander Brown, "Sir Thomas West, Third Lord De La Warr," 9 *Magazine of American History* 18 (1883); J. Frederick Fausz, "West, Thomas, third Baron De La Warr (1577–1618)," *Oxford Dictionary of National Biography* (2004), online ed., October 2008, available at http://www.oxforddnb.com/view/article/29100.

9. See Kupperman, *The Jamestown Project*, 151, 243; Miller, *The First Frontier*, 18.

10. See Carville V. Earle, "Environment, Disease, and Mortality in Early Virginia," in *The Chesapeake in the Seventeenth Century: Essays on Anglo-American Society*, ed. Thad W. Tate and David L. Ammerman (1979), 96.

11. See Dennis B. Blanton, "Drought as a Factor in the Jamestown Colony, 1607–1612," *Historical Archaeology* 34 (2000): 74, 78; Kupperman, *The Jamestown Project*, 163, 227; Bailyn, *The Barbarous Years*, 53.

12. On Shakespeare's inspiration, see Bernhard, *A Tale of Two Colonies*, 3; Kieran Doherty, *Sea Venture: Shipwreck, Survival, and the Salvation of Jamestown* (2008), 163.

13. Where necessary for clarity, old English is translated into contemporary English throughout this book. On the "starving time," see Miller, *The First Frontier*, 22; Paula Neely, "Jamestown Colonists Resorted to Canibalism," *National Geographic*, May 1, 2013, available at http://news.nationalgeographic.com/news/2013/13/130501-jamestown-cannibalism-archeology-science/.

14. West's commitment to the Virginia Company was one of the subjects he touched upon in Sir Thomas West, "The Relation of the Lord De-La-Ware" (1611), reprinted in Lyon Gardiner Tyler, *Narratives of Early Virginia, 1606–1625* (1907), 209.

15. On de Luna's ill-fated effort in Pensacola, see William S. Coker, "Pensacola, 1686–1821," in *Archaeology of Colonial Pensacola*, ed. Judith Ann Bense (1999), 5. On the Lost Colony of Roanoke, see Kupperman, *The Jamestown Project*, 3–5, 32, 100.

16. See "A True and Sincere Declaration of the Purpose and Ends of the Plantation Begun in Virginia," originally published in 1610 and reprinted in Alexander Brown, *The Genesis of the United States* (1890), 1:338; Kupperman, *The Jamestown Project*, 241; Bailyn, *The Barbarous Years*, 66, 72.

17. Miller, *The First Frontier*, 23; Kupperman, *The Jamestown Project*, 23–24.

18. See Bailyn, *The Barbarous Years*, 66–67; Frank E. Grizzard, *Jamestown Colony: A Political, Social, and Cultural History* (2007), xxxiii.

19. See Alexander Brown, *The Genesis of the United States* (1891), 2:1049; Alexander Brown, "Sir Thomas West. Third Lord De La Warr," 9 *The Magazine of American History* 18, 28, 30 (1883).

20. See William Robert Scott, *The Constitution and Finance of English, Scottish, and Irish Joint-Stock Companies to 1720* (1951), 1:255; Wesley Frank Craven, *The Virginia Company of London, 1606–1624* (1993), 31–34; Kupperman, *The Jamestown Project*, 261.

21. Scott, *The Constitution and Finance of English, Scottish, and Irish Joint-Stock Companies*, 1:255; Craven, *The Virginia Company of London*, 31–34; Kupperman, *The Jamestown Project*, 261; Miller, *The First Frontier*, 26.

22. See Jack Beatty, "The Corporate Roots of American Government," in *Colossus: How the Corporation Changed America*, ed. Jack Beatty (2001), 17; Theodore K. Rabb, "Sir Edwin Sandys and the Parliament of 1604," 69 *American Historical Review* 646 (1964); Henrietta Elizabeth Marshall, *This Country of Ours* (1917), 75–76; Bailyn, *The Barbarous Years*, 75.

23. See Craven, *The Virginia Company of London*, 140; Beatty, "Corporate Roots," 17–18.

24. See Kupperman, *The Jamestown Project*, 293.

25. See Sir William Throckmorton, Richard Berkeley, et al., "Ordinances Direc-

tions and Instructions to Captaine John Woodlefe" (September 4, 1619), in *The Records of the Virginia Company of London*, ed. Susan Myra Kingsbury (1933), 3:207; Charles E. Hatch, *The First Seventeen Years: Virginia, 1607–1624* (2009), 44; H. Graham Woodlief, "History of the First Thanksgiving, Virginia Thanksgiving Festival," available at http://virginiathanksgivingfestival.com/history/; Gloria Peoples-Elam, *An American Heritage Story: Tracing the Ancestry of William Henry Peoples & Elizabeth Washington Peoples* (2014), 86.

26. Bailyn, *The Barbarous Years*, 82–87; Kupperman, *The Jamestown Project*, 287, 320.

27. See Bailyn, *The Barbarous Years*, 322.

28. See Kupperman, *The Jamestown Project*, 2–3.

29. On how the corporate form influenced the institutions and practices of American democracy, see David A. Ciepley, "Is the U.S. Government a Corporation? The Corporate Origins of Modern Constitutionalism," 111 *American Political Science Review* 418 (2017); Stephen Innes, "From Corporation to Commonwealth," in *Colossus: How the Corporation Changed America*, ed. Jack Beatty, 18; Andrew C. McLaughlin, *The Foundations of American Constitutionalism* (1932).

30. On the history of the Massachusetts Bay Company and its charter, see Frances Rose-Troup, *The Massachusetts Bay Company and Its Predecessors* (1930); Charles J. Hilkey, *Legal Development in Colonial Massachusetts, 1630–1686* (1910); Stephen Innes, *Creating the Commonwealth: The Economic Culture of Puritan New England* (1995); Barbara A. Moe, *The Charter of the Massachusetts Bay Colony: A Primary Source Investigation of the 1629 Charter* (2002). The text of the charter can be found at http://avalon.law.yale.edu/17th_cen tury/mass03.asp.

31. Corporate offices were themselves likely modeled on medieval English governmental officeholding practices, which heavily influenced American constitutionalism. See Karen Orren, "Officers' Rights: Toward a Unified Field Theory of American Constitutional Development," 34 *Law & Society Review* 873 (2000).

32. See McLaughlin, *The Foundations of American Constitutionalism*, 39; Scott, *The Constitution and Finance*, 313–315. On Winthrop, see Francis J. Bremer, *John Winthrop: America's Forgotten Founding Father* (2003); Rose-Troup, *The Massachusetts Bay Company*, 28 et seq.; Innes, *Creating the Commonwealth*, 64 et seq.

33. See McLaughlin, *The Foundations of American Constitutionalism*, 42–45; Innes, *Creating the Commonwealth*, 19–20.

34. See Hilkey, "Legal Development," 22–23.

35. See McLaughlin, *The Foundations of American Constitutionalism*, 55–56.

36. See Bernard Schwartz, *The Great Rights of Mankind: A History of the Bill of Rights* (1992), 36–39.

37. Ibid., 41–51; John Phillip Reid, *Constitutional History of the American Revolution: The Authority of Rights* (2003), 159–160.

38. See McLaughlin, *The Foundations of American Constitutionalism*, 47.

39. On the East India Company, see H. V. Bowen, *The Business of Empire: The East India Company and Imperial Britain, 1765–1833* (2006); Marguerite Eyer Wilbur, *The East India Company: And the British Empire in the Far East* (1945). On Elihu Yale, see Wilbur, *The East India Company*, 311.

40. On the East India Company's finances, see Benjamin L. Carp, *Defiance of the Patriots* (2010), 13–23; Wilbur, *The East India Company*, 307–311.

41. Bowen, *The Business of Empire*, 30–31.
42. See Carp, *Defiance of the Patriots*.
43. See Bernard Bailyn, *The Ideological Origins of the American Revolution* (1992), 189–191, 201, 222.
44. See Reid, *Constitutional History of the American Revolution*, 145, 160–167.
45. Ibid., 189.
46. Ibid., 174, 188; Schwartz, *The Great Rights of Mankind*, 52.
47. On the colonial protests, see Gary B. Nash, *The Unknown American Revolution: The Unruly Birth of Democracy and the Struggle to Create America* (2006), 45–49; Carp, *Defiance of the Patriots*, 65–68.
48. See Ray Raphael, *A People's History of the American Revolution: How Common People Shaped the Fight for Independence* (2012), 18.
49. See Wilbur, *The East India Company*, 313–314.
50. See Robert Allison, *The American Revolution: A Concise History* (2011), 16–17.
51. The value of the tea thrown overboard is subject to some dispute. The figure in the text comes from Wilbur, *The East India Company*, 314–315.

CHAPTER 2: THE FIRST CORPORATE RIGHTS CASE

1. On the Bank of the United States, see Edward S. Kaplan, *The Bank of the United States and the American Economy* (1999); James O. Wettereau, "New Light on the First Bank of the United States," 61 *Pennsylvania Magazine of History and Biography* 263 (1937); John H. Wood, *A History of Central Banking in Great Britain and the United States* (2005); James Stuart Olson, "Bank of the United States," in *Encyclopedia of the Industrial Revolution in America* (2002), 21.
2. See Henry Clay, "On a National Bank" (1811), in *The Life and Speeches of Henry Clay*, ed. James Barrett Swain (1843), 1:80.
3. See Jerry W. Markham, *A Financial History of the United States: From Christopher Columbus to the Robber Barons* (2002), 1:126.
4. On the Bank of North America, see Kaplan, *The Bank of the United States*, ix; Simeon E. Baldwin, "American Business Corporations Before 1789," 8 *American Historical Review* 449, 458–459 (1903); Lawrence Lewis, *A History of the Bank of North America* (1882); Todd Wallack, "Which Bank is the Oldest? Accounts Vary," *Boston Globe*, December 20, 2011, available at http://www.bostonglobe.com/business/2011/12/20/oldest-bank-america-accounts-vary/WAqvIlmipfFhyKsx8bhgAJ/story.html.
5. See Wood, *A History of Central Banking*, 124–125.
6. See Wettereau, "New Light on the First Bank," 272, 284.
7. See Markham, *A Financial History of the United States*, 1:124–126, 281.
8. See Markham, *A Financial History of the United States*, 1:126; Charles W. Calomiris, "Banking: Modern Period," in Joel Mokyr, *Oxford Encyclopedia of Economic History* (2003), 1:227–228.
9. See W. Calvin Smith, "Banks, Law, and Politics: The Origins, Outcome and Significance of the Deveaux Case," *Proceedings of the South Carolina Historical Association*, Spring 1991, 9, 11; Wettereau, "New Light on the First Bank," 276–277.
10. See Smith, "Banks, Law, and Politics," 11.
11. On Peter Deveaux, see Lucian Lamar Knight, *Georgia's Landmarks, Memorials, and Legends* (1914), 539; Wm. Overton Harris, "A Corporation as a Citizen in Connection With the Jurisdiction of the United States Courts," 1 *Virginia Law*

Review 507 (1914); Georgia Historical Society, "Deveaux, Peter, 1752–1826," available at http://georgiahistory.pastperfect-online.com/37659cgi/mweb.exe?request=record;id=Deveaux,%20Peter,%201752-1826;type=702; George White, *Historical Collections of Georgia* (1855), 219. For a detailed history of the Deveaux litigation, see Smith, "Banks, Law, and Politics," 9.

12. See Stuart Banner, *Anglo-American Securities Regulation: Cultural and Political Roots, 1690–1860* (2002), 75–80; Ron Harris, "The Bubble Act: Its Passage and Its Effects on Business Organization," 54 *Journal of Economic History* 610 (1994); Pauline Maier, "The Revolutionary Origins of the American Business Corporation," 50 *William and Mary Quarterly* 51 (1993).

13. James Stancliffe Davis, *Essays in the Earlier History of American Corporations* (1917), 332 et seq.; John Adams, Letters to John Taylor, of Caroline, Virginia, in Reply to His Strictures on Some Parts of the Defence of the American Constitutions, in *The Works of John Adams, Second President of the United States*, ed. Charles Francis Adams (1856), 510.

14. On Roman *societas* and *societas publicoranum*, see Ulrike Malmendier, "Law and Finance 'at the Origin,'" 47 *Journal of Economic Literature* 1076 (2009); Ulrike Malmendier, "Roman Shares," in William N. Goetzmann and K. Geert Rouwenhorst, eds., *The Origins of Value: The Financial Innovations that Created Modern Capital Markets* (2005), 31. For a somewhat contrary view, see Andreas M. Fleckner, "Roman Business Associations" (unpublished manuscript, 2014), available at http://papers.ssrn.com/sol3/papers.cfm?abstract_id=2472598. For earlier studies of Roman corporations, see Andrew Stephenson, *A History of Roman Law* (1912), 371–74; William Livesey Burdick, *The Principles of Roman Law and Their Relation to Modern Law* (1938), 282 et seq.

15. See Kevin J. R. Rosman et al., "Lead from Carthaginian and Roman Spanish Mines Isotopically Identified in Greenland Ice Dated from 600 B.C. to 300 A.D.," 31 *Environmental Science and Technology* 3413 (1997).

16. On the many different kinds of late medieval corporations, see Eric Enlow, "The Corporate Conception of the State and the Origins of Limited Constitutional Government," 6 *Washington University Journal of Law & Policy* 1, 3–8 (2001); John Micklethwait and Adrian Wooldridge, *The Company: A Short History of a Revolutionary Idea* (2003), chapter 1. Even the monarchy was seen as a corporation. See Frederic Maitland, "The Crown as a Corporation," 17 *Law Quarterly Review* 131, 134–135 (1901).

17. On Blackstone, see Lewis C. Warden, *The Life of Blackstone* (1938), 13–14; David A. Lockmiller, *Sir William Blackstone* (1938), 10. On his influence, see Albert W. Alschuler, "Rediscovering Blackstone," 145 *University of Pennsylvania Law Review* 1 (1996); Ian Williams, "Book Review: Blackstone and His Commentaries: Biography, Law, History," 71 *Cambridge Law Journal* 223 (2012); Wilfred Prest, "Blackstone as Architect: Constructing the Commentaries," 15 *Yale Journal of Law & the Humanities* 103 (2003).

18. See William Blackstone, *Commentaries on the Laws of England*, ed. Robert Malcolm Kerr (1876), 1:446.

19. On the human individual as the "paradigmatic legal actor," see Meir Dan-Cohen, *Rights, Persons, and Organizations: A Legal Theory for Bureaucratic Society* (1986), 13.

20. In time, the principle that corporate acts beyond the charter were void came to be known as *ultra vires*. See H. Kent Greenfield, "*Ultra Vires* Lives!: A Stake-

holder Analysis of Corporate Illegality (With Notes on How Corporate Law Could Reinforce International Law Norms)," 87 *Virginia Law Review* 1279 (2001); Stephen Griffin, "The Rise and Fall of the *Ultra Vires* Rule in Corporate Law," 2 *Mountbatten Journal of Legal Studies* 1 (1998).

21. See Cedric Kushner Promotions, Ltd. v. King, 533 U.S. 158 (2001).

22. On Binney, see William Strong, *An Eulogium on the Life and Character of Horace Binney* (1876), 5–21; Robert R. Bell, *The Philadelphia Lawyer: A History, 1735–1945* (1992), 145–155; John Hays Gardiner, *Harvard* (1914), 161.

23. See Smith, "Banks, Law, and Politics," 12–13.

24. On corporate nationality, see Linda A. Mabry, "Multinational Corporations and U.S. Technology Policy: Rethinking the Concept of Corporate Nationality," 87 *Georgetown Law Journal* 563, 581 (1999). See also Society for the Propagation of the Gospel v. Wheeler, 22 Fed. Cas. 756 (C.C.D. New Hampshire 1814).

25. See Bank of the United States v. Deveaux, 9 U.S. 61 (1809).

26. On veil piercing in corporate law, see Maurice Wormser, "Piercing the Veil of Corporate Entity," 12 *Columbia Law Review* 496, 500, 501 (1912); Peter B. Oh, "Veil Piercing," 89 *Texas Law Review* 81, 83 (2010–2011); Lorraine Talbot, *Critical Company Law* (2015), 24. For a comprehensive study of piercing-the-veil cases in corporate law, see Robert B. Thompson, "Piercing the Corporate Veil: An Empirical Study," 76 *Cornell Law Review* 1036 (1991).

27. See Bank of the United States v. Deveaux, 2 Fed. Cas. 692, 692–693 (Cir. Ct. GA 1808).

28. See Justin Crowe, *Building the Judiciary: Law, Courts, and the Politics of Institutional Development* (2012), 1; Robert G. McCloskey, *The American Supreme Court* (5th ed., 2010), 1. On the business-friendly tendency of the Supreme Court, see Ian Millhiser, *Injustices: The Supreme Court's History of Comforting the Comfortable and Afflicting the Afflicted* (2015).

29. See Anon., "The Supreme Court—Its Homes Past and Present," 27 *American Bar Association Journal* 283 (1941); William C. Allen, *History of the United States Capitol: A Chronicle of Design, Construction, and Politics* (2001), 89, 107. There is some disagreement about whether Long's Tavern was located where the current Supreme Court sits or across the street to the south, where the Library of Congress sits. According to Allen, Long's Tavern was renovated and renamed the "Brick Capitol." According to Kenneth Jost, *The Supreme Court A–Z* (2013), 212, the Supreme Court Building is located where the Brick Capitol used to be. Yet Jost also says that Long's Tavern is where the Library of Congress is currently located. Suffice to say the exact location of the pub remains uncertain.

30. See Bank of the United States v. Deveaux, 9 U.S. 61 (1809).

31. See Hope Insurance Company v. Boardman, 9 U.S. 57 (1809). On Adams, see Harlow G. Unger, *John Quincy Adams: A Life* (2012); Fred Kaplan, *John Quincy Adams: American Visionary* (2014). See also William G. Ross, "John Quincy Adams," in *Great American Lawyers: An Encyclopedia*, ed. John R. Vile (2001), 1:9; Charles Warren, *The Supreme Court in United States History, 1821–1855* (1922), 1:390, 2:347. Adams is also credited with winning a later 1810 case, Fletcher v. Peck, 10 U.S. 87 (1810), but that case was in fact argued prior to the *Hope Insurance* case.

32. See Allen Sharp, "Presidents as Supreme Court Advocates: Before and After the White House," 28 *Journal of Supreme Court History* 116, 118 (2003).

33. See Marc Leepson, *What So Proudly We Hailed: Francis Scott Key, A Life* (2014); Smith, "Banks, Law, and Politics."

34. For a discussion of competing theories of the corporation, see Eric W. Orts, *Business Persons: A Legal Theory of the Firm* (2013), 9–51. Some scholars argue that corporate rights discussions should avoid metaphysical abstractions like personhood or associationalism. See, e.g., Richard Schragger and Micah Schwartzman, "Some Realism about Corporate Rights," in Micah Schwartzman et al., *The Rise of Corporate Religious Liberty* (2016), 345.

35. See John Quincy Adams, *Memoirs of John Quincy Adams*, ed. Charles Francis Adams (1874), 546.

36. See Alexander M. Bickel, *The Least Dangerous Branch: The Supreme Court at the Bar of Politics* (1962), 1. See generally Jack Rakove, *Revolutionaries: A New History of the Invention of America* (2010), 377.

37. Mary Sarah Bilder, "The Corporate Origins of Judicial Review," 116 *Yale Law Journal* 502 (2006).

38. See Marbury v. Madison, 5 U.S. 137 (1803).

39. See Hope Insurance Company v. Boardman, 9 U.S. 57 (1809).

40. See Bank of the United States v. Deveaux, 9 U.S. 61 (1809).

41. See Margaret M. Blair and Elizabeth Pollman, "The Derivative Nature of Corporate Constitutional Rights," 56 *William & Mary Law Review* 1673, 1680 (2015).

42. See Smith, "Banks, Law, and Politics," 13; McCulloch v. Maryland, 17 U.S. 316 (1819).

43. See Richard S. Grossman, *Unsettled Account: The Evolution of Banking in the Industrialized World Since 1800* (2010), 225; Murray N. Rothbard, *History of Money and Banking in the United States: The Colonial Era to World War II* (2002), 69–72.

CHAPTER 3: THE CORPORATION'S LAWYER

1. On Webster, see Robert Vincent Remini, *Daniel Webster: The Man and His Time* (1997); Maurice Glen Baxter, *Daniel Webster & the Supreme Court* (1966); Everett Pepperrell Wheeler, *Daniel Webster: The Expounder of the Constitution* (1904). The quotes are from Baxter, 16, 245, and Remini, 8. The fish story is recounted in Seth P. Waxman, "In the Shadow of Daniel Webster: Arguing Appeals in the Twenty-First Century," 3 *Journal of Appellate Practice & Process* 521, 522 (2001).

2. See Remini, *Daniel Webster: The Man and His Time*, 146.

3. See Gregg D. Crane, *Race, Citizenship, and Law in American Literature* (2002), 235 n. 99; Baxter, *Daniel Webster & the Supreme Court*, 15–16, 153–154.

4. See Baxter, *Daniel Webster & the Supreme Court*, 84 (quoting Story).

5. See Francis N. Stites, *Private Interest & Public Gain: The Dartmouth College Case, 1819* (1972), 23–26; R. Kent Newmyer, *John Marshall and the Heroic Age of the Supreme Court* (2007), 245; R. Kent Newmyer, "John Marshall as a Transitional Jurist: *Dartmouth College v. Woodward* and the Limits of Omniscient Judging," 32 *Connecticut Law Review* 1665, 1668 (2000).

6. On the *Dartmouth College* case generally, see Stites, *Private Interest & Public Gain*. Dartmouth College's 1769 charter can be found at http://www.dartmouth.edu/~library/rauner/dartmouth/dc-charter.html?mswitch-redir=classic.

7. See Baxter, *Daniel Webster & the Supreme Court*, 7.

8. See Henry Cabot Lodge, *Daniel Webster* (1911), 75; Stites, *Private Interest & Public Gain*, 6–22.

9. On the mixed public and private nature of the corporation, see David Ciepley, "Beyond Public and Private: Toward a Political Theory of the Corporation," 107 *American Political Science Review* 139 (2013).

10. See Richard S. Grossman, *Unsettled Account: The Evolution of Banking in the Industrialized World Since 1800* (2010), 224; Thomas Linzey, "Awakening A Sleeping Giant: Creating a Quasi-Private Cause of Action for Revoking Corporate Charters in Response to Environmental Violations," 13 *Pace Environmental Law Review* 219, 232–233, 239 (1995); Oscar Handlin and Mary F. Handlin, "Origins of the American Business Corporation," 5 *Journal of Economic History* 1, 22 (1945). See also Scott Bowman, *The Modern Corporation and American Political Thought: Law, Power, and Ideology* (1996), 50 ("eighteenth-century English law regarded corporate enterprise as an instrumentality of the state").

11. See Stites, *Private Interest & Public Gain*, 53–54 (quoting opinion).

12. Ibid., 40–41.

13. See Everett Pepperrell Wheeler, *Daniel Webster: The Expounder of the Constitution* (1904), 28 (quoting Story); Rufus Choate, "A Discourse Commemorative of Daniel Webster," in *Addresses and Orations of Rufus Choate* (1897), 241 (quoting Goodrich); Baxter, *Daniel Webster & the Supreme Court*, 80.

14. See Lodge, *Daniel Webster*, 84; Stites, *Private Interest & Public Gain*, 66–67.

15. See Baxter, *Daniel Webster & the Supreme Court*, 32–33; Timothy R. Johnson, *Oral Arguments and Decision Making on the U.S. Supreme Court* (2004), 2.

16. See Wheeler, *Daniel Webster: The Expounder of the Constitution*, 29–31 (quoting Story).

17. Lodge, *Daniel Webster*, 72; Remini, *Daniel Webster: The Man and His Time*, 27–28.

18. Choate, "A Discourse Commemorative of Daniel Webster," 272 (quoting Goodrich). Webster's argument is available in Edwin P. Whipple, *The Great Speeches and Orations of Daniel Webster* (1879), 1–23.

19. Wheeler, *Daniel Webster: The Expounder of the Constitution*, 30–31.

20. See Dartmouth College v. Woodward, 17 U.S. 518 (1819).

21. On Parliament's right to alter corporate charters, see also Baxter, *Daniel Webster & the Supreme Court*, 100.

22. Marshall was wrong about the absence of state contributions to Dartmouth, and may have known it. See Stites, *Private Interest & Public Gain*, 67.

23. See Ciepley, "Beyond Public and Private."

24. On Marshall's basing corporate rights on the rights of the members, see Newmyer, *John Marshall and the Heroic Age of the Supreme Court*, 251.

25. Ibid., 245–247. See also R. Kent Newmyer, "John Marshall as a Transitional Jurist: *Dartmouth College v. Woodward* and the Limits of Omniscient Judging," 32 *Connecticut Law Review* 1665 (2000).

26. See Stites, *Private Interest & Public Gain*, 103; Herbert Hovenkamp, "The Classical Corporation in American Legal Thought," 76 *Georgetown Law Journal* 1593, 1616–1619 (1988) (on reservation clauses and quoting Cooley); James W. Ely Jr., "The Protection of Contractual Rights: A Tale of Two Constitutional Provisions," 1 *New York University Journal of Law & Liberty* 370, 373, 400 (2005); James W. Ely Jr., "Whatever Happened to the Contract Clause?," 4 *Charleston Law Review* 371 (2010); Sue Davis, *Corwin and Peltason's Understanding the Constitution* (17th ed. 2008), 157.

27. See Baxter, *Daniel Webster & the Supreme Court*, 108–109.

28. On the life of the Second Bank of the United States, see Edward S. Kaplan, *The Bank of the United States and the American Economy* (1999).

29. See McCulloch v. Maryland, 17 U.S. 316 (1819); Baxter, *Daniel Webster & the Supreme Court*, 177–178.

30. On Taney, see Carl Brent Swisher, *Roger B. Taney* (1961); Bernard Christian Steiner, *Life of Roger Brooke Taney: Chief Justice of the United States Supreme Court* (1922).

31. See Mira Wilkins, *The History of Foreign Investment in the United States to 1914* (1989), 38, 61; Andrew Jackson, Veto Message on the Bank of the United States, July 10, 1832, available at http://avalon.law.yale.edu/19th_century/ajveto01.asp; Remini, *Daniel Webster: The Man and His Time*, 356–357, 400; John H. Wood, *A History of Central Banking in Great Britain and the United States* (2005), 123–130. On Jackson's populist slogan, see Robert C. McGrath, *American Populism: A Social History, 1877–1898* (1993), 52.

32. See J. Willard Hurst, *The Legitimacy of the Business Corporation in the Law of the United States, 1780–1970* (1970), 120; Maier, "The Revolutionary Origins of the American Business Corporation," 51.

33. See Hovenkamp, "The Classical Corporation," 1634–1635; P. M. Vasudev, "Corporate Law and Its Efficiency: A Review of History," 50 *American Journal of Legal History* 237, 255–256 (2008–2010).

34. See Andrew Jackson, Veto Message on the Bank of the United States, July 10, 1832, available at http://avalon.law.yale.edu/19th_century/ajveto01.asp.

35. See Larry Schweikart, "Bank of the United States," in *Conspiracy Theories in American History: An Encyclopedia*, ed. Peter Knight (2003), 1:112; Kaplan, *The Bank of the United States*, x.

36. See Remini, *Daniel Webster: The Man and His Time*, 400, 421.

37. See James F. Simon, *Lincoln and Chief Justice Taney: Slavery, Secession, and the President's War Powers* (2007), 24.

38. On the animosity between Webster and Taney, see Samuel Tyler, *Memoir of Roger Brooke Taney* (1872), 234; Simon, *Lincoln and Chief Justice Taney*, 24–33; Baxter, *Daniel Webster & the Supreme Court*, 23–25; Remini, *Daniel Webster: The Man and His Time*, 435–460. On Taney's nominations, see Joseph Pratt Harris, *The Advice and Consent of the Senate: A Study of the Confirmation of Appointments by the United States Senate* (1953), 63–64.

39. See Remini, *Daniel Webster: The Man and His Time*, 437; Harris, *The Advice and Consent of the Senate*, 63–64.

40. See Baxter, *Daniel Webster & the Supreme Court*, 23 (italics in original)

41. See Charles River Bridge Company v. Warren Bridge Company, 36 U.S. 420 (1837).

42. See Roscoe Pound, "The Charles River Bridge Case," 27 *Massachusetts Law Quarterly* 17 (1942); Bernard Schwartz, "Supreme Court Superstars: The Ten Greatest Justices," in *The Supreme Court in American Society: Equal Justice Under the Law,* ed. Kermit Hall (2001), 495.

43. See Remini, *Daniel Webster: The Man and His Time*, 444.

44. See Bank of Augusta v. Earle, 38 U.S. 519 (1839).

45. See Baxter, *Daniel Webster & the Supreme Court*, 181–193; Timothy S. Huebner, *The Taney Court: Justices, Rulings, and Legacy* (2003), 186; Howard Jay Graham,

Everyman's Constitution: Historical Essays on the Fourteenth Amendment, the "Conspiracy Theory," and American Constitutionalism (1968), 73–75.

46. See Bank of Augusta v. Earle, 38 U.S. 519 (1839); Huebner, *The Taney Court*, 122.

47. See 1 *The Hunt's Merchants' Magazine and Commercial Review* 511 (1939). See also Simon, *Lincoln and Chief Justice Taney*, 36; Huebner, *The Taney Court*, 122.

48. Webster's argument was recounted in 38 U.S. 519, 549–567 (1839). On the argument, see Charles Grove Haines and Foster H. Sherwood, *The Role of the Supreme Court in American Government and Politics, 1835–1864* (1957).

49. On Ingersoll, see Haines and Sherwood, *The Role of the Supreme Court*, 65; Eric Monkkonen, "Corporate Growth v. States' Rights: Bank of Augusta v. Earle," in *Historic U.S. Court Cases: An Encyclopedia*, ed. John W. Johson (2d ed., 2001), 474, 478.

50. On Taney and his expansive view of the federal courts in the commercial arena, see Gregory A. Mark, "The Court and the Corporation: Jurisprudence, Localism, and Federalism," 1997 *Supreme Court Review* 403 (1997), 437; Paul Finkelman, "Roger Brooke Taney," in *The Supreme Court Justices: A Biographical Dictionary*, ed. Melvin I. Urofsky (1994), 465; Frank Otto Gatell, "Roger B. Taney," in *The Justices of the United States Supreme Court*, ed. Leon Friedman and Fred L. Israel (1997), 1:337.

51. See Bank of Augusta v. Earle, 38 U.S. 519 (1839).

52. See Baxter, *Daniel Webster & the Supreme Court*, 190–191.

53. See ibid., 192; Haines and Sherwood, *The Role of the Supreme Court*, 69–72.

54. On Alexander Marshall and the B&O Railroad, see Haines and Sherwood, *The Role of the Supreme Court*, 83–87; James D. Dilts, *The Great Road: The Building of the Baltimore and Ohio, the Nation's First Railroad, 1828–1853* (1993), 324–352.

55. See Dilts, *The Great Road*, 335.

56. On railroad development, see John Murrin et al., *Liberty, Equality, Power: A History of the American People* (6th ed., 2013), 1:191–193. On Morse, see Kenneth Silverman, *Lightning Man: The Accursed Life of Samuel F. B. Morse* (2010).

57. See Alfred D. Chandler Jr., *The Visible Hand: The Managerial Revolution in American Business* (1977), 81 et seq.; H. W. Brands, *American Colossus: The Triumph of Capitalism, 1865–1900* (2011), 24–25; Bowman, *The Modern Corporation and American Political Thought*, 54.

58. See David H. Gans and Douglas T. Kendall, "A Capitalist Joker: The Strange Origins, Disturbing Past, and Uncertain Future of Corporate Personhood in American Law," 44 *John Marshall Law Review* 643 (2010).

59. See Louisville, Cincinnati & Charleston Railroad Company v. Letson, 43 U.S. 497 (1844). On the Letson case, see Haines and Sherwood, *The Role of the Supreme Court*, 76–81; Dudley O. McGovney, "A Supreme Court Fiction: Corporations in the Diverse Citizenship Jurisdiction of the Federal Courts," 56 *Harvard Law Review* 853, 875–879 (1943).

60. Marshall v. Baltimore & Ohio Railroad Company, 57 U.S. 314 (1853).

61. See Austin Allen, *Origins of the Dred Scott Case: Jacksonian Jurisprudence and the Supreme Court, 1837–1857* (2006), 126–132.

62. See Dred Scott v. Sandford, 60 U.S. 393 (1857).

CHAPTER 4: THE CONSPIRACY FOR CORPORATE RIGHTS

1. On Waite's view of Conkling, see Alfred Ronald Conkling, *The Life and Letters of Roscoe Conkling: Orator, Statesman, Advocate* (1889), 3:697. Justice Miller's view was recounted in David M. Jordan, *Roscoe Conkling of New York: Voice of the Senate* (1971), 417. These are both excellent sources on Conkling generally.

2. See Conkling, *The Life and Letters of Roscoe Conkling*, 3:451, 462, 676–677.

3. For a thorough account of the controversy, see Howard Jay Graham, *Everyman's Constitution: Historical Essays on the Fourteenth Amendment, the "Conspiracy Theory," and American Constitutionalism* (1968); Malcolm J. Harkins III, "The Uneasy Relationship of *Hobby Lobby, Conestoga Wood*, the Affordable Care Act, and the Corporate Person: How a Historical Myth Continues to Bedevil the Legal System," 7 *Saint Louis University Journal of Health Law & Policy* 201 (2014).

4. On the Supreme Court's courtroom in the 1880s and the society women who attended oral argument, see Clare Cushman, *Courtwatchers: Eyewitness Accounts in Supreme Court History* (2011), 20, 105–106.

5. See Graham, *Everyman's Constitution*, 409–413. See also San Mateo County v. Southern Pacific Railroad, 116 U.S. 138 (1885).

6. On Stanford, Huntington, and their two partners, see Richard Rayner, *The Associates: Four Capitalists Who Created California* (2009). See also Norman E. Tutorow et al., *The Governor: The Life and Legacy of Leland Stanford* (2004). On the Southern Pacific's taxes, see Graham, *Everyman's Constitution*, 397–398.

7. See Graham, *Everyman's Constitution*, 31; "The Railroad Tax Cases," *Daily Alta California*, February 10, 1886, 2 ("There were in all some sixty-three of these railroad tax cases pending. . . . The sixty-three cases are for the collection of taxes of 1880, 1881 and 1882"). The docket numbers of these sixty-three cases are listed in California Attorney General's Office, *Special Report on Railroad Tax Cases and Railroad Taxation* (1893).

8. See Graham, *Everyman's Constitution*, 398, 400, 416, 419.

9. See Jordan, *Roscoe Conkling of New York*, 35–36; Conkling, *The Life and Letters of Roscoe Conkling*, 3:12, 36, 361–363, 370.

10. See Jordan, *Roscoe Conkling of New York*, 82, 104, 126–127.

11. On the spectators' galleries in Congress and Conkling's relationship with Grant, see Conkling, *The Life and Letters of Roscoe Conkling*, 3:95–96, 451.

12. See Jordan, *Roscoe Conkling of New York*, 394, 413.

13. See Alfred D. Chandler Jr., *The Visible Hand: The Managerial Revolution in American Business* (1977), 81 et seq.; H. W. Brands, *American Colossus: The Triumph of Captialism, 1865–1900* (2011), 24–25; Scott R. Bowman, *The Modern Corporation and American Political Thought: Law, Power, and Ideology* (1995), 54.

14. See Mark Wahlgren Summers, "To Make the Wheels Revolve We Must Have Grease: Barrel Politics in the Gilded Age," 14 *Journal of Policy History* 49 (2002); Richard White, "Information, Markets, and Corruption: Transcontinental Railroads in the Gilded Age," 90 *Journal of American History* 19 (2003); Ted Nace, *Gangs of America: The Rise of Corporate Power and the Disabling of Democracy* (2003), 93; Robert Justin Goldstein, *Political Repression in Modern America From 1870 to 1976* (1978), 7.

15. On the controversy over the Fourteenth Amendment's ratification, see Joseph B. James, *The Ratification of the Fourteenth Amendment* (1984); David Lawrence, "There is No 'Fourteenth Amendment'!," *U.S. News & World Report*, Septempber 27, 1957, 140; Douglas H. Bryant, "Unorthodox and Paradox: Revisiting the Ratification of the Fourteenth Amendment," 53 *Alabama Law Review* 555 (2002).

16. On Campbell, see Timothy L. Hall, "John Archibald Campbell," in *Supreme Court Justices: A Biographical Dictionary*, 127–131; Robert Saunders Jr., *John Archibald Campbell: Southern Moderate, 1811–1889* (1997).

17. On the lawsuits, see Ronald M. Labbe and Jonathan Lurie, *The Slaughterhouse Cases: Regulation, Reconstruction, and the Fourteenth Amendment* (2003); Pamela Brandwein, *Rethinking the Judicial Settlement of Reconstruction* (2011). See also Michael A. Ross, *Justice of Shattered Dreams: Samuel Freeman Miller and the Supreme Court During the Civil War Era* (2003), 189 et seq.

18. On Miller, see Ross, *Justice of Shattered Dreams*; Lou Falkner Williams, "Samuel Freeman Miller," in *Supreme Court Justices: A Biographical Dictionary*, 317–322.

19. The Slaughter-House Cases, 83 U.S. 36 (1872).

20. See United States v. Cruikshank, 92 U.S. 542 (1876); United States v. Reese, 92 U.S. 214 (1876).

21. On Garfield and Conkling, see Robert C. Byrd, *The Senate, 1789–1989: Addresses on the History of the United States Senate* (1989), 326.

22. See Conkling, *The Life and Letters of Roscoe Conkling*, 3:24, 680.

23. See ibid., 3:105.

24. See Graham, *Everyman's Constitution*, Appendix A.

25. See ibid., 74–75, 383–385; Insurance Company v. New Orleans, 1 Woods 85 (1871).

26. On Beard, see Clyde W. Barrow, *More Than A Historian: The Political and Economic Thought of Charles A. Beard* (2000). See Charles A. Beard, *An Economic Interpretation of the Constitution of the United States* (1935), ix.

27. See Charles A. Beard and Mary R. Beard, *The Rise of American Civilization* (1914), 2:112–114; Graham, *Everyman's Constitution*, 23.

28. On Graham, see Felicia Kornbluh, "Turning Back the Clock: California Constitutionalists, Hearthstone Originalism, and *Brown v. Board*," 7 *California Legal History: Journal of the California Supreme Court Historical Society* 287 (2012).

29. See Graham, *Everyman's Constitution*, 82–87, 447, 490, 493 n. 211.

30. Ibid., 31, 93.

31. Ibid., 25, 44, 417.

32. On Field, see Carl Brent Swisher, *Stephen J. Field: Craftsman of the Law* (1930); John Norton Pomeroy, *Some Account of the Work of Stephen J. Field* (1895); Paul Kens, *Justice Stephen Field: Shaping Liberty from the Gold Rush to the Gilded Age* (1997).

33. See Walker Lewis, "The Supreme Court and a Six-Gun: The Extraordinary Story of *In re Neagle*," 43 *American Bar Association Journal* 415 (1957).

34. See In re Neagle, 135 U.S. 1 (1890).

35. See Pomeroy, *Some Account of the Work of Stephen J. Field*, 7, 18–22.

36. See ibid., 7–8; Swisher, *Stephen J. Field: Craftsman of the Law*, 22.

37. On Field's strong personality, see Willard L. King, "Melville Weston Fuller: 'The Chief' and the Giants on the Court," 36 *American Bar Association Journal* 293 (1950).

38. Ibid.

39. On Field and Stanford, see David C. Frederick, *Rugged Justice: The Ninth Circuit Court of Appeals and the American West, 1891–1941* (1994), 49–50; Swisher, *Stephen J. Field: Craftsman of the Law*, 245, 265.

40. On Waite's letter to Field, see Nace, *Gangs of America*, 90.

41. On Field's ideology, see Graham, *Everyman's Constitution*, 110–119; Swisher, *Stephen J. Field: Craftsman of the Law*, 77–81; Charles W. McCurdy, "Justice Field and the Jurisprudence of Government-Business Relations: Some Parameters of Laissez-Faire Constitutionalism, 1863–1897," 61 *Journal of American History* 970 (1975).

42. On Field's first trip to California, see Swisher, *Stephen J. Field: Craftsman of the Law*, 24–26. On railroad freight, see Justice Field's circuit court opinion in Santa Clara County v. Southern Pacific Railroad, 18 F. 385 (Circuit Court, D. California, [1883]).

43. See Graham, *Everyman's Constitution*, 400.

44. On Field's inappropriate involvement with Stanford, see Kens, *Justice Stephen Field: Shaping Liberty*, 239–240; Howard Jay Graham, "Four Letters of Mr. Justice Field," 47 *Yale Law Journal* 1100, 1106 (1938).

45. See Graham, *Everyman's Constitution*, 426.

46. Ibid., 437 n. 155.

47. See Santa Clara County v. Southern Pacific Railroad, 18 F. 385 (Circuit Court, D. California [1883]. See also Harkins, "The Uneasy Relationship."

48. See Morton J. Horwitz, "*Santa Clara* Revisited: The Development of Corporate Theory," 88 *West Virginia Law Review* 173 (1985–1986); Gregory A. Mark, "The Personification of the Business Corporation in American Law," 54 *University of Chicago Law Review* 1447 (1987). See also Herbert Hovenkamp, "The Classical Corporation in American Legal Thought," 76 *Georgetown Law Journal* 1593, 1630–1632 (1988) (on the railroads' association-based portrayal of the corporation in another series of cases decided in the Gilded Age).

49. See Paul v. Virginia, 75 U.S. 168 (1868).

50. See Welton v. Missouri, 91 U.S. 275 (1876).

51. See Timothy L. Hall, "Morrison Remick Waite," in *Supreme Court Justices: A Biographical Dictionary*, 168–172.

52. See Graham, *Everyman's Constitution*, 563; Munn v. Illinois, 94 U.S. 113 (1876).

53. See Hall, "Morrison Remick Waite," 171; Graham, *Everyman's Constitution*, 570.

54. See Santa Clara County v. Southern Pacific Railroad, 118 U.S. 394 (1886).

55. See San Bernardino County v. Southern Pacific Railroad, 118 U.S. 417 (1886) (Field, J., concurring).

56. On the Supreme Court reporter, see Frank D. Wagner, "The Role of the Supreme Court Reporter in History," 26 *Journal of Supreme Court History* 9 (2001).

57. On Davis, see John A. Garraty and Mark C. Carnes, "J. C. Bancroft Davis," in *American National Biography* (1999), 6:168; Thom Hartmann, *Unequal Protection: How Corporations Became "People"—And How You Can Fight Back* (2d ed., 2010), 44–48.

58. On the growth of law schools and the transformation of legal practice in the late 1800s, see Lawrence M. Friedman, *History of American Law* (rev. ed., 2010), 606 et seq. On public libraries, United States Office of Education, *Public Libraries in the United States of America* (1876), 778.

59. On Davis's strained relationship with the justices, see James W. Ely, *The Chief Justiceship of Melville W. Fuller, 1888–1910* (1995), 49; Loren P. Beth, *John Marshall Harlan: The Last Whig Justice* (1992), 164–165. On Davis's controversial list, see Charles A. Beard and Alan F. Westin, *The Supreme Court and the Constitution* (1912), 17–18.

60. Harlan's complaint is reported in Beth, *John Marshall Harlan: The Last Whig Justice*, 165. Brewer's rebuke appeared in United States v. Detroit Lumber Co., 200 U.S. 321 (1906).

61. See Graham, *Everyman's Constitution*, 566.

62. See Harkins, "The Uneasy Relationship," 249–250.

63. On "Ninth Circuit Law," see Graham, *Everyman's Constitution*, 570–575. On Field's racism, see Thomas Wuil Joo, "New 'Conspiracy Theory' of the Fourteenth Amendment: Nineteenth Century Chinese Civil Rights Cases and the Development of Substantive Due Process Jurisprudence," 29 *University of San Francisco Law Review* 353 (1995).

64. See Graham, *Everyman's Constitution*, 137; Lochner v. New York, 198 U.S. 45 (1905); E. S. Corwin, "The Supreme Court and the Fourteenth Amendment," 7 *Michigan Law Review* 643, 653 (1909). The 1897 case was Allgeyer v. Louisiana, 165 U.S. 578 (1897).

65. See Pembina Consolidated Silver Mining Company v. Pennsylvania, 125 U.S. 181 (1888).

66. On Fuller, see Ely, *The Chief Justiceship of Melville W. Fuller*. On the incorporation of Mark Twain, see "Mark Twain Turns Into A Corporation," *New York Times*, December 24, 1908; "In Vacation," 15 *Virginia Law Register* 982 (1910).

67. Minneapolis & St. Louis Railway Co. v. Beckwith, 129 U.S. 26 (1889) (citations omitted).

68. On the publication process of Supreme Court opinions, see Ruth Bader Ginsburg, "Informing the Public About the Supreme Court's Work," 29 *Loyola University of Chicago Law Journal* 275 (1998), 283 ("There was a long time in the U.S. Supreme Court's history, indeed until Chief Justice Melville Fuller's 1888–1910 tenure, during which justices did not routinely circulate their draft opinions among their colleagues prior to delivery"). See also Harkins, "The Uneasy Relationship," 286–287.

69. For illustrative opinions citing *Santa Clara*, see Charlotte, C. & A. R. Co. v. Gibbes, 142 U.S. 386, 391 (1892); Covington & Lexington Turnpike Road Co. v. Sanford, 164 U.S. 578, 592 (1896); Gulf, C. & S. F. R. Co. v. Ellis, 165 U.S. 150, 154 (1897); Smyth v. Ames, 169 U.S. 466, 522 (1898); Blake v. McClung, 172 U.S. 239, 259 (1898); Kentucky Finance Corp. v. Paramount Auto Exchange Corp., 262 U.S. 544, 550 (1923).

70. See Charles Wallace Collins, *The Fourteenth Amendment and the States* (1912), 129–138. Illustrative cases include Allgeyer v. Louisiana, 165 U.S. 578 (1897); Lochner v. New York, 198 U.S. 45 (1905); Adair v. United States, 208 U.S. 161 (1908); Coppage v. Kansas, 236 U.S. 1 (1915); and Hammer v. Dagenhart, 247 U.S. 251 (1918).

71. See Collins, *The Fourteenth Amendment*, 126, 127 n. 1 (quoting Arthur T. Hadley); Charles Wallace Collins, *Whither the Solid South? A Study in Politics and Race Relations* (1947); Joseph E. Lowndes, *From the New Deal to the New Right* (2008), 11–29; Victoria Hattam and Joseph Lowndes, "The Ground Beneath Our Feet: Language, Culture, and Political Change," in *Formative Acts: American*

Politics in the Making, ed. Stephen Skowronek and Matthew Glassman (2008), 199, 206.

72. See Ruth H. Bloch and Naomi Lamoreaux, "Corporations and the Fourteenth Amendment," in *Corporations and American Democracy*, ed. Naomi R. Lamoreaux and William J. Novak (2017), 286.

73. See Plessy v. Ferguson, 163 U.S. 537 (1896); Collins, *The Fourteenth Amendment*, 137–138.

CHAPTER 5: THE CORPORATE CRIMINAL

1. See DeLancey Nicoll, *3 Representative Men of New York: A Record of their Achievements*, ed. Jay Henry Mowbray (1898), 130; Fred C. Kelly, *The Wright Brothers: A Biography* (2012), 269; Dan H. McCullough, "The Sunset of the Criminal Lawyer," 50 *American Bar Association Journal* 223 (1964); George Derby and James Terry White, "De Lancey Nicoll," in *The National Cyclopedia of American Biography* (1910), 14:297. On Hale, see "Trusted Men in Jail for Large Defalcation," *New York Times*, September 29, 1905.

2. See generally Transcript of Record, Hale v. Henkel, 201 U.S. 43 (1906).

3. On Taft, see Henry Waters Taft, Obituary Record of Graduates of Yale University Deceased During the Year 1945–1946, *Bulletin of Yale University* 7 (1947). See also Henry Waters Taft, "The Tobacco Trust Decisions," 6 *Columbia Law Review* 375 (1906).

4. See Naomi R. Lamoreaux, *The Great Merger Movement in American Business, 1895–1904* (2011).

5. See Theodore Roosevelt, State of the Union Message, December 3, 1901, available at http://www.theodore-roosevelt.com/images/research/speeches/sotu1 .pdf; Richard Kluger, *Ashes to Ashes: America's Hundred-Year Cigarette War, the Public Health, and the Unabashed Triumph of Philip Morris* (1996), 46.

6. See Kathleen F. Brickey, "Corporate Criminal Accountability: A Brief History and an Observation," 60 *Washington University Law Quarterly* 393 (1982), 396.

7. See Helen Silving, "The Oath: I," 68 *Yale Law Journal* 1329 (1959), 1361–1364.

8. See "Trusted Men in Jail for Large Defalcation." The transcript of the grand jury proceeding can be found in Transcript of Record, Hale v. Henkel, 201 U.S. 43 (1906).

9. On licorice, see Kluger, *Ashes to Ashes*, 48; Rosemarie Boucher Leenerts, "Licorice," in *Encyclopedia of Cultivated Plants: From Acacia to Zinnia*, ed. Christopher Martin Cumo (2013), 579.

10. On Duke, see Robert F. Durden, *Bold Entrepreneur: The Life of James B. Duke* (2003); "Tobacco Trust," in *Gale Encyclopedia of U.S. Economic History*, ed. Thomas Carson et al. (1999), 1008; Kluger, *Ashes to Ashes*, 30 et seq.; "Tobacco Trust Tells Its Plan," *New York Times*, October 15, 1911.

11. On Dodd, see John M. Dobson, *Bulls, Bears, Boom, and Bust: A Historical Encyclopedia of American Business Concepts* (2007), 203.

12. On the knights and the rise of trust law, see David A. Thomas, "Anglo-American Land Law: Diverging Developments from a Shared History," 34 *Real Property, Probate, and Trust Journal* 143 (1999).

13. Charles R. Geisst, *Wall Street: A History* (1997), 100, 106; Morton J. Horwitz, *The Transformation of American Law, 1870–1960: The Crisis of Legal Orthodoxy* (1992), 80.

14. See Horwitz, *The Transformation of American Law, 1870–1960*, 83–87; Ralph Nader et al., *Taming the Giant Corporation* (1976), 52.

15. See Dobson, *Bulls, Bears, Boom, and Bust*, 203; Geisst, *Wall Street: A History*, 100, 106; Charles F. "Bostwick, Legislative Competition for Corporate Capital," 7 *American Lawyer* 136, 140 (1899); Horwitz, *The Transformation of American Law, 1870–1960*, 83–84.

16. On the race to the bottom, see William L. Cary, "Federalism and Corporate Law: Reflections Upon Delaware," 83 *Yale Law Journal* 663, 666 (1974). On Delaware, see Leslie Wayne, "How Delaware Thrives as a Corporate Tax Haven," *New York Times*, June 30, 2012.

17. See "Tobacco Trust," *Gale Encyclopedia of U.S. Economic History*, ed. Thomas Carson et al. (1999), 1008.

18. American Tobacco's purchase of MacAndrews and Forbes is detailed in court opinions, including United States v. American Tobacco, 221 U.S. 106 (1911) and United States v. MacAndrews & Forbes Co., 140 F. 823 (S.D. N.Y. 1906).

19. On Lloyd, see John L. Thomas, *Alternative America: Henry George, Edward Bellamy, Henry Demarest Lloyd, and the Adversary Tradition* (1983). Lloyd's exposé of Standard Oil can be found at http://www.theatlantic.com/magazine/archive/1881/03/the-story-of-a-great-monopoly/306019/. On the Sherman Antitrust Act, see "Trust-Busting," in *Gale Encyclopedia of U.S. Economic History*, ed. Thomas Carson et al. (1999), 1025.

20. See Theodore Roosevelt, State of the Union Message, December 3, 1901, available at http://www.theodore-roosevelt.com/images/research/speeches/sotu1.pdf; Kluger, *Ashes to Ashes*, 46.

21. On indicting a ham sandwich, see Ronald Wright and Marc Miller, "The Screening/Bargaining Tradeoff," 55 *Stanford Law Review* 29, 51 n. 70 (2002). On grand juries more generally, see Kevin K. Washburn, "Restoring the Grand Jury," 76 *Fordham Law Review* 2333 (2008); Akhil Reed Amar, *The Bill of Rights: Creation and Reconstruction* (1998), 83–85.

22. Nicoll's smoking habit was described in Allan Nevis, "Henry Ford: A Complex Man" in *Henry Ford: Critical Evaluations in Business and Management*, ed. John Cunningham Wood and Michael C. Wood (2003), 1: 47, 52. His sentiments about criminal justice were recounted in Timothy J. Gilfoyle, "'America's Greatest Criminal Barracks': The Tombs and the Experience of Criminal Justice in New York City, 1838–1897," 29 *Journal of Urban History* 525 (2003). See also Betty Glad, *Charles Evans Hughes and the Illusions of Innocence* (1966), 62.

23. See "Witness in Contempt in Tobacco Inquiry," *New York Times*, May 9, 1905; "English Anarchist Loses," *New York Times*, November 8, 1903.

24. See Transcript of Record, Hale v. Henkel, 201 U.S. 43 (1906).

25. See "Trusted Men in Jail for Large Defalcation."

26. On the prevalence of Fourth and Fifth Amendment cases today, see Ashlyn Kuersten and Donald Sonder, *Decisions of the U.S. Courts of Appeals* (2014), 35.

27. See Boyd v. United States, 116 U.S. 616 (1886). Additional cases included railroad companies. See Counselman v. Hitchcock, 142 U.S. 547 (1892); Brown v. Walker, 161 U.S. 591 (1896).

28. See Brickey, "Corporate Criminal Accountability: A Brief History and an Observation," 60 *Washington University Law Quarterly* 393 (1982); Daniel Lipton, "Corporate Capacity for Crime and Politics: Defining Corporate Personhood at the Turn of the 20th Century," 96 *Virginia Law Review* 1911, 1954 (2010);

William Blackstone, *Commentaries on the Laws of England*, ed. Robert Malcolm Kerr (1876), 1:464.

29. See Harold J. Laski, "The Personality of Associations," 29 *Harvard Law Review* 404 (1916); John Dewey, "The Historical Background of Corporate Legal Personality," 35 *Yale Law Journal* 655 (1926); P. Q. Johnson, "Law and Legal Theory in the History of Corporate Responsibility: Corporate Personhood," 35 *Seattle University Law Review* 1135 (2012); New York Central & Hudson River Railroad Co. v. United States, 212 U.S. 481 (1909).

30. See Transcript of Record, Hale v. Henkel, 201 U.S. 43 (1906).

31. See Lochner v. New York, 198 U.S. 45 (1905).

32. See E. Allgeyer & Company v. Louisiana, 165 U.S. 578 (1897).

33. On Peckham, see "Rufus Wheeler Peckham, Jr.," in Melvin Urofsky, *The Supreme Court Justices: A Biographical Dictionary* (2015), 351. On Allgeyer's influence, and that of the *Lochner* era it began, see David E. Bernstein, *Rehabilitating Lochner: Defending Individual Rights Against Progressive Reform* (2011).

34. On *Lochner* revisionism, see Bernstein, *Rehabilitating Lochner*; Howard Gillman, *The Constitution Besieged: The Rise and Demise of the Lochner Era Police Powers Jurisprudence* (1995). For an excellent review of some of the early literature, see Gary D. Rowe, "Lochner Revisionism Revisited," 24 *Law & Social Inquiry* 221 (1999).

35. On the distinction between property rights and liberty rights in the *Lochner* era, see Ruth H. Bloch and Naomi Lamoreaux, "Corporations and the Fourteenth Amendment," in *Corporations and American Democracy*, ed. Naomi R. Lamoreaux and William J. Novak (2017), 286.

36. Northwestern National Life Insurance Company v. Riggs, 203 U.S. 243 (1906).

37. Meyer v. Nebraska, 262 U.S. 390 (1923). On property and liberty rights more generally, see Henry Monagham, "Of 'Liberty' and 'Property,'" 62 *Cornell Law Review* 405, 411–412 (1977); Wayne McCormack, "Property and Liberty: Institutional Competence and the Functions of Rights," 51 *Washington & Lee Law Review* 1, 29 (1994).

38. See Hale v. Henkel, 201 U.S. 43 (1906); "Federal Jury Indicts Tobacco Trust Men," *New York Times*, June 19, 1906.

39. See Henry Billings Brown and Charles Artemis Kent, *Memoir of Henry Billings Brown, Late Justice of the Supreme Court of the United States* (1915), 88; Robert M. Warner, "Henry B. Brown," in *The Supreme Court Justices: Illustrated Biographies*, ed. Clare Cushman (2012), 229.

40. There were pragmatic reasons for *Hale*'s split outcome on corporate rights. See William J. Stuntz, "Privacy's Problem and the Law of Criminal Procedure," 93 *Michigan Law Review* 1016, 1053–1054 (1995); William J. Stuntz, "The Substantive Origins of Criminal Procedure," 105 *Yale Law Journal* 393, 422–433 (1995).

41. On the property-rights basis of *Hale*, see Lipton, "Corporate Capacity for Crime and Politics: Defining Corporate Personhood At the Turn of the Twentieth Century," 96 *Virginia Law Review* 1911, 1943–1945.

42. See Hale v. Henkel, 201 U.S. 43 (1906). On *Hale*'s recognition of the differences between humans and corporations, see Bloch and Lamoreaux, "Corporations and the Fourteenth Amendment."

43. See Roscoe Pound, "Visitatorial Jurisdiction Over Corporations in Equity," 49 *Harvard Law Review* 369, 371 (1936); William Blackstone, *Commentaries on the Laws of England*, ed. Robert Malcolm Kerr (1876), 1:455.

44. See "Federal Jury Indicts Tobacco Trust Men."
45. See United States v. American Tobacco, 221 U.S. 106 (1911); Standard Oil Co. v. United States, 221 U.S. 1 (1911); Kluger, *Ashes to Ashes*, 52–53.
46. See Colonnade Catering Corp. v. United States, 397 U.S. 72 (1970); United States v. Biswell, 406 U.S. 311 (1972); Marshall v. Barlow's Inc., 436 U.S. 307 (1978); United States v. Morton Salt Co., 338 U.S. 632 (1950). See Peter J. Henning, "The Conundrum of Corporate Criminal Liability: Seeking A Consistent Approach to the Constitutional Rights of Corporations in Criminal Prosecutions," 63 *Tennessee Law Review* 793, 802, 826 et seq. (1996); Darrell A. H. Miller, "Guns, Inc.: *Citizens United, McDonald*, and the Future of Corporate Constitutional Rights," 86 *New York University Law Review* 887, 919 (2011). On the application of another criminal right to corporations, see Elizabeth Salisbury Warren, "Note, The Case for Applying the Eighth Amendment to Corporations," 49 *Vanderbilt Law Review* 1313 (1996).

CHAPTER 6: PROPERTY, NOT POLITICS

1. On the Great Wall Street Scandal and the resulting campaign finance reform, see Adam Winkler, "'Other People's Money': Corporations, Agency Costs, and Campaign Finance Law," 92 *Georgetown Law Journal* 871 (2004); Morton Keller, *The Life Insurance Enterprise, 1885–1910: A Study in the Limits of Corporate Power* (1963); "Probing the Insurance Companies," *New York Times*, October 1, 1905, 1. On Perkins and the insurance investigation, see John A. Garrity, *Right-Hand Man: The Life of George W. Perkins* (1957), 164 et seq.
2. On Hughes's being "scarcely known," see Lindsay Russell, "Charles E. Hughes, The Pilot of the Insurance Investigation," 17 *Green Bag* 633 (1905). On Hughes's lack of affiliation with major firms, see Mark Sullivan, *Our Times: The United States, 1900–1925* (1930), 3:51–52. On Hughes's life and career more generally, see Dexter Perkins, *Charles Evans Hughes and American Democratic Statesmanship* (1956); Betty Glad, *Charles Evans Hughes and the Illusions of Innocence* (1966); Merlo J. Pusey, *Charles Evans Hughes* (1951).
3. On Perkins, see Garrity, *Right-Hand Man*; "George W. Perkins," in *Wall Street People: True Stories of the Great Barons of Finance*, ed. Charles D. Ellis and James R. Vertin (2001), 2:84–87.
4. See Winkler, "'Other People's Money,'" 887–888; Louis Filler, *Crusaders for American Liberalism* (1939), 196; Mark Sullivan, *Our Times: The United States, 1900–1925: Pre-War America* (1930), 3:34.
5. See Garrity, *Right-Hand Man*, 165.
6. Ibid., 166–167.
7. The account of Perkins and Hughes's private conversation came from Hughes himself. See *The Autobiographical Notes of Charles Evans Hughes*, ed. David J. Danelski and Joseph S. Tulchin (1973), 125–126.
8. On Keppler's cartoon, see Donald Dewey, *The Art of Ill Will: The Story of American Political Cartoons* (2008), 229.
9. On the "industrial revolution" in electoral politics and candidates' increasing need for new sources of financing, see Mark Wahlgren Summer, "'To Make the Wheels Revolve We Must Have Grease': Barrel Politics in the Gilded Age," in *Money and Politics*, ed. Paula Baker (2002), 49. On the changes in the electoral process, see Adam Winkler, "Voters' Rights and Parties' Wrongs: Early Politi-

cal Party Regulation in the State Courts, 1886–1915," 100 *Columbia Law Review* 873 (2000).

10. On Hanna, see Herbert David Croly, *Marcus Alonzo Hanna: His Life and Work* (1912); William T. Horner, *Ohio's Kingmaker: Mark Hanna, Man and Myth* (2010).

11. On Bryan, see Michael Kazin, *A Godly Hero: The Life of William Jennings Bryan* (2006).

12. See Croly, *Marcus Alonzo Hanna: His Life and Work*, 212–213; Thomas J. Baldino and Kyle L. Kreider, *U.S. Election Campaigns: A Documentary and Reference Guide* (2011), 3.

13. See Croly, *Marcus Alonzo Hanna: His Life and Work*, 146; *Oxford Dictionary of American Quotations*, ed. Hugh Rawson and Margaret Miner (2006), 526.

14. See Croly, *Marcus Alonzo Hanna: His Life and Work*, 219.

15. On Hanna's solicitations of businessmen, see ibid., 326; Steven G. Koven, *Responsible Governance: A Case Study Approach* (2008), 46; Baldino and Kreider, *U.S. Election Campaigns*, 5; Bradley A. Smith, *Unfree Speech: The Folly of Campaign Finance Reform* (2001), 22.

16. See Smith, *Unfree Speech: The Folly of Campaign Finance Reform*, 22.

17. On New York Life's dealings with the Texas inquiry, see "N.Y. Life Men Made Oath in Flat Conflict," *New York World*, September 28, 1905, 1; "Sworn Statement of N.Y. Life Officials That Disagree," *New York World*, September 28, 1905, 1.

18. On the rumors of corporate contributions, see Perry Belmont, "Publicity of Election Expenditures," 180 *North American Review* 166 (1905); George Thayer, *Who Shakes the Money Tree? American Campaign Finance Practices From 1789 to the Present* (1973), 49–50; Keller, *The Life Insurance Enterprise*, 228. Parker's charges were recounted in "Parker Barred the Trusts from Democratic Fund," *New York Times*, November 6, 1904, A1.

19. On Frick's reaction to Roosevelt, see Sean Dennis Cashman, *America Ascendant: From Theodore Roosevelt to FDR in the Century of American Power, 1901–1945* (1998), 15.

20. See Tom Lansford, *Theodore Roosevelt in Perspective* (2005), 73; "Roosevelt Speaks; Cortelyou Charges Called Monstrous," *New York Times*, November 5, 1904, A1.

21. See Glad, *Charles Evans Hughes and the Illusions of Innocence*, 62.

22. On the press reaction to Perkins's revelations, see *The Autobiographical Notes of Charles Evans Hughes*, ed. David J. Danelski and Joseph S. Tulchin, 125–126.

23. On insurance company contributions, see Testimony Taken Before the Joint Committee of the Senate and Assembly of the State of New York to Investigate and Examine into the Business and Affairs of Life Insurance Companies Doing Business in the State of New York (1905), 1:751–753; State of New York, Report of the Joint Committee of the Senate and Assembly of the State of New York Appointed to Investigate the Affairs of Life Insurance Companies, Assembly Document Number 41 (1906), 106; Winkler, *Other People's Money*, 892–893; James K. Pollock Jr., *Party Campaign Funds* (1926), 128.

24. See Adolf A. Berle and Gardiner C. Means, *The Modern Corporation and Private Property* (1991 ed.), 68.

25. See Keller, *The Life Insurance Enterprise*, ix; "The Life Insurance Upheaval," *Collier's*, October 7, 1905, 11; Melvin Urofsky, *Louis D. Brandeis: A Life* (2009), 158.

26. See "Light on a Missionary Enterprise," *Collier's*, October 28, 1905, 13; James F. Simon, *FDR and Chief Justice Hughes: The President, The Supreme Court, and the Epic Battle over the New Deal* (2012), 30–31.

27. See Winkler, *Other People's Money*, 901–905.

28. See Alfred D. Chandler Jr., *The Visible Hand: The Managerial Revolution in American Business* (1977), 15–49, 287–289; James C. Bonbright and Gardiner Means, *The Holding Company: Its Public Significance and Its Regulation* (1932), 56; Charles S. Tippetts and Shaw Livermore, *Business Organization and Control: Corporations and Trusts in the United States* (1932), 229; Winkler, *Other People's Money*, 906–909. Hughes's conclusion was stated in State of New York, Report of the Joint Committee of the Senate and Assembly of the State of New York Appointed to Investigate the Affairs of Life Insurance Companies, Assembly Document No. 41 (1906), 6.

29. See Charles J. Bullock, "Life Insurance and Speculation," 97 *Atlantic Monthly* 629, 639 (1906).

30. Burton J. Hendrick, "Governor Hughes," *McClure's* 30 (1908): 521, 534.

31. See James W. Breen, "How the Banks Filled Hanna's War Chest," *New York Herald*, April 12, 1906; Winkler, *Other People's Money*, 896–898; F. P. Dunne, "Mr. Dooley on the Life Insurance Investigation," *Collier's*, November 4, 1905, 12.

32. See Winkler, *Other People's Money*, 898–899.

33. See Testimony Taken Before the Joint Committee of the Senate and Assembly of the State of New York to Investigate and Examine into the Business and Affairs of Life Insurance Companies Doing Business in the State of New York (1905), 1:761; State of New York, Report of the Joint Committee of the Senate and Assembly of the State of New York Appointed to Investigate the Affairs of Life Insurance Companies, Assembly Document No. 41 (1906), 59; Winkler, *Other People's Money*, 899.

34. See Winkler, *Other People's Money*, 894–895.

35. See Urofsky, *Louis D. Brandeis: A Life*, 164.

36. See "Probing the Insurance Companies," *New York Times*, October 1, 1905, 4.

37. On Brandeis generally, see Urofsky, *Louis D. Brandeis: A Life*; Jeffrey Rosen, *Louis D. Brandeis: American Prophet* (2016); Alpheus Thomas Mason, *Brandeis: A Free Man's Life* (1946); Philippa Strum, *Louis D. Brandeis: Justice for the People* (1984).

38. Brandeis biographer Melvin Urofsky pinpoints the insurance scandal as Brandeis's initial articulation of the "curse of bigness" and "other people's money" corruption ideas. See Urofsky, *Louis D. Brandeis: A Life*, 157–162. For Brandeis's own scholarship, see Samuel Warren and Louis D. Brandeis, "The Law of Ponds," 3 *Harvard Law Review* 1 (1889); Samuel Warren and Louis D. Brandeis, "The Right to Privacy," 4 *Harvard Law Review* 193 (1890). On the influence of the privacy article, see Melville B. Nimmer, "The Right of Publicity," 19 *Law and Contemporary Problems* 203 (1954).

39. See Urofsky, *Louis D. Brandeis: A Life*, 157.

40. Brandeis's speech is available at https://archive.org/stream/lifeinsuranc eabu00branrich#page/n1/mode/2up and is discussed in detail in Urofsky, *Louis D. Brandeis: A Life*, 160 et seq. On how Brandeis's role as counsel to the New England Policy-Holders Committee reflected his sometimes problematic "independence" from his clients, see Clyde Spillenger, "Elusive Advo-

cate: Reconsidering Brandeis as People's Lawyer," 105 *Yale Law Journal* 1445 (1996).

41. See Thomas K. McCraw, *Prophets of Regulation* (1984), 80 et seq.; Urofsky, *Louis D. Brandeis: A Life*, 161, 300-326.

42. See Urofsky, *Louis D. Brandeis: A Life*, 308-309. On Brandeis as intellectual heir to Jefferson's populism, see Rosen, *Louis D. Brandeis: American Prophet*.

43. Quoted in Urofsky, *Louis D. Brandeis: A Life*, 170.

44. Louis K. Liggett Company v. Lee, 288 U.S. 517 (1933) (Brandeis, J., dissenting).

45. See Louis D. Brandeis, *Other People's Money: And How the Bankers Use It* (1914).

46. On Cabot and the Muscovy Company, see Richard Biddle, *A Memoir of Sebastian Cabot: With A Review of the History of Maritime Discovery* (1831); J. T. Kotilaine, *Russia's Foreign Trade and Economic Expansion in the Seventeenth Century* (2005), 15; Anon., *The Origin and Early History of the Russia or Muscovy Company* (1830); John Micklethwait and Adrian Wooldridge, *The Company: A Short History of a Revolutionary Idea* (2003), 8; T. S. Willan, *The Early History of the Russia Company, 1553-1603* (1956). On Columbus's financing, see D. B. Quinn, "The Italian Renaissance and Columbus," 6 *Renaissance Studies* 359 (1992). On Cabot's Italian inspiration, see C. E. Walker, "The History of the Joint Stock Company," 6 *Accounting Review* 97 (1931). On early European stockholding, see Fernand Braudel, *The Wheels of Commerce* (1982), 323 et seq. The firm's multiple reorganizations have led to some disagreement about when it ceased to operate.

47. See William G. Roy, *Socializing Capital: The Rise of the Large Industrial Corporation in America* (1997), xiii, 197; Charles R. Geisst, *Wall Street: A History* (1997), 105.

48. See State of New York, Report of the Joint Committee of the Senate and Assembly of the State of New York Appointed to Investigate the Affairs of Life Insurance Companies, Assembly Document Number 41 (1906), 393.

49. "President in Conference over Campaign Funds," *New York World*, September 21, 1905, 1; "Probing the Insurance Companies," *New York Times*, October 1, 1905, 4; Theodore Roosevelt, State of the Union Message, December 5, 1905, available at http://www.presidency.ucsb.edu/ws/index.php?pid=29546.

50. See Winkler, *Other People's Money*, 922.

51. On Greenberg's dispute with the Western Turf Association, see "Jury Verdict for Greenberg," *San Francisco Chronicle*, March 23, 1900, 9; "Corrigan Has a Black List for Enemies," *San Francisco Call*, March 21, 1900, 12; Greenberg v. Western Turf Association, 73 P. 1050 (Cal. 1903); Bennett Liebman, "The Supreme Court and Exclusions by Racetracks," 17 *Jeffrey S. Moorad Sports Law Journal* 421, 426-430 (2010); Transcript of Record, Western Turf Association v. Greenberg, 204 U.S. 359 (1907). On Tanforan, see "Tanforan Park," *San Francisco Call*, December 17, 1899, 45; Laura Hillenbrand, *Seabiscuit: An American Legend* (2001), 113 et seq.

52. See Western Turf Association v. Greenberg, 204 U.S. 359 (1907).

53. For an excellent account of the *Berea College* case, see David E. Bernstein, "*Plessy* versus *Lochner*: The *Berea College* Case," 25 *Journal of Supreme Court History* 93 (2000). See also Berea College v. Commonwealth, 94 S.W. 623 (1906).

54. See Bernstein, "*Plessy* versus *Lochner*," 99-101.

55. See Berea College v. Kentucky, 211 U.S. 45 (1908).

56. See Amy Mittelman, *Brewing Battles: A History of American Beer* (2008), 28-62.

57. Ibid., 38–39; Lisa M. F. Anderson, *The Politics of Prohibition: American Governance and the Prohibition Party, 1869–1933* (2013); Daniel Okrent, *Last Call: The Rise and Fall of Prohibition* (2010).
58. See Okrent, *Last Call*, 58; Mittelman, *Brewing Battles*, 61.
59. See People v. Gansley, 158 N.W. 195 (Mich. 1916).
60. See "John Stone," *Michigan Supreme Court Historical Society*, available at http://www.micourthistory.org/justices/john-stone/.
61. See Okrent, *Last Call*, 58; Mittelman, *Brewing Battles*, 61; "Many Brewers Indicted by Grand Jury," *Reading Eagle*, March 3, 1916, 29; United States v. United States Brewers Association, 239 F. 163 (W.D. Pa. 1916).
62. See United States v. American Tobacco, 221 U.S. 106 (1911); Standard Oil Co. v. United States, 221 U.S. 1 (1911). For examples of Roosevelt biographies that skip over the campaign finance scandal, see Lewis L. Gould, *Theodore Roosevelt* (2012); Louis Auchincloss, *Theodore Roosevelt* (2002). An exception is Edmund Morris, *Theodore Rex* (2010).
63. See Winkler, *Other People's Money*, 914–915; Garrity, *Right-Hand Man*, 190–191.
64. See New York ex rel. Perkins v. Moss, 80 N.E. 383 (N.Y. 1907).
65. See Garrity, *Right-Hand Man*, 253–275.

CHAPTER 7: DISCRETE AND INSULAR CORPORATIONS

1. The number of cases decided and majority opinions written was compiled from the following sources: Albert P. Blaustein and Roy M. Mersky, *The First One Hundred Justices: Statistical Studies on the Supreme Court of the United States* 89 (1978); Lee Epstein et al., *The Supreme Court Compendium: Data, Decisions, and Developments* 88–90 (5th ed., 2012); *Journal of the Supreme Court of the United States*, October Terms 2010–2014, available at http://www.supreme-court.gov/orders/journal.aspx. For the cases listed by name, see Brown v. Board of Education, 347 U.S. 483 (1954); Reynolds v. Sims, 377 U.S. 533 (1964); Obergefell v. Hodges, 135 S. Ct. 2071 (2015).
2. On Stone, see Alpheus Thomas Mason, *Harlan Fiske Stone: Pillar of the Law* (1968); Samuel J. Konefsky, *Chief Justice Stone and the Supreme Court* (1946); John W. Johnson, "Harlan Fiske Stone," in *The Supreme Court Justices: A Biographical Dictionary*, ed. Melvin Urofsky (1994), 425. On the opposition in the Senate, see Joseph Pratt Harris, *The Advice and Consent of the Senate: A Study of the Confirmation of Appointments by the United States Senate* (1953), 118.
3. See United States v. Carolene Products Co., 304 U.S. 144, 152–153 n. 4 (1938).
4. On the Sedition and Espionage Acts and the persecution of marginalized people, see Ernest Freeberg, *Democracy's Prisoner: Eugene V. Debs, the Great War, and the Right to Dissent* (2008). On Stone and Columbia, see Robert McCaughey, *Stand, Columbia: A History of Columbia University* (2003), 215; Mason, *Harlan Fiske Stone: Pillar of the Law*, 518.
5. On Long, see Richard White, *Kingfish: The Reign of Huey P. Long* (2006).
6. On Long's battle with the newspapers, see Richard C. Cortner, *The Kingfish and the Constitution: Huey Long, the First Amendment, and the Emergence of Modern Press Freedom in America* (1996). See also Samuel R. Olken, "The Business of Expression: Economic Liberty, Political Factions and the Forgotten First Amendment Legacy of Justice George Sutherland," 10 *William & Mary Bill of Rights Journal* 249 (2001–2002).

7. See Cortner, *The Kingfish and the Constitution*, 24–32.

8. Ibid., 26–31, 47–50.

9. Ibid., 35, 96–97.

10. Ibid., 76, 95; Olken, "The Business of Expression," 284.

11. See Cortner, *The Kingfish and the Constitution*, 79–82; Olken, "The Business of Expression," 286.

12. On the pre–World War I free speech debates, see David M. Rabban, *Free Speech in Its Forgotten Years* (1997).

13. See Freeberg, *Democracy's Prisoner*, 4.

14. See Geoffrey R. Stone, *Perilous Times: Free Speech in Wartime from the Sedition Act to the War on Terrorism* (2004), 135 et seq.; "Sedition Act of 1918," in *The United States in the First World War: An Encyclopedia*, ed. Anne Cipriano Venzon (2013), 536.

15. On Holmes's evolution, see Thomas Healy, *The Great Dissent: How Oliver Wendell Holmes Changed His Mind—and Changed the History of Free Speech in America* (2013).

16. See Abrams v. United States, 250 U.S. 616, 624–631 (1919) (Holmes, J., dissenting). On the origins and flaws of the marketplace metaphor, see Joseph Blocher, "Institutions in the Marketplace of Ideas," 57 *Duke Law Journal* 821 (2008).

17. See Gitlow v. New York, 268 U.S. 652 (1925).

18. See Near v. Minnesota, 283 U.S. 697 (1931); Fred W. Friendly, *Minnesota Rag* (2013).

19. Cortner, *The Kingfish and the Constitution*, 92.

20. On Deutsch and Phelps, see ibid., 21, 31, 99–100; S. L. Alexander et al., *The Times-Picayune in a Changing Media World* (2014), 33; E. P. Deutsch, "A Louisiana Lawyer," *New York Times*, January 18, 1980, B5.

21. See Cortner, *The Kingfish and the Constitution*, 114.

22. Ibid., 33–34, 55.

23. On Porterie, see Harnett T. Kane, *Huey Long's Louisiana Hayride* (1971), 249; E. Phelps Gay, "History of the Louisiana Bar: Kingfish's Legacy?," 60 *Louisiana Bar Journal* 466, 469 (2013).

24. On Porterie and Rivet's mistakes, see Cortner, *The Kingfish and the Constitution*, 137, 161.

25. See "Henry Ford Explains Why He Gives Away $10,000,000," *New York Times*, January 11, 1914; M. Todd Henderson, "The Story of *Dodge v. Ford Motor Company*: Everything Old is New Again," in *Corporate Law Stories*, ed. J. Mark Ramseyer (2009), 37.

26. See Dodge v. Ford Motor Company, 170 N.W. 668 (Mich. 1919); Kent Greenfield, "Corporate Law's Original Sin," *Washington Monthly* (2015), available at http://washingtonmonthly.com/magazine/janfeb-2015/sidebar-corporate-laws-original-sin/.

27. Greenfield, "Corporate Law's Original Sin."

28. See Dodge v. Ford Motor Company, 170 N.W. 668 (Mich. 1919).

29. See Milton Friedman, "The Social Responsibility of Business Is to Increase Its Profits," *New York Times Magazine*, September 13, 1970.

30. On the shareholder wealth maximization norm, see Stephen M. Bainbridge, "In Defense of the Shareholder Wealth Maximization Norm," 50 *Washington & Lee Law Review* 1423 (1993). On its flaws, see Lynn Stout, *The Shareholder Value*

Myth: How Putting Shareholders First Harms Investors, Corporations, and the Public (2012); Joel Bakan, *The Corporation* (2005).

31. See Cortner, *The Kingfish and the Constitution*, 139.
32. See ibid.
33. Ibid., 91.
34. See Olken, "The Business of Expression," 292 n. 215.
35. See G. Edward White, *The Constitution and the New Deal* (2002), 81, 296–297.
36. On Cardozo, see Richard Polenberg, *The World of Benjamin Cardozo: Personal Values and the Judicial Process* (1999).
37. See Olken, "The Business of Expression," 293–307.
38. Ibid., 298–299; Grosjen v. American Press Co., 297 U.S. 233 (1936).
39. On the freedom of the press, see Garrett Epps, *The First Amendment: Freedom of the Press: Its Constitutional History and the Contemporary Debate* (2008); A. J. Liebling, "Do You Belong In Journalism?," *New Yorker*, May 14, 1960, 105. See also New York Times v. Sullivan, 376 U.S. 254 (1964); New York Times v. United States, 403 U.S. 713 (1971).

CHAPTER 8: CORPORATIONS, RACE, AND CIVIL RIGHTS

1. On the NAACP, see Patricia Sullivan, *Lift Every Voice: The NAACP and the Making of the Civil Rights Movement* (2009); Mark Tushnet, *Making Civil Rights Law: Thurgood Marshall and the Supreme Court, 1936–1961* (1994). See also Taylor Branch, *Parting the Waters: America in the King Years, 1954–1963*.
2. On Patterson, see Gene L. Howard, *Patterson for Alabama: The Life and Career of John Patterson* (2008).
3. Details of the NAACP litigation can be found in Tushnet, *Making Civil Rights Law*, 283 et seq.; John D. Inazu, *Liberty's Refuge* (2012), 77 et seq. See also Branch, *Parting the Waters*.
4. See Connecticut General Life Insurance Company v. Johnson, 303 U.S. 77 (1938) (Black, J., dissenting).
5. See Richard R. W. Brooks, "Incorporating Race," 106 *Columbia Law Review* 2023, 2025–2026 (2006).
6. See ibid., 2047 et seq. The Supreme Court decision ending racially restrictive covenants was Shelley v. Kraemer, 334 U.S. 1 (1948).
7. Late Corporation of the Church of Jesus Christ of Latter-Day Saints v. United States, 136 U.S. 1 (1890).
8. See People's Pleasure Park Company, Inc. v. Rohleder, 61 S.E. 794 (Va. 1908).
9. See Robert L. Carter, *A Matter of Law: A Memoir of Struggle in the Cause of Equal Rights* (2012).
10. See Brief for Petitioner, NAACP v. Alabama ex rel. Patterson, 357 U.S. 449 (1958), 18, 23.
11. See Brief for Respondent, NAACP v. Alabama ex rel. Patterson, 357 U.S. 449 (1958), 10, 26.
12. On Black, see Roger K. Newman, *Hugo Black: A Biography* (1997); Burlington Howard Ball, *Hugo L. Black: Cold Steel Warrior* (1996). See also "Justice Black Dies at 85," *New York Times*, September 25, 1971.
13. See Newman, *Hugo Black: A Biography*, 54; Ball, *Hugo L. Black: Cold Steel Warrior*, 66.

14. Connecticut General Life Insurance Company v. Johnson, 303 U.S. 77, 83 (1938) (Black, J., dissenting).
15. See Merlin Owen Newton, *Armed With the Constitution: Jehovah's Witnesses in Alabama and the U.S. Supreme Court, 1939–1946* (1995), 106–132.
16. See Lovell v. City of Griffin, 303 U.S. 444 (1938); Schneider v. State, 308 U.S. 147 (1939); Cantwell v. Connecticut, 310 U.S. 296 (1940); Minersville School District v. Gobitis, 310 U.S. 586 (1940); West Virginia Board of Education v. Barnette, 319 U.S. 624 (1943). On the string of landmark Jehovah's Witness cases, see Newton, *Armed with the Constitution.*
17. Marsh v. Alabama, 326 U.S. 501 (1946).
18. See Peter Drucker, *Concept of the Corporation* (1946). On Drucker and his influence, see John Tarant, *Drucker: The Man Who Invented the Corporate Society* (2009).
19. See Adolph A. Berle Jr., "Constitutional Limitations on Corporate Activity: Protection of Personal Rights from Invasion Through Economic Power," 100 *University of Pennsylvania Law Review* 933, 942–953 (1952).
20. See Carl E. Schneider, "Free Speech and Corporate Freedom: A Comment on *First National Bank of Boston v. Bellotti*," 59 *California Law Review* 1227, 1247 (1986).
21. See Tinsley E. Yarbrough, *John Marshall Harlan: Great Dissenter of the Warren Court* (1992), 126–127.
22. On Harlan, see ibid. Harlan's decision can be found at NAACP v. Alabama ex rel. Patterson, 357 U.S. 449 (1958).
23. See NAACP v. Alabama ex rel. Patterson, 357 U.S. 449, 460–461 (1958); NAACP v. Button, 371 U.S. 415 (1963); Evelyn Brody, "Entrance, Voice, and Exit: The Constitutional Bounds of the Right of Association," 35 *University of California Davis Law Review* 821 (2002).
24. See Bains LLC v. ARCO Products Company, 405 F.3d 764 (9th Cir. 2005); Brooks, "Incorporating Race," 8.
25. On the emergence of minority business enterprise programs, see Daniel R. Levinson, "A Study of Preferential Treatment: The Evolution of Minority Business Enterprise Assistance Programs," 49 *George Washington Law Review* 61 (1980).
26. On the benefits to whites from equal protection law generally, see Derrick A. Bell Jr., "*Brown v. Board of Education* and the Interest Convergence Dilemma," 93 *Harvard Law Review* 518 (1980); Kimberlé Williams Crenshaw, "Race, Reform, and Retrenchment: Transformation and Legitimation in Antidiscrimination Law," 101 *Harvard Law Review* 1331 (1988).
27. Regents of the University of California v. Bakke, 438 U.S. 265 (1978).
28. See Thinket Ink Information Resources, Inc. v. Sun Microsystems, Inc., 368 F.3d 1053, 1058 (9th Cir. 2004); City of Richmond v. J. A. Croson Company, 488 U.S. 469 (1989); Adarand Constructors, Inc. v. Peña, 515 U.S. 200 (1995).

CHAPTER 9: THE CORPORATION'S JUSTICE

1. A transcript of Cullman's tribute to Powell can be found at http://legacy.library .ucsf.edu/tid/sfc34e00. The toast was first brought to my attention by Jeffrey D. Clements, *Corporations Are Not People: Reclaiming Democracy from Big Money and Global Corporations* (rev. ed., 2014).

2. According to David Vogel, there were sixty-two federal laws enacted to protect consumer health and safety between 1964 and 1979, compared to only sixteen such laws in the Progressive and New Deal eras combined. See David Vogel, "The 'New' Social Regulation in Historical and Comparative Perspective," in *Regulation in Perspective*, ed. Thomas K. McCraw (1981), 155, 162. On faith in industry, see Thomas Byrne Edsall, *The New Politics of Inequality* (1985), 113.

3. "Meet Ralph Nader," *Newsweek*, January 22, 1968, cover, 65; "The U.S.'s Toughest Customer," *Time*, December 12, 1969, cover, 89.

4. On the Powell Memorandum and its impact, see Benjamin C. Waterhouse, *Lobbying America: The Politics of Business From Nixon to NAFTA* (2013), 58–60; Kim Phillips-Fein, *Invisible Hands: The Businessmen's Crusade Against the New Deal* (2010), 156–160. A copy of the memorandum can be found at http://law .wlu.edu/deptimages/Powell%20Archives/PowellMemorandumPrinted.pdf. On the reform movement led by Nader, see Edsall, *The New Politics of Inequality*, 107–114; Vogel, "The 'New' Social Regulation," 170–173.

5. On Nathaniel Powell, see Frank E. Grizzard, "Powell, Captain Nathaniel," in *Jamestown Colony: A Political, Social, and Cultural History*, ed. Frank E. Grizzard and D. Boyd Smith (2007), 173.

6. See John Calvin Jeffries, *Justice Lewis F. Powell, Jr.: A Biography* (2001).

7. Ibid., 550 (quoting ACLU legal director Burt Neuborne).

8. On Powell's appearance, see Robert Schnakenberg, "Lewis Powell," in *Secret Lives of the Supreme Court* (2009), 183; Clements, *Corporations Are Not People*, 20. On Powell's views on crime, see Jeffries, *Justice Lewis F. Powell, Jr.*, 210; U.S. Congress, Senate, Committee on the Judiciary, *Nominations of William H. Rehnquist and Lewis F. Powell: Hearings before the Committee on the Judiciary*, 92nd Congress, 1st session (1971), 216.

9. On Sydnor, see Phillips-Fein, *Businessmen's Crusade*, 156–160; Matthew D. Lassiter, *The Moderates' Dilemma: Massive Resistance to School Desegregation in Virginia* (1998), 112; "House Unit Hears Wage Bill Clash," *New York Times*, February 21, 1961.

10. On Nader, see Evan Osborne, *The Rise of the Anti-Corporate Movement: Corporations and the People Who Hate Them* (2007), 59; "The U.S.'s Toughest Customer," *Time*, December 12, 1969, 89; Charles McCarry, "A Hectic, Happy, Sleepless, Stormy, Rumpled, Relentless Week on the Road with Ralph Nader," *Life*, January 21, 1972, 45; Jack Doyle, "GM & Ralph Nader, 1965–1971," PopHistoryDig.com, March 31, 2013, available at http://www.pophistorydig.com/ ?tag=ralph-nader-time-magazine; Barbara Hinkson Craig, *Courting Change* (2004), 1–32. See Ralph Nader, *Unsafe at Any Speed: The Designed-In Dangers of the American Automobile* (1966).

11. Justin Martin, *Nader: Crusader, Spoiler, Icon* (2002), 57.

12. See Doyle, "GM & Ralph Nader"; "The U.S.'s Toughest Customer," *Time*, December 12, 1969, 89.

13. Charles McCarry, *Citizen Nader* (1972), 29; Doyle, "GM & Ralph Nader" (quoting the *Washington Post*); McCarry, "Relentless Week," 91; "Nader's Zenith," *Washington Post*, August 30, 1966, A18.

14. See Michael T. Kaufman, "Joseph F. Cullman 3rd, Who Made Philip Morris a Tobacco Power, Dies at 92," *New York Times*, May 1, 2004. The transcript of

Cullman's *Face the Nation* appearance can be found at http://legacy.library
.ucsf.edu/tid/jiz28eoo/pdf.

15. Phillips-Fein, *Businessmen's Crusade*, 160–161.

16. "The U.S.'s Toughest Customer," *Time*, December 12, 1969, 91.

17. On Morrison, Nader, and the Public Citizen Litigation Group, see Craig, *Courting Change*, 33 et seq.

18. Nader quoted in ibid., 32.

19. Ibid., 4; Alan B. Morrison, "How We Got the Commercial Speech Doctrine: An Originalist's Recollections," 54 *Case Western Reserve Law Review* 1189, 1190 (2004).

20. Ben A. Franklin, "Woman's Drive for Drug-Price Ads Ends Victoriously After 2 Years," *New York Times*, May 25, 1976, 12; Craig, *Courting Change*, 129. See also Randall P. Bezanson, *Speech Stories: How Free Can Speech Be?* (1998), 157.

21. See Morrison, "How We Got the Commercial Speech Doctrine," 1192.

22. On Chrestensen's suit, see the facts recounted in the lower court opinion in Chrestensen v. Valentine, 122 F.2d 511 (2d Cir. 1941), and in the Supreme Court opinion, Valentine v. Chrestensen, 316 U.S. 52 (1942). See also Tom Gerety, "The Submarine, the Handbill, and the First Amendment," 56 *University of Cincinnati Law Review* 1167 (1988); "Federal Court Finds Ordinance of City Discriminatory," *New York Times*, August 31, 1940, 15; Alex Kozinski and Stuart Banner, "Who's Afraid of Commercial Speech?," 76 *Virginia Law Review* 627 (1990).

23. On Chrestensen's alimony dispute, see "Never Let Your Husband Buy A Submarine," *Milwaukee Sentinel*, October 2, 1938, 23. On Commissioner Valentine, see "Lewis J. Valentine Dies in Hospital, 64," *New York Times*, December 17, 1946. For a copy of the handbill, see http://digitalcommons.law.scu.edu/cgi/viewcontent.cgi?article=1158&context=historical.

24. See Valentine v. Chrestensen, 316 U.S. 52 (1942).

25. See Craig, *Courting Change*, 45. For classic statements of free speech theory, see Alexander Meiklejohn, *Free Speech and Its Relation to Self-Government* (1948); C. Edwin Baker, "Scope of the First Amendment Freedom of Speech," 25 *UCLA Law Review* 964 (1977); Martin H. Redish, "The Value of Free Speech," 130 *University of Pennsylvania Law Review* 591 (1982).

26. See Morrison, "How We Got the Commercial Speech Doctrine," 1192.

27. See Martin H. Redish, "The First Amendment in the Marketplace: Commercial Speech and the Values of Free Expression," 39 *George Washington Law Review* 429 (1971).

28. The audio and transcript of the *Virginia Pharmacy* oral argument can be found at http://www.oyez.org/cases/1970-1979/1975/1975_74_895.

29. On White, see Dennis J. Hutchinson, *The Man Who Once was Whizzer White: A Portrait of Justice Byron R. White* (1998). On what might be termed the "Supreme Basketball Court," see Gina Holland, "Legal Eagles Tip Off in 'Highest Court in the Land,'" *Los Angeles Times*, September 8, 2002, available at http://articles.latimes.com/2002/sep/08/news/adna-court8.

30. See Roe v. Wade, 410 U.S. 113 (1973); Linda Greenhouse, *Becoming Justice Blackmun: Harry Blackmun's Supreme Court Journey* (2005), 186.

31. See Virginia Pharmacy Board v. Virginia Citizens Consumer Council, 425 U.S. 748 (1976).

32. On Powell's reaction to *Virginia Pharmacy*, see Powell Conference Notes,

November 14, 1975, Papers of Justice Lewis Powell, Virginia State Board of Pharmacy Case File, available at http://law.wlu.edu/deptimages/powell%20 archives/74-895_VirginiaBoard.pdf. On the Nixon proposals, see John D. Morris, "U.S. Moves to End Bans on Drug Ads," *New York Times*, November 28, 1971, 70; Burt Schorr, "Fuss Over Fees: Professional People Slowly Lose Insulation from Antitrust Laws," *Wall Street Journal*, August 7, 1975, 1; Karen Jo Elliott, "Retail Druggists May be Required to Post Prices," *Wall Street Journal*, May 30, 1974, 3. On the antitrust suit, see "Two Pharmacist Groups Are Sued by U.S. Over 'Code of Ethics' Barring Drug Ads," *Wall Street Journal*, November 25, 1975, 2.

33. See Jeffrey Clements, "The Conservative versus the Corporatist: Justice Rehnquist's Opposition to Justice Powell's Drive to Create 'Corporate Speech' Rights," American Constitution Society Blog, September 3, 2014, available at https://www.acslaw.org/acsblog/the-conservative-versus-the-corporatist-justice -rehnquist%E2%80%99s-opposition-to-justice-powell%E2%80%99s#_ftn1.

34. See Craig, *Courting Change*, 137 (quoting the *New York Times*); Linda Matthews, "High Court Voids Ban on Prices in Drug Ads," *Los Angeles Times*, May 25, 1976, B1. See Bates v. State Bar of Arizona, 433 U.S. 350 (1977) (lawyer advertising).

35. See Lorillard Tobacco Co. v. Reilly, 533 U.S. 525 (2001) (tobacco ads); Greater New Orleans Broadcasting Assn v. United States, 527 U.S. 173 (1999) (casino broadcast ads); Edenfield v. Fane, 507 U.S. 761 (1993); Pacific Gas & Electric Co. v. Public Utility Commission, 475 U.S. 1 (1986) (utility); International Dairy Foods Association MIF v. Amestoy, 92 F.3d 67 (2d Cir. 1996) (growth hormone); Robert Weisman, "Let the People Speak: The Case for a Constitutional Amendment to Remove Corporate Speech From the Ambit of the First Amendment," 83 *Temple Law Review* 979 (2011). For a thorough and persuasive account, see Tamara R. Piety, *Brandishing the First Amendment: Commercial Expression in America* (2012).

36. On the Ad Council, see Wendy Melillo, *How McGruff and the Crying Indian Changed America: A History of Iconic Ad Council Campaigns* (2013).

37. See Phillips-Fein, *Businessmen's Crusade*, 161–162.

38. See Chamber of Commerce of the United States, Business Response to the Powell Memorandum, Washington Report, November 26, 1973; Phillips-Fein, *Businessmen's Crusade*, 162; Vogel, "The 'New' Social Regulation," 176; Jack Doyle, "Nader's Raiders, 1968–1974," PopHistoryDig.com, March 31, 2013, available at http://www.pophistorydig.com/?p=14452; Clements, *Corporations Are Not People*, 26.

39. See Waterhouse, *Lobbying America*, 60–66; Edsall, *The New Politics of Inequality*, 120.

40. On the Chamber, see Richard Hume Werking, "Bureaucrats, Businessmen, and Foreign Trade: The Origins of the United States Chamber of Commerce," 52 *Business History Review* 321 (1978); Cathie Jo Martin and Duane Swank, *The Political Construction of Business Interests: Coordination, Growth, and Equality* (2012), 101–104; ; *U.S. Chamber of Commerce: The Early Years* (2012), available at https://www.uschamber.com/sites/default/files/uscc_HistoryBook.pdf.

41. On the Chamber's politicization and electoral activity, see Phillips-Fein, *Businessmen's Crusade*, 199–203; Edsall, *The New Politics of Inequality*, 123–127; Waterhouse, *Lobbying America*, 58–62; Carol D. Leonnig, "Corporate Donors

Fuel Chamber of Commerce's Political Power," *Washington Post*, October 19, 2012; Ben Jacobs, "U.S. Chamber of Commerce's Big Money Fail in 2012," *The Daily Beast*, November 17, 2013; "U.S. Chamber of Commerce Outside Spending Summary 2012," available at http://www.opensecrets.org/outsidespending/detail.php?cmte=US+Chamber+of+Commerce&cycle=2012.

42. See Thomas Dye and Harmon Zeigler, *The Irony of Democracy: An Uncommon Introduction to American Politics* (2008), 200; Phillips-Fein, *Businessmen's Crusade*, 190-198; Mark Green and Andrew Buchsbaum, "The Corporate Lobbies: The Two Styles of the Business Roundtable and Chamber of Commerce," in *The Big Business Reader: On Corporate America*, ed. Mark Green et al. (1983), 204; Edsall, *The New Politics of Inequality*, 113-114.

43. See Robert A. Bennett, "Boston Bank Chief Yields Post," *New York Times*, November 25, 1982; Boston Urban Study Group, *Who Rules Boston?* (1984); Bank of Boston Corporation, *International Directory of Company Histories* (1990), available at http://www.encyclopedia.com/doc/1G2-2840600083.html.

44. See First National Bank of Boston v. Attorney General, 359 N.E.2d 1262 (Mass. 1970); Lustwerk v. Lytron, 183 N.E.2d 871 (Mass. 1962).

45. See Bennett, "Boston Bank Chief Yields Post"; First National Bank of Boston v. Attorney General, 359 N.E.2d 1262 (Mass. 1970); First National Bank of Boston v. Bellotti, 435 U.S. 765 (1978). The best account of First Bank's fight against the graduated tax is Nikolas Bowie, "Corporate Democracy: How Corporations Justified Their Right to Speak in 1970s Boston" (unpublished manuscript, 2017).

46. See Rick Perlstein, *The Invisible Bridge: The Fall of Nixon and the Rise of Reagan* (2014), 478-479. The *Fortune* article was quoted in Vogel, "The 'New' Social Regulation," 163. On business sentiment in Massachusetts during the Dukakis years, see R. Scott Fosler, *The New Economic Role of the American States* (1988), 34-36.

47. On Frankfurter, see H. N. Hirsch, *The Enigma of Felix Frankfurter* (1981). His view of the political thicket was stated in Colegrove v. Green, 328 U.S. 549 (1946).

48. See Buckley v. Valeo, 424 U.S. 1 (1976). On the impact of *Buckley*, see Richard L. Hasen, *The Supreme Court and Election Law* (2003).

49. Audio and transcription of oral argument in the *Bellotti* case are available at http://www.oyez.org/cases/1970-1979/1977/1977_76_1172.

50. On amicus briefs in the Supreme Court, see Joseph D. Kearney and Thomas W. Merrill, "The Influence of Amicus Curiae Briefs on the Supreme Court," 148 *University of Pennsylvania Law Review* 743 (2000); Stuart Banner, "The Myth of the Neutral *Amicus*: American Courts and Their Friends, 1790-1890," 20 *Constitutional Commentary* 111 (2003); Paul M. Collins, *Friends of the Supreme Court: Interest Groups and Judicial Decision Making* (2008). See Clements, *Corporations Are Not People*, 26; Waterhouse, *Lobbying America*, 61; Ann Southworth, *Lawyers of the Right: Professionalizing the Conservative Coalition* (2009), 15; Phillips-Fein, *Businessmen's Crusade*, 162.

51. See Memorandum to William Rehnquist from Lewis Powell, April 17, 1978, Bellotti Case File, Papers of Lewis Powell, available at http://law.wlu.edu/dept images/powell%20archives/76-1172_FirstNationalBellotti1978April.pdf.

52. Powell Conference Notes, November 11, 1977, Bellotti Case File, Papers of Lewis Powell, 1977, available at http://law.wlu.edu/deptimages/powell%20archive /76-1172_FirstNationalBellotti1977.pdf; Draft Dissent of Byron White, March 7,

1978, Bellotti Case File, Papers of Lewis Powell, available at http://law.wlu.edu/deptimages/powell%20archives/76-1172_FirstNationalBellotti1978Mar.pdf.

53. See Preliminary Memorandum, April 6, 1977, Bellotti Case File, Papers of Lewis Powell, 1977, available at http://law.wlu.edu/deptimages/powell%20archives/76-1172_FirstNationalBellotti1977.pdf; Memorandum by Lewis Powell, August 9, 1977, Bellotti Case File, Papers of Lewis Powell, 1977, available at http://law.wlu.edu/deptimages/powell%20archives/76-1172_FirstNationalBellotti1977.pdf.

54. On Brennan, see Seth Stern and Stephen Wermiel, *Justice Brennan: Liberal Champion* (2010); Linda Greenhouse, "An Activist's Legacy: From Personal Liberties to Voting Rights, Brennan Led Way in Changing the Nation," *New York Times*, July 22, 1990; Alex Kozinski, "The Great Dissenter," *New York Times*, July 6, 1997. On the Warren court, see Morton J. Horwitz, *The Warren Court and the Pursuit of Justice* (1999). See Furman v. Georgia, 408 U.S. 238 (1972); Roe v. Wade, 410 U.S. 113 (1973); Craig v. Boren, 429 U.S. 190 (1976).

55. Memorandum to the Conference from William Brennan, December 1, 1977, Bellotti Case File, Papers of Lewis Powell, 1977, available at http://law.wlu.edu/deptimages/powell%20archives/76-1172_FirstNationalBellotti1977.pdf. On the drafting of *Bellotti*, see Clements, "The Conservative versus the Corporatist."

56. See Letter to the Conference from William Brennan, December 1, 1977, Bellotti Case File, Papers of Lewis Powell, 1977, available at http://law.wlu.edu/deptimages/powell%20archives/76-1172_FirstNationalBellotti1977.pdf; Memorandum to the Conference from Lewis Powell, December 6, 1977, Bellotti Case File, Papers of Lewis Powell, 1977, available at http://law.wlu.edu/deptimages/powell%20archives/76-1172_FirstNationalBellotti1977.pdf.

57. Memorandum to William Brennan from Warren Burger, December 6, 1977, Bellotti Case File, Papers of Lewis Powell, 1977, available at http://law.wlu.edu/deptimages/powell%20archives/76-1172_FirstNationalBellotti1977.pdf.

58. Letter to William Rehnquist from Lewis Powell, April 6, 1978, Bellotti Case File, Papers of Lewis Powell, available at http://law.wlu.edu/deptimages/powell%20archives/76-1172_FirstNationalBellotti1978April.pdf.

59. See Greenhouse, *Becoming Justice Blackmun*; Tinsley Yarbrough, *Harry A. Blackmun: The Outsider Justice* (2008).

60. On Powell's reaction to *Virginia Pharmacy*, see Powell Conference Notes, November 14, 1975, Papers of Justice Lewis Powell, Virginia State Board of Pharmacy Case File, available at http://law.wlu.edu/deptimages/powell%20archives/74-895_VirginiaBoard.pdf.

61. Bregstein's bio can be found at https://www.law.upenn.edu/cf/faculty/nbgordon/. On women partners in Washington, DC, law firms in the late 1970s and early 1980s, see Cynthia Fuchs Epstein, *Women in Law* (2012), 193–194.

62. Bench Memorandum by Nancy Bregstein to Lewis Powell, September 13, 1977, Bellotti Case File, Papers of Lewis Powell, 1977, available at http://law.wlu.edu/deptimages/powell%20archives/76-1172_FirstNationalBellotti1977.pdf.

63. Powell Conference Notes, November 11, 1977, Bellotti Case File, Papers of Lewis Powell, 1977, available at http://law.wlu.edu/deptimages/powell%20archives/76-1172_FirstNationalBellotti1977.pdf; Memorandum from Nancy Bergstein to Lewis F. Powell, Jr., January 30, 1978, Bellotti Case File, Papers of Lewis Powell, available at http://law.wlu.edu/deptimages/powell%20archives/76-1172_FirstNationalBellotti1978JanFeb.pdf.

64. See J. W. Sullivan, *Direct Legislation By the Citizenship Through the Initiative*

and Referendum (1892); Matthew Manweller, *The People vs. the Courts: Judicial Review and Direct Democracy in the American Legal System* (2005), 22–23.

65. Liz Essley White, "Big Business Crushed Ballot Measures in 2014," Center for Public Integrity, February 5, 2015, available at https://www.publicintegrity.org/2015/02/05/16693/big-business-crushed-ballot-measures-2014.

66. See Michael T. Kaufman, "Joseph F. Cullman 3rd, Who Made Philip Morris a Tobacco Power, Dies at 92," *New York Times*, May 1, 2004; Richard Kluger, *Ashes to Ashes: America's Hundred-Year Cigarette War, the Public Health, and the Unabashed Triumph of Philip Morris* (1996), 170.

67. See Clements, *Corporations Are Not People*, 26; Waterhouse, *Lobbying America*, 61; Southworth, *Lawyers of the Right*, 15; Adam Liptak, "Justices Offer Receptive Ear to Business Interests," *New York Times*, December 18, 2010.

68. Riegel v. Medtronic, 552 U.S. 312 (2008).

69. See Jeffrey Rosen, "Supreme Court Inc.," *New York Times Magazine*, March 16, 2008, available at http://www.nytimes.com/2008/03/16/magazine/16supreme-t.html?mcubz=1; Tony Mauro, "The Supreme Court's Majority Flexes Its Muscles," *Legal Times*, February 25, 2008.

CHAPTER 10: THE TRIUMPH OF CORPORATE RIGHTS

1. See James Bennett, "The New Price of American Politics," *The Atlantic*, October 2012, available at http://www.theatlantic.com/magazine/archive/2012/10/the/309086/. On "the wild west," see Mary Beth Schneider, "Hoosier's Campaign-Finance Crusade Pays Off," *Indianapolis Star*, August 26, 2012, available at http://www.indystar.com/story/news/politics/2014/04/02/hoosiers-campaign-finance-crusade-pays/7228163/.

2. See "A Conversation with James Bopp, Jr.," *Legally Speaking*, October 2013, available at https://www.youtube.com/watch?v=LHyKHdC__Ak; Stephanie Mencimer, "The Man Behind Citizens United Is Just Getting Started," *Mother Jones*, May/June 2011, available at http://www.motherjones.com/politics/2011/05/james-bopp-citizens-united/.

3. See James Bopp Jr. and Richard Coleson, "Vote-Dilution Analysis in *Bush v. Gore*," 23 *St. Thomas Law Review* 461 (2011).

4. On partisan realignment and polarization, see Jeffrey M. Stonecash, "The Two Key Factors Behind Our Polarized Politics," in *Political Polarization in American Politics*, ed. John Sides and Daniel J. Hopkins (2015), 69.

5. See Marcia Coyle, *The Roberts Court: The Struggle for the Constitution* (2007), 200; Robert Costa, "Trump Enlists Veteran Operative David Bossie as Deputy Campaign Manager," *Washington Post*, September 1, 2016, available at https://www.washingtonpost.com/news/post-politics/wp/2016/09/01/trump-enlists-veteran-operative-david-bossie-as-deputy-campaign-manager/?utm_term=.2bb173ebc109.

6. See Jeffrey Toobin, "Money Unlimited," *New Yorker*, May 12, 2012, available at http://www.newyorker.com/magazine/2012/05/21/money-unlimited.

7. Bipartisan Campaign Reform Act, 52 U.S.C. §§ 30101-30146.

8. See Michael Hollister, *Hollywood* (2004); Simon Louvish, *Cecil B. DeMille: A Life in Art* (2008).

9. See Scott Eyman, *Empire of Dreams: The Epic Life of Cecil B. DeMille* (2010).

10. See David J. Sousa, "'No Balance in the Equities': Union Power and the Making

and Unmaking of the Campaign Finance Regime," 13 *Studies in American Political Development* 374 (1999); Edwin M. Epstein, "The PAC Phenomenon: An Overview," 22 *Arizona Law Review* 356 (1980); Robert E. Mutch, *Buying the Vote: A History of Campaign Finance Reform* (2014).

11. Sousa, " 'No Balance in the Equities,' " 380–382.
12. Ibid., 383.
13. On money as water, see Samuel Issacharoff and Pamela S. Karlan, "The Hydraulics of Campaign Finance Reform," 77 *Texas Law Review* 1705 (1999). On CIO-PAC, see Sousa, " 'No Balance in the Equities,' " 382.
14. See Pipefitters Local Union No. 562 v. United States, 407 U.S. 385 (1972).
15. See Mutch, *Buying the Vote*, 134; Edwin M. Epstein, "The Business PAC Phenomenon: An Irony of Electoral Reform," *The American*, June 5, 1979, available at https://www.aei.org/publication/the-business-pac-phenomenon-an-irony-of -electoral-reform/.
16. See Federal Election Commission, PAC Activity Continues to Rise, June 27, 2002, available at http://www.fec.gov/press/press2002/20020627pacstats/20020 627pacstats.html.
17. See Coyle, *The Roberts Court*, 207.
18. See Austin v. Michigan Chamber of Commerce, 494 U.S. 652, 655 (1990); Randall P. Bezanson, *Speech Stories: How Free Can Speech Be?* (1998), 59 et seq. Elsewhere, I have analyzed how *Austin* sought to protect shareholders. See Adam Winkler, "Beyond *Bellotti*," 32 Loyola of Los Angeles Law Review 133 (1998).
19. McConnell v. Federal Election Com'n, 540 U.S. 93, 205 (2003).
20. Federal Election Com'n v. Wisconsin Right to Life, Inc., 551 U.S. 449, 457 (2007).
21. Citizens United v. Federal Election Comm'n, 530 F. Supp. 2d 274, 279 (D.D.C. 2008).
22. See Bopp Jr. and Coleson, "Vote-Dilution Analysis in *Bush v. Gore*," 461; Author Interview of Jim Bopp, March 6, 2013.
23. See Bopp Jr. and Coleson, "Vote-Dilution Analysis in *Bush v. Gore*," 468. Olson addressed equal protection in his rebuttal argument, at the very end of the hearing when it had become clear the justices were interested in that aspect of the case.
24. Bush v. Gore, 531 U.S. 98, 110–111 (2000).
25. See Schneider, "Hoosier's Campaign-Finance Crusade Pays Off"; Sweatt v. Painter, 339 U.S. 629 (1950).
26. Stephanie Mencimer, "Hillary's Hero: Judge Royce Lamberth," *Mother Jones*, January 13, 2008, available at http://www.motherjones.com/politics/2008/01/ hillarys-hero-judge-royce-lamberth.
27. On Olson's honor, see Tony Mauro, "Debate Party: GOP Lawyers Toast Ted Olson," *National Law Journal*, October 20, 2008. On the Capitol Hill Club, see Ken Silverstein, "Inside the Capitol Hill Club," *Harper's Monthly*, February 15, 2008, available at http://harpers.org/blog/2008/02/inside-the-capitol-hill-club -private-home-away-from-home-for-republican-lawmakers/.
28. On Kilberg, see his profile on the Gibson Dunn website, available at http:// www.gibsondunn.com/lawyers/wkilberg.
29. On the elite Supreme Court bar, see Richard J. Lazarus, "Advocacy Matters Before and Within the Supreme Court: Transforming the Court by Transforming the Bar," 96 *Georgetown Law Journal* 1487 (2008); Joan Biskupic et al., "At America's Court of Last Resort, A Handful of Lawyers Now Dominates the Docket," Reuters, December 8, 2014.

30. See Lincoln Caplan, "The Supreme Court's Advocacy Gap," *New Yorker,* January 6, 2015; Biskupic et al., "At America's Court of Last Resort"; Janet Roberts et al., "In an Ever-Clubbier Specialty Bar, 8 Men Have Become Supreme Court Confidants," Reuters, December 8, 2014.

31. See Lazarus, "Advocacy Matters Before and Within the Supreme Court," 1498. On the skew toward business interests, see Biskupic et al., "At America's Court of Last Resort." On the pro-business tendencies of the Roberts Court, see Lee Epstein et al., "How Business Fares in the Supreme Court," 97 *Minnesota Law Review* 1431 (2013); Jeffrey Rosen, "Supreme Court Inc.," *New York Times Magazine,* March 16, 2008, 38; Debra Cassens Weiss, "Supreme Court Grants Cert and Rules for Businesses in Growing Percentage of Cases," *American Bar Association Journal,* December 20, 2010.

32. On Olson, see Jo Becker, *Forcing the Spring: Inside the Fight for Marriage Equality* (2014). Olson's corporate clients before the Supreme Court were determined by reviewing his briefs filed with the Supreme Court.

33. See Tim Wu, "Did Laurence Tribe Sell Out," *New Yorker,* May 6, 2015; "Peabody Hired Gun Laurence Tribe Also Working for Coal Giant to Kill Life-Saving Mercury/Toxic Standards," *Clean Air Watch,* March 24, 2015, available at http://www.cleanairwatch.org/2015/03/peabody-hired-gun-laurence-tribe-also.html.

34. See Mary Beth Schneider, "Hoosier's Campaign-Finance Crusade Pays Off."

35. See Coyle, *The Roberts Court,* 225.

36. Ibid.

37. Matthew Walther, "Sam Alito: A Civil Man," *American Spectator,* May 2014, available at http://spectator.org/articles/58731/sam-alito-civil-man.

38. Lorraine Woellert, "Why Big Business Likes Alito," *Bloomberg News,* October 31, 2005; Ledbetter v. Goodyear Tire & Rubber Co., Inc., 550 U.S. 618 (2007); Lee Epstein et al., *The Behavior of Federal Judges: A Theoretical and Empirical Study of Rational Choice* (2013).

39. Debra Cassens Weiss, "Alito and Roberts Are the Most Pro-Business Justices Since 1946, Study Finds," *American Bar Association Journal,* May 7, 2013; Epstein et al., *The Behavior of Federal Judges.*

40. Transcript of Oral Argument, March 24, 2009, Citizens United v. Federal Election Comm'n, 508 U.S. 310 (2010) (No. 08-205), available at https://www.supremecourt.gov/oral_arguments/argument_transcripts/08-205.pdf.

41. See Jim Bopp Jr. and Richard E. Coleson, "*Citizens United v. Federal Election Commission*: 'Precisely What WRTL Sought to Avoid,'" 2009–2019 *Cato Supreme Court Review* 29, 47 (2010).

42. Author Interview of Jim Bopp, June 19, 2014; Coyle, *The Roberts Court,* 235. The author attempted on several occasions to interview Ted Olson for this book but Mr. Olson did not make himself available.

43. Transcript of Oral Argument, March 24, 2009, Citizens United v. Federal Election Comm'n, 508 U.S. 310 (2010) (No. 08-205).

44. See Steven G. Medema, "Chicago Law and Economics" (June 2013), available at https://papers.ssrn.com/sol3/papers2.cfm?abstract_id=560941; Leo E. Strine Jr. and Nicholas Walter, "Originalist or Original: The Difficulties of Reconciling *Citizens United* with Corporate Law History," 91 *Notre Dame Law Review* 877, 910 (2016).

45. For an overview of the nexus of contracts theory of the corporation, see Frank H. Easterbrook and Daniel R. Fischel, *The Economic Structure of Corporate Law*

(1991); Stephen M. Bainbridge, "The Board of Directors as Nexus of Contracts," 88 *Iowa Law Review* 1 (2002); William W. Bratton, "The 'Nexus of Contracts' Corporation: A Crticial Appraisal," 74 *Cornell Law Review* 407 (1989).

46. See Austin, 494 U.S. at 681–687 (Scalia, J., dissenting).

47. Transcript of Oral Argument March 24, 2009, Citizens United v. Federal Election Comm'n, 508 U.S. 310 (2010) (No. 08-205).

48. Author Interview of Jim Bopp, June 19, 2014; Memorandum in Support of Plaintiff's Summary Judgment Motion, Citizens United v. Federal Election Commission, No. 07-2240 (D.C.C. May 16, 2008).

49. See "Chief Justice Says His Goal Is More Consensus on Court," *New York Times*, May 22, 2006.

50. Scalia's retort can be found in *A Conversation on the Constitution: A Debate Between Antonin Scalia and Stephen Breyer*, December 5, 2006, available at https://www.youtube.com/watch?v=4OyRHiFQp40.

51. On the dynamics of the justices' deliberations over *Citizens United* after the first oral argument, see Toobin, "Money Unlimited"; Coyle, *The Roberts Court*, 251–252.

52. Citizens United v. Federal Election Commission, 558 U.S. 310, 398 (2010).

53. On the Tea Party, see Theda Skocpol and Vanessa Williamson, *The Tea Party and the Remaking of Republican Conservatism* (2013).

54. Transcript of Oral Argument, September 9, 2009, Citizens United v. Federal Election Comm'n 558 U.S. 310 (2010) (No. 08-205), available at https://www.supremecourt.gov/oral_arguments/argument_transcripts/08-205%5BR eargued%5D.pdf.

55. Transcript of Oral Argument, McConnell v. Federal Election Com'n, 540 U.S. 93, 205 (2003) (No. 02-1674), available at http://www.democracy21.org/uploads/%7B8158ECE3-B325-43F3-A647-AB06B229DD36%7D.PDF.

56. Opinion Announcement, Citizens United v. Federal Election Comm'n, 508 U.S. 310 (2010) (No. 08-205), available at https://www.oyez.org/cases/2008/08-205.

57. On *Citizens United* and "disfavored" corporations, see Tamara R. Piety, "Why Personhood Matters," 30 *Constitutional Commentary* 361 (2015); Tamara R. Piety, "*Citizens United* and the Threat to the Regulatory State," 109 *Michigan Law Review First Impressions* 16 (2010).

58. See Thomas Wuil Joo, "Corporate Speech and the Rights of Others," 30 *Constitutional Commentary* 335 (2015); Larry Ribstein, "The First Amendment and Corporate Governance," 27 *Georgia State University Law Review* 1019 (2011).

59. See Coyle, *The Roberts Court*, 272–273.

60. See Morse v. Frederick, 551 U.S. 393, 404–405 (2007); Garcetti v. Ceballos, 547 U.S. 410 (2006). For an insightful analysis of corporate constitutional rights fleshing out Stevens's theory, see Ryan Azad, "Can a Tailor Mend the Analytical Hole? A Framework for Understanding Corporate Constitutional Rights," 64 *UCLA Law Review* 452 (2017).

61. See Regan v. Taxation With Representation of Washington, 461 U.S. 540 (1983).

62. See Bluman v. Federal Election Commission, 132 S. Ct. 1087 (2012); Bluman v. Federal Election Commission, 800 F. Supp. 2d 281 (D. DC 2011).

63. David Bossie's statement to the media after *Citizens United* is available at https://www.c-span.org/video/?291571-1/citizens-united-v-federal-election-commission-reactions&start=335.

64. Philip Rucker, "Citizens United used 'Hillary: The Movie' to take on McCain-

Feingold," *Washington Post*, January 22, 2010, available at http://www.washing tonpost.com/wp-dyn/content/article/2010/01/21/AR2010012103582.html?sid= ST2010012104871.

65. See Toobin, "Money Unlimited."

66. On Super PACs generally, see Adam Gabbatt, "Citizens United Accounts for 78% of 2012 Election Spending, Study Shows," *The Guardian*, September 24, 2012, available at https://www.theguardian.com/world/2012/sep/24/super-pac-spending-2012-election?INTCMP=SRCH. On Chevron, see Dan Eggen, "Chevron donates \$2.5 million to super PAC," *Washington Post*, October 26, 2012, available at https://www.washingtonpost.com/news/post-politics/wp/2012/10/26/chevron-donates-2-5-million-to-gop-super-pac/?utm_term=.798d5f26aa1e; Anna Palmer and Abby Phillip, "Corporations Don't Pony Up for Super PACs," *Politico*, March 8, 2012, available at http://www.politico.com/news/stories/0312/73804.html.

67. On Qualcomm, see Nicholas Confessore, "Qualcomm Reveals Its Donations to Tax-Exempt Groups," *New York Times*, February 22, 2013, available at https://cityroom.blogs.nytimes.com/2013/02/22/qualcomm-agrees-to-reveal-dona tions-to-tax-exempt-groups/. On Merck, Dow Chemical, and Prudential, see Mike Mcintire and Nicholas Confessore, "Tax-Exempt Groups Shield Political Gifts of Businesses," *New York Times*, July 7, 2012, available at http://www.nytimes.com/2012/07/08/us/politics/groups-shield-political-gifts-of-busi nesses.html.

68. On total 2012 new political spending due to *Citizens United*, see Reity O'Brien and Andrea Fuller, "Court Opened Door to \$933 Million in New Election Spending," The Center for Public Integrity, January 16, 2013, available at https://www.publicintegrity.org/2013/01/16/12027/court-opened-door-933-million-new-election-spending. On increases in state and local campaign spending, see Chisun Lee et al., "After *Citizens United*: The Story in the States," Brennan Center for Justice (2014), available at https://www.brennancenter.org/publication/after-citizens-united-story-states.

69. See Dan Eggen, "Poll: Large Majority Opposes Supreme Court's Decision on Campaign Financing," *Washington Post*, February 17, 2010, available at http://www.washingtonpost.com/wp-dyn/content/article/2010/02/17/AR201002170115 1.html; Greg Stohr, "Bloomberg Poll: Americans Want Supreme Court to Turn Off Political Spending Spigot," *Bloomberg News*, September 28, 2015, available at https://www.bloomberg.com/politics/articles/2015-09-28/bloomberg-poll-americans-want-supreme-court-to-turn-off-political-spending-spigot.

70. See Todd Gitlin, *Occupy Nation: The Roots, the Spirit, and the Promise of Occupy Wall Street* (2012); Heather Gautney, "What is Occupy Wall Street? The History of Leaderless Movements," *Washington Post*, October 10, 2011, available at https://www.washingtonpost.com/national/on-leadership/what-is-occupy-wall -street-the-history-of-leaderless-movements/2011/10/10/gIQAwkFjaL_story .html; "A Resolution to End Corporate Personhood," Occupy Wall Street, avail- able at http://occupywallstreet.net/story/resolution-end-corporate-personhood.

71. Mattathias Schwartz, "Map: How Occupy Wall Street Chose Zuccotti Park," *New Yorker*, November 18, 2011, available at http://www.newyorker.com/news/news-desk/map-how-occupy-wall-street-chose-zuccotti-park.

72. See John Nichols, "America's Most Dynamic (Yet Under-Covered) Movement: Overturning 'Citizens United,'" *The Nation*, July 5, 2013; Allegra Pocinki, "16

States Call to Overturn 'Citizens United,'" July 8, 2013, available at http://www
.publicampaign.org/blog/2013/07/08/16-states-call-overturn-%E2%80%98citizens
-united%E2%80%99.

73. Author Interview of Jim Bopp, June 19, 2014.

CONCLUSION: CORPORATE RIGHTS AND WRONGS

1. Ashley Parker, "'Corporations Are People,' Romney Tells Iowa Hecklers Angry Over His Tax Policy," *New York Times*, August 11, 2011, available at http://www .nytimes.com/2011/08/12/us/politics/12romney.html.
2. National Federation of Independent Business v. Sebelius, 567 U.S. 519 (2012).
3. Verified Complaint, Hobby Lobby Stores, Inc. v. Sebelius, 2012 WL 4009450 (W.D.Okla. September 12, 2012) (No. CIV-12-1000-HE).
4. See 42 U.S.C. §2000bb(a)(2)–(4).
5. Burwell v. Hobby Lobby Stores, Inc., 134 S. Ct. 2751 (2014).
6. On the religious liberty rights of corporations, see Micah Schwartzman et al., *The Rise of Corporate Religious Liberty* (2016); David Gans and Ilya Shapiro, *Religious Liberties for Corporations? Hobby Lobby, the Affordable Care Act, and the Constitution* (2014). On Hobby Lobby's piercing-the-corporate-veil reasoning, see Schwartzman et al., "Introduction," in *The Rise of Corporate Religious Liberty*, iii; Elizabeth Pollman, "Corporate Law and Theory in Hobby Lobby," in *The Rise of Corporate Religious Liberty*, 149. On a corporate law defense of piercing the veil in corporate religious liberty cases, see Stephen M. Bainbridge, "Using Reverse Veil Piercing to Vindicate the Free Exercise Rights of Incorporated Employers," 16 *The Green Bag* 2d 235 (2013).
7. Leo Strine Jr., chief justice of the Delaware Supreme Court, delivered the 2015–2016 Judge Ralph K. Winter Lecture on Corporate Law and Governance on October 13, 2015. Chief Justice Strine's lecture was entitled "Corporate Power Ratchet: The Courts' Role in Eroding 'We the People's' Ability to Constrain Our Corporate Creations," and is available for viewing at https://www.law.yale .edu/yls-today/yale-law-school-videos/leo-strine-corporate-power-ratchet.
8. On Strine, see Len Costa, "Boss of the Bosses," *Legal Affairs*, July/August 2005, available at https://www.legalaffairs.org/issues/July-August-2005/feature_costa _julaug05.msp.
9. Liz Hoffman, "Leo Strine Nominated to Head Delaware Supreme Court," *Wall Street Journal*, January 8, 2014, available at https://www.wsj.com/articles/SB100 01424052702304347904579308432948927494.
10. Leo E. Strine Jr. and Nicholas Walter, "Conservative Collision Course?: The Tension between Conservative Corporate Law Theory and Citizens United," 100 *Cornell Law Review* 335 (2015).
11. See Burnet v. Clark, 287 U.S. 410 (1932).
12. See Amicus Curiae Brief of Corporate and Criminal Law Professors In Support of Petitioners, Sebelius v. Hobby Lobby Stores, Inc., available at http://www .americanbar.org/content/dam/aba/publications/supreme_court_preview/ briefs-v3/13-354-13-356_amcu_cclp.authcheckdam.pdf.
13. For an argument in a similar vein, see Daniel J. H. Greenwood, "Essential Speech: Why Corporate Speech Is Not Free," 83 *Iowa Law Review* 995 (1998).
14. For Olivas's interview, see "US Region Bans Oil and Gas Drilling," Al Jazeera English, May 27, 2013, available at https://www.youtube.com/watch?v=Suqp

SzNxLDE. On Olivas and the fracking ban, see Ernie Atencio, "The Man Behind a New Mexico County's Fracking Ban," *High Country News*, June 24, 2014, available at http://www.hcn.org/issues/46.11/the-man-behind-a-new-mexico-countys-fracking-ban; Staci Matlock, "Federal Judge Overturns Mora County's Drilling Ordinance," *The Santa Fe New Mexican*, January 20, 2015, available at http://www.santafenewmexican.com/news/local_news/federal-judge-overturns-mora-county-s-drilling-ordinance/article_dddd444a-6ae8-56ea-b8a7-999c562a77b8.html; Statement of County Commissioner John Olivas, Chairman, Mora County, New Mexico Board of Commissioners, March 20, 2014, available at http://celdf.org/2014/03/statement-of-county-commissioner-john-olivas-chairman-mora-county-new-mexico-board-of-commissioners/; Nina Bunker Ruiz, "How Residents of a Rural New Mexico County Fought the Fracking Barons and Won—For Now," *Yes! Magazine*, September 15, 2014, available at http://www.yesmagazine.org/issues/the-end-of-poverty/how-residents-of-a-rural-new-mexico-county-fought-fracking-barons-and-won.

15. On Browning, see Kyle Marksteiner, "From Sacks to Sentencing: Federal Judge Jim Browning," *Focus New Mexico*, October 9, 2015, available at http://focusnm.com/articles/2015/10/9/from-sacks-to-sentencing-federal-judge-jim-browning.htm.

16. See Swepi, LP v. Mora County, 81 F.Supp.3d 1075 (D. N.M. 2015).

CREDITS

—

Frontspiece: "We the Corporate Personhood," by Brian Corr. Originally for The Subjective Theatre Company.

Page xii: Courtesy of New York City Parks Photo / Art & Antiquities.

Page 1: Private Collection © at Look and Learn / Bridgeman Images.

Page 8: Courtesy of Library of Virginia.

Page 12: Courtesy of National Park Service and Colonial National Historical Park.

Page 20: Courtesy of Salem Athenæum.

Page 33: Courtesy of Ed Uthman.

Page 46: Courtesy of Historical & Special Collections, Harvard Law School Library.

Page 52: Courtesy of National Gallery of Art, Washington.

Page 58: *John Quincy Adams*, by Pieter Van Huffel, 1815, oil on canvas, National Portrait Gallery, Smithsonian Institution; gift of Mary Louisa Adams Clement in memory of her mother, Louisa Catherine Adams Clement, 1950.

Page 65: Courtesy of Historical & Special Collections, Harvard Law School Library.

Page 72: *Daniel Webster*, by Francis Alexander, 1835, oil on canvas, National Portrait Gallery, Smithsonian Institution; bequest of Mrs. John Hay Whitney.

Page 80: Hood Museum of Art, Dartmouth College, Hanover, New Hampshire: gift of the Estate of Henry N. Teague, Class of 1900.

Page 89: Courtesy of the Bruce C. Cooper Collection of Historic US Documents.

Page 91: Courtesy of US Senate Collection.

Page 96: Courtesy of Library of Congress, Prints & Photographs Division, LC-DIG-cwpbh-00789.

Page 98: *Daniel Webster*, by Francis D'Avignon, copy after Mathew B. Brady, 1850, lithograph on paper, National Portrait Gallery, Smithsonian Institution.

Page 111: Courtesy of Donald Duke, Security Pacific National Bank Collection / Los Angeles Public Library.

Page 116: (top right) *Justice Stephen J. Field*, photography by Mathew Brady Studio, c. 1870, collection of the Supreme Court of the United States. (bottom left) *Reporter of Decisions J. C. Bancroft Davis*, by Robert C. Hinckley, c. 1900, Collection of the Supreme Court of the United States. (bottom right) Courtesy of California State University, Chico, Meriam Library Special Collections, sc#14034.

Page 126: *Associate Justice John A. Campbell*, photograph by Mathew Brady, c. 1857, Collection of the Supreme Court of the United States.

Page 141: Courtesy of the California History Room, California State Library, Sacramento, California.

Page 147: *Chief Justice Morrison R. Waite*, photograph by Mathew Brady, c. 1877, Collection of the Supreme Court of the United States.

Page 162: Courtesy of Library of Congress, Prints & Photographs Division, LC-DIG-ggbain-03468.

Page 166: Courtesy of Library of Congress, Prints & Photographs Division, LC-DIG-ggbain-05808.

Page 169: "The trust giant's point of view. What a funny little government?," illustration by Horace Taylor, *The Verdict* (New York), vol. 3, no. 7, January 22, 1900, pp. 8–9. Collection of Original Works of Art on Paper (Collection Original 99), UCLA Library Special Collections, Charles E. Young Research Library, UCLA.

Page 171: "Reidsville Plant of the American Tobacco Company, Reidsville, N.C.," Rockingham County, North Carolina Postcard Collection (P052), North Carolina Collection Photographic Archives, Wilson Library, UNC–Chapel Hill.

Page 178: Courtesy of Library of Congress, Prints & Photographs Division, LC-USZ62-55730.

Page 182: Courtesy of Library of Congress, Prints & Photographs Division, LC-USZ62-56711.

Page 186: *Associate Justice Henry B. Brown*, photograph by Parker Studio, 1906, Collection of the Supreme Court of the United States.

Page 193: (left) Courtesy of Library of Congress, Prints & Photographs Division, LC-DIG-ggbain-06150. (right) Courtesy of Library of Congress, Prints & Photographs Division, LC-DIG-ggbain-00632.

Page 196: Courtesy of US Senate Collection.

Page 218: *Theodore Roosevelt*, by Adrian Lamb, oil on canvas, 1967, copy after 1908 original, National Portrait Gallery, Smithsonian Institution; gift of the Theodore Roosevelt Association.

Page 225: Courtesy of Forest Parke Library and Archives, Capital Area District Libraries, Lansing, Michigan.

Page 229: Photograph by Josh Howell.

Page 233: Courtesy of Library of Congress, Prints & Photographs Division, LC-USZ62-137254.

Page 235: Courtesy of Library of Congress, Prints & Photographs Division, LC-USZ62-111008.

Page 239: Courtesy of Library of Congress, Prints & Photographs Division, LC-USZ62-47817.

Page 246: Courtesy of Library of Congress, Prints & Photographs Division, HAER, HAER MICH,82-HAMT,1--313.

Page 252: Photograph by Harris & Ewing, Collection of the Supreme Court of the United States.

Page 258: Courtesy of Alabama Department of Archives and History.

Page 266: Portrait by John Pelham Black after Yousuf Karsh, Collection of the Supreme Court of the United States.

Page 268: Marx-19003-Ben_Franklin, Julius E. Marx Collection, The Doy Leale McCall Rare Book and Manuscript Library, University of South Alabama.

Page 273: Justice John M. Harlan II authored the Supreme Court's opinion in *NAACP v. Alabama ex rel. Patterson. Associate Justice John M. Harlan*, photograph by Harris & Ewing, c. 1956, Collection of the Supreme Court of the United States.

Page 284: *Associate Justice Lewis F. Powell Jr.*, photograph by Chase Studios, c. 1972, Collection of the Supreme Court of the United States.

Page 287: Courtesy of Library of Congress, Prints & Photographs Division, LC-U9- 31644-24.

Page 288: Photo by Bettman / Contributor via Getty Images.

Page 301: "Economic Education on TV, The Competitive Enterprise System, detail. Courtesy of Hagley Museum and Library, from the Chamber of Commerce of the US Records (Acc. 1960), Box 93, Vol. Chamber Publications, 1973, A-H. Hagley Museum & Library, Wilmington, DE, 19807.

Page 303: The Powell Papers, Lewis F. Powell Jr. Archives.

Page 306: Photo by William Ryerson / *The Boston Globe*, via Getty Images.

Page 313: Robert S. Oakes, *National Geographic*, courtesy of the Supreme Court of the United States.

Page 328: Photo by Gage Skidmore.

Page 331: Courtesy of the Academy of Motion Picture Arts and Sciences.

Page 337: AP Photo / J. Scott Applewhite.

Page 342: Courtesy of Citizens United.

Page 345: Courtesy of Gibson, Dunn & Crutcher LLP.

Page 363: Courtesy of Steve Petteway, Collection of the Supreme Court of the United States.

Page 371: Courtesy of Reuters / Jonathan Ernst.

Page 378: Associated Press / Charlie Neibergall.

Page 384: Photograph by Harold Shapiro.

INDEX

—

Page numbers in *italics* refer to illustrations.

ABOUT THE AUTHOR

ADAM WINKLER is a professor at the University of California, Los Angeles School of Law. His scholarship has been cited by the Supreme Court of the United States on the constitutional rights of corporations and on the Second Amendment. His writing has appeared in the *New York Times, Wall Street Journal, Washington Post, Los Angeles Times, New Republic, Atlantic, Slate,* and SCOTUSblog. Prior to joining the UCLA faculty, he clerked on the US Court of Appeals for the Ninth Circuit, practiced law in Los Angeles, and was a John M. Olin Fellow at the University of Southern California Law School's Center in Law, Economics, and Organization. A graduate of the Georgetown University School of Foreign Service, he earned a law degree at New York University and a master's in political science from UCLA. He lives in Los Angeles with his wife, daughter, and kitten.